Christopher Hill

Christopher Hill

The Life of a Radical Historian

Michael Braddick

VERSO

London • New York

For my parents, Bill and Ann

This paperback edition first published by Verso 2026
First published by Verso 2025
© Michael Braddick 2025
Every effort has been made to identify copyright holders and secure permission for images
reproduced herein. If any oversight or error has been made, the publisher will endeavour to
correct the text at the earliest opportunity. Uncredited pictures are in the public domain or
the property of the author.

The moral rights of the author have been asserted

1 3 5 7 9 10 8 6 4 2

Verso
UK: 6 Meard Street, London W1F 0EG
US: 207 East 32nd Street, New York, NY 10016
versobooks.com

Verso is the imprint of New Left Books

ISBN-13: 978-1-83674-358-3
ISBN-13: 978-1-83976-079-2 (US EBK)
ISBN-13: 978-1-83976-078-5 (UK EBK)

British Library Cataloguing in Publication Data
A catalogue record for this book is available from the British Library

The Library of Congress Has Cataloged the Hardback Edition as Follows:

Names: Braddick, M. J. (Michael J.), 1962– author.
Title: Christopher Hill : the life of a radical historian / Michael
  Braddick.
Other titles: Life of a radical historian
Description: London ; New York : Verso, 2025. | Includes bibliographical
  references and index.
Identifiers: LCCN 2024049306 (print) | LCCN 2024049307 (ebook) | ISBN
  9781839760778 (hardback) | ISBN 9781839760792 (ebk)
Subjects: LCSH: Hill, Christopher, 1912-2003. | Hill, Christopher,
  1912–2003 - Political and social views. | Historians - England - Biography.
  | Socialists - England - Biography. | Marxian historiography - Great
  Britain. | Great Britain - History - 20th century. | Great
  Britain - History - Puritan Revolution, 1642–1660 - Historiography.
Classification: LCC DA3.H55 B73 2025 (print) | LCC DA3.H55 (ebook) | DDC
  907.2/02 - dc23/eng/20241230
LC record available at https://lccn.loc.gov/2024049306
LC ebook record available at https://lccn.loc.gov/2024049307

Typeset in Minion Pro by MJ & N Gavan, Truro, Cornwall
Printed in the UK by CPI Group (UK) Ltd, Croydon, CR0 4YY

Contents

Preface

History has to be rewritten in every generation, because although the past does not change the present does; each generation asks new questions of the past, and finds new areas of sympathy as it re-lives different aspects of the experiences of its predecessors.

Christopher Hill, *The World Turned Upside Down*, 1972

In February 1944 Christopher Hill, then a young academic away on war service, wrote to an Oxford colleague with news of the birth of his first child, Fanny. Mother and daughter were both well, he said, noting with characteristic wit that Fanny 'is universally stated to be (a) very ugly (b) exactly like me'. He can hardly have thought, as he made the quip, that the letter would be opened by the secret services, still less that they would keep a copy. As the file records, Hill's correspondence that year with Beryl Smalley, the colleague in question, was 'concerned entirely with scholastic matters', albeit leavened with some personal chat.[1] It seems all the more remarkable, therefore, that it can now be read among government records in the National Archives.

Over the following decades Hill emerged as one of the leading historians of his generation, and his interpretation of English history in the seventeenth century became essential reading for a generation of ambitious sixth-formers and serious undergraduates. However, although he was undoubtedly a major establishment figure – Fellow of the British Academy and Master of Balliol College, Oxford – he was also seen as a threat to that establishment and its values. Well known as a Marxist scholar, he was for twenty years a member of the Communist Party, monitored by Special Branch and the secret service between 1935 and

1962, and publicly accused in the 1980s of having been a Soviet agent of influence during the war. It was a Cold War life, as well as a scholarly one.

Coming of age in the 1930s Hill saw middle-class certainties collapsing around him in the profound aftershocks of the First World War and the Wall Street Crash. The Great Depression revealed the limitations of bourgeois parliamentary government, which seemed simply to be the management committee for the capitalist class. Later, in the 1960s, he recalled that as he went to Oxford in 1931 it was clear that the labour movement had abandoned the working class: Ramsay MacDonald's government had cut unemployment benefit and imposed means tests. At the same time, Rowntree's survey revealed that 30 per cent of the working-class population of York, Hill's hometown, was living below the poverty line. The 'facile' optimism of nineteenth-century liberals – that life would improve continuously through the application of human reason – was given the lie by the trauma of the Great Depression. Twentieth-century liberals seemed to have no answers.

Meanwhile international relations were increasingly chaotic and war appeared to be a permanent feature of a world made up of bourgeois states. The Japanese occupation of Manchuria, the Italian occupation of Abyssinia and the rise of German fascism all suggested that a world of competing bourgeois states was inevitably, and increasingly, anarchic. In Hill's view only the USSR was committed to peace during the 1930s.

He was, however, also preoccupied with a search for personal authenticity, a prominent theme in the literature he was reading at the time. Literary modernism articulated feelings of profound dissociation between individuals and the world around them, and as a serious-minded adolescent Hill read T.S. Eliot, D.H. Lawrence, Stephen Spender, W.H. Auden and James Joyce. There he found evocations of profound alienation which reflected a general tension between personal feelings and impulses on the one hand and, on the other, expected forms of expression and conduct. He was soon to abandon the respectable Methodism of his youth, one element of his dissatisfaction its apparent preoccupation with respectability, even censoriousness, rather than the real root of the matter.

Marxism offered a way to make sense of both the crisis of bourgeois states and this pervasive sense of personal alienation, and by the time he graduated he had abandoned Methodism and embraced Marxism as an intellectual system. Following a visit to the Soviet Union in 1936 he joined the Communist Party of Great Britain and remained a member until 1957. This was a political strategy, however, of less enduring significance than his embrace of Marxism: his most enduring commitment was to the writing of Marxist history as a way to make sense of the present and give hope for the future. By the 1970s Hill had achieved remarkable prominence in academic life and in British literary and political culture. As a result, he became a target in the culture wars of the 1980s; the reception of his work was increasingly overshadowed by politics, both his own and those of his critics.

My interest in this life is twofold. Firstly, Hill's work has done more to shape the study of seventeenth-century England than that of any other historian in my lifetime; secondly, he wrote history that spoke directly to the politics of his own day, revealing the shifting relationship of the British left to the British past.

Hill's undergraduate lectures at Cardiff and Oxford in the 1930s set an agenda which is still recognisable nearly 100 years later, and is certainly much closer to current concerns than the preoccupations of S.R. Gardiner, the great Victorian historian whose interpretation of seventeenth-century England Hill set out to challenge. Gardiner saw in the seventeenth century a 'Puritan revolution': as puritan ideas took hold they destabilised a constitution based around king and church, eventually leading to a reduction in the power of both. Hill argued instead that the appeal of puritan ideas depended on the context in which they were being expressed – they did not win out simply because they were more true than older ideas, but because they made more sense in the social and political conditions that were developing alongside them. These destabilising ideas, and the revolution they produced, were a symptom of the birth of bourgeois culture, the culture whose crisis he thought he was now witnessing.

This interest in the origins of bourgeois culture could be glossed as an interest in the economic, intellectual and political roots of modern society. Understood this way, his work resonated widely among non-Marxists in his lifetime: many political problems were viewed through that lens and proposed reforms were often framed as 'modernisation'. At the same time, understanding England's route to modernity was believed to be of particular importance because it had the first constitutional revolution, the first industrial revolution and was at the core of the largest empire of the modern world. England's route to modernity shaped not only Britain's experience of modernisation but that of the whole globe. Hill's interests reflected these central preoccupations in academic life and resonated more widely because so much of British life from the 1950s to the 1980s was debated in these terms.

It is this core interest that has really shaped the way the seventeenth century is now studied, rather than Hill's specifically Marxist interpretation of these developments. His stock rose and fell along with the appeal of the political views he shared, while his working methods have been criticised, and improved upon; but he is still a major historian because his questions remain fundamental to how we think about the significance of this period.

Secondly, because his work was political in inspiration and intent, it offers a window onto the relationship between the British left and the British past. Hill hoped that a clearer understanding of the past would make better sense of the present, and so help us to shape the future – part of his reaction against liberal historians in the 1930s was that they simply threw up their hands in the face of events.

This ambition to inform the present led him in different directions as the world around him changed. In the 1940s and 1950s he wrote about the development of the bourgeois state; in the 1960s, about the promise of scientific and rational thought and the social conditions that allowed it to thrive; in the later '60s and 1970s about radical ideas, particularly those relating to personal freedom and self-expression. By the 1980s it was the radicals' experience of defeat and disappointment that dominated his writing. His published output was vast – depending on how you count, eighteen books and seven volumes of essays, as well as major source editions and hundreds of reviews and other journalism. There is no space here to adjudicate each in detail; instead, I try to contextualise what he wrote at each stage of his career as part of this dialogue between the past and the present.

Christopher Hill is not an easy subject for a biographer. Although warm, unpretentious and wry, he was notoriously reserved and hard to know with any intimacy, particularly in professional contexts. Many of those who knew him profess ignorance of much of his inner life. As an adult, he was comfortable with silence, and although he would answer questions that were put to him he was not prone to voluntary revelation of his interior life: 'a genial but very reserved and private man' remembered his niece, the historian Penelope Corfield, 'laconic in speech and witty, even sardonic, in humour'.[2] His surviving papers are spare and often chaotically written, and they contain hardly any personal correspondence. They are working papers, not personal papers, and as working papers they say much more about his working practices than the development of his thought or the relationships that shaped it. Most of the time his internal life is hidden, both by temperament and political caution, as it was to many of his contemporaries.

What follows therefore is more an intellectual life than a biography: an account of one trajectory through the twentieth century on the British left, and of the development of a particular way of engaging with the British past to try to make sense of the present.

1

Methodism, Modernism, Marxism and the Crisis of Bourgeois Culture: 1912–36

Man is not merely a social animal, but an animal which can develop into an individual only in society.

Christopher Hill, *Listener*, 1967, quoting Karl Marx

[M]y parents, I think, had these very good things which went with their nonconformity but were not of the God-y part of it, you see what I mean. I reacted rather against the God-y part of it, but there are certain basic instincts that I am very glad I was brought up with.

Christopher Hill, interview with Penelope Corfield, 1988

Christopher Hill was born at 7.30 am on 6 February 1912 in Norfolk House, Bishopthorpe Road, York, twenty-one inches long and weighing in at a healthy seven pounds. After three weeks he was six inches across the chest and at ten weeks weighed 12 pounds. He didn't crawl for nearly a year, but he took his first step at almost the same time, on 7 January 1913. The first recognisable words of this famously taciturn man were 'night-night' and 'dad-dad'. At birth he had blue eyes, although they became brown. His pet name was 'The Imp': despite a marked personal reserve, many people noted the twinkle in his eye over the following ninety years.[1]

Hill's 'Baby's Record' reflects the solid respectability of his Methodist background. He was baptised on 30 March 1912, also at Norfolk House, by the Reverend G.E. Scutt: there were no godparents but a number of witnesses beyond the family. His first drive was within two weeks of his birth – that the family had access to a car in 1912 was a testament to their social status. He rode in a pram for the first time on 13 March and took his first trips to Bridlington, Castle Howard, Weston Rawcliffe and Leeds between April and July.[2]

Samuel Beer, a fellow student at Balliol, recalled that in Oxford Hill had appeared rather classless, and Beer had assumed he was from a poor background until he and his wife visited the Hill family in 1935. The Hills were then living at The Lodge, Huntington: 'A high wall stretched round grounds which ran down to a little river and had a tennis-court. A servant brought us lunch at a table on the lawn', he remembered. They had a gardener, a cook and a live-in maid and there was a library of three or four thousand books in which the young Hill immersed himself.[3]

Christopher's father, Edward Harold Hill, was a prosperous solicitor, rather shy and reserved but neither severe nor forbidding, 'a strict, but genial puritan'. During the Beers' visit 'Father' had been the centrepiece, a man of wealth now committed to doing good works, 'quiet in manner in contrast to Mrs. Hill's talkative vivacity, but agreeable'. Penelope Corfield, Hill's niece, agrees that Christopher's mother, Janet Augusta, was 'more relaxed and lively'. Twice each Sunday the family rode to church on bicycles, returning home for intense discussion of the sermon, particularly between Christopher and his mother. Although not 'personally severe',

The Lodge, Huntington, York, Hill's childhood home.

Sundays were 'observed punctiliously as days of worship and abstinence from all worldly activities'.[4] The Hills came from a line of such people: Eliza Hill had spent her last hours in 1856 'sending out garments for the poor, praying ... and sharing in the joys of Christian fellowship', while her son, Christopher's great uncle David, had been an 'inspirational' missionary in China in the 1870s and 1880s.[5] A.L. Rowse (another Oxford historian but by no means a reliable witness, it has to be said) thought that the family had wanted Christopher to be a missionary too.[6]

It was a hearty, sporty, no-nonsense, Yorkshire kind of Methodism. The wider Hill family in fact had fielded its own cricket team and as a boy Hill's 'highest ambition' had been to play for Yorkshire ('I practised and practised ... but I wasn't any good').[7] He grew to be a sturdy man of no great height – 5' 7" according to the passport issued in 1931, 5' 7¾" according to the army in 1940.[8] Physically robust, a rugby player, cyclist and walker, he was capable of testing his niece's mettle on long walks into his middle age.[9]

This heartiness was linked to a marked poetic and literary sensibility, associated in part with his adolescent love of the upland landscapes, and that love both of the moors and of exertion remained with him. Of the Dales he wrote in 1940: 'It is enormously good country – a bit bleak and strenuous, but springy to the feet and with heather about one's ankles; something to grapple with: pretty individualist country, really.' It also had an 'unexpected tenderness', the skies, walls and sheep prompting trains of 'philosophical reflection'. Having conquered them on foot and by bike he would now enjoy 'cheating by going by car to near the top of the hills I know and running very fast down'.[10] On his visit in 1935 Beer discovered in Christopher a previously unsuspected enthusiasm for Wordsworth, particularly 'The Excursion', and the poetry of the Romantics more generally.[11]

It was also an egalitarian upbringing, centred on a view that we are all one in the eyes of the Lord, and therefore also sceptical about authority and (some) social convention. Hill recalled, for example, that he was brought up with 'a lack of any sense of racial distinction, discrimination', and his parents had a similar view of sexual equality too: when Hill got into Oxford, the first of his family to go to university, it was assumed that his sister would go too.[12]

From 1923 to 1931 Hill attended St Peter's School, York, initially as a day-boy and then as a boarder. Clearly outstandingly able, in 1930 he won a County Major Scholarship as well as the Headmaster's prize both for

History and Latin Prose.[13] His reading diary for May–July 1928, when he was fifteen, is intimidating: Belloc, Dante, Wells, Butler, Trevelyan, Goethe, Plato, Tolstoy and Langland, as well as a list of school books bought and read which consisted mainly of English literature mixed with classical texts, foreign literature and history.[14] Returning home following graduation from Oxford, he pointed to the window seat in the living room of his parents' house, 'and remarked with emotion, "That is where I spent all those hours reading".'[15]

So impressive was his schoolwork that he seems to have been actively recruited by Balliol. The tale has probably grown in the telling, but Patrick Renshaw, an Oxford-trained historian of the generation after Hill, heard at second hand that the historian V.H. Galbraith had been marking Higher School Certificate scripts when he came across a couple by a young man who wrote answers 'with very few facts but lots of interesting ideas'. In short, a student who showed signs of developing an original view of the past. Galbraith was so keen to get him to read history at Balliol that he wrote and asked him to enter their open scholarship exams. Hill replied he was down for Trinity, Cambridge, but he sat the Balliol exam nonetheless. 'But you know what he's like', Galbraith said. 'He got anxious during the week he was here and we had to go to his room and buck him up.' A 'very shy, callow and unsophisticated boy', Hill had sat despondently in a cold Balliol room feeling that he had 'failed' in his interview. Galbraith and another tutor burst into his room unannounced, staging an argument which they hoped would provoke him to join in. '"What good", said Galbraith, "ever came out of the Church of England."' Hill was finally tempted to intervene, saying one word, 'Swift', after which he had to improvise a defence of the famous satirist.[16]

While Balliol was considering Hill's application, however, he had apparently gone ahead and accepted the offer from Trinity. Hearing this the other Balliol tutor, Kenneth Bell, drove to York to persuade him to come to Oxford. 'Informed by Mrs Hill that her son was preparing to go to Cambridge, Kenneth replied that, no, he was coming to Balliol.'[17] This he did, entering Balliol as a Brackenbury scholar in 1931.

According to Richard Southern, the medieval historian and lifelong friend of Hill's, Galbraith also 'bludgeoned his parents into letting him go to Germany'. This was, he said, 'the kind of thing Balliol tutors did in those primitive days'. As a result Hill spent six months in the country in 1931, and a further two months there in 1933, having also spent six weeks in Paris in 1932.[18] He was a good linguist, who read both French and German (in fact taking notes from German texts in German), as well as the Russian he learned later and put to work in translating Soviet scholarship for English-speaking audiences. As a teenager, he was capable of composing passable German love poetry and in later life he seems to have read Italian too.[19]

Galbraith was the Balliol tutor who most influenced him. Son of the secretary of a Sheffield steel works, Galbraith had studied at Manchester with some of the great medievalists of the early twentieth century: T.F. Tout, James Tait and Maurice Powicke. During the First World War he had served as a company commander in Palestine and France, earning the Croix de Guerre avec palme. Now in his early forties, he had taught at Manchester and worked at the Public Record Office before coming to Oxford in 1928, where he was particularly known for his close and imaginative reading of documents.[20] He took an interest in Hill, and it was he who helped to draw out the 'shy and stammering Christopher' and encouraged him to combine literature and history, having recognised how bored Hill was 'by the way some parts of history were being taught'.[21]

It was more Galbraith's teaching style than his historical interests which impressed Hill, however: 'his easy egalitarianism … and his irreverence'. Galbraith took pleasure in the character assassination of his colleagues, particularly the Master of the College, 'before shocked but delighted undergraduates'. Tutorials did not convey facts or conclusions but encouraged discussion 'between equals', dismantling established interpretations and building new ones through 'joint work on the relevant documents'. Assuming that any orthodoxy must be wrong, he 'encouraged one to debunk orthodoxies of any kind'; 'a uniquely stimulating tutor' he was also 'the most generous of men'. In fact, he once gave a student top marks for an essay on the grounds that he 'disagreed with every word of it'.[22] Hill was to emulate much of this as a tutor, particularly the insistence that students should form their own opinions. As he wrote to Shiela Grant Duff in 1941, 'I have a sort of physical revulsion from taking one's thought from other people, which seems to me the sin against the Holy Ghost.'[23]

Another key figure in Balliol was Kenneth Bell, who was, according to the Oxford classicist and Fellow of Balliol Oswyn Murray, 'perhaps the most remarkable tutor in Balliol in the first half of the twentieth century, and one of the most important men in Oxford during that period'. Bell's father made a precarious living, partly by painting watercolours and partly from the family publishing firm, G. Bell and Sons. Bell had gone to Balliol in 1903, where he rowed in the first eight, was elected a Fellow of All Souls, took a lectureship at Toronto University, and worked as a director of the family firm. In 1914, before war broke out, he volunteered, and was a successful major in heavy artillery, serving in Flanders throughout. He won the Military Cross at Passchendaele. His letters home reveal that he relished the comradeship of the war, and he seems to have found it easy to make connections across class lines with men serving under him.[24]

He was also a hearty, muscular Christian. Elected to a Fellowship at Balliol in 1919, he had something of a reputation as an 'Ex-Army, back-slapping … beer-drinking man of action'. The novelist Graham Greene thought him 'the most brilliant lecturer in Oxford, on the Tudor period, full of ideas, swears like a Billingsgate fish porter, and married to a very fascinating … wife'.[25] A.B. Rodger's obituary for Bell celebrated the fact that 'Class distinctions and educational distinctions meant simply nothing to him' since he valued 'generosity of soul' above all other virtues.[26] Hill likewise retained a profound Christian egalitarianism throughout his life, and the heartiness probably appealed to him too: 'heartiness has always been a skeleton in my cupboard' he once admitted, and he felt a justified pride that while an undergraduate he had scored a decisive try for Balliol in the inter-collegiate cup final.[27] Rodger recalled Bell telling students, 'Give me the facts and I will give you the ideas',[28] and this may also have influenced Hill, shaping his working method. His many surviving notebooks show him squirrelling away facts to which he would later apply his ideas, a technique that, as we will see, eventually led to criticism – that he decontextualised quotations and facts to the extent of cherry-picking.[29]

Another lasting influence was A.D. 'Sandie' Lindsay, Master of Balliol: Hill 'was an affectionate and cynical observer of Lindsay's mixture of high conscience and low cunning', remembered Hugh Stretton, and 'its funniest expositor'.[30] The admiration was clear though. Lindsay was the son of a minister with a powerful commitment to social activism. Like Bell and Galbraith, he had a good war, rising to be deputy controller of labour in France and mentioned in despatches several times. In politics he was a committed democrat, believing it 'was learned in the self-government of small communities'; he discerned that view in the seventeenth-century English Levellers and supplied a foreword to A.S.P. Woodhouse's selection of documents on *Puritanism and Liberty*, which became critical to teaching in Balliol. For Lindsay, education and democracy were closely connected, and he celebrated 'the great democratic commonwealth of learning, which transcends division of class, religion and nationality, which takes the co-operation of all for granted,

Alexander Dunlop Lindsay in 1938.

and which has worked out a wonderful technique of co-operative think-ing'. In the service of this vision, he published on Kant, Hobbes and Plato for a wider reading public.[31]

He is also remembered for his highly effective tenure as vice-chancellor of Oxford, and for his broad and progressive approach to education. He led the fundraising efforts that helped to expand science departments and to establish Nuffield College – the first co-educational graduate college – and had been instrumental in the development of 'Modern Greats', the hugely successful degree in Philosophy, Politics and Economics. Beyond Oxford he was active with the Workers' Educational Association (WEA) and later led the establishment of the University of Keele, with its highly innovative degree programme. This educational activism was of a piece with his work during the 1930s with the National Council of Social Service and unemployed clubs, as an adviser to the Labour Party and the Trades Union Congress (TUC), and to the International Missionary Council on its work in India.[32]

Hill did not regard Lindsay as a major thinker, and he believed him capable of both hypocrisy and authoritarianism. Nonetheless, many of Lindsay's values were important to him, and he admired Lindsay for 'his utter freedom from affectation and self-importance, his profound sense of the dignity and equality of all human beings', as well as 'a quite exceptional human sympathy which made him always ready to help a colleague or undergraduate in trouble'.[33] Hill also admired the fact that 'Lindsay was always shocking the stuffy in Oxford', for example by organising an undergraduate conciliation committee in 1926 as an alternative 'to sending them away to break the General Strike by driving buses', or by entertaining Gandhi in the Balliol Lodgings.[34] In the 1938 Oxford by-election, Lindsay stood as an independent candidate against the appeasers and the Munich Agreement.

What most attracted Hill though was Lindsay's 'fantastic moral energy'. Lindsay was not motivated 'by considerations of self-aggrandisement or display, or of what was expected of him: he did [all these things] because he thought he ought to'. He was 'a great teacher, and a man who probably did more to make his world a better place than all but a handful of his contemporaries'.[35] Later, as Master of Balliol himself, Hill displayed many of these qualities as an academic administrator; less ruthless perhaps, and more willing to compromise, but also, like Lindsay, willing to recognise 'the dignity and equality of all', or at least (as Hill put it, quoting Cromwell) those who he believed to have 'the root of the matter in them'.[36]

By the time he graduated, besides becoming an exemplary Oxford historian, Hill had also become a Marxist and was soon to join the Communist Party. In some ways, it was a long journey from the respectable provincial Methodism of his youth to become one of the leading Marxist scholars of his generation, but Hill did not leave all of it behind. He later wrote that seventeenth-century radical religion had been willing to challenge orthodoxy: 'It was like wine ... while the censoriousness of Victorian nonconformity had turned the wine into bitter vinegar.'[37] During his time at Oxford he seems to have come to regard the formal restraint of Methodism as a concern merely with forms, codes and rules, rather than the real spirit.

Hill stopped going to Chapel in Oxford during 1931 and, returning home after his first term, he took his younger sister to the theatre, causing a family crisis, expressed in tense silences rather than shouted anger.[38] Four years later, when Samuel Beer and his wife visited, they had 'surreptitiously' gone to the pub, eating liquorice sweets to cover the smell on their breath before they returned to dinner: 'Christopher's [pretended] innocence was beautiful.'[39] By then he had stopped going to chapel in York too and had revealed to his 'anguished' parents that he had lost his faith. There was quite a family crisis, leading to 'acceptance that the generations had moved apart on questions of religion'.[40]

He remained close to his family, although by the later 1930s he had a slightly weary, satirical view of his mother's respectability. He spent Christmas 1939 at the family home, and when his girlfriend (or soon to be girlfriend) Shiela Grant Duff bought him a scarf for Christmas it elicited the verdict from his mother that 'no nice girl would want to be seen dead in it, but she could see no harm in it for a man'. That autumn he wrote to Shiela, 'I have had a letter from the family and cheques (small) and my mother very sordidly told me to buy myself a pair of trousers.'[41] There were political differences too, and he regretted a row with his father 'about the morality of Mr Chamberlain's policy'.[42] The underlying affection was enduring, however: prompted by his first major radio appearance in 1953, his mother wrote a letter full of comfortable gossip. She reported that they had enjoyed watching the coronation on Mr Shaw's TV so much that they had gone to see the film for the colour,

Reproduced by permission of Penelope J. Corfield

The Hill family, at Edward Hill's 80th birthday party, 1961: Christopher (5th left, back row), was wearing a neck brace while suffering neck strain. Also pictured are his sister Irene (2nd right, back row), his mother Janet and father Edward (2nd and 3rd left, front row), and his niece, Penelope Corfield (2nd left back row, next to her father Tony).

but regretted that the weather had prevented them taking part in many events. The weather also affected missionary week, and not having a car was an inconvenience – 'buses are tiresome'. Missionary week and the coronation were hardly likely to be enthusiasms Christopher shared, and yet there was no hint of discomfort or hesitation in her talking to him about them. This was essentially a warm and familiar letter from a proud parent free to tell her son about the things that mattered to her.[43]

Hill's embrace of Marxism was certainly not a simple response to his loss of faith, or a replacement for it. In 1978 Raphael Samuel asked him about this directly – whether rationalism and the secularist movements had led him and others into Marxism. Samuel was particularly interested in Archibald Robertson, who had published biblical criticism and history, and wrote regularly for the *Daily Worker* in the 1950s. Hill disavowed both – Robertson because 'I thought him a dreadful old Stalinist dogmatist' (although 'I expect he was a worthy figure in his earlier career'). On the broader point his reply was revealing: he remembered feeling that Archibald and others 'tended to have a very religious approach to irreligion, substituting one form of dogmatism for another'.[44] When Hill left Methodism he took with him a deep suspicion of dogmatisms of all kinds.

He also, however, retained an obvious respect for the seriousness of socially engaged Christian belief. T.S. Gregory, an inspirational Methodist minister, whose preaching he heard in York in 1929, made a deep impression on him, something reflected in the dedication to Gregory of *The Intellectual Origins of the English Revolution*, published in 1965.[45] Gregory's preaching was marked by an evangelical urgency, aimed at social and personal renewal: 'He made it his duty to denounce the smugness and hypocrisy of his largely bourgeois congregation and to preach to them the political consequences of their belief in the equality of all souls.' Leaning forward, his eyes sweeping the congregation, he urged the congregation to see God in the eyes of every fellow sinner, 'even the poorest beggar or the most abandoned prostitute or the most vicious wretch in the city streets'. Gregory later became a Catholic, drawn by its spiritual universalism rather than ceremony, something that gave Hill wry amusement.[46]

As Corfield puts it: 'Marxism combined an underlying moral belief in equality with a sweeping view of historical destiny that predicted its eventual achievement.'[47] Hill never lost the imprint of Methodism's serious social and political engagement, of the potentially transformative power of ideals, and there is a clear line to be drawn between that

Christian egalitarianism and his communism, not least in his enduring fascination with Gerrard Winstanley, the visionary who led an experiment in communal living under the direction of God's laws in 1651.

The connection, however, may have been more fundamental: Gregory recognised parallels between Hill's Marxist interests and the concerns he had pursued in his own religious life. Gregory had been flattered by the acknowledgement in 1965, writing to Hill that it was 'a high honour and of course I shall value it very highly'. 'I had no idea that the youngest member of the congregation was listening so closely, but I remember you very well. You were a shy and quiet young man. We have travelled in apparently different directions but I think perhaps it is largely a matter of appearance.' What he meant by that is clear in his advice about how to formulate an insight that Hill wanted to include in the preface, that 'all accepted truths, just because they become accepted, tend to become lies':

> I think it would be nearer to what I used to say, and easier for the public to digest if you say 'tend to become' instead of 'are probably'. A truth could not as such be anything but itself. But it does make sense to say that the process of being accepted, of being established, kills its truthfulness, turns it into a fiction or a myth or an abstraction or a conditioned reflex. Kills it anyhow. It becomes unreal. What becomes is your business as an historian and as a dialectical materialist, and was my business in describing religious experience.[48]

Like Methodism, Marxism explained the world and how to act in it. Both provided a holistic worldview and also the promise that conditions would one day be right for the realisation of its ideals. Marxism explained why equality had not been possible in past societies, but also that 'the cause of justice was not lost' and could be won by human action.[49] The dynamics of social and political life would eventually create the right environment for the triumph of egalitarianism – intellect, social life and personal affect would be harmonised as a result.

It is hard to be precise about Hill's intellectual development as he left Methodism behind, perhaps more difficult than for many people; in fact, Galbraith used to enjoy saying that at Oxford there had 'been a conservative Christopher'.[50] Hill later claimed that, rather than his teachers, the main influence on him had been other students, including Norman O. Brown, who in the late 1960s and early 1970s became the doyen of student revolutionaries in California. Brown had apparently urged on him a moral responsibility to join the Communist Party (although Brown may not have done so himself).[51] Hill had been part of G.D.H. Cole's Pink Lunch Club, along with later luminaries such as Isaiah Berlin, Richard Crossman, Roy Harrod, Stuart Hampshire, J.L. Austin and E.H.M. Jones. Membership was subsequently taken to be a badge of anti-fascist pride.[52] He was also a member of the Labour Club and the October Club (named for the Russian Revolution), and remembered being thrilled when, in the course of a lecture on the global economy, Cole had said, 'Personally, I hope that the whole thing is going to smash.'[53] Another significant figure was A.L. Rowse, a rising star in the historical world, son of a working-class Cornish family, who had achieved remarkable social mobility. He knew Hill well enough to introduce him in 1935 to Harold Laski, a key figure in left-wing intellectual life, and Rowse (who was not prone to underestimating his own importance in the world) claimed at least part responsibility for Hill's Marxism.[54]

In truth there is no great mystery about the gravitation of young idealists to Marxism and communism in Oxford in the 1930s: Rodney Hilton, another leading historian and life-long friend of Hill's, recalled that in those days 'a Marxist intellectual could not fail to be involved in politics and the almost inescapable choice in the late 1930s was the Communist Party'.[55] Denis Healey, later a Labour MP and cabinet member, who was himself briefly a party member, thought that in 1939 the Communist Club had 200 undergraduate members; '[n]ot many outstanding undergraduates on the left did not join'. Many others belonged to the predominantly Marxist Labour Club.[56]

The exact chronology and detail of Hill's intellectual influences is harder to trace. Looking back on the origins of his worldview, he liked to claim that it was the metaphysical poets rather than Marx that led him to the English Revolution; and Beer confirms the impression that his interest in the revolution preceded his Marxism.[57] Eric Hobsbawm thought that Britain was distinctive in developing a cadre of Marxist *historians* rather than philosophers and theorists, something he attributed in part to the fact that 'on the arts side of British sixth-forms literature took the space left vacant by the absence of philosophy'. Prominent Marxists like Hill, Victor Kiernan, A.L. Morton, E.P. Thompson and Raymond Williams all arrived at historical analysis 'from, or with, a passion for *literature*'.[58] Hobsbawm also noted the influence of the anti-Marxist F.R. Leavis on Cambridge Marxists, an influence that Hill was to acknowledge in 1984 in a letter to Margot Heinemann, the writer, academic and former comrade from the Communist Party of Great Britain (CPGB):

'I secretly suspect I was rather more over-awed by Leavis in the 30s and 40s than you suggest – after all, he had his good sides?'[59] The appeal lay perhaps in Leavis's opposition to the literary establishment, and his desire to demystify literature.[60]

In the same letter to Heinemann he wrote that his line about metaphysical poetry was a 'quarter truth anyway'.[61] It was, in a way, a deflection that reflected his 'dislike of "confessional" types of conversation; and from his impish sense of humour' – it aimed at disarming questioners expecting an answer about Hitler,[62] but it was an answer he gave more than once, and that he developed at length in an article for the *Listener* in 1967.[63] It certainly contained a real truth: Hill's personal papers from the 1930s reveal him struggling to find forms of authentic personal expression. A profoundly serious person, he was troubled by the world around him, and he was seeking answers in literature rather than economic theory. He wrote and transcribed poetry on peace, love and even an acerbic view of the life of a Don. He seems to have planned to write a novel too.[64]

In what looks like a miscellany from the mid-1930s, Hill reflected on art, self-expression and the crisis of the contemporary world. It is the record of a profound literary sensibility but also a powerful concern with sexual expression:

> The impulse to art is a need like hunger. But unlike hunger, a desire to give parallels the desire to receive. Closest correspond[ence] copulat[ion], giving and receiving. So with crit: in both art and sex there are certain fundamentals wh[ich] must be there if satisfact[ion] is to be received at all: and these are immutable standards.[65]

Hill was clearly concerned about the debasement of art and with it authentic sexual desire:

> The seven and sixpenny novel is the whore – cash down, fills in the time, and purges. Like sex, art may be perverted to barren ends; to narcissism; may have the external trappings without fulfilling the essential function; may be diverted, distracted, impotent, too thin, too inexperienced, too sophisticated. At its best it has fresh full healthy giving, in wh[ich] its own want is satisfied: and this is the basis of all g[rea]t art.[66]

These failings of both art and feeling lay in the 'apathy of modern life … There is none of the intellectual activity of Athens and Florence. All is dead, dumb, listless, bored.' The young Hill expresses profound disillusionment and alienation:

> Things happen, but we do not mind. They are not for us, not by us. We
> have got used to inaction now. To keep us alive we need repeated emo-
> tional stimulus: and being a democracy we get them – wireless, cinema,
> jazz, novels, newspapers, sentimentality. These things are not bad in
> themselves, not very bad. But they exhibit a dreadful state of mental
> inertia. We do not think: it is too hard work. Instead we buy the Daily
> Mail. Besides thinking would get us nowhere: it is a mechanical age.

Intellectual life is denuded: 'Second-rate thought is definitely discouraged, and without that you can never have first-rate thought.' As a result
'there is no creative art. We admire past greatness from afar, and pathet-
ically imitate it. But our admiration is traditional, our imitation slavish.'[67]

In all, 'Greatness is not worthwhile nowadays. Education is "practical"
and promotes anything but thought.' All this is a reflection of the scale
and anonymity of modern life: 'Life in a city state [like Athens or Flor-
ence] was concentrated: we are oppressed and stultified by our own size,
and lose interest in government and all its ramifications, whilst to be a
Mayor is confession of social inferiority.' There is not much reflection on
music, but he took notes on Brahms and Dvořák; perhaps the interest
there was in their power of emotional expression and their engagement
with folk traditions.[68]

Here are some of the hallmarks of a profound intellectual and personal crisis. 'I don't really know what I want', he wrote, among a series
of notes that reveal him reflecting in an unclear way on the relationship between books, self-control and desire, in part a reflection on D.H.
Lawrence. The body is, or is greater than, the soul, he writes, and there
are disjointed notes on what this might mean for him: 'Whatever a man
desires, better for him to have than to refuse himself'; 'But must have
courage and objectivity to find what really is desired'. Achieving a comfortable union of body and mind seems to be the key: 'Unio mystica of
2 bodies the only hope: if God not there, nowhere.'[69]

The relevance of the metaphysical poets to this crisis was that, as
T.S. Eliot claimed, they achieved an 'integrated sensibility' capable of
authentic expression which had subsequently been lost. Samuel Johnson
had noted in the eighteenth century that these poets shared a style in
which 'the most heterogeneous ideas are yoked by violence together';
Eliot thought it was their capacity to harmonise apparently conflicting
ideas that subsequent generations (including Johnson) had lost.[70] In a
1967 article Hill cited the opening statement by the soul from Marvell's
'Dialogue between the Soul and the Body': that it is enslaved by the body,

with its 'vain head, and double-heart'.[71] For Eliot it was their ability to deal with complexity that made the metaphysicals remarkable; that, at their best, they 'engaged in the task of trying to find the verbal equivalent for states of mind and feeling'. He connected this directly to the struggle of leading writers of his own time, expressed in literary modernism. For the current age, wrote Eliot, 'it appears likely that poets in our civilization, as it exists at present, must be *difficult*'. In the face of the complexity of modern life, the poet had to be 'more comprehensive, more allusive, more indirect, in order to force, to dislocate if necessary, language into his meaning'.[72] Hill's work on early modern literature consistently addressed this same problem – of how language was stretched in order to convey new meaning.

The alienation of feeling and the fragmented meaning of social life in Hill's notes seem to echo Eliot's poetry, in 'Prufrock' or 'The Wasteland', for example, and perhaps also Joyce's *Ulysses*. In fact, he later thought he was 'rather … overwhelmed' by Eliot's poetry, although there was 'not much good about his ideology'.[73] He seems also to have been reading Freud and other psychoanalytic work, as well as de Sade, and Stuart Gilbert's 1930 study of *Ulysses*, completed with Joyce's participation.[74] Apparently, though, neither modernism nor psychoanalysis provided him with a satisfying resolution of what he saw as the profound tensions in contemporary life; Eliot's writing was for him a provocation rather than an exemplar. Hill later denounced him (as well as Graham Greene, with whom he corresponded in the late 1960s) for responding to the problems of contemporary life by trying to revive the 'priestly magic' that the Elizabethans had thrown off.[75] It was Eliot's insights into thought and feeling that attracted him, not his worldview.

Hill also took notes on D.H. Lawrence's *Lady Chatterley's Lover* which again reveal this concern to harmonise thought and feeling. The novel is normally interpreted in exactly this way: in terms of the alienation of individuals from their feelings, trapped in the structures and practices of their society. Constance (Lady Chatterley) is denied emotional and physical intimacy in her marriage, in part because her husband, Sir Clifford, had been paralysed from the waist down by a war injury. She finds these fulfilments in a transgressive affair – outside her marriage and across class lines – expressed in equally transgressive language. It was this that made the novel unpublishable, and the subject of an obscenity trial as late as 1960.

At Oxford, Hill was said to be easy in female company and his notebooks reveal respect for women: he notes, for example, that there has never been a female buffoon, not because they lack humour, but because they are steady and thoughtful; and (more pithily) that all the greatest English kings have been queens.[76] It was sex, not women, that concerned him, and he could not find in English literature satisfactory means to express a healthy attitude towards it: 'The only realistic attitudes to sex are the glorification of D.H. L[awrence] or the fear and disgust of Joyce. Other attitudes are conventional – the romantic conventionalises glorification, the repressive conventionalises fear. Sh[akespeare] always fear when not conventionally romantic.'[77] This perhaps informs his view that in the end Lawrence showed a lack of nerve: overall, Hill found *Lady Chatterley's Lover* a 'curiously reactionary moral story. Vice defeated, virtue rewarded, ends on reconciling note of wedding sermon, and live happily ever afterwards.'[78] It is easy to see here how his provincial Methodism was failing to satisfy: how the vinegar of nineteenth-century nonconformist formalism about conventional sexual and social relations was failing to offer him spiritual refreshment.

Many of these reflections seem to date from 1933 and 1934, the period in which Corfield says that Hill became a convinced Marxist.[79] Those who knew Hill at that time do not describe a person in crisis. Samuel Beer's wife found him 'nimble, witty, warm, and handsome'. He worked very hard and 'moments of self-revelation were rare'. While this was clearly not the whole story, to the outside world he presented a wry and sardonic front, a development perhaps of the 'Imp' first noted in 1912. Beer recalled that Hill was never 'clever at other people's expense [and] the objects of his ridicule were not personal'. A 'pervasive sense of the ridiculous made him great fun to be with', although that humour also had a defensive function, 'helping him to avoid any serious discussion of his personal feelings or thoughts about the world'.[80]

These notes reveal therefore a profound reflection on what was important to him, and on how to live well, rather than symptoms of a personal breakdown as he left Methodism. Some of them move beyond reflections on alienation, personal and social, but not in an obviously Marxist direction. They range from philosophical observations ('Some things can be more different to one another than if they were exactly opposite: by appealing to different faculties of the mind, not to alternative aspects of the same faculty') to more challenging, but not particularly Marxist, views on social development. For example, he noted the thought that 'Civilisation generally means the artificial preservation of the unfit, but in times of mental upheaval (Reformation, Fr[ench] Rev[olution], ab[olition] of slave trade) "Progress" comes only at the price of human life: then usually the unfit.' Civilisation protects the mediocre, he writes: 'Imagine most of us if convention broke down as the result, e.g., of another world war.' Fear of another war was of course not idle speculation, and he returned to the thought: 'By developing their intellectual powers to a greater extent, [the unfit] manage to defend themselves. But the average brutal man gradually assimilates their inventions and new advances have to be made.' The pace of this process, he speculated, increases until the brutes catch up and there is Armageddon.[81]

There are of course notes on Hegel, Marx, Engels, Lenin and others (although again hard to date),[82] but it seems that he was primed for Marxism, as he often claimed, more by feelings of personal and social alienation than more narrowly political discontents – his route into Marxism was humanist, not via politics and economy.

Marx, Engels and Lenin are more often associated with a profound economic critique of capitalism; for example, that it is prone to cyclical crises as capital accumulates and investment returns decline, creating financial bubbles and crashes. At the same time, it polarises wealth and power, creating a class with no real stake in the system who will eventually overthrow it in favour of something more stable, rational and just. The classic work in this strand of Marxism is *Capital*, published in parts from the late 1860s onwards. But Hill seems to have been drawn to Marxism by the promise that the alienation and dissociation of sensibility felt by so many in the 1930s would be resolved in a successor system – that a more just society would emerge from the crisis which would allow for more fulfilled individual lives. It was not the economic critique that drew him in so much as the humanistic promise of a society that allowed individual and collective flourishing.

There the key thought is that the economic life of society (the mode of production) generates social roles and expectations. In the capitalist mode of production, these roles fail to satisfy our authentic desires or essential humanity. Bourgeois economic life creates expectations with which many people feel patently unhappy. The collapse of the capitalist economic order promised greater human fulfilment because it would do away with the institutions, roles and expectations that left so many people alienated and unfulfilled. The crucial text here is *The German Ideology*, largely written in the 1840s but not published until 1932. In a way it took its departure from the philosopher Ludwig Feuerbach's reflection that humans created God and then became his slaves: that cultural beliefs and social practices are human products but are experienced by individuals as constraints. Marxists stressed how such cultural and social practices are products of the pattern of production that underpins social life. Hill's reflections in the 1930s seem to lead more directly to this element of Marxism than to the critique of political economy: a particular mode of production leads us to imagine roles for ourselves, which sustain that economic order, but which are also prisons of our own collective making.

In a collection of notes on Christianity and Hegel's and Marx's views on religion, Hill speculates that up until the seventeenth century it was possible for an 'average cultivated man (and their tutors – Marvell, Hobbes) to attempt to cover all knowledge'. It was the subsequent development of a new division of labour – specialised agricultural and industrial techniques, and the services that worked with them – that made it 'impossible to embrace all culture'. By the eighteenth century, country house culture and its literature had become separated from their agricultural base. This was what made sense 'of all this talk about the integrated sensibility of the metaphysicals' and why it had been lost.[83] The central insight is that the organisation of production reflects but also shapes how we comprehend the world: the metaphysical poets were able to achieve what they did because they inhabited a world where material conditions still allowed an integrated sensibility.

Hill said in a later lecture that he first read *Capital* as an undergraduate, but 'found it pretty tough going'. Over the following three or four years he read Marx's 'more historical works' and was much influenced by them, though he was careful not to say too much about Marx in his final exam papers.[84] In general, the notes on Marxist writers in his papers are philosophical, historical and sociological: there are notes on Lenin and the state, but not, in the papers that survive, on *Capital*. It is easy to see the attraction for him of Lenin's *The State and Revolution* (1917); for instance, the idea that the state arose to arbitrate battles of social interest in favour of the dominant class. Institutions arise and take shape on an economic basis, and then help to sustain that mode of production; social and political institutions, and their shortcomings, reflect the material base on which they are constructed. Lenin was here building on Engels's earlier work *The Origin of the Family, Private Property and the State* (1884), which analysed connections between family forms, modes of production and class formation; for example, that ideals of bourgeois marriage reflected the demands of maintaining private property. Hill took notes on that too. He seems to have been primarily interested in this aspect of Marxist analysis: how material interests interacted with culture to produce dysfunctional forms of behaviour such as the defence of privilege, the sanctity of the bourgeois family or the belligerence of bourgeois states. In sum, although there are no notes on *The German Ideology* (it had only recently been published, in the Soviet Union), Hill's Marxism seems to have been inspired more by that strand of Marxism than by the critique of capitalist economy in *Capital*.

There are also extensive notes on historical materialism.[85] One of the central problems in Marxism was whether the mode of production determined everything else or, if not, how we should think about its relationship to society and culture. Hill resisted 'determinist' views of the relationship between material life and social and cultural practices – the claim that the mode of production determined everything else – not least because it denied people any role in making their own history. To defend the role and importance of ideas was at the same time to hold out the hope that people could actively change their world for the better rather than simply waiting on historical development. Historical materialism, in his view, argued for a dialectical relationship between economy and culture – what people thought shaped the economy as much as the economy set limits on their thinking. New thoughts could help create a new society.

Dialectics are critical to Marxism in a more fundamental way – the story of the human past is one of modes of production and the societies erected on them being challenged by new modes and new thinking. This confrontation, between 'thesis' and 'antithesis', results in a new form of life, the synthesis, which itself then becomes open to challenge. The bourgeois challenge to feudal society had produced a synthesis – modern capitalism – which was itself now under challenge by its antithesis, socialism. Hill believed that the challenge came from new ideas, not just the collapse of the capitalist system under the weight of its own contradictions. He was interested in how people made their own history.

Hill's mature thinking about personal authenticity was also dialectical in form: the oppositions of thought and feeling, body and soul, civilisation and brutality, for example. As he explained in 1967 in relation to metaphysical poetry, the key advantage of a Marxist analysis was that it related the dualisms and tensions in the poetry to the social strains and stresses of the wider society that produced that writing: a period, he wrote, 'like that in which we lived'. Marxism was attractive because of its determination 'to see society as a whole, to relate philosophy, literature and science to the society from which they sprang'.[86] 'Just as the poetry of Eliot and Auden and Spender and so on seemed to us to have a direct relationship to the crisis of the 1930s, so ... it seemed to me perfectly obvious that metaphysical poetry had a relation to the crisis of the seventeenth century.' The key to understanding this dissociation of sensibility was the analysis of the contradictions in the society that produced it: 'Man is not merely a social animal, but an animal which can develop into an individual only in society.'[87]

Seen this way, Marxism offered a persuasive analysis of a contemporary social, political and economic crisis. That crisis and the associated problems of personal alienation were for Hill symptoms of a collapse of middle-class certainties during the 1930s, leading him to ponder how society could be organised to allow human flourishing and a more rational, stable and just political order. Marxism offered a response to personal alienation that modernism and psychoanalysis seemed to lack, and for this reason it also offered a constructive response to collapsing political certainties.

Looking back some time later, he said that for him the story of the political crisis started in August 1931, just as he went to Oxford. Britain's position as a 'top nation' could no longer be taken for granted, and following the Crash in 1929 London banks had been lending all over the world. Ramsay MacDonald, the Labour prime minister, had sold ordinary people out, cutting unemployment benefit and imposing means tests. The National Government, with a 500-seat majority, then took sterling off the gold standard with no discernible benefit. The labour movement, Hill said, had never forgotten the betrayal. Mass unemployment produced demoralisation and despair. For Hill, the mood was captured by Walter Greenwood's social realist novel about life in Salford during the Great Depression, *Love on the Dole*, a morality tale about how working-class lives and life chances were shaped by a crisis of the world around them that was not of their making.[88]

In that context, he later wrote, Marxism offered an antidote to the 'facile' liberalism of the nineteenth and early twentieth centuries, with its naive certainties about progress. Earlier thinkers had done much to challenge such certainties. Rousseau in particular had argued that the rise of civilisation had been accompanied by a decline in morality, and Marx and Engels had extended that thought, showing that capitalism produces increased inequality and injustice, but also creates the conditions of its own demise and, hence, of the emergence of a better society. As Hill summarised their views: 'Loss of control over production by the majority, and its concentration in the hands of a privileged minority, produced the pretence that the interests of the ruling class were the same as the interests of society as a whole.' But Marx had also shown that the end point of economic development was a return to a classless society and primitive equality. This replaced the need for the 'vulgar optimism' of the nineteenth-century bourgeoisie: 'History is a tragedy but it need not be a meaningless tragedy. Nor are we mere spectators: we have our parts in the action.'[89]

The grim domestic picture was the counterpoint to a lawless international order: the rise of Hitler, the Japanese occupation of Manchuria, and the Italian occupation of Abyssinia. In the long shadow cast by the First World War, the League of Nations preferred non-military sanctions, and certainly anti-war feeling and pacifism were a marked feature of life in Oxford. The divisions were stark, between desire for collective security and the cultural feeling reflected for example in *All Quiet on the Western Front*, *Death of a Hero* and *Journey's End*.[90] In February 1933 the Oxford Union, the student debating society, discussed the motion, 'This House will under no circumstances fight for its King and country'. It was carried by 275 votes to 153, causing uproar in the press. Hill later said he learned more from this controversy 'than from any other single incident in my undergraduate career'. The motion had attracted not just pacifists but also those who saw in the Soviet Union hope for a different world order; much of the commentary after the fact sought to disentangle the conviction that war was futile from expressions of support for Moscow, based on the idea that class war was inevitable and that the problem was capitalism.[91]

Hill was not a pacifist. He saw the Anglo-German naval agreement of June 1935, which regulated the relative size of the two navies, as a sell-out; he had no time for the Hoare–Laval Pact with Mussolini, which sought peace in Ethiopia by ceding most of Abyssinia to Italy; and he thought sanctions in Rhodesia and Manchuria 'bogus'. Above all he was disgusted by the non-interventionist response to the Spanish Civil War which began after a military coup in 1936 against the democratically elected Popular Front government. He later said that he would have fought 'if braver', recalling that 'I rather half-heartedly volunteered and was told I should not [go to fight] … I must admit I did not push my volunteering very hard.' Here he quoted Auden: 'To-morrow, perhaps the future … But to-day the struggle.'[92] In that struggle he had more faith in the Soviet Union than in the British government.

The failures of the League of Nations, the Japanese invasion of China in 1937, the *Anschluss* and the Munich Agreement all spoke of spiralling international disorder: Munich, Hill remembered, had not involved consultation with the Soviet Union, and was marked by both relief and shame.[93] In the face of all this, A.D. Lindsay offered an inspiring lead. He stood as an independent candidate against appeasement in the 1938 Oxford by-election and took a large bite out of Quintin Hogg's majority in a conventionally very safe Tory seat. Remembering it fifty years later, Hill said, with a characteristic twinkle, that the fight was 'good against evil, democracy against Fascism, Balliol against All Souls'.[94]

The 1930s had opened with a profound shock to the City of London and the old regime, marking the end of London as the centre of the capitalist world. There had followed a fundamental challenge for the labour movement posed by the policies of the Labour Party and non-intervention. The result was fragmentation on the left and a distrust of traditional politicians, leading many to an admiration for the Soviet Union and into the Communist Party. The contrast Hill drew was between the actions of the Soviet Union and the capitalist response to global depression – such as dumping Brazilian coffee into the sea in order to bolster the price rather than allowing its consumption.[95] Richard Southern, a contemporary of Hill's (they were born only two days apart), shared his memory of the crisis: 'the experience of those years "cut our minds loose from their traditional moorings and launched them on a sea of speculation over which they at last floated to a great diversity of havens"'. He and Hill found very different havens (Southern was a devout Anglican), but the shared experience of the crisis bound them together throughout their lives.[96]

Hill was consistently more forthcoming on these matters of state than on his interior life, and it is easy to see how a serious-minded young man coming to political consciousness in these years would have been drawn to Marxism and the state built on its principles, the USSR. Although in his early career, and particularly during his active membership of the Communist Party, the focus of his Marxism was on the state, revolution and political economy, in the longer run his interests were more clearly expressed in terms of a Marxist humanism for which the key question, as the historian Barbara Epstein puts it, was 'what sort of society would be most conducive to human thriving?'[97] The advantage Marxism held over psychoanalysis or the subjectivism of modernist literature was that it offered a science both of society and the individual, of state politics and individual fulfilment.

After graduating in 1934, having won a Goldsmith's Senior Studentship and the University's Lothian Prize for an essay on the Jansenists of Port Royal, Hill was elected to a Fellowship at All Souls College.[98] By that time he was a Marxist but had not joined the CPGB despite his membership of the October Club. Becoming a convinced Marxist and joining the party were quite different processes: one the adoption of an intellectual position, the other a judgement about political tactics.

Following graduation Hill had been uncertain on the question of political strategy and how he would make a difference in the world. During 1935 he did some work with the Fabian Society, to which he had direct connections through Cole and Rowse. Cole had established the Fabian Research Bureau in 1931, including a Political Section which met in Theo Chorley's rooms at the LSE. Between 1932 and 1934 the Section produced papers on the reorganisation of government departments and ministerial functions, the position of the prime minister in relation to the crown and the cabinet, electoral reform, the need for a redistribution of seats, and devolution. The membership included Harold Laski, who in November 1933 had been asked to prepare a memorandum on 'Ought there to be a second chamber? If so, what?' At the same time Rowse was being proposed as a possible member and was invited to prepare a memorandum on 'The case against the House of Lords'. H.R.G. Greaves was asked to write one on the press and public opinion.[99]

It was Hill, however, who took on both projects: a memorandum on the House of Lords and a draft pamphlet on the press and public opinion. His thoughts on the press were presented in February 1935 and discussed at a meeting in March, where it was decided to wait on comments from professional journalists. A full pamphlet produced in June was due for discussion in July, and although it was not published, notes on the 'constructive points' he made were taken up by Richard Commyns Carr in preparing a memorandum on 'A socialist policy for the press'. Hill presented his thoughts on the House of Lords on 22 July.[100]

The tone of both papers is outspoken. His discussion of the House of Lords is in itself fairly conventional – whether there should be a second chamber, and if so how constituted, how to define its function and how to ensure its subordination to the Commons. For him there was clear frustration that the democratic will could be thwarted by a permanent Tory majority in the Lords, but his proposal was fairly modest: a modified version of the Norwegian arrangement of a second house nominated by the first house and completely renewed at each election. What drew more disapproval – from the Labour politician W.T. Wells (another Balliol man) – were his thoughts about political tactics. It could safely be assumed that the Lords would not support legislation for their own abolition, and this could potentially create a two-year paralysis while legislation took effect without that consent. Hill discussed various ways of applying pressure in such an interim, including the threat of a General Strike used to pressure the king to support reform and bring the Lords into line.[101]

He had also, and perhaps improbably, tried to become the BBC's parliamentary correspondent, but it was the Fellowship of All Souls that was to give direction to his life. This was not because it offered a direct path into an academic career. In fact he had hesitations about academic life and Oxford, and felt particularly ambivalent about All Souls. As he told Richard Pares, 'the one thing I don't want to be is an academic. If I become an academic I shall regard that as the ultimate defeat.' Taking up his Fellowship, he later claimed, 'had nothing to do with history. Rather, it gave you two years free time … Doing nothing. No questions asked.'[102] In November 1935 he had told Isaiah Berlin that 'Pares had written to me about [the possibility of a Fellowship at] Wadham. I still have hankerings for the wider world.' Two months later he was still of the same mind: 'I don't think I want to come back to Oxford: do any provincial universities yearn for a historian? Or should I join the *Daily Worker*, which has become an excellent paper?'[103] He remained ambivalent (at best) about All Souls for his entire career. Ved Mehta, the Indian-born writer who was at Balliol while Hill was Master, recalled Hill saying that his experience at All Souls contributed to his decision to join the Communist Party: seeing the devotion of the Fellows to the good life, a 'lot of junior Fellows felt, as I did, that the college was just a place of privilege'. The author's biography he supplied for his final collection of essays mentioned St Peter's School, York, University College, Cardiff, Balliol and visiting positions at The Open University and Lancashire Polytechnic, but made no mention of All Souls.[104]

The Fellowship at All Souls was formative, therefore, but not for the reasons one might expect: rather, it made possible an extended visit to the USSR. More than one Oxford don has told me (only half-jokingly) that in those days, and indeed until much later, the college was opposed to the writing of PhDs, in part because it would have meant that a Fellow of All Souls had to submit to the judgement of a Fellow of another college. In any case, Hill did not write a PhD, but was encouraged to travel by Humphrey Sumner, a specialist in Russian history and one of his Balliol tutors, who had been a Fellow of All Souls and was later to be elected Warden there.[105] It was in the USSR that it became clear to Hill what he should do in the face of the crisis of bourgeois culture.

Christopher Hill in 1940.

On 13 July 1935, soon after his final exams and as the Fabians were discussing his pamphlets, he embarked on the *Smolny* at Hays Wharf, London, bound for Leningrad, his hair swept back in the style of Joe Stalin.[106] His purpose was to learn Russian and to get to know the Soviet scholarship on English history, something the librarian at Worcester College had also encouraged him to do.[107] The following six months were to be a defining experience, during which his Marxism and admiration for the USSR were consummated with membership of the Communist Party, which he joined on his return in May 1936.[108]

He later referred to this period of Soviet history as a Golden Age, sandwiched between the horrors of collectivisation and the purges to come.[109] While in Moscow he lodged with the wife of a kulak, a member of the wealthy peasant class seen as an obstacle to the creation of collective agriculture and subject to brutal repression – official policy was that the kulaks should be liquidated as a class. When Hill arrived his host's husband was 'doing time in Siberia' for speculation, but he turned up during Hill's stay, 'in the bloom of health'. Hill concluded from this 'that kulaks could not be having as bad a time in concentration camps as foreign reports said'. Similarly, when the first purges began, again during his stay, Hill assumed that the victims were guilty as charged;

he rationalised the purges of 1938 in the same way, having by then 'long experience with the whoppers [told by] the English press'. Clearly, as he later admitted, it was during this period that he 'got some of my illusions about the Soviet Union': having gone to Moscow 'favourably disposed; I came back committed'.[110] When he disembarked at Harwich from the Hook of Holland eight months later, on 23 February 1936, it was said 'he has the appearance of a communist' and his luggage was searched. A few months later he returned to Leningrad, at the end of May 1936, embarking from Hay's Wharf aboard the *Cooperatzia*, having joined the CPGB earlier that month.[111] His Marxism was now firmly tied to his admiration for the USSR, and he had come to see the CPGB as the best hope for progressive change in Britain.

The best insight we have into this key period of Hill's life is a notebook with fragments of what appears to be a mixture of a semi-autobiographical novel and memoir. The date is unclear but it has chapters set in Moscow, around the British Library, and in Cardiff, where Hill worked from 1936 to 1938, and some of the notes are written on the back of a letter dated 1937, folded into the book. One set of fragments relates to a scene in Oxford, where the narrator has taken his younger sister. At the railway station they bump into another academic, who takes offence at the narrator's effusive greeting. The sister, 'Mary', is galvanised by the visit and talks about her School Certificate all the way home. Irene, Hill's younger sister, went to St Anne's College, Oxford, in 1938.[112]

It is likely then that the drafts date from shortly after Hill's return from the Soviet Union. In the fragments relating to Moscow, the narrator celebrates the Soviet Golden Age as a matter not of material well-being but of the honesty of Soviet society: '[t]he real absence', he writes, 'of class hostilities, suspicions … is the 1st thing one notices here'. For '70% of the pop[ulation] life is, on the material side, less pleasant than in Eng[land]. But on the non-material side there is no [comparison]: that is more important to me than all your promises of physical comfort in the near future, though I believe them too.' An element of that honesty of Soviet society is emotional and sexual self-expression: 'Its such a relief to be in a sane country. Where wages have some connection with work done, where power has no connection with money, where sex is not a matter of rubber shops and lavatory jokes.'[113] Soviet society seemed to realise the possibility of a social organisation that harmonised individual authenticity with social justice.

The narrator expresses these thoughts to Tanya, his married Russian teacher, for whom he feels a doomed love. Hill had an affair in Russia and he, or at least his narrator, records the sense of loss on his departure: 'in fact the limb did not pain me until it was amputated. That is what love had been: custom, comfort, unnoticed mutual selfidentification, definable only by abs[ence] and regr[ets]. Sceptic that I am I didn't really know how different it was from kindliness till it was over.' Hill was later to refer to his affair in letters to Shiela Grant Duff, and with a clear memory of the pain.[114] This revelation of personal feeling was associated too with admiration for the Soviet system which allowed such authenticity. Tanya 'was as impressed as I meant her to be' by the narrator's political declarations: 'you have at least the advantage of not being a hypocrite, she said'.[115]

Did the narrator belong in the USSR though, and if not, what could he do in Britain? Two days later, in place of the usual lesson, Tanya takes him to the theatre, and in the interval they view an exhibition of paintings, 'Interventionists in Samara', that includes work by her husband Kostya. The exhibition turns out to represent a response to Czech intervention in the civil war.[116] Two German tourists discussing the paintings speculate about whether the death and sacrifice depicted were worth it: 'Does anybody really remember the martyrs, not just lip-service? This state is built on their bones, suckled with their blood; and they are a series of not v[ery] good pictures on the wall that tourists are taken to see and criticize.' To the narrator these seem self-contradictory thoughts – if a state had been built then how could the 'pouring out of life' have been 'pointless'? It seemed 'the maddest individualism to deny the triumph in that'.[117] To him this sacrifice had been remarkable, and meaningful.

However, between Hill's narrator and Tanya there lay a vast gulf of experience, for she had direct knowledge of this sacrifice and suffering. She had met her husband Kostya in an orphanage – they had both lost parents in the civil war. Kostya had learned to paint and earned a scholarship to Moscow, where he had students and sold art abroad before being ordered to the Caucasus. Sometime later Tanya, by then also having been at University in Moscow, was by chance sent there too. She shows the narrator a painting by Kostya that expresses something she shares with him: 'A lot of our people were shot. The picture is of a detachment of them being led off to be executed. And to the first man in the picture – a big strong man you may have noticed – Kostya gave his father's face. And down in a corner, where some women are watching – did you see? – one of those is like his mother.'[118]

Lacking this shared experience, the narrator is convinced by Bolshevism but unsure what it might mean in Britain or for him. In part it was a question of personal qualities ('It is no good my going down to the working cl[ass] and preaching bloody rev[olution] in an Oxford accent', he writes), but also of the social and political conditions in 'England' (the term Hill habitually used). The narrator is sceptical about the CPGB, identifying the Labour Party as the genuine working-class party. The 'handful of univ[ersity] bourg[eois] intellectuals and lumpen proletariat that calls itself the CP' achieved nothing by simply attacking the working-class party. Hill had also been put off by the egotism of Frank Meyer, a prominent figure in communist circles in Oxford in the 1930s: 'A very nasty, shrill, neurotic show-off, who was one of the main reasons why I didn't join the Party when I was an undergraduate.'[119] In a verdict that resonates with a lot of Hill's historical writing, however, the real point for the narrator was the connection between ideas and social conditions: the CPGB 'is imitating the Bolsheviks in a totally different situation.'[120]

During the late 1920s and early 1930s, confronted by the Labour Party's betrayal of the working class and the formation of the National Government, and encouraged by the Great Depression to think that a revolutionary situation was developing, the CPGB had adopted a policy of 'class against class', refusing to cooperate with reformists. Middle-class reformists were regarded as 'social fascists' and in the coming years no strong distinction was drawn between fascist and imperialist regimes, both of which were regarded as forms of bourgeois state resorting to desperate measures in the face of terminal failure. These views were championed by Rajani Palme Dutt, the leading British communist intellectual, but they followed closely the Comintern line. Established in 1919 to coordinate the global struggle for communism, the Comintern had in practice become a means by which the Soviet party directed the actions of other national parties. After 1928 it had encouraged this class against class line, confidently predicting the collapse of the bourgeois order.[121] Clearly, to Hill's narrator, this line was misguided and seemed to be condemning British communists to political irrelevance.

The narrator himself was a different person in different social conditions. The scepticism of the German tourists 'struck an answering chord on which I played frequently in Eng[land] but wh[ich] was silent here … a sceptic in England; a Marxist here – because it is easier?' The main point was that Soviet society enabled personal authenticity. He disagreed with Tanya's view that he was not a hypocrite, 'describing my self-consciousness as giving that form of dualism bet[ween] thought and action wh[ich] in many Englishmen abroad is the ground for the accusat[ion] of hypocrisy justly due to many of their fellows who stay at home.'[122]

If Bolshevism was out of place at home, though, what should he do? This is the real point of this fragment of a novel. The phrase 'sane country' turns out to have been borrowed from an American Polish Jew who, despite the sanity of the USSR, was returning to the United States because 'one doesn't feel quite comfortable here after a time'.[123] Hill was actually rather wry about life in the Soviet Union in letters from Moscow to Isaiah Berlin, a contemporary at All Souls. In part it was a matter of minor personal discomforts: the inefficiencies of Intourist, the Russian tourist agency for foreign visitors to the Soviet Union, and the Russian postal system, the queues, the cold and the food. 'Starvation has begun: we feed on bread and sausage, keep ourselves warm with tea.'[124] Hill's narrator was happy to allow such small criticisms of Soviet society because on the largest questions Soviet society was sane; in England by contrast 'there is no point in making small crit[icism]s: there are so many big ones to be cried in the wilderness'.[125]

Nonetheless, to stay in the USSR would be to run away, or to be seen to be doing so. The narrator says, 'I know I [couldn't] be much use in Engl[and] – I am not the stuff proto-martyrs are made of', but the thought of staying made him uneasy. He had not shared in the sacrifice that had built the state, had not shared the suffering that had earned this paradise. Soviet sacrifices had made this new order; 'for me to run away from labour to go and live on another's harvest – how c[oul]d I justify that to the dead?' The narrator felt 'the sullen street-corner hopeless faces that had driven me out of Engl[and] were easier to convince than the motionless masks of the [Soviet] dead. Rest was not to be found in Engl[and]: for rest had to be earned; but at least I sh[oul]d have the chance of earning it there.' It is easy to see here the imprint of a Methodist upbringing – 'rest is a wage, not an inheritable property' – but the narrator also commends a recent article by Anna Louise Strong about the new Soviet work ethic. If you do not like the factory you work in, you should not leave for a better one but rather improve the one you are in: if it is not as good as the next factory, 'That is a reason for staying on, not clearing out.'[126]

What could he do to improve his own factory, to make a difference in England? To Berlin he observed that at the Lenin Library he had been reading history 'which when true is not Marxist and _____'.[127] Perhaps this related to the revelation for the narrator that he should return to his original academic purpose: 'I thought it might be as important, taking the longer view, to work out a satisfact[ory] Marxist hist[ory] of Engl[and].'[128]

Such thoughts were surely the basis of Hill's own decision to go home and join the CPGB. Although fictional, the feelings of Hill's narrator in the novel resonate powerfully with his writing in his own voice. It is also worth noting that two telegrams from Russia survive from the time of his visit to Moscow and Leningrad nearly twenty years later. One lists a series of artists supplies that he could bring from the UK; the other, from Tatiana, thanks him for the letters and sends love to him and his daughter Fanny: surely these are from Kostya and Tanya.[129]

It was a propitious moment for Hill to join the CPGB. At the 7th Congress of the Comintern in 1935, the party line had changed from class against class, and the politics of the Popular Front had begun to crystallise. In Britain there had already been some movement away from class against class at a grassroots level. A loss of faith in the imminent development of a revolutionary situation, and the urgency of the battle against fascism at home, had bred an atmosphere of cooperation on the left, reinforced by the rise of Nazism and Spanish fascism. There was no electoral alliance with Labour, and the CPGB was refused affiliation, but there was nonetheless cooperation between communists and others in what was presented as an extension of Labour reformism. It was associated too with an intellectual openness – these Popular Front years gave left-wing intellectuals, writers and artists an important role in the party in building cultural support for the cause. Hill's historical ambitions were potentially useful to this effort: the CPGB was no longer preaching bloody revolution, but was encouraging a broad cultural initiative to build support for its critique of capitalist society.[130]

In the late 1930s Hill had been active in a number of causes: working with the Fabians, becoming a branch member of the Association of University Teachers, and joining the Oxford Co-operative, the Society for Cultural Relations between the People of the British Commonwealth and the USSR (SocCR) and 'similar organizations'. In fact he remained a member of the Labour Party until 1939.[131] He acted as treasurer for a fundraising effort to support out-of-work Welsh miners attending a summer school for the unemployed at Clifton Hampden between 13 July and 10 August 1935. The school was under the direction of the Oxford Trades Council, collaborating with the South Wales Miners' Federation and the London District Council of the National Unemployed Workers' Movement. Here perhaps is a sign of the direct influence of Lindsay: these were organisations close to Lindsay's role coordinating voluntary work with the unemployed and, specifically, with the South Wales educational settlement at Maes-yr-Haf, founded in 1927 to help the unemployed following the General Strike.[132]

Hill's time in the Soviet Union, however, transformed and focused these broad left commitments. Experience of life in the USSR showed how Soviet communism promised both personal authenticity and an effective response to the crisis of capitalism – a harmony of head and heart, a means of both personal and societal renewal. To that extent it offered a solution to the crises evident in his papers from earlier in the decade. The task of the narrator, convinced of the virtues of Bolshevism, was to improve England, and the changed strategy of the CPGB offered him a party-political home. He would promote social change not by 'preaching bloody revolution' but, with some hesitation and self-doubt, by filling 'the need for Engl[ish] teachers, for a Marxist hist[ory] of Engl[and] that w[oul]d be acceptable to academic historians'.[133]

2

Academic Life, Communism and the Authentic Self: 1936–40

> *It is struggle that wins reforms, just as it is struggle that will retain the liberties which our ancestors won for us. … We still have much to learn from the seventeenth century.*
>
> Christopher Hill, 'The English Revolution, 1640', 1940

On his return from the USSR, despite his hesitations about academic life, Hill took up a teaching position at Cardiff, 'appointed', according to his colleague Gwendolyn Whale, 'for two years, [with] the tacit assumption … that he would then be returning to Oxford'. He came on the recommendation of the great medieval historian Maurice Powicke, who was Lindsay's brother-in-law and who had taught Galbraith at Manchester.[1] Twin commitments – to the CPGB and to an academic life – shaped the next twenty years. Of the two, in retrospect, the party seems the less fundamental, although at the time Hill may have seen it the other way around.

At Cardiff he was regarded with some suspicion, although more for his obvious Oxford manners than his politics. The Principal, J.F. Rees, was delighted to have a Fellow of All Souls on the staff, but some of Hill's colleagues 'did not take immediately to the self-assurance of this young man from Balliol and All Souls'.[2] He was remembered as a conscientious and effective teacher, although not a charismatic speaker, and his lecturing style was affected by a stammer. As a young man he found that harder to manage. The effect was variable; although the secret services heard that he was a 'Good tutor, but stammers badly (does not lecture)', another report noted that 'the stammer is not a bad one; he can lecture without difficulty. It apparently emerges in times of stress.'[3]

Hill certainly thought stress made it worse. In 1940 he wrote to Shiela Grant Duff that separation from her was affecting his speech: 'my stammer was worse again yesterday evening at my WEA lecture. Not as bad as it will be next week but still your absence was already noticeable and I am already getting terrified of the progressive deterioration that is to be expected in the week.' A few days later he wrote, 'it is so marvellous that you may be coming back on Sunday because that will just save my Monday lecture from being one long splutter.'[4] In later life he had much better control, although he was never renowned as a great lecturer.

His teaching at Cardiff was less formal than was conventional there, and his 'more intimate Oxford manner' was appreciated by his students, 'especially by the best of them'. Whale recalled that he took a close interest in each of them, and he was able to speak 'succinctly and perceptively' about individual students, their qualities and attainments at departmental meetings.[5]

For his part, he seems to have enjoyed the experience. 'I am working a strenuous four hours a week am good at solving problems whose existence I had hardly suspected [about the degree regulations in Cardiff].' He relished Welsh culture: 'Most of the conversation in the common room is in Welsh, which on the whole I think a good thing: it is spoken nowhere else in Cardiff. I already regard it as normal that my Professor should say Come in pleass when I knock.'[6] Cardiff students appealed to him for 'their pleasant and unsophisticated manner'. He wrote to Berlin wryly but appreciatively about his students, recounting the verdict of 'one of my best-intentioned female students on the Reflections on the French Revolution: "Burke, shut off from the struggle, might well talk"'; another summed up Frederick II: 'His father described him as unwashed and effeminate. But this was only a phase.' On his return from Cardiff he found 'Balliol men … a bit of a trial'.[7]

He chose the 'Puritan revolution' as his main field of teaching, 'the social, economic, and intellectual dimensions of the conflict' seeming to provide 'the perfect blend of interests': his central purpose was to explore the relationship between ideas and their social, economic and political environment. The values and principles championed by seventeenth-century parliamentarians may have been puritan, but they did not take hold and triumph simply because they were better ideas. His target here was idealism, which treated the force of ideas as if they operated independently of their social and political context; he was not denying the importance of puritanism but seeking to understand why it gained force. Although his teaching did prompt some students to ask, 'Does he believe in God?', what struck his colleague Gwendolyn Whale was 'his deep and deepening knowledge of the sermons and theological writings of the Puritans'.[8] As he observed to Berlin rather archly, 'I am a member of the Faculty of Theology.'[9]

His starting point was a sharp rupture in the history of ideas: the passage from a world of theories about the divine right of kings, Jean Bodin's view of sovereignty and English arguments for the royal prerogative to a world of rights and contract. Rather than authority descending from God, being embodied in the king and being obeyed by his subjects, there was a human arrangement – a deal in which power was acknowledged in return for rights guaranteed. His students were introduced to Bulstrode Whitelocke and Edward Coke, whose historical and legal studies aimed at retrieving an ancient constitution with common rights that pre-dated the powers of the crown (the royal prerogative) and were therefore superior to them, and a common law whose authority also lay beyond the power of kings. Students then learned about parliamentarian arguments against the divine right of kings during civil war and revolution: Coke again, but also the legal reforms proposed in the 1650s that might have constituted a Code Cromwell, every bit as epochal as the Code Napoleon of the French Revolution. Hill also lectured on the thought of John Milton and James Harrington, of religious independents (who opposed the existence of a hierarchical national church) and of political levellers (who argued in favour of popular sovereignty and electoral reform). Restoration political thought was represented by Richard Baxter – the interest perhaps being that he was a convinced puritan who made peace with the Anglican regime – and the first Marquess of Halifax, perhaps significant as a 'trimmer', who took a pragmatic approach to the monarch's religion in defending the stability of the kingdom. Trimmers had given up on imposing the True Religion as a task of government, favouring civil peace over religious purity and certainty. Religion played a smaller role in politics, and politics were less dominated by royal power and prerogative.

In some ways this was a standard outline of the period, but the detail of the notes reveals how Hill's Marxism inflected his teaching, framing questions that engaged him for decades after: it was not a term he used, but this was a modernising political crisis. After the revolution, witch beliefs no longer produced prosecutions, and Hobbes's successors did not need to fear (as he had) that their political theories would get them burned as heretics. As late as 1680 Chief Justice Scroggs had said that 'there is no such thing as a liberty of the press'; in 1696 pre-publication censorship was abandoned.

However, what lay behind this transformation of the intellectual world was a social and economic transformation – the 'main changes' of the period were economic and social. The new thinking was a product of the interregnum, and of the rise to power of a new capitalist class. They passed, for example, the Navigation Act, which used state power to protect and promote overseas trade and the associated growth of trade and colonisation. They abolished feudal tenures, allowing a free market in land, which became more clearly a source of profit and a means of capital accumulation. They ended monopolies and established free internal trade, and curbed the royal (court) bureaucracy. With their influence, so grew religious nonconformity along with rationalism and the new science: intellectual systems built on reason and evidence, not authority. Coke's common law thinking also triumphed: 'bourgeois law', which championed common rights and the legal agency of individuals. The Tudor state had been structured in essentially feudal ways, but within that state a bourgeoisie had emerged. The resulting stresses were largely resolved in a constitutional revolution in 1641, although that did not forestall civil war. As a result there was a second revolution, in 1649, that was potentially about the rights of ordinary people. It was partially successful and the restoration of the monarchy in 1660 was a compromise, not a reversal of the gains of the interregnum: a closing of the ranks against the more radical potential of a democratic revolution, but not a reversion to the quasi-feudal state of the Tudors.

Hill's students were encouraged to analyse political theory not as pure thought, but in its 'historical framework' as a 'response to social needs, political and economic needs'. The 'Important thing', he wrote, is 'not the "truth" of a theory, but what was its purpose?' He summed up by saying that the century saw the establishment of 'the domination of the new class', which was 'reflected in the tone of the political theories of both sides in the party game'. There had been a 'transition from one realm of ideas to another, from divine right, witches, arguments from biblical texts and Anglo-Saxon precedents, to deism, rationalism, The Royal Society and Locke'. That revolution in thought corresponded to a revolution in society and was to influence the thinking of men who drove 'an even more radical revolution in France'.[10] It was not a lecture course about social and economic change, but about ideas, making a case for their 'correspondence' to social and economic change.

The implied target was S.R. Gardiner's interpretation of the seventeenth century as a 'Puritan revolution', in which Protestant doctrines and the desire to free the conscience led to demands for political freedoms. For Gardiner it was the development of human understanding and the power of ideas that drove political progress. Gardiner's interpretation emerges over fourteen volumes of political narrative, written consecutively over several decades, in a way that can make the thread of the argument more or less invisible. He had been subject to polemical dissection by Usher on those grounds, and it was a criticism that Hill shared.[11] However, his main objection to the idea of the Puritan revolution was methodological: the force of ideas does not depend simply on their truth. Puritanism triumphed because of the influence of those to whom it appealed.

Relating ideas to economic, social and political change was not a specifically or uniquely Marxist ambition. Indeed, A.L. Rowse championed Hill on exactly this issue in the letters pages of the *Spectator* in 1938. It was, he said, simple-minded to think that understanding someone's conscious motivation explained their behaviour and belief: 'People in general are apt to be so unconscious of what really moves them.' Rowse commended Hugh Trevor-Roper (certainly no Marxist) for the argument that the Reformation was a struggle for power and not simply a conflict of doctrine, and Hill for making a similar point in a review of a biography of John Lambert. As one of the great soldiers of the revolutionary period, Lambert came as close as anyone to being a rival to Cromwell in the 1650s. 'Twenty years ago, no doubt, people would have seen Lambert's career in terms of religious principle and conflict, as they did Cromwell's. Only the out of date and those incompetent to judge would do that now.' 'This is what the younger people think', wrote Rowse, 'indeed they have come to regard it as commonplace.'[12]

An influence here was Lewis Namier, who delivered the Ford Lectures in Oxford in 1934, relating political life in eighteenth-century England to networks of patronage and connection rather than the force of ideas. Namier is now conventionally seen as a conservative figure, but this analysis was a radical departure and a stimulus to the development of a social history of England, tracing the real forces at work in historical development which were otherwise concealed by an emphasis on the accounts people gave of themselves and their motives. The mood was turning against idealism in many ways, and it was not only Marxists who were suspicious of it as a form of historical explanation.[13]

Nor was Hill the first to try to understand the relationship between

Protestant ideas and capitalism. The German sociologist Max Weber and the British historian R.H. Tawney had both explored the relationship between the Protestant ethic and the spirit of capitalism, seeing in the Protestant faith an encouragement of habits of thought and behaviour that helped create a striving, acquisitive, commercial society. Hill's approach was distinct in two ways, however. Weber and Tawney approached the question as a matter of personal psychology – Protestantism acted on individuals in a way that made them capitalist. Hill, by contrast, addressed it as a sociological question, analysing its appeal for particular social groups rather than the personal psychology of belief and the 'spirit of capitalism'. Secondly, following Laski, Hill said that Weber and Tawney had made a 'grave chronological error' – the capitalist spirit had pre-dated the triumph of Protestantism and explained that triumph. In effect Weber and Tawney had the causal arrow pointing in the wrong direction.[14]

While in Cardiff, Hill moved in communist circles, where he clearly felt at home. He lodged with the Awberrys, 'a family closely connected with the Communist Party', on a housing estate in North Cardiff, and was 'in touch with lots of political people in the valleys'. Also lodging there was Will Paynter, later general secretary of the NUM and at the time very involved in the unemployed worker's movement (with whom Hill had worked in Oxfordshire in 1935). Hill addressed meetings of the Left Book Club and was branch secretary of the SocCR. Above all, he committed wholeheartedly to working with Basque refugees from the Spanish Civil War, at Caerleon, one of a number of centres at which they were housed: 'I was secretary of the committee that ran it, and my two years in Cardiff were really much more occupied with the Basque children than with history. I learned an awful lot from them, of course, a tremendous lot.' The work was educational, running alongside effective language tuition.[15] He retained a strong affection for the refugee children and a sense of obligation to them. Writing to Berlin, jokingly, he asked whether he would 'like to adopt a Basque child? I have 57 to dispose of.' Sometime later, as the residents in Caerleon were being dispersed, he wrote to Shiela: 'forgive me in advance if I am rather gloomy because I was for days after the last batch went because for 2 years or so these kids really were my life.' For the rest of his life he kept an autograph book signed by them and the affection was apparently reciprocated: Josefina Savery, one of the children, certainly remembered him very clearly years later, and seems to have sent him Christmas cards as late as the 1990s.[16]

Hill's stay in Cardiff was short, however. As he entered his second year of teaching he was being courted by Balliol, although there was clearly another possibility in the air too: 'Balliol has coyly suspended its advances for Christmas', he wrote to Berlin, 'so urgency lapses. I incline to favour Balliol on the ground that I shall save money by less frequent dress shirts.'[17]

In the event it was to Balliol that he returned. There his lecture course offered a similar view to his Cardiff teaching, albeit with a more obviously dialectical approach. He encouraged his students not to take sides, but to see a dialectic in which 'points' were made on both sides, with an outcome that was ultimately progressive. The crises resulted in constitutional compromise but one that converged on a synthesis of ideas expressed by the two opposing parties in relation to trade, landholding, foreign policy, law and legal practice and the Church.

Religious institutions were of course a key arena in which these conflicts played out. Puritanism began first to permeate, then capture religious institutions, leading to confrontation with the bishops and the church establishment anxious to reassert control. But this was not simply a Puritan revolution because there were other issues in play: the Church was a landlord and press censor, and there was much overlap between the personnel of Church and state, including in judicial roles. The church had a monopoly on 'the manufacture of public opinion': the control the bishops were defending was political, economic and social, not simply theological. Against them were ranged new social interests whose social and political roles were restricted by this establishment. At heart the analysis is about the relationship between ideas and the contexts in which ideas make sense and achieve political influence.

Hill's broad left social activism was consistent both with his early Methodism and with some of his Balliol mentors. It suited his temperament and beliefs, therefore, and he had kept the specifically Marxist content of his political beliefs relatively quiet. His Cardiff colleagues were subsequently rather shocked by the appearance in 1940 of the overtly Marxist 'The English Revolution, 1640', and 'pressed hard to know whether [knowledge of his communist sympathies] had been concealed when he was appointed'. Rees, the Principal so pleased to have landed a Fellow of All Souls, was himself upset, although the warmth he felt for Christopher survived the revelation.[18]

❧

Back in Oxford, as war approached, Hill fell in love with Shiela Grant Duff. A year younger, she had gone to Lady Margaret Hall, one of the handful of women's colleges in Oxford, to study Philosophy, Politics and Economics. There, she was taught by Isaiah Berlin and entered into a relationship with Goronwy Rees – another Fellow of All Souls, later tainted by association with his close friend Guy Burgess. Rees and Grant Duff had travelled together to Ruthenia in 1933,[19] and at that time Hill was clearly known to all of them.[20]

Following graduation she became a foreign correspondent in order to follow international affairs more closely, writing on German and Czech affairs for the *Observer*. Appalled by the indifference of the British establishment to the plight of the Czechs and the brutality of the Nazi regime, she became passionately anti-Nazi and a stern critic of the appeasers. She wrote *Europe and the Czechs* in response, which was published by Penguin and delivered to British parliamentarians on the day that Chamberlain returned from Munich. She is perhaps best remembered now for her friendship with Adam von Trott zu Solz, who was to become a leading figure in the conservative resistance to Hitler, and who was eventually executed for plotting Hitler's assassination. While at Oxford

Shiela Grant Duff in 1938.

they moved in similar circles and kept in touch after he left. The following year she and Rees visited Trott in Germany, following which he was for three years in the Far East, and as war approached it became harder for them to meet. They met again in 1938 in Paris and twice in England the following year, but they fell out when he conveyed a deal to Chamberlain which would have ceded parts of Poland and the city of Gdańsk to Germany in return for withdrawal from Bohemia and Moravia. His purposes in offering this deal were unclear – whether it was German nationalist expansion by other means or a compromise to buy Hitler off – but in any case it was hard to reconcile with Duff's increasingly convinced anti-appeasement stand.[21]

By the time war broke out she was working at the Royal Institute of International Affairs (Chatham House), which was relocated to Balliol College on 2 September 1939. Balliol was continuing to operate, although most of the college buildings had been requisitioned for war service and the rapidly dwindling number of students had moved to Trinity College, next door (in 1938 there had been 264 undergraduates at Balliol, an average that was to fall below 100 during the war). In 1939, however, Hill was still at work in the college.[22] He and Grant Duff had many shared personal connections, at Balliol and All Souls, and were both deeply engaged in the politics of the international situation, although Grant Duff was no communist.

During the autumn of 1939 their friendship turned to romance, the intensity of feeling matched by the frequency of their correspondence, sometimes daily, which lasted until May 1941. The first postcard that Shiela kept is relatively reserved: 'Dear Shiela', Hill writes, 'sorry to seem silly. Not sulking – really; just busy. Could we have lunch or play squash some time? Yours Christopher.' By December he was signing 'xxxxx', and in another letter from around that time he says he has written in terms suitable 'from a don to his girlfriend'.[23] In January 1940 he had met her mother, although he and Shiela apparently still felt the need for discretion in at least some social situations.[24]

These letters give almost unique access to Hill's views on love, sex, morality and respectability. For Hill, 'Love after all isn't just sleeping with; its only a sort of physiological accident that after a certain stage love can't go on developing smoothly without sleeping with.' In this he ran up against Shiela's more conventional morality. For him, her resistance to physical intimacy suggested that she misunderstood the whole experience by concentrating on only one aspect. Love, he urged, is like being a sea anemone. When the sea comes in, one opens and flowers and spreads ones t[endrills?], and is refreshed and strengthened deep down inside; when the sea goes away, one turns in on oneself, smaller, and is stumpy and blunt and tough and resilient and fresh with inner resources to stand the bludgeonings of the sun: and when one is tired, the sea flows back again, and caresses, and one sleeps. But if the sea never comes, then, darling Shiela, one dies. And though one may fight on bravely for a time, shoulders humped and vulnerable heart out of sight, drawing on one's little roots, still one dies in the end: and in the mean time one never flowers, never opens as one safely can when the tender and gentle sea flows in.[25]

Much of the correspondence consists of attempts by him to persuade her to commit further to a physical relationship: 'Feelings can't just go on increasing in intensity without an outlet, and it would be impossible to get back to the old basis, because that would mean fearful and increasingly frequent rows, and become intolerable.' Quoting Hobbes, he told her that to blush 'is a sign of the love of good reputation; and commendable: In the old it is a sign of the same; but because it comes too late, not commendable. How old are you?'[26]

Some of the urgency came from the times: 'This is such a wicked, wicked, wicked world', he wrote in April 1940, 'that I don't wonder you're afraid of being hurt. But there are some nice people in it.'[27] He clearly had some success and from around that time onwards there was an explicitly passionate tone to some of his letters.

The letters reveal great intimacy and fondness, and the mutual support of two people in love. The previous year Shiela had been involved in a car accident which left her bedridden. Hill sympathised about 'that horrible old dragon', presumably a carer, from whom he expected no civility. Around this time he wrote in another letter, 'it's made me so happy getting you on top again like that, all sparkling and lovable and clear and in the foreground, and making me want to kiss and hug you'.[28] He promised that on his return from York after Christmas 1939, 'you can come and see me in my room soon when you are all tired and angry after your beastly day's work in that silly Chatham House and I can soothe and stroke you and restore your balance and tell you how wonderful it all is really'.[29] They also shared jokes about mutual acquaintances, for example John Fulton, who was at the time a philosophy don at Balliol, for his rejection of Denis Pritt's views on the international situation in advance of having read them.[30]

One obstacle to their relationship was their political differences. Although they were both appalled by fascism, and deeply opposed to Chamberlain's foreign policy, Duff did not share Hill's diagnosis that the problem lay with the natural bellicosity of capitalist states, including Britain and France. Hill was clearly anxious about the damage these differences were doing, and sought to overcome them with jokes, some of which seem startlingly unlikely to have worked: 'Darling Shiela, how angry your stupidity makes me'; 'Shiela you are awfully nice and the world is a better place for you being in it so I do hope you will be sensible and I don't have to shoot you.' He loved her despite her flawed political understanding:

> really of course I ought to be angry with the wicked system which abuses and perverts your wonderful and kind and good and fairly clever ideas and not with simple you. Yes, that will do, won't it? So you really can be wonderful after all and rather a pitiful abused object with its arm in a sling battling blindfold against a wicked fascist system, and here is brave St. Christopher helping only you haven't found him yet but it is difficult blindfold.[31]

In late 1939 in particular he was often apologetic about his behaviour in these political arguments, but 'a passionate character like me has to be passionate about something'.[32]

Another serious problem for them was that Shiela felt pulled between her feelings for Hill and for someone they both referred to as 'the baron'. That tension was complicated by what seems to have been her more conventional view of morality in relation to love and sex. It is not clear who the baron was, but it seems likely they were referring to von Trott zu Solz, although no public acknowledgement of a relationship between the two of them exists.[33] Trott had proposed to Shiela though, hoping to prevent her from marrying Rees, and it seems clear that Grant Duff hoped for more than friendship, despite the circumstances.[34] In the period in which she was involved with Hill, however, she was not able to see Trott at all, separated as they were by war. In December 1939 Hill commended the new Conrad Veidt film, *The Spy in Black*, in which a female British double agent in a relationship with a British spy is drawn to a charismatic and honourable German U-Boat commander, despite the fact that war made them enemies: 'It is all about us', he wrote.[35]

When Shiela did commit to Hill, on condition that her attachment to the baron was recognised between them, Hill likened it to his lingering feeling for 'my baroness in Moscow': 'suppose my job for the War Office was in Moscow, wouldn't I go back if I could? Like a shot. That's where I belong too, wenn nur der weite Raum nicht trennte [if only we were not separated by such a distance].'[36]

Shiela had worried that, with these reservations, physical intimacy would not be moral. Hill reassured her that it was 'Love not Lust' and 'Anyway all these fine metaphysical distinctions of good and bad are only the sort of things nice girls invent for themselves so as to know how nice it is to be naughty and virtuous at the same time by calling it something else.' At the time he was working on what would become an influential paper on Andrew Marvell. Making the distinctions she did between good and bad, he wrote, is 'why nice girls are liberals and not revolutionaries like Marvell, and oh dear Shiela do read His Coy Mistress again and tell me I am right because it is so clever if I am'.[37] Against the complexities of their position – she apparently in love with someone else, he in love with a woman who also loved another man – and with war looming, he urged Marvell's view: 'let's be grand together until God strikes. If we cannot make our sun stand still at least we'll make him run.'[38]

These complications led Hill to express a personal morality far removed from the bourgeois respectability of his youth. He also reflected a little on his own selfishness, which he says he disguised 'in order to have an excuse to give myself a greater degree of pleasure than my non-conformist conscience allows me to think is virtuous'.[39] Following his call up in September 1940 he wrote that these complications posed no moral problem for him 'because my monogamous desires fit with my monogamous nature'. Shiela, however, had to reconcile 'the situation to (a) her nature (b) certain conventional standards which she wants to accept. As (a) and (b) contradict one another this is difficult.' The truth was that she was 'fundamentally polyandrous in the nicest possible way'. As things stood she was 'making absurd gestures to (b) when she says sleeping with me would stop complete concentration on the baron'.

The real point, he felt, was personal authenticity: 'If she is polyandrous why pretend not to be and draw artificial lines? Is there or is there not deception in our relationship now?'

> If only it was simple and straightforward being good, and someone would tell you what it was. But I say being good is being You because you are wonderful; and being sordid isn't a thing one avoids by a particular mode of behaviour but by being a particular sort of person. And the beginning of sordidness is bothering about whether one is being (and seeming) sordid, and to that extent stopping being a real person of one's own.[40]

Overall, he advised her, 'don't be monogamous. As long as your poly-androus nature lets you be directed to me when I am there and my monogamous nature goes on being directed to you.'[41]

In the end they seem to have committed to the affair on the understanding that it might not last: 'in this bloody world short term happiness, if it is real happiness, ought to be taken with both hands oughtn't it?', he wrote; '[b]ut I agree we ought to have eyes open, so thank you very much for telling me so clearly. We know exactly where we are and where we aren't.'[42]

They had slept together before Hill signed up in the summer of 1940. Arriving at barracks he wrote that 'sleeping between army blankets and on straw is not quite as nice as sleeping between your arms and on your tummy. And oh what a wonderful tummy you have.'[43] And it continued to be for him a lyrical experience: 'Oh dear ich möchte dich küssen Tausend und eine Nacht [I want to kiss you for a thousand and one nights] but I suppose I shall have to do without the thousand for the time being.'[44] Later he wrote, 'didn't you give me a lovely time, beds if no baths, and such a lot of sin? … all I know is it is something … both aching and absolutely wonderful, and I suppose that is love.'[45]

Much of the correspondence from August 1940 onwards is about how they will manage to meet up – his leave arrangements and postings; train services – but there had evidently been a crisis in October 1940, when he wrote as if the relationship was over. Meeting up after a long time apart he had felt for the first time as though they were 'pretending'. Their different commitments to authenticity made them averse to such pretence. 'I think perhaps you were right', he wrote, 'it is much better to have had something wonderful and then to have a big hurt, than to let it die away in pretences and mutual irritations.'[46]

There followed a gap in their correspondence until December, when she had second thoughts about their situation and Hill tried to force a resolution by proposing marriage. He now felt that she resorted to her feelings for the baron only when other arguments against committing to the relationship failed. The proposal would make her choose. The terms, though, were again beyond those of a conventional morality, and perhaps not best chosen to woo a conventionally minded lover:

> Marriage on the one hand attracts you, because it is after all if success-ful a desirable state; and on the other hand frightens you because of its finality … [Y]ou take a more prayer book and catastrophic view than I do of marriage: I regard it as a necessary (sometimes) evil which bears no

relation to intensity of feeling. So to that extent my suggesting marriage was tactical, hoping it might be a way of getting you, by making things easier and holding out prayer-book vistas.

Despite his pragmatic view of marriage and his acceptance of polyandry, Hill did also feel the pull of more conventional bourgeois aspirations:

> let's have a wonderful cottage somewhere and keep pigs. That will appeal to both of us won't it? And then when summer comes we can sit out in our little garden, and perhaps dig a bit in the evening, and then go and look at our pigs and think how much better we are than they because we in our poor and different ways try to do something for humanity and what do they do for piggery? Nothing.[47]

Part of that was a desire to have children.[48]

Shiela was apparently resistant to marriage partly on the grounds that it would be a distraction from her other purposes. For Hill this too was a mistake: 'Celibacy isn't a cure', he wrote to her, 'it is only a different disease. What is important for achieving purposes is to be in mental and physical and psychological health … Temptations and time-frittering are not caused by marriage: on the exact contrary, I think they are caused much more by fear of combined with a need for – a sort of Hassliebe not toward me so much as toward Liebe.' In all, he rejected these bourgeois pieties: 'To hell with your pigeon-holes.'[49]

By March 1941 she seemed to be close to accepting his proposal. In the end though she did not, and apparently urged him to end the relationship, save his dignity and protect his best interests by cutting his losses. He persisted: 'I'd like to have another try because I still think it's possible and dignity and bravery would hurt much and leave life so dreary without you.' He did, however, agree that it would be better to stop altogether than allow their relationship to 'peter out sordidly'. Again, his unconventional morality might have been ill-judged as a romantic proposition: 'the great superiority my former lovers (except Taya) had over you was that I didn't want them all that much anyway. So naturally I was flattered by their affection till I got bored with it.'[50]

The end was near. In late April 1941 he wrote saying he had not heard from her and suspected she was following a 'best interests' policy. Around this time, he withdrew the offer of marriage: 'if that is how you think you are likely to go on feeling about the baron, then the offer of marriage had better be off and stop putting you down in the dumps. But if ever you change your mind, or if ever it could be useful to you, there it is. And meanwhile let's make the best and the most of the situation as it is.'[51] By May it was over, and he wrote that 'We needn't go on writing epitaphs for each other need we?'[52]

Following their break-up, he recalled how at their last meeting he had locked his shoes in a suitcase so that he could not run after her: he was not putting a brave face on his disappointment. Using his leave to go to Oxford rather than to visit her, he had 'bravely kissed a girl I knew to be engaged' and then gone to York, which had been restful 'because my mother is very tactful and hates the war anyway, and my father has been out all the time organizing missionary meetings'. An uncle had got him some illegal petrol so he had been able to reconnect with the moors, and he visited an Austrian refugee woman 'who turns out to be a wicked semi-Trotskyist but quite nice'. He had begun burying himself in work on an edition of Gerrard Winstanley's writing and had 'found a lot of unpublished works of Hill here and re-read them and suddenly realized how good they were and what a tragedy it would be for the world if they weren't ever published, so shan't I be busy and sublimated?'[53]

They were subsequently rather distant. In August 1943 he wrote to Shiela from Cambridge, where he had been posted; this was clearly her first notice of that. He regretted the coldness of her most recent letter, and sought to avoid an argument: 'after all there is more common ground politically between us now than ever in all the years we have known each other, so wouldn't it be silly to choose that moment to quarrel?'[54] Terms were somewhat restored after the war, after both had married other people, but they were only ever intermittent correspondents after this.[55]

The affair had led Hill to express a personal morality that was far from respectable, but to some extent such truths were inexpressible, even by a don. 'Words', he wrote to Shiela, 'are what Hill has been good at ever since Sumner described him as a scholarship candidate as a nice little man who can write interminably on any subject.' They had always served him well, and writing letters had previously got him out of awkward situations, including with previous girlfriends. Now, however, 'wanting more than ever before to express himself with passionate eloquence, his medium breaks down'. Physical intimacy was far more expressive of such things: 'If I were lying there by your side I could look or stroke, and then you would know all about it.'[56]

In this letter and others, there is a sense that he can write more freely and directly than he can speak, his stammer perhaps reflecting a deeper inhibition about how openly he expressed himself in speech. Mehta commented on Hill's habit of sniffing, thinking it a symptom of shyness. He was, Mehta later wrote, 'an extremely clever man, and said everything he had to say much more rapidly than the people he was talking to could take it in – a habit that inevitably led to long pauses'.[57] Throughout his career he was interested in language, from the struggles of the metaphysical poets for authentic expression to the relationship between the 'plain style' of the seventeenth century and the gathering triumph of rationalism and empiricism. It is perhaps tempting to relate this to his own relative verbal inarticulacy – his stammer and a lecture style that was, even to his most ardent supporters, less than charismatic.

Some of his reserve was more straightforwardly temperamental though. He apologised to Shiela for resorting to flippancy, admitting that it 'is a disguise worn by sentimental but nonconformist Marxist dons'. Although confessing to being a 'fumbling, inarticulate, defeatist' sort of person, 'flippanting it over bravely', he was not apologising, but rather explaining: 'flippancy and fumble are not *necessarily* evidence of lack of the real thing. Perhaps they are, but not necessarily. At least they are me, and I want to be loved for myself alone.'[58]

'Roger', a mutual acquaintance who often seemed to act as an intermediary, wondered if 'the army is undermining [Hill's] inhibitions'.[59] But despite the psychoanalytic references which occasionally pop up – inhibitions, sublimation, or mentions of Freud – Hill's main frame of reference in matters of love and desire was poetry. Marvell figured, of course, but also some of his own. He sent Shiela a poem he had written in German in 1931, when he was fifteen, musing on how possession was the enemy of love. At another point he commended Rilke to her, and he frequently referred to German literature, with which she was also familiar.[60] This romantic sensibility, as noted by Beer on his visit to York in 1935, was also associated with the landscape. 'If I have roots at all', Hill wrote to Shiela from Oxford in 1940, 'I have decided, it is in the Yorkshire moors. We went there on Saturday to visit my horrible maiden aunt, and then to the hills and walked; and it all came back to me. I know one bit of 20–25 miles each way absolutely backwards, having cycled it bravely and toughly all alone when I was young, doing thinking.' He waxed equally lyrical about Dartmoor on Christmas Day 1941, describing the landscape and musing on the nature of beauty from the cab of an army lorry.[61]

As well as revealing some unconventional views about love, sex and marriage, these letters therefore reveal something about Hill. Above all, his more reflective letters were concerned with personal authenticity, particularly in relation to conventional expectations. Being true to oneself might very well put one at odds with what was required in the world. He distinguished between '(1) the world one has to work in, to make it better and (2) the person one really is'. The world as it is encountered is 'our unescapable burden – I am not Oxford any more than you, but it is my political job – but one has to be taut and braced and girded to stand its strain, and one just can't do that unless one has a firm root'. That was distinct from one's authentic self, a condition in which 'one can take one's armour off and be a real person ... And that is what we can give one another'.[62] He and Shiela seem in fact to have shared some emotional distance from Oxford academic life, a sense that their real selves were elsewhere. After an evening with Isaiah Berlin and Goronwy Rees in December 1939, he claimed to Shiela that we 'are both also very anti-intellectual or at any rate non-intellectual – though we rationalize about our politics a bit, the intellectualism is an after thought isn't it?' The conversation between Berlin and Rees was 'why I hated [All Souls] though I pretended I despised it politically'.[63]

This juxtaposition, of the authentic self and the conduct required to operate in an imperfect world, led him to 'wonder if I am morally brave?' Whereas Shiela was 'immediately braver at making gestures, ... I intrigue and deceive'. His was perhaps 'a sort of obstinacy that serves as moral courage', reflected also in his aversion to simply following the opinions of others.[64] The personal reserve so many people noted about him was a shield, worn while out and about, meeting the demands of the fallen world. It was matched, though, by a stringent morality and a seriousness about his own principles, which made him respectful of the principles of others: as he wrote to Shiela at one point, 'I so much admired your right ideas even when they perversely led to the wrong conclusion'.[65]

Hill had not published much by the end of the 1930s. A short article appeared pseudonymously in *Communist International* in 1938, marking the 250th anniversary of the Glorious Revolution. The pseudonym was necessary, noted Hill's fellow Marxist historian Rodney Hilton, 'for already in those days it was prudent for someone in the early stages of a career as a university teacher not to blazon attachment to a political organisation still considered to be revolutionary'.[66] Hill argued that the Glorious Revolution, in which James II was forced from the throne in favour of William III, was the capstone of a bourgeois revolution that had started in 1640. Charles I was overthrown by a bourgeois class that mobilised the energies of the lower orders but, when a real democratic revolution threatened, closed ranks with elements of the old order to protect their shared social interests. In 1660 Charles II was restored not to the monarchy his father had inherited, but 'as defender of the essentials of the revolution against attack from the Left'. It was this settlement that was preserved again in 1688/9: 'power had passed from the feudal-bureaucratic monarchy to an alliance of bourgeoisie and gentry' but not to the 'more revolutionary and democratic petty bourgeoisie'. This outcome reflected the balance of class forces.

Hill's analysis had direct relevance to contemporary society. The contemporary working class was 'the progressive class, the class with whom the future lies, the class with revolutionary energy'. Its revolution would contain no contradictions like the bourgeois revolution of the seventeenth century because 'by its position it is not an oppressing class, and so need be hampered by no fear of its natural allies'. The parliamentary gentry had been an exploiting class, and it feared what these lower-class allies might in the end desire if they were not excluded from political power. The twentieth-century working class, however, would not need to impose such limits on its democratic revolution: it could make good on the claims for liberty made in the seventeenth century, establishing them as 'realities for the whole population'.[67] Hill made a similar case more briefly in a review for the *Spectator* of Trevelyan's *The English Revolution, 1688–89*.[68]

This article drew Hilton's admiration, excited by the prospect of a Marxist version of the national story, but Hill had not published much besides, or anything of any great substance.[69] His principal mainstream academic publications had been an article reporting a variety of Soviet interpretations of English history in the seventeenth century which offered differing class analyses of aspects of the crisis, and another outlining the arguments of the Soviet historian S.I. Arkhangelsky about agrarian legislation during the English Revolution. Arkhangelsky saw this as accelerating the development of management of lands to allow capital to be extracted, rather than to sustain family lineage, status or display, developments that came at the expense of the crown and its feudal landholding dependents.[70] Hill had also written book reviews for other journals, but none were major statements.[71]

His review of H.A.L. Fisher's recently reissued *History of Europe* in *Modern Quarterly* was a slightly more substantial statement of his own views. Fisher claimed not to see any pattern in the past, simply the effect of events in the course of which, sometimes, good might triumph.

Behind this lay value judgements that Hill abhorred. This history, he wrote, 'is bankrupt and an absconding bankrupt at that. Its denial of the possibility of interpretation conceals its own bland assumption of the absoluteness of the narrow standards of the English ruling class, its impartiality turns out to be a synonym for Liberal politics.' In reviewing recent constitutional histories published by D.L. Keir (soon to be Master of Balliol) and M.A. Thompson, he gave them half a cheer for trying to take constitutional history out of the vacuum in which it was usually studied and to consider it as part of the wider history of the societies in which the constitutions were made. But he went on to use their material to make an argument of his own, about the balance of class forces that lay behind these constitutional settlements, the social forces they were seeking to balance.[72]

These were innovative and interesting interventions but there was nothing in this list that answered the ambition to write an academically acceptable Marxist history of England, except in the most preliminary, ground-clearing kind of way. It did reveal, though, how infuriating he found the '"maddening fatalism" of the Liberals and Liberal tradition', and the 'historical smug right' that Fisher represented. For Hill, Fisher seemed 'totally fatalistic. Nothing anyone can do about history. History just happens. Nothing is explained. No causes. No results. Just waves.' By contrast Marxism offered analysis and prescription. Marx saw society as a whole, 'dominated at different periods by different parties and the state as being by and large the property of the ruling class at the time and not the sort of neutral thing that it was then depicted as being'. In those inadequate liberal analyses, 'states did things and reforms happened, because people got wiser and better', not because, as the more convincing analysis had it, there were 'interest groups involved'.[73]

Before enlisting, however, Hill did make a major statement in a long essay included in a volume that he edited for Lawrence and Wishart, publisher to the CPGB and one of the few presses amenable to explicitly Marxist writing. The essay was prompted by Dona Torr, a major figure in the Marxist left. It is not clear where they met but she clearly exerted a profound influence on him. A generation older than Hill, she was the daughter of a clergyman and had been educated at home by private tuition before studying at Heidelberg and University College, London. At UCL between 1911 and 1914 she had studied English and Greek philosophy, combining that with organising student debates, becoming vice-president of the women's committee and serving on the editorial board of the union magazine.[74]

Dona Torr.

The way an anonymous obituarist characterised the roots of Torr's communism resonates strongly with Hill's own biography. She was, they write: 'one of those generous spirits who, finding the contrast between the privileges of her own class and the sufferings of the lower class intolerable, selflessly devote their lives to the service of the latter; but who, because they are intelligent, rationalize their emotions'. She was also a very talented linguist who added many proletarian colloquialisms to her English vocabulary. That was not true of Hill. Although he shared her marked lack of affectation in personal manners, he also confessed that 'I have spent a lifetime warding off Chris', although some members of the party referred to him that way. For Torr the CBGB offered 'an intellectual as well as a spiritual home', allowing her to write and teach, and the party gave more space to such ambitions during the Popular Front period.[75]

Torr clearly meant a lot to Hill and was also a major influence on his long-time associates and fellow Marxist historians John Saville and Victor Kiernan. In fact, it seems that Hill first got to know Saville through their work on a festschrift for Torr.[76] On the other hand, she and fellow Communist Party historian Eric Hobsbawm were not close. Torr found Hobsbawm uncongenial – he was perhaps too egotistical, and she was sceptical about the value of his work. E.P. Thompson was more to her taste, particularly his 'liveliness'. For his part, 'Eric never shared our devotion to her', wrote Hill, 'and I suspect they found themselves mutually incompatible.'[77]

The essay from Hill, prompted by Torr, was 'The English Revolution, 1640'. Although abbreviated and schematic, it remedied the fact that he had made no major statement about the English Revolution. It was published alongside two other essays: the first by the poet and critic Edgell Rickword, on 'Milton: the revolutionary intellectual'; and the second by the historian Margaret James on 'Contemporary materialist interpretations of society in the English Revolution'. Rickword was a grammar-school boy, son of a borough librarian, who had enlisted in 1916 as soon as he could. He won the Military Cross but was invalided out of the army having lost an eye to septicaemia. Thereafter he worked as a journalist and wrote poetry, and he was regarded as an astute interpreter of modernist poetry; along with Douglas Garman he founded the *Calendar of Modern Letters*. He joined the CPGB in 1934 and gave up poetry around the same time, concentrating on journalism as founder of the party-affiliated journals *Left Review* and *Our Time*. Like Hill, he admired the metaphysical poets, perceiving 'insipidity' in much contemporary poetry.[78]

Ten years or so older than Hill, Margaret James was the author of *Social Problems and Policy during the Puritan Revolution* (1930), a book which Hill admired and which was republished in the 1960s. She had graduated from Girton College, Cambridge, in 1924 and went on to do postgraduate work at the LSE, where she worked with Tawney. Through him she must have been close to the circles that had drawn Hill to the Fabians in the mid-1930s. She was lecturer in History at Royal Holloway between 1927 and 1931, but by the time of the war had returned to her hometown, Nottingham, where she was lecturing in the Adult Education Department. Hill wrote to her at length about the politics of the war in 1940, and clearly had immense respect for her. In the 1980s he said he thought that his own essay in the collection looked more rounded alongside hers (his was subsequently published, and is most often read, in isolation from the other essays). James died tragically young in 1942, a verdict of suicide returned after she fell from a second-floor window of her home having suffered a temporary imbalance of mind: her brother said at the inquest that she had eye trouble which caused depression and meant that she could not concentrate on her scholarly work.[79] Hill later wrote that 'Her tragic early death during World War II, at the height of her powers, was an incalculable loss to 17th-century scholarship'; he dedicated *Change and Continuity* (1974) to her along with John Buckatzsch: 'Both died tragically and prematurely, but not before they had opened up new areas of research which historians are still exploring.'[80]

Hill's was the main contribution though, both in length and influence. The essay worked out a line that would have been familiar to a student who had taken his courses in either Cardiff or Oxford. The Tudor and early Stuart state defended, and was defended by, the reactionary forces of the established church and conservative landlords. However, economic change had undermined the social basis of the system as a more commercially minded exploitation of land fuelled the growth of an agrarian capitalist class, particularly associated with the manufacture of woollen cloth and commercial farming. This class of capitalists could not be accommodated by the system in the same way that merchant capital had been in the Middle Ages, because it demanded a change in the way land was regulated and exploited. That worked inevitably to undercut the economic position of the old landed class, the crown and the church.

The result was a change of morals, 'which are always bound up with a given social order'. No longer were peasants protected by paternalistic landowners: rents were racked up and there was pressure to make it easier to trade in land. Economic interests ran up against the legal order of the old moral code, and the same was true in industry and trade, where protectionist policies, privileges and monopolies inhibited the pursuit of profit. These were the fundamental pressures behind the conflicts of the seventeenth century. New social groups offered a receptive audience for puritan ideas, whereas the established church, with its protected financial privileges, was on the side of the established order. In moving to protect and exploit the old system, the Stuarts were effectively supporting feudal interests against the growth of commercial society.

During the civil war the bourgeoisie mobilised the support of the petty bourgeoisie and the working class, the men who made up the victorious New Model Army. Those groups developed their own political and religious agenda: more fully democratic and in favour of religious freedom expressed in congregational independence. However, having defeated the feudal reaction, the bourgeoisie and gentry realigned with the landed order, shutting the door on further reform in favour of an oligarchic parliamentary settlement and a national church that guarded against religious radicalism.

In effect, England had a revolution like that in France in 1789. '[T]he period 1640–60', Hill wrote, 'saw the destruction of a whole social order – feudalism – and the introduction of a political structure within which capitalism could freely develop.' The pretence that 1660 saw a 'restoration' was tactical: that settlement actually gave 'sanctity and social stamp to a new social order. The important thing is that the social order was new and could not have been won without revolution.' Economic growth, science, technology and trade were all set free in the restoration settlement.[81]

There were many contemporary parallels: the defenders of the old order in Tudor and Stuart England, looking back nostalgically on a stable peasant society in the Middle Ages, had the same role 'as that of many liberals at the present day who think how nice it would be if capitalism could still work in the "liberal" nineteenth-century way, without having to resort quite so frequently to fascism and war'. Liberals were on the wrong side of history no less than Charles, his church and feudal supporters had been: 'Fine words alter no historic processes.'[82]

Hill tried to avoid determinism by arguing that religion mattered, but not in a *simply* theological way. Theology was expressed in concrete social conditions that gave shape to abstract precepts: 'It is not … denied that the "Puritan Revolution" was a religious as well as a political struggle; but it was more than that', he wrote. 'What men were fighting about was the whole nature and future development of English society.' The fight for control of the church was of fundamental significance because 'whoever controlled its doctrine and organisation was in a position to determine the nature of society'.[83] For Hill that latter task, of determining the nature of society, was a religious *and* political task, not simply an expression of a theological position.

He also stressed that the story of the revolution was a hopeful one. What had produced both progress and reaction in the seventeenth century had at the same time planted the seeds of progress in the current century. History was not the hopeless drift of events depicted by the liberals. He quoted Thomas Rainsborough, the New Model Army officer and radical politician: 'It is struggle that wins reforms, just as it is struggle that will retain liberties which our ancestors won for us.'[84] Two of the arguments to which Hill was most committed were here: that England had a revolution comparable to the French; and that there was a radical, progressive tradition in England that, if remembered, would empower future progressive change.

While at Aldershot doing basic training Hill heard news of 'a wicked review of my book in the New Statesman'.[85] It was by George Orwell, who, like many subsequent commentators on Hill's work, chose to denounce Marxism rather than to review the book. He accepted what Hill had worked so hard to do, to 'represent [the civil war] as a struggle between a rising capitalism and an obstructive feudalism, which in fact it was'.

However, 'men will not die for things called capitalism or feudalism, and will die for things called liberty or loyalty, and to ignore one set of motives is as misleading as to ignore the others.' He claimed that a single passage demonstrated Marxism's cardinal weakness in dealing with human motives:

> The fact that men spoke and wrote in religious language [wrote Hill] should not prevent us realising that there is a social content behind what are apparently purely theological ideas. Each class created and sought to impose the religious outlook best suited to its own needs and interests. But the real clash is between these class interests.

Orwell glossed this argument as the 'cocksure' assumption that religion, morality and patriotism could be written off as 'a sort of hypocritical cover-up for the pursuit of economic interests', a view he then dismissed.[86]

Hill's position on the relationship between ideas and their context was more complex than that, but the relationship had not been spelt out clearly in the essay. His attack on the idealism of Gardiner had aimed at establishing what Orwell accepted as axiomatic: that a rising capitalism was confronting an obstructive feudalism. It is ironic, given the intellectual crisis that lay behind Hill's move from Methodism to Marxism, that he was being accused of a lack of interest in the power of ideas, and of religious ideas in particular. Nonetheless, this early tract was open to that reading by those primed to hear Marxist arguments that way: he clearly does prioritise an account of the clash of material interests over an explanation of how that gave force to particular ideas, and this is still the piece to which people turn to demonstrate that Hill was basically a determinist. The review in the *Times Literary Supplement*, by something of a contrast, claimed that the economic context of the revolution was old hat, and that Hill and the others had done nothing original or convincing to illuminate the connections between that economic context and the ideas used to animate the conflict.[87] Hill was himself a little diffident about this early essay, and as A.L. Merson pointed out, he did not recommend it as further reading in his later textbook, *The Century of Revolution*.[88] Nonetheless, it has been influential, and was published separately in 1955 and in subsequent editions.

Reflecting on it more than forty years later Hill said, 'I saw it as my last will and testament. I expected to be killed in the war. I wrote it very fast and angrily.' The anger was about 'bloody stuffy Whig constitutional history, I suppose. English exceptionalism. The idea that revolutions were the sort of things that happened in other countries and couldn't happen in England.' But it was also about the war: 'it was a war I and my friends had tried to stop.' He admitted though to some embarrassment about the 'dogmatisms' of this piece.[89] As academic writing it is crude by comparison with his later work, but that is partly because it was not intended as academic writing. It combines a manifesto for the Marxist analysis of the crisis, in opposition to Gardiner's idealism, with a sense of how such an analysis could contribute to contemporary life. Here was something a young man with an Oxford accent could do.

3

Fighting the Wrong War: 1939–45

Wars are no good unless socialism (= peace) comes out of them: otherwise they are all to do over again … It is the class structure of a state that determines its foreign policy, not the niceness or otherwise of the individuals in the government or even its advisory departments.

Christopher Hill, letter to Margaret James, late 1939

Hill's political disagreements with Shiela about the coming war reveal his own political views in some detail. Where Shiela took a liberal line, that the democratic states had to defeat fascism and free the Czechs and other victims of Nazi aggression, Hill believed that the war was a product of the system of capitalist states rather than of the evils of particular politicians. In the long-term, peace would depend on a coalition of progressive parties seeking democratic change in all states.

He had read Norman Angell's influential book, *The Great Illusion*, a foundational text in international relations, published in 1909 and republished in 1933. Angell (who had been invited to speak at the controversial King and Country debate at the Oxford Union in 1933 but had pleaded a prior engagement) argued that economic interdependence rendered militarism obsolete: war was self-defeating for capitalist powers and military ambition was an outdated impulse in capitalist statecraft. Hill took full notes both on Angell and on Maurice Dobb's counter-argument that Angell's argument only worked if there was complete rational planning, something absent from capitalist states.[1] Hill was more convinced by the argument, as a *New Statesman* correspondent put it, that 'capitalist governments are by nature anarchic'.[2] This was fundamental to his response to the international crises of the 1930s.

The CPGB line set out in October 1939 was that if fascist aggression resulted in a new war, then communists would work for victory and the overthrow of the fascist regimes. However, they would also 'demand and work to achieve the immediate defeat of Chamberlain and a new government in Britain, representing the interests of the common people and not the rich friends of fascism'.[3] Hill took this line, but for him it was not a revolutionary ambition: his hopes lay with the broadly reformist Otto Wille Kuusinen in Finland and Maurice Thorez in France (in conscious preference to Gustave Bouvet, the anarchist would-be assassin of the French president in 1922).[4]

War was, of course, a horror to be avoided, and Hill thought the Allied Powers had not done enough to prevent it. That failure demonstrated that the origins of the war lay in the capitalist system, rather than the evil intentions of particular leaders. He felt that an alliance with the USSR against fascism before 1939 would have forestalled war, while democratic reform would make the imperial powers less warlike. Like others on the left, he supported collective security through the League of Nations but not rearming the National Government, which he regarded as highly regressive, and he did not trust Baldwin and Chamberlain. The resistance to Hitler had come too late, by which time war was inevitable: he continued to think decades later that the war could have been prevented, and that the Spanish war had been the one to fight. It was only after Dunkirk that the arguments of the appeasers collapsed; prior to that their conduct suggested that they preferred Hitler to the Bolsheviks. Semi-sympathisers with the Nazis and Mussolini included, Hill thought, Churchill himself, and the prevalence of such sympathy meant that Britain had not stood up until it was too late. The 'peace ballot' of 1935 had revealed huge majorities in favour of membership of the League of Nations and the reduction of armaments by international agreement, as well as economic and non-military measures against international aggression.[5] Hill was probably optimistic about the interest of ordinary Britons in foreign policy and the promise of the League of Nations, but he was sincere in his belief that more democracy would have prevented another world war.[6]

For Hill, the Soviet Union really was a new kind of state. Fundamental to his view of politics in 1939 was the idea that the USSR was a heroic experiment and a force for progress, and he regarded stories about torture and executions at the Lubyanka (the secret police headquarters), for example, as fabrications of the capitalist press. It was for this reason that he found the Nazi–Soviet Pact of August 1939 so shocking when it became known in Britain. Victor Kiernan remembered it as 'an astounding volte face' and Hill later referred to that as the worst day of his life.[7] It was followed by the German invasion of Poland, the declaration of war by the British and the Soviet invasion of Finland, but for eight months there was no actual fighting between Britain and the Axis Powers – the period of so-called Phoney War.

Hill's turmoil at the time reflected that of the party as a whole. Harry Pollitt, the working-class activist who had become general secretary of the CPGB, had favoured a struggle on two fronts against the National Government and fascism, and nurtured a real revulsion at the latter. During the 1930s, however, the Comintern line had been to stand aloof from the looming conflict, which it saw as a war among capitalist states, and this mirrored official Soviet policy. Neutrality about fascism had been hard enough for Pollitt; to be in semi-alliance with the fascists, as communists were following the 1939 pact, was a bitter pill indeed. He was apparently nearly broken by the stress of reconciling his personal views with the party line, although he never publicly broke with party discipline (and in fact kept a portrait of Stalin on his wall until his own death).[8] He did, though, temporarily lose his position as general secretary to Palme Dutt, who was far more willing to toe the new line. For Hill, the Pact signalled that the neat opposition of malign, adventurist capitalist countries versus the people's peace-loving democracy no longer held. His certainties, he recalled, 'collapsed 8/39'. That did not mean that Chamberlain had been right, however, but that the remedies Hill had earlier favoured were now obsolete. Nor even did it mean, for Hill, that the Soviet Union was necessarily wrong, since its policy was rational given the British refusal to make an alliance.[9]

Hill elaborated these views in 1939–40 in letters to Shiela and to Margaret James, with whom he was at the time working on her contribution to the volume of essays published in 1940. Hill's differences with James over the war were quite as marked as his disagreements with Shiela.

Although they were allies against fascism, he said to Shiela, 'We wouldn't be on the same side in England because in England the enemy is Chamberlain and the filthy system he represents and justifies and tells liberal lies for.' Shiela drew a clear line between fascism and the democracies, but for Hill 'It is one struggle all over the world.' The 'biggest and only' encouragement to German workers would not be dropping leaflets about the evils of Hitler and Nazism, 'but to overthrow Chamberlain and [Édouard] Daladier [French signatory to the Munich Agreement] and show the German and Czech people there is a government that can be trusted not to do a Versailles or a Munich on them.'[10]

As he put it to James, fascism was simply a form of 'capitalism in a very bad jam indeed – capitalism not rich in colonies, hit by inflations and slumps etc.' The British and French states were equally capable of brutality and would have resorted to it if they had to. Both fascists and liberal capitalists aimed at the same thing: to 'beat down wages, prevent independent working-class organization and criticism, monopolize government power in the hand of the financier-oligarchical clique'. This they did through a tame press (apart from the *Daily Worker*) owned by millionaires, and a labour leadership that collaborated with the ruling class in industrial conciliation and damping down revolutionary movements, 'generally acting as shock-absorber'.[11] Fascism represented 'a tightening up of the organization [of capitalist society] for the purpose of war'. War served rather than undermined capitalist interests – on this he commended Palme Dutt's *Fascism and Social Revolution* (1934). War was a product of the system, not of the wickedness of particular politicians or peoples, so 'it can't be opposed by just goodness'.[12]

The alliance against fascism could only be temporary unless it led to the reform of the capitalist democracies. However, socialism, not Hitler, was Chamberlain's enemy number one: 'Again and again he could have saved peace and overthrown fascism if he had been willing to run the risk of socialist revolution.'[13] At Munich, British imperialists would not take on Hitler single-handed, and they opposed a peace front with democratic Czechoslovakia and socialist USSR because of the implications that might have for their own states. By 1939, however, they were in a different position – hectic rearmament made them confident they could do it single-handedly, and they felt that a revolution of the left in Germany and independence movements in Czechoslovakia could be controlled.[14] It had been a race, he told Shiela: hence the unconditional offer of Soviet help, and also its rejection by the Czech nationalists recognised by Chamberlain and Daladier.[15]

This was the context in which to understand Soviet policy. From 1935 onwards the Comintern had promoted a peace front of peoples versus governments, to force capitalist governments to pursue a policy they did not want to follow. It was not using peace as a pawn, but trying to make people see that opposing Hitler and fascism meant also opposing Chamberlain and promoting socialism. The failure of this policy did not mean that it had been wrong.[16] Acknowledging Shiela's bitterness, he said: 'It is easy … to forget to be bitter about the things Chamberlain wants you to forget' – British conduct in India, for example.[17]

When Chamberlain did finally stand up to Hitlerism, therefore, the communist left was in a quandary: thinking about it decades later Hill quoted Graves, 'was this exactly what they had meant?' He had wanted an earlier alliance with the USSR to forestall war; what they now got was a war against Nazism without, initially at least, a strong alliance with the USSR.[18] At the time he asked Shiela why they should now place any faith in Chamberlain – simply because he had 'started publishing white papers about the atrocities he had hushed up and helped for 6 years? Or when his government announced that wages mustn't go up with prices?'[19] This was not 'as cynical as it sounds', he wrote. 'There is no short cut, no easy salvation, no clean hands, no unsullied conscience.' It depended on informing masses of people, equipping them to make proper choices. James thought communism 'just another ... exploiting racket', but on the basis of his time in the USSR Hill thought 'there is no economic reason it should want ignorance and deception'.[20] By supporting the men of Munich, he told Shiela, 'you support one of the 2 rival groups of thugs trying to impose its own puppet government on them, instead of fighting to overthrow all capitalist thuggery, fascist or imperial'.[21] He did not think the USSR cynical for branding Britain and France aggressors, since the real hope was 'to get at public opinion v. Chamberlain' and gain support for the real path to peace.[22]

So, when James said the point of the war is that 'we must stand up to Hitler', Hill's question was who is the 'we'? Or as he put it to Shiela: 'Wars between rival ruling classes don't interest me except in so far as they are likely to create a revolutionary situation.'[23] This was to flirt with the revolutionary defeatism propounded by Lenin in 1914: losing the war would create a revolutionary situation. The CPGB, however, did not take this line, lacking confidence that there was a potentially revolutionary situation in Britain.[24] Nonetheless, Hill had no enthusiasm for this capitalist war, and certainly not in the name of free countries. That term, he thought, made no sense: 'Individuals can be free, a country can contain more or less free individuals: but a free country? ... Can one be free with a doped press? Is parliamentary democracy the only test of freedom? Is one free on the dole? How is one freer in a French than a German concentration camp?' 'There aren't free countries, there are countries in which certain classes – broader or less broad – are free.' He did concede, though, that 'other things being equal one prefers to live in a capitalist state rich enough to afford formal democracy'.[25]

All this mattered because real peace could only be achieved by a radical change of government. Only socialism could forestall war: 'It is the class structure of the state that determines its foreign policy', wrote

Hill, 'not the niceness or otherwise of the individuals in the government or even its advisory departments.'[26] German defeat last time had not liberated ordinary Germans and Czechs since the first action of the British and French puppet government in Prague in 1919 had been 'to massacre the workers of Hungary and Transylvania, [and] to continue intervention in the USSR'. He contrasted that with '22 years of socialist *achievements* in the USSR. The Comintern has made mistakes but it has never betrayed.'[27]

These political judgements expressed an underlying Marxist analysis about the relationship between ideas and their context. Good intentions were not enough. It was essential to study 'historical tendencies, the existing forces – often not nice forces – and using the less evil at any time to get to the clearly defined goal of the abolition of exploitation of man by man'. There would be disappointments and let-downs, he wrote, but 'if we are quite sure where we are going, what we are doing, what our ideals involve', then we will avoid simply adopting slogans in words that we then betray in our deeds. James would only get the peace she wanted, Hill thought, by getting rid of the system. Where James thought that if individuals acted decently we would have a decent society, Hill thought social reform was necessary to create 'a decent society within which the decency of all of us is not frustrated, wasted, side-tracked'.[28] Or, as he put it to Shiela, she should not be trying to help him escape, but 'fighting to create the sort of society where good people like me don't need to escape'.[29]

In Moscow in 1936 his narrator had thought that the pouring out of life in the Russian civil war had been meaningful because of what had been created. It was not at all obvious to Hill that the impending pouring out of human life on behalf of British and French imperialism would create anything new. His heroes in these conflicts were therefore the communists working for a fundamental change of government – Kuusinen, in alliance with the Soviets in Finland, Thorez in France, and Klement Gottwald and Rudolf Slánský in Czechoslovakia.

If the Nazi–Soviet Pact had been the worst day in his life, a visit to South Wales in December seems to have restored these certainties. Being back 'among all my old comrades', he wrote to Shiela, had been 'a wonderful thing … and restored my perspective and made me aware of the extent to which Oxford (and you) had been getting me down'. He was no longer miserable about the Soviet invasion of Finland, 'because I have got the whole thing linked up – with Spain, and Czechoslovakia and England and Germany. In Finland my people are fighting the sort of people Franco describes as "an ideal state" and I am with them.' Shiela might go and fight for Mannerheim in Finland: the former White opponent of the Russian Revolution now leading resistance to the Soviet invasion. For his part, though, Hill felt 'I mustn't let down my friends who were killed in Spain.'[30]

The German invasion of the USSR in June 1941 brought British and Soviet interests back into alignment and relieved these tensions. However, the twists and turns of CPGB policy in the period before that have brought it little credit.[31] For his part Hill recognised that his views were not immediately practical, and he joked that he would not be shot for them because they were not dangerous in the current situation. But he had been encouraged by the conversation of soldiers overheard on a train so crowded it resembled 'a capitalist film of Russian trains'. 'Naturally they were fed up', he wrote to Shiela, 'but they were fed up for the right reasons too – prices, allowances to dependents, political black-out, class structure of the army, what do we get out of all this. All their unorganized discontent only needed a focus, and I was proud to belong to an organization which is trying in face of great difficulties to express these needs of ordinary people.'[32]

In January 1940 Hill came to the defence of the University Labour Federation, a student body that had recently debated the war and concluded, among other things, that the Allies were as guilty as Hitler, since they had rejected the peace front solution. For this they been threatened with an end to financial support from the state for their studies. 'Freedom is, indeed, in peril', he wrote in a letter to the *Spectator*, 'if academic grants are to be subject to a political test.'[33] Denis Healey also intervened, pointing out that such views had been aired before, and that 'within a year nearly all the supporters of the U.L.F. resolution will be risking their lives to defend, not their own beliefs, but "Janus" [the *Spectator* columnist] and the million others with whom they profoundly disagree.'[34] In May, on the eve of signing up, Hill wrote in the *New Statesman and Nation* that the Soviet invasion of Finland was a consequence of western policy – the Allies had been laying mines and looking for an anti-Soviet territorial base. This was not to give comfort to the Nazis but to stand for a third option: as Lenin had said of the last war, the alternatives were not restricted to Kaiser or Czar – 'it was possible to defeat both.'[35]

Reflecting on this decades later Hill could see more 'snags' to his politics than were obvious at the time, admitting he had been naive. By then it seemed more a choice between alternative nightmares than he had realised, but he felt he would still have chosen the nightmare that he did.[36] In thinking about the crisis he had been more in the hands of the party and activists in the South Wales coalfields than of his Oxford colleagues – it was to South Wales that he went for reassurance after the shock of the Nazi–Soviet Pact.

Despite these views, and while the CPGB was still maintaining an anti-war position, Hill volunteered for the Field Security Police in June 1940, and within two days was offered an officer's training course.[37] He had been recruited with seven other dons, among them J.L. Austin, later a very eminent philosopher, who he already knew – they were contemporaries at Balliol and All Souls, and both moved in Isaiah Berlin's orbit. Hill was vetted in February 1940, the return coming back 'Nothing Recorded Against' him. He was vetted again by the Air Ministry at the time of his call up, and again the return was N.R.A.[38]

In July he reported to Aldershot for basic training, writing en route, 'I am rather excited about it all now that I really am a real soldier.' But it was not to last. Billeted that night near Winchester, he had been given straw to sleep on, and not having anything to do had asked if he could visit the town. The mess sergeant had been quite friendly, but taken him to the Sergeant Major, whose decision it was. There the reception was less friendly: 'Wants to go out? But he's only just arrived.' Hill thought the Sergeant Major was 'brutal for brutality's sake', and although Hill was given permission to go out for longer than the mess sergeant had suggested, the Sergeant Major's parting shot was 'get your hair cut while you're there. Tell them you're in the army now.'[39]

Once in Aldershot he reported that 'Physically life isn't too bad.' One of the dons, he claimed, 'is worse at drill than I am'; he was no longer sleeping on straw, a pillow was on its way, and he had two blankets. Nor was the food bad. For much of his time in training he was preoccupied with trying to see Shiela: 'There is really only one thing in the world I want, and it is such a long way from Oxford to Aldershot. I get off most evenings after 4.30, though I am supposed to be reading their silly stuff then.' Having arrived late he was in a different barrack from the 'rest of my platoon, and spend most of my time running anxiously backwards and forwards trying to find out what I ought to be doing'. On the whole, he was not rebellious, just waiting for something more meaningful to happen: 'I regard my period here as one of those times, you know, which are only interims, nothing in themselves and only something at the end of them, and one just lives through them. Not bad, you know, just nothing.'[40] 'At its worst there is nothing actually unpleasant or wrong or bad about this place. The worst is the rudeness of it all.'[41]

Much of his comment on the army is of this kind: complaints about the routine and apparently meaningless tasks he was required to do, like fetching food and a 'sinister drink called Pepsi-Cola (non-alcoholic)' for the officers.[42] He was irreverent about his responsibilities as a corporal of the night guard at Aldershot, and later, after his posting to Ashburton, about commanding men digging holes while he took a seat in a pub: he could not dig himself without making it obvious that he was less good at it.[43] For their part the men were happy, since 'making a hole in the ground is the nearest they ever get to constructive work'.[44] He often wrote to Shiela while on (boring) duty and mentioned the risk of being caught neglecting his duties: 'Here I am bravely guarding a railway line taking my eyes off the enemy to write to you.' On that occasion his writing was frequently interrupted 'because officers keep coming round and then I am looking efficiently and fearlessly to my front and the pen and paper suddenly aren't there'.[45] He was also sarcastic about disciplinary measures, writing that 'we have been naughty boys and given an extra drill parade every evening 5.15 to 6.0 for the next 10 days'.[46]

He joked self-deprecatingly about his military competence. For example, on first firing a Bren gun he said he had scored 'a very brave and creditable bull, which is rare at the first time of firing. A thousand pities it was on somebody else's target.' Worse still, having marched miles in the rain he had dropped his cape in the butts and could not retrieve it until all the firing was done. In the meantime it had continued to pour with rain. 'But I will make a soldier yet', he wrote, 'and know very nearly all the names of all the parts of all the weapons now.'[47]

The eagerness of the recruits to achieve competence reduced them, he thought, to a kind of 'animal level', wanting to succeed 'not because one believes it or it makes any difference but just because it is there on paper and panders to one's pride however meaninglessly'. This came after he had been given a good first monthly report by the platoon commander: 'Until that happened I had the utmost contempt for him and his judgement, but now I see things to be said for him and perhaps he isn't such a bad chap after all.' He had been gloomy on arrival because at Oxford he had believed in the power of Oxford, but here 'one believes only in the power of the machine and stupidity and has a helpless horror of its immorality'. Becoming competent, though, helped to mollify the monster: 'One is still a cork on the waters, but out of the trough and on the crest.'[48]

To the extent that he was critical of the army's effectiveness he reached for a class explanation. He was outraged on the behalf of two cadets sent back to their battalions despite being good soldiers. The explanation he was sure, was snobbery: they had risen from the ranks and spoke with regional accents. The first case had caused general outrage and left the rest of the men 'seething with revolutionary indignation'. By such means the army 'has lost a good officer, and will have hundreds of gentlemanly twirps'. Following the second case one of his 'nonpolitical' colleagues remarked: 'This army is run on a firmly class basis.'[49] He was satirical about the 'very old world atmosphere' of church parade in Ashburton, Devon: 'village church, commanding officer (believer) reading the lessons, fanatical chaplain literally trying to put the fear of hell into the men. All very 18th century.'[50] With a glee and relish that would have shocked his parents, he asked Shiela whether it was 'you who told me about there being no prostitutes in East London because they had all joined the ATS? Well they've all just been drafted to Aldershot, and liven up the cookhouse quite a lot.'[51]

The eight Oxford dons seem to have signed up with the expectation that they would get work in intelligence. That hope drove Hill to try to pass muster as a soldier, but it was at odds with his rather sardonic view of army life in general. Austin, on the other hand, was very keen. '[A]fter appearing extravagantly glad I was coming here', Hill wrote, he 'now ignores me and concentrates on a man called Peck: also Oxford. They "swot" a great deal, as we call it here.' Hill made common cause with Robert Zaehner, an expert in Persian languages and literature from Christ Church and a friend of Berlin's. They spent their time 'drinking and making cynical remarks about the swots' and getting 'other people to put our equipment together'.[52] It gave him no little satisfaction, therefore, to witness in September 'the spectacular collapse of Austin, who has at last seen the folly of swotting' after all the cadets got low marks on their second monthly reports.[53]

In fact Hill was not a bad soldier and could not help taking a little pride in that. There was something in him that wanted to do well: 'I thoroughly and unreservedly enjoy the drill', and acquiring military swagger, he wrote, '[m]akes me feel I really am somebody'.[54] He celebrated being one of the two best in his platoon at grenade throwing, and that he did as well as Austin on map reading with a score only bettered by five others.[55] After one long tactical exercise in which he had to assess the situation and give out appropriate orders, he boasted that he had done 'better than some of the real soldiers'.[56] Military competence also emboldened him to patronise his colleagues while on leave in Oxford, giving 'them tips about when they are soldiers too'. He even 'had the first civil conversation I have had with the Master since the war, so won't he think the army has done me good?'[57] (Lindsay, of course, had a distinguished war record.)

Hill was physically resilient too, spending one Sunday cycling to London from Aldershot and back, which had greatly increased his standing in his new barrack room. So much so in fact, that he now had the confidence to use his hot water bottles, having 'shown I'm not a cissy civvy really'.[58] An Oxford acquaintance had embarrassed him at Ashburton by telling the others that 'I am a Fellow of All Souls and I am afraid of even darker things from my past'. Hill's retaliation was to tell them 'how awfully good he used to be at rugger because they are getting up a team, and he didn't like that much because he is so fat'.[59] On exercises he was among the more robust recruits, surviving one charge – which left three men sick, one with a twisted ankle and another with a knee injury – with nothing worse than a burst belt buckle.[60] He came through another, 'an 8 mile march in full equipment, and then two bayonet charges of half a mile each at the double', although he did think the exercise 'ludicrous, because by the time we reached the objective a German bullet would have been a merciful release'.[61]

On the other hand, he resented being drawn into caring about such things: 'The thing about the army is one doesn't ever really do any thinking at all [which] is very evil in itself and why the fascists like armies as ends in themselves'. Trying to do well was a distraction from misery and despondency, while dwelling on optimistic hopes of someone 'pulling chestnuts' for him by securing him an intelligence job that would save him from infantry service. Life was gloom, 'and a gloom in which things blow up. But as my friend Bunyan wisely said We dare not despair, so we've got to go on adapting.'[62]

Despite the flippancy and scepticism, both Hill and Shiela had immediate experience of the Battle of Britain as it raged around them. In August 1940 Hill was caught out in the open during an air raid, German bombers directly above, the 'air thick with flying bullets' and 'bombs a few hundred yards away that killed people'. He described an oddly detached response, in which he was interested rather than terrified, somehow feeling that it was not 'anything that could happen to me'.[63] Soon after they had a general invasion warning and Hill asked anxiously if Shiela had been in London in the thick of it all.[64] Around that time he reported that 'Hundreds of bombs were dropped all around us last night, shaking ground and windows and terrifying everybody except me who was bravely asleep at the most dangerous period.' There was a 'delayed-action bomb in the barracks just next to us', and they were now waiting for an explosion.[65]

His letters also record serious routine disruption of train, telephone and telegram services, and large raids on London. These appear mainly as things that made life difficult for them, although they expressed sympathy with the victims and awareness of what might be coming. Following another invasion warning, in which they were genuinely expecting parachutists to land, he wrote 'even the most patriotic people yesterday evening were secretly more anxious to get the horrible business over even than to win'.[66] Confined to barracks every other day during September, he wrote to advise Shiela about gas attacks: stay indoors, and because there might be gases undetectable by taste or smell, 'be somewhere where you will be told and if a real invasion starts put your gas-mask on quite a stupid amount and pretend you are getting used to wearing it'. The absence of air raids became ominous, and night operations took on a more threatening tone.[67] Shiela's brother had gone missing early in the war, causing much anguish as she waited for news; and she was close to the Blitz.[68] In September 1940 she had been upset by the bombing of Mulberry Walk, in Chelsea, in response to which he encouraged her, not for the first time, to get out of London.[69] They had lost contact with a mutual friend, Archie, who they presumed was in an internment camp in Greece.[70] In the darkest moments he wrote that in the event of the real thing: 'Remember… we both stay in England if we can and get in touch.'[71]

In September an exercise looking for parachutists in pouring rain and wet bracken elicited the usual sardonic comment, the air of unreality accentuated by the fact that he and Shiela had once enjoyed a beautiful walk nearby. There was also, though, a sombre realisation of the potential reality he faced: 'The parachutists killed hundreds of us even though they hadn't tommy guns and 20 could easily immobilise 200+ troops. So 2000 scattered about would be one hell of a nuisance.'[72] Hill was one of the appreciative readers of Tom Wintringham's *New Ways of War*, almost a manifesto for a people's guerrilla war against an occupying army, which had 'shocked the War Office' but for Hill said 'all the things I wanted to say'.[73]

During his basic training it became clear that intelligence postings were not going to be automatic, and their adjutant agreed that the dons had been treated badly.[74] As early as August they had heard that only two-thirds of a previous group of 'intelligence people' had actually been given intelligence jobs, the others having become infantry subalterns.

To Hill this was an appalling fate. He wrote to Shiela that he would have preferred the ranks, with no responsibility for things he did not approve of, and avoiding life as a military incompetent forever 'in his sergeant's hands'. This raised the stakes in trying to demonstrate military competence: 'shall I swot more, or doesn't swotting help and is it decided only on languages? Or is it decided on general character and what are my enemies doing about all that?'[75] In September he told Shiela: 'I have to go very seriously with a regiment for many months, perhaps for ever: in fact all that intelligence stuff seems to have been a pooh-trap for dons, and we are all now just infantry officers.'[76]

If at first 'Politics and even the war' had seemed 'very far off from all this routine', he was now more conscious that his political beliefs were a potential obstacle to his ambitions for a job in intelligence.[77] He felt he was in the wrong war, defending British imperialist capitalism against German fascist capitalism, and complained to Shiela about the 'the spreading of this bloody war, and the feeling of impotence it gives one'.[78] He worried that his hostile review for *Scrutiny* of H.B. Parkes's *Marxism: A Post-mortem*, a 'wicked anti-Marxist book', would not do him 'any good with the intelligence people': 'will a review or two stop them? Who knows?'[79] There did not seem to be any rhyme or reason to these decisions: a mutual acquaintance had been refused an intelligence posting 'because of his white Russian wife. Aren't they insane?'[80]

As his passing out approached, he began to worry about which regiment to put his name down for, asking Shiela's advice as someone from a military family. His own main interest was where he would be stationed,[81] although it may have appealed a little to his vanity too: 'being measured for [an officer's] uniform and don't I look smart and like a real officer really?'[82] When it came, the news was bad: 'Of the seven Oxford dons enlisted for M.I. with me, they are taking one, and 6 are going to regiments. We are not very pleased.'[83] Hill was posted to the 1st Bucks Light Infantry at Ashburton, from the 168th Officer Cadet Training Unit. His record noted that he had served with the CTC at St Peter's School (something he never mentioned) and according to his OCTU reports, 'After a good start he continued to do well. He should be an asset to his regiment.' He was appointed to a commission on 1 November 1940 and by February 1941 was a staff lieutenant.[84]

He continued to hope for a posting to intelligence, however, or to the War Office in Cheltenham, pinning his hopes on rumours of a place on an intelligence course at Matlock, although there were doubts about the quality of his German.[85] In January 1941 he got disappointing news.

He would not be going to Matlock; although his name had been put forward there was no vacancy. At that point there was no news from Cheltenham either. Redemption came the same day, however. Having been told at 4.30 pm that he was not going to Matlock he had been cast into the deepest gloom, only to hear at 8 pm that he would be going on an intelligence course in Cambridge: 'The army is indeed the quaintest of institutions.'[86]

Zaehner had assumed some importance in this: recruited by the Special Operations Executive, he was perhaps the one of the eight who had been taken on by intelligence straight away.[87] For Hill the opportunity of a desk job did present itself early in 1941 in a posting to the War Office in Cheltenham: not an intelligence job but not infantry service either. He thought there might be ignominy in this partial posting; on the other hand 'Zaehner does seem to think M.I. have taken against me.' Failing Military Intelligence twice, Hill thought, 'would condemn me to battalion forever'.[88] He worried, however, that it was dishonourable to want a desk job, and was pleased to have Shiela's approval for the move. When he tested out his fellow officers on the issue he was relieved to find them all 'frankly envious': none had suggested that honour was in question. After a frustrating day of slow operations ending with a discussion about low morale in the battalion, he was firmly resolved to accept the War Office posting.[89]

Any political difficulty was relieved by the German invasion of the Soviet Union in June 1941. From this point on British communists were wholehearted supporters of the war effort and regarded as such by the government. Harry Pollitt returned to his position as general secretary of the CPGB, and the Comintern formally renounced Dutt's very critical line about Churchill's government (a line it had previously supported).[90] In September, Hill was recommended for employment as a liaison officer with the Soviet forces: his German might not have been good enough for intelligence, but his 'Knowledge of Russian [was] said to be that of the standard of a Second Class Interpreter'. In December it was noted that he would 'make a most useful personal assistant to the Head of a Military or Politico-Economic Mission to the USSR'. This was indeed the direction his service took. He joined the Intelligence Corps as a second lieutenant in February 1942, and by April was an acting captain in Military Intelligence Section 1.x (M.I.1.x).[91]

There were by now some rumours about his politics. When his name came up in July 1942 in connection with an official history of the principal departments in the current war, it was said that one department, perhaps the Ministry of Economic Warfare, had previously decided against employing him because of his 'Communist leanings'. This claim was denied by Sir David Petrie, the head of the intelligence service, who said that quite to the contrary, they had informed M.I.1.x in the previous year that there was nothing recorded against him. Asked for more information about the rumours, Petrie's correspondent backed down: 'I had received nothing in writing from anybody' but had 'misinterpreted an oral message making a quite clearly mistaken' inference.[92]

In any case, now that the Soviets were on the same side, the British government generally regarded communists positively. Hill's name came up again in conversation among Communist Party leaders in August 1942, monitored by the secret services, discussing who might be helpful to put forward to the intelligence services. The Soviets did not trust the British government, which had refused to open a second front against the Nazis, and in that context British communists were likely to have an easier hearing with the Soviets than representatives of a government whose foreign policy had been so disappointing to them in the previous decade. It was certainly not a conversation about illicit infiltration, but about how they might be employed to support the war effort in this way.[93] This fits with the offer made to Hill in October 1942 of employment at the British Embassy in Kuibyshev with the Ministry of Information. Again the return on his vetting was N.R.A. and his indefinite release from the army was recommended, although in the end the move did not take place: 'officer unwilling'.[94]

In December he was appointed acting captain in the Russian Liaison Group of the Ministry of Information and by June 1943 was acting major instructing in the Civil Affairs Centre. For Hill the posting was great news: 'I am wonderfully happy, more so than ever since the war began – speaking of course purely of the ideological and occupational side.' The work was hard, but the training was excellent: '[we] have first class teachers for language, and the most startlingly liberal selection of lecturers on economic – political – military subjects'. Many of them were old friends or acquaintances and 'others clearly ought to be'. In intelligence he was among his own: 'The people on the course, whites and all, are charming.'[95] That month, he was released from military service and transferred to the Foreign Office; sanction was given to pay Major Hill the relatively generous salary of £900 p.a. His file reveals that his membership of the Communist Party was known at that point, but not from Hill himself; a notification is stamped as received in June 1945, making a cross-reference to a report from 1943.[96]

The British government clearly wanted to promote positive views of the Soviet Union and was relaxed about making appropriate use of Soviet sympathisers. (My own mother and father recall how, at school in Dorset and Cornwall respectively, in the middle of the war they were suddenly made aware of the great virtues of the Soviet people, as Ministry of Information posters appeared extolling the virtues of Stakhanovite labour and life on collective farms – while steering clear of an endorsement of communism, of course.)[97] Hill's political sympathies were hardly unique, and they were not always a bar to service in intelligence; a 1945 report on Hill's connections noted among them Peter Shinnie (later an eminent archaeologist), known to have been an active communist since his undergraduate days, who nonetheless 'was for a time employed on secret work in Italy'.[98] These shared war aims made for odd bedfellows: Hill later recounted 'with some affection how his boss in the Foreign Office, a convinced Tory of the old school, kept a huge map of Russia on his wall, on which he moved little red flags to mark the Soviet resistance to Hitler'.[99]

The promotion of cultural awareness and understanding became one of Hill's main responsibilities at the Foreign Office. It had set up a Committee on Russian Studies in June 1944, with three sub-committees. Hill was appointed secretary of one of them, dealing with facilities for teaching Russian studies, and was principal assistant to Geoffrey Wilson, a career civil servant, who was secretary of the main committee. Hill's sub-committee was chaired by Professor Le Gros Clark and the whole enterprise was chaired by Orme Sargent.[100] Although he recognised the academic credentials of the committee, Hill was sceptical about its work both at the time and after. In fact he was later quite withering about the Russia Desk in general: 'So far as I know', he wrote, 'there was no special scheme for training diplomats in things Russian … *No one* in the Northern Dept. knew *anything* about the USSR except two temporaries, of whom I was one.'[101] He was also characteristically self-deprecating about the importance of this work, later telling John Jones, author of the standard history of Balliol, that he was ill-informed about college affairs in 1944 because at that time 'I was bravely defending my country in Whitehall.'[102]

His approach to the task seems to have been more Oxford than pro-Soviet. Isaiah Berlin wrote to him from the British Embassy in Washington in May 1945, stressing the importance of post-war Russian studies and therefore the importance of securing the services of serious scholars. Hill replied, sympathetic to the problem and lamenting the appointment in Oxford of Sergey Konovalov to a lectureship in Slavonic Studies, an appointment Berlin had found 'somewhat depressing'. Berlin also seemed to share a scepticism about Sir Bernard Pares, an influential Russian expert hostile to the Soviet Union.[103] Hill had previously shared his doubts about Pares with both Shiela Grant Duff and Berlin, and he and Berlin also shared regret that Humphrey Sumner would be difficult to tempt back to Oxford from his Chair in Edinburgh (although he was later to return as Warden of All Souls).[104] An element of this was worry about the dependence on White Russians for such roles, which Berlin thought had served the Library of Congress very badly. For Berlin, 'British scholars on the subject are miserably lacking, and there are no native Americans, e.g. who are much good'; the main priority should be 'to stop British universities electing local hacks'.[105]

Their exchange was gossipy and academic, including gossip about academic appointments. They both displayed a sceptical attitude towards the Foreign Office Russia Desk (FORD). In fact Berlin had been sounded out about taking over the Desk, and in refusing had struggled to 'use language calculated not to offend T[oynbee] and yet indicate quite clearly that I would rather be unemployed and starve than work in the atmosphere in which I discovered you all to be enveloped in 1944'. For his part, Hill said he would have thought Berlin 'mad if you had gone to FORD'.[106]

In response to the shortage of suitably qualified staff, the Committee eventually recommended that employing Soviet citizens would help diplomatic relations, and Russians who were not Soviet citizens should only be employed in junior posts or teaching literature. Given later accusations about his role in this, it is important to note that no action seems to have been taken by the time Hill left to return to academic life.[107]

Favourable attitudes to the Soviet people persisted after the war when, for a 'brief period … it seemed as though the wartime friendship between England and the Soviet Union would continue to prosper'.[108] Hill contributed here too. He wrote a book, *Two Commonwealths*, for a series edited by John MacMurray, an academic philosopher and yet another Balliol man (in fact a student of A.D. Lindsay's). MacMurray's preface explained that the purpose was 'to help us in Britain understand the people of the Soviet Union by comparing and contrasting their way of life with our own'. Hill wrote the book with Foreign Office knowledge but, as protocol demanded, under a pseudonym (K.E. Holme – Russian for Hill). It promised to explain how 'The Soviet system is the answer to Russian needs and the solution to a Russian problem.' Neither MacMurray nor the publisher, Harrap, are now associated with communism or pro-Soviet sympathies; Harrap had a reputation primarily for educational publications.[109]

In the book Hill laid out the Russian system and aspects of its constitutional arrangements in the most sympathetic way, and often offset acknowledgement of difficulties by comparison with spots on the British past: on the first page, in fact, he pointed out that in England Afro-Caribbeans were subject to discrimination, whereas in the USSR a colour bar was illegal, and Pushkin's African grandfather had been welcome at the court of Peter the Great. The history of freedom was not all on one side, in other words. He acknowledged that those kulaks who 'opposed collectivisation and sabotaged production ... were evicted and driven away into exile or forced labour', but compared this to enclosure in eighteenth-century England, which had driven peasants to the workhouse or factory: it was the price paid for more efficient agriculture. The constitutional structure, the soviets, the party system, bureaucracy, notions of freedom, collective farms, trade unions and collective planning were distinctive to the USSR, but not inferior to western economic and political arrangements: they answered to the different logic of Russia's rapid modernisation in the twentieth century. Although this now seems very credulous, to say the least, there was nothing sinister about the pseudonym which, as MacMurray noted, the author was obliged to use, and Hill openly identified himself as the author in another publication in 1949.[110]

Hill seems to have maintained a political life in the early years of the war, although it is not well documented. In his letters to Shiela there are references to the Thursday lunch club throughout the spring of 1940, to the Labour Club and, occasionally, to his 'London friends'. At one point he recounted meeting an unnamed CPGB member on the platform of Oxford station, from where they were to travel on Party business. Hill's companion was ill, but very keen to go; 'the day before like a good commissar I had tried to arrange for some one else to go instead of him', because 'he was so steeled and bolshevik but so ill and pathetic and sorry for himself'.[111]

Hill's name had been noted by the secret service in August 1942, after it came up in conversation among communist leaders, and in 1944 they picked up his connection with the leader of a communist group at Oxford: Beryl Smalley, a medieval historian at St Hilda's College. A daily report on correspondence to his London address was imposed for one week in March 1944. The official file contains copies of intercepted letters between him and Smalley dealing with academic and personal matters. Further checks were set up in October 1944 and May 1945.[112]

The purpose of the surveillance was to understand networks of connection and loose talk as much as to catch spies: 'to show', one report noted, 'the type of party member with whom Christopher HILL is in contact and the risk of leakage through him of secret information, particularly on Russian affairs'.[113] A report from August 1945 shows that, through Smalley, Hill was connected to the economist Maurice Dobb (another old friend of Smalley's). By then Hill was married to Inez Waugh, and through her he was connected to Claud Cockburn, the communist journalist and veteran of the Spanish Civil War. John Lewis, the Marxist philosopher, and Dona Torr are both noted as friends, as was her husband, Walter Milton Holmes, of the *Daily Worker*. Hill had stayed at the flat of Tony Barnett in Great Portland Street, another old friend of Smalley's and convenor of an undercover group of party members. It was not an exclusively communist milieu, however. He and Inez had also hosted a visit from Alexander Baykov, an economist of White Russian background who had been in exile in Czechoslovakia and had Balliol connections: hardly an obvious focus of a search for communists, even if one conclusion from the report was that Baykov might not be what he seemed. There had in fact been some tension between Baykov and his neighbours Yvonne and Leonard Craven, both Communist Party members, after their political differences became clear. There was some connection too with Nicholas Kaldor, the eminent Hungarian economist, and others whose links to the party seem tenuous or non-existent, such as Peggy Joseph and Phyllis Auty, about whom the security services could find nothing suspicious. Hill wrote to comrades brokering introductions, sometimes for anonymous friends, but in general it seems likely that this was a relatively broad intellectual church even though the party was critical to the Hills' social connections.

Following his demobilisation, the surveillance of Hill continued on the grounds that it would be 'useful to discover the kind of work on which he was engaged, and it might also be valuable to place a check on his correspondence in order to discover more about his friends in official circles'. His subscription to *Soviet War News* was noted from the mail check on his London address at Hereford Square, as was his recent marriage to Inez, who had previously worked for the paper: here was a connection of 'particular interest'. The only specific charge, however, was that 'we have information from [a] secret source [in the party] of a leakage to the Communist Party, through Diane PYM, of Foreign Office information, though there is nothing to show whether HILL was the culprit'.[114] Again, the worry seemed to be about leakage, loose talk, rather than active espionage.

The most damaging connection of which the secret service was aware was that Hill had stayed in the house of Heinz Koestler. Koestler was of German origin but naturalised in 1928, and he had attracted the attention of Oxford City Police early in the war. Suspicion had been aroused by his open celebration of Nazi victories, and his keen interest in aerodromes on the east coast. In May 1940 he had been overheard engaging a serving officer, Lieutenant Peter Cadogan (a CPGB member), in conversation about military matters and troop movements in France. Cadogan's fiancée was also of interest: she was the daughter of Konni Zilliacus, later an MP but previously suspected of 'Russian interests and revolutionary designs, [who] has been guilty of careless talk'. Koestler seems mainly to have escaped problems because a man in the secret services vouched for Cadogan.[115] These were hardly strong indications of guilt or guilt by association, and the decision about Hill was that no action should be taken except to bear these connections in mind if any leakage recurred, and 'to bring him out for an airing if (i) we hear nothing of him for some time or (ii) you ever find yourself with time on your hands'.[116]

This imperfect but potentially broad interest of the secret service had failed to unearth anything much. In any case, Hill's work was not sensitive and, as Penelope Corfield notes, the latter part of the war was one of the few periods in his life when his own views aligned well with British foreign policy.[117] It later became clear that Hill had not known that he had been vetted, but his politics were certainly well known to anyone qualified to answer questions about him, and his Communist Party membership was known to many, not only the secret services.

His letters to Shiela during the war reflected not so much pro-Soviet intent as the subversiveness and scepticism of authority expressed by many who were caught up in the war. Once the war arrived he did not want a Nazi victory any more than anyone else; where he differed from the army command was in wanting an Allied victory to be followed by a transformation of the British state. It may be that this latter hope was what really worried the secret services. In April 1941, prior to giving a talk to troops about British history, he told Shiela: 'I am rather panicky because I find it so difficult to open my mouth nowadays without saying things that will get me denounced.'[118] Roger Simon, the communist lawyer who later inherited his father's title, Baron Simon of Wythenshawe, had been barred from an infantry commission for fear that he would spread subversion among the troops. This was despite regular reports of his good conduct: 'good conduct is of course in conformity with the present attitude of the Communist Party', noted Alan Johnston of MI5 in February 1945.[119] Hill clearly thought the army could give men a political education, seeing political potential in the discontents he heard expressed on the trains. He would have been keen to impart such an education, and the one thing the security services did clearly resist was his appointment as a civilian lecturer in the Southern Command following the war.[120]

Immediately after the war Hill was hopeful about the prospects of significant political change in Britain; it was the topic of a paper he wrote in the early autumn of 1945 that was well received in the party. Everywhere in Europe, he argued, the old state apparatus had broken down. It was too early to say what would happen in Germany, but in liberated countries in the Soviet sphere the state would be rebuilt by a proletariat that could take a political lead against those who had collaborated with the Nazis. The prospects for socialism and democracy appeared bright. In the Anglo-American sphere, by contrast, the old state apparatus now enjoyed support from the Allied forces, and Hill thought there would be a struggle between remnants of the pre-war state and proletarian movements that had led the resistance and liberation.

Britain was a special case in these terms: the state machine had not been smashed and the pre-war elites had survived, but one fraction of the governing class had made an alliance with the USSR, which would prevent the resumption of Britain's former imperial policies. At the same time, Hill wrote, it brought 'a great accession of strength to the democratic forces in Britain'. The alliance with the USSR greatly restricted the government's 'freedom of action in the coming struggle against opposition at home'. In this situation, he argued, reform was the best hope for progressive change: in the oldest and strongest centre of capitalism the government would have to make concessions to the proletariat. In Britain this opportunity would last only so long as the threat of revolution did not provoke a powerful reaction. Revolutionary activity would therefore be counter-productive, provoking the forces of Anglo-Imperial reaction, while Soviet diplomacy and international trade union pressure were the best defences against it.[121] In this he was once again in line with the CPGB as a whole, which had emerged from the war largely shorn of any immediately revolutionary ambition, and willing to cooperate on reform.[122] Having fought and won the wrong war, Hill had high hopes for domestic reform, although these were soon to be dashed by the onset of Cold War.

4

Cold War, Marxism and the British Past: 1945–53

The connexions between different groups of ideas are subtle and difficult to analyse, but they exist: they exist because of the unity of the individual and of the society in which he lives. It is to the structure of society that we must look for the key to interpretation. Otherwise we shall distort and do violence to the history we are studying.

Christopher Hill, *Economic Problems of the Church*, 1956

Following the war, a reformist rather than a revolutionary, Hill returned to the project of writing a Marxist history of Britain. Thomas Hodgkin remembered party meetings in Hill's rooms: 'a sect, no doubt, consisting of a few moderately devoted, mainly nice people, like some of those Christopher discusses in *The World Turned Upside Down*'. They were modest in ambition and largely ineffectual, but Hodgkin was impressed by 'Christopher's understanding, gentle, patient guiding of our deliberations, the same Arts as did maintain, later, the Power of the Mastership [of Balliol].'[1] They were, Hill later recalled, 'days of very great optimism', the Labour government 'coming in with this astonishing sweep and everybody had what now, I suppose, seem rather utopian hopes for a change in society'.[2] It soon became clear, however, that communists were living in an increasingly hostile environment, and secret service surveillance intensified.[3] It was, Hill later wrote, 'dangerous to one's reputation to say anything good about the USSR', and party members became even more cautious in conversation and correspondence, preferring terms such as 'the American expert', 'your American friend' or 'an English expert' to real names.[4]

As Cold War attitudes settled in, Hill denounced the threatened purges of civil servants 'suspected of being associates of the Communist Party', noting the potential for arbitrary power if 'Alleged Communists or "fellow travellers" are to be dismissed … with no right of appeal to an impartial tribunal'. He was withering about the secret services that would wield this power: 'During the war I had the opportunity of seeing something of the working of M.I.5, and what most impressed me was its inability to distinguish between Communists and the most apparently innocuous members of the Labour Party.'[5] It was at this point that vetting concluded Hill would be unsuitable as a lecturer in Southern Command – it 'would give him the opportunity, which he might well take, of expressing Communist views to military audiences'.[6] These were not ungrounded fears. Hill continued to think there was radical potential in the British Army and in 1948 wrote a popular piece for the *Communist Review* about the New Model Army, the first democratic army and the body that came closest to achieving a democratic revolution in the seventeenth century: 'it would give our Whitehall brass-hats the creeps if anything like it existed today'.[7]

Before the war, he had been careful not to offend his colleagues in Cardiff with his political views, and when they became known it caused a stir. As Rodney Hilton later said, it was already prudent for an early career academic to be cautious about revealing communist sympathies.[8] In Cold War conditions the problem became even more pronounced. In 1948 Hill had told Jack Dunman, a party official, that the dons 'were very upset about victimisation, and [Hill] was raising the question whether they shouldn't go underground again'. The concern was about 'young dons not getting jobs', but even Hill, 'who did make a fight in coming out apparently, was "feeling wobbly about it now"'.[9] When Andrew Rothstein lost his position at the School of Slavonic and East European Studies in 1950, Hill wrote to the *New Statesman and Nation* to defend him, prompting Max Beloff, the historian, to reply, saying that it was a matter of the academic autonomy of the School of Slavonic Studies. Three months later Beloff wrote a very hostile review of Rothstein's history of the Soviet Union in the *Manchester Guardian*, which made only one specific criticism (that it underplayed the role of the Comintern) but which assumed that Rothstein would have no interest in telling the truth. That Rothstein's tone was 'studiously moderate' and that he cited non-Marxists including Namier was no defence against a sarcastic dismissal.[10]

According to Eric Hobsbawm this was the opening of the 'darkest period of public anti-communism', in the shadow of the Korean War and, in 1951, the defection of the spies Burgess and Maclean.[11] Hill told Ved Mehta he was lucky that he had tenure at Balliol 'or I would have been thrown out in the fifties'. Certainly, lots of people could not get jobs, the effect of 'a cold purge, conducted in a discreet and gentlemanly English way, so that people victimised politically seemed to be passed over for other reasons'.[12]

In this atmosphere it was not unusual to hear the claim that Marxist writing was not just poor scholarship but, as Henry St Laurence Beaufort Moss put it in a review of Jack Lindsay's book *Byzantium into Europe* (1952), 'fundamentally opposed to the canons of western scholarship'. Lindsay was a prolific writer and party member, and Moss took the opportunity of the review to make the general claim that historical materialism starts with 'immutable dogmas, revealed truths to which the facts must be made to conform', making a nonsense of western scientific methods. The growing influence of Marxist scholarship therefore 'raises the question', he wrote, 'whether, in fairness to his pupils', communists should be allowed to hold teaching positions.[13]

Not the least of the possible objections to this was that Lindsay had never had, and never did have, any responsibility for the teaching of history. Hill, however, took on the more serious principle, 'deploring the suggestion that any heretics should be regarded as unfit to teach *by reason of their heresy* and of that alone'. He wrote his own review of Lindsay's book in the *Modern Quarterly* in explicit refutation of that in the *TLS*, making a point of criticising the book, to show that Marxists had scholarly disagreements, but arguing that the real problem liberals had with it was with the solid base of scholarship which challenged their views.[14]

In April 1953 Victor Kiernan wrote to Hill partly about the possibility of a post in Cardiff. He was reluctant to put his referees to any trouble 'if the political tone is bad there [since] it would be a very long shot'. He also wanted to avoid competition with Hill for professorial positions at Exeter and Leeds, the latter much more promising for Hill than Kiernan since Kitson Clark, the prominent Cambridge historian, had influence there: 'He may not know you much', wrote Kiernan, but 'he knows me'.[15] Academics lived, and still do, with this awareness of who their enemies might be for jobs and grants, but there was clearly a more serious political concern behind these worries. Around this time Hill himself had missed out on the founding chair of History at University

College of North Staffordshire (later to become the University of Keele), 'not because there was anything intrinsically wrong with [being a Communist]' but because A.D. Lindsay, soon to be its first vice-chancellor, worried that 'his appointment might … make difficulties for an experimental university through its early years'.[16]

The atmosphere made others cautious about their connections. Rosamond Lehmann, the novelist, anti-fascist campaigner and one-time lover of Goronwy Rees, was invited to speak at a conference in Oxford discussing the implications of the retention of American bombing bases in the UK. Wary of becoming associated with communism, she agreed, but asked them not to invoke her name as a supporter, for fear she would be assumed to hold 'political opinions which, intellectually or morally, I cannot share'.[17]

On the other hand, there was a perception among non-Marxists that the Marxists hunted as a pack. Hugh Trevor-Roper, the eminent Oxford historian, complained in 1955 that he was 'sick of these Marxists. Every time I write in the [*New Statesman and Nation*] one of the London Academic Marxists – Rothstein, Hobsbawm etc – pops up and lays down the law to me. But I suppose I should relish being selected as their academic enemy no. 1.'[18] He was, however, hopeful that their academic fortunes were failing. In 1956 he wrote to Berlin, who had fallen out with Hill over the latter's book on Lenin. 'I hear', wrote Trevor-Roper, 'that Goronwy Rees has published a violent attack on G. Burgess and announced in print that Anthony Blunt is still a communist. Please tell me all. I have often wondered whether G. Rees is sound on that point. I hate them all, the communists and (even more) the ex-communists. How is X. Hill surviving the destalinisation of history?'[19]

The charge that, unlike liberals, the work of Marxist scholars was warped by their political commitments, was a serious one. Hill's sensitivity on this point was plain. Writing to John Sparrow following his election as Warden of All Souls in March 1952, Hill's congratulations were tempered by the memory 'that you once accused me of being a deliberate distorter of historical fact'. He also noted that Isaiah Berlin apparently now included 'E.H. Carr among perverters of historical truth'. Hill's irritation is clear: 'I do wish you would either investigate the matter for yourself or contemplate the possibility that "lie" may mean no more than "interpretation with which I disagree"'.[20] Sparrow evidently responded generously, and Hill conceded self-deprecatingly that he could not expect him to change his mind on the issue: 'I do … tend to think that all right-minded people would agree with me if they seriously investigate the problems on which we appear to disagree: otherwise I should not agree with myself.'[21]

Revelations of espionage by Soviet sympathisers were uncomfortable for their liberal friends. Rees's denunciation of Burgess, sometimes attributed to his need of money, was motivated at least in part by fear of the damage Burgess could now do to others including himself. Rees's denunciation shocked both Berlin and Grant Duff.[22] All Marxists and communists were tainted by association, even though they did not necessarily know or like each other. Hill was, for instance, horrified by the former communist Frank Meyer's testimony in February 1957 to a subcommittee of the US Senate about Soviet activities in the United States; Hill had already disliked Meyer when they were both in Oxford communist circles in the 1930s: 'I knew he had gone to the radical right, but this piece is loathsomely cold-blooded.'[23]

By 1951 Hill was known to the secret services as 'one of the leading Communists at Oxford University [who] plays a prominent part in all the Party's cultural work'. Close surveillance, it was claimed, would 'increase our knowledge of Communism at the Universities'.[24] During 1952 and 1953 they cast the net widely in their search, but unearthed precious little evidence that Hill was effectively or dangerously subversive. In 1952, for example, MI5 toyed with the idea of tipping off the FBI about the historians David Underdown and Peter Marshall, then both working at Yale. Neither was remotely identifiable as communist at the time or subsequently, but correspondence with Hill was sufficient to cast suspicion on them. Klaus Berentzen, then serving in the RAF, was under scrutiny after getting in touch with Hill for support in getting academic work – the connection was, it seems, Balliol rather than communism. Anna Lingard, who worked at the Oxford University Press, was investigated after having written warmly to Hill in the summer of 1953, as was Valerie Pearl, the far-from-Marxist historian, after staying with the Hills in December that year; they also looked into Dorothy Marshall, again not notably a Marxist historian, following some correspondence with Hill.[25] For all these people there was clearly a risk in association with Hill, of which they were almost certainly unaware.

The surveillance was quite thorough, including a check on whether Hill had applied for an amateur wireless licence in Malaya.[26] If some of this zeal suggests simple-minded excess, that might not be far off the mark. In December 1952 Hill became aware of the surveillance when he received a letter which, having been opened and read, was put back in the wrong envelope. Checks on his mail were suspended 'in case the matter was raised in the House of Commons'.[27] A little oddly, the secret services also kept press cuttings of articles in the public domain and abstracted a bibliography of Hill's publications down to 1948.[28]

All this effort failed to reveal much more than prosaic activity in alliance with other communists and a broader group of left-leaning figures – factory gate meetings, leafleting and selling the *Daily Worker* in support of Labour's campaign in a High Wycombe by-election, and Hill lending Ernie Keeling, the party's South Midlands district organiser, his car to give a talk in Banbury.[29] The secret services were aware of an Anglo-French conference of communist historians in December 1952, as well as an invitation to the communist writer James Klugmann to address a meeting including non-party members about the Nineteenth Party Congress in Moscow, and they intercepted a letter from Hill to Diana St John suggesting readings for a group working on a textbook on working-class history.[30] In 1953, they also noted a visit to Oxford by Arnold Kettle to talk about Marxist views of Shakespeare, an event hosted by Hill.[31]

Hill's main contribution in fact lay in this cultural work of the party, a relatively minor but potentially difficult role. Rajani Palme Dutt, writing in the *Communist Review* in 1932, had taken a stringent line on the role of intellectuals, prompted in part by Maurice Dobb's efforts to organise an intellectual caucus in the party.[32] Later, in light of the controversy sparked by Hill's *English Revolution*, Dutt confessed that 'he was never much of an enthusiast for "the academic brigade" within the party: "incurable professional types", who were apt to "contaminate" their Marxist exegetic with the language of "bourgeois liberalism"', or to confuse '"intellectual agreement" with the Communist position and "real revolutionary consciousness"'.[33] This suspicion of academic Marxists was also prominent in the later controversies of 1956/7, and clearly Hill was vulnerable to this line of criticism, committed as he was to what might seem liberal individualist values of personal flourishing and independence of thought.

Immediately after the war, however, such tensions were less marked. Harry Pollitt, the party general secretary and veteran organiser, had spoken to a meeting of communist professionals in London hoping to foster the 'maximum contribution every progressive citizen in the country can make'. The party needed 'the best writers, actors, singers, doctors, teachers, research workers, mathematicians, playwrights and so on'; they must reach the highest standards so that 'our work reflects the nobility of Communism'. The duty of a communist mathematician was to be a good mathematician, while communist historians could not continue 'to teach history in a way indistinguishable from that of bourgeois historians'. This sense of the importance of intellectual and cultural work was balanced by an awareness of class tensions: intellectuals should drop any sense of superiority and not be upset if their reception in party circles was sceptical. Intellectuals should neither be flippant about manual workers, nor in awe of them, and 'at the same time avoid irresponsibility about and towards the party sometimes expressed in flippant wisecracks about its jargon and organisational defects'. Intellectuals would be crucial in combatting the forces of reaction and in constructing a good society ('People want to know and understand the political situation'), and they should try not to worry if 'unkind things are said to them because of misunderstandings as to what they are driving at'. This latter danger could be avoided by a proper understanding of what 'the masses themselves are interested in'.[34]

This was part of a broader cultural effort in the post-war years which aimed at building support for communist ambitions through a cultural programme as well as (cautious) cooperation with the broader left. There was no return to the class against class sectarianism of the late 1920s and early '30s, although the suspicion of reformism remained, and policy was inconsistent.[35] In May 1947, however, the Cultural Committee of the party discussed the possibility of a union of intellectuals. While the long-term goal would be to build up 'a broad and democratic organisation of all workers in the cultural and scientific field', the more immediate aim 'should be to get common action on issues as they arise, to examine the best ways of helping to extend work of existing organisations, such as Arts Council, etc., and especially, to consider how to advance British culture, fighting against reactionary American ideas etc'. There was to be a broad effort in the arts, humanities and science to improve the democratic life of society, and the Committee was to receive reports from the newly founded Historians' Group.[36]

As early as November 1944 Dona Torr had spoken of the need for 'Marxist publications and methods of popularising the Marxist creed', and Hill's name was raised in that context by Emile Burns, an economist and a leading figure in this cultural effort. Burns was then in his early sixties, from a bourgeois background (he was the son of the harbourmaster of St Kitts and a graduate of Trinity College, Cambridge). He thought Hill's knowledge of Russian affairs would be of 'inestimable value for them' and that a healthy advance on publishing royalties would incentivise him.[37] The following January the Political Committee of the party heard about plans for a new scientific journal to be led by Burns, the relaunched *Modern Quarterly*, and in February the editorial board noted that Hill would be 'privately consulted' about the journal immediately and might formally join the board later. By July the following year he was attending the meetings and did so regularly until its dissolution in 1953. Other board members included J.D. Bernal, the radical scientist, Maurice Dobb, J.B.S. Haldane and Margot Heinemann, with whom Hill remained close until the end of his life.[38] He was also a member of the National Cultural Committee, although his main formal connection with it seems to have been through his activity on the Historians' Group, effectively one of its sub-committees.[39] The latter group was launched in 1946 and Hill remained active in it until 1953.

The publication of *The British Road to Socialism* in 1951 committed the party to reform rather than revolution, and this provided the context for further concerted thought about the role of the professional classes. At the same time, the *Modern Quarterly* had formally committed to cooperation with non-Marxists 'in the struggle for international peace' given the global situation.[40] The result was the promotion of the work of writers, lawyers, architects, musicians, lawyers, painters, sculptors and fine artists, as well as the historians, all in line with the vision spelt out by Pollitt in the immediate aftermath of the war.[41] In 1954 the Central Committee of the party established a commission on the place of the middle classes in the struggle and their role in relation to the British road.[42]

One of the purposes the Cultural Committee agreed in April 1947 was to keep in touch with the cultural activities of communist parties in other countries, and Hill actively promoted academic exchange between the Eastern Bloc and the West.[43] He reported on British historical work for academic audiences abroad, in Russia, France and Japan, and brought more Soviet writing to the attention of English-speaking audiences.[44] This work also interested Special Branch, which noted his return from the 'Congress of Intellectuals in Defence of Peace' at Wrocław on 1 September 1948, as well as a visit to Prague the following year to give historical lectures. The report noted that a luggage search had proved impossible because the bags had already cleared customs.[45] In December 1952 he helped promote the visit of the Soviet historian Eugene Kosminsky, and was in contact with Jean-Marie Chesnoux, visiting the UK in the course of PhD studies (presumably the same 'Genoux' with whom Hill and others later stayed in Paris on their way back from the International Congress of Historians in Rome in September 1955).[46]

Some of this work appears to have been a more broad-based cultural exchange rather than partisan activism, but it was a hard line to draw. In

November 1951 he had been active with Rothstein in organising events and hosting Vladimir Semenovich Kemenov, the eminent art historian, on his visit to Oxford. Hill had been infuriated when it turned out that the visit was official and included a member of the Russian embassy: this had embarrassed Hill, who had invited, among others, Ernst Gombrich, hardly a slavish devotee of the party. In the event Gombrich and a number of others 'failed to appear' and the whole thing was considered an 'abject failure' by both Rothstein and the Russians.[47]

As seen through the eyes of the security services, Hill's work for the CPGB outside the university left little doubt about his party loyalty down to the mid-1950s, but it was far from dangerously subversive and sat a little uncomfortably with the party's view of itself as a working-class movement. Anne Connolly Manduit, who lodged with the Hills during that period, remembered their kitchen at Northmoor Road in Oxford being 'constantly filled with amused and cynical car-factory workers of the "pur and dur" [ideologically pure and committed] calibre'. There, they mixed with 'bemused and earnest academics – fellow travellers – discussing the new religion'. In an early sign of later tensions perhaps, she noted that 'The former despised the latter and over countless pots of tea (made by bourgeoise Inez and me) they did not hesitate to show their disdain.'[48] This was not a world in which Hill could obviously take a lead.

He had said as much to the party leadership in 1950. He noted the difficulty of balancing day-to-day branch work with his work as a party intellectual, but his main worry was that he lacked leadership qualities, something very evident since his appointment to the party's Cultural Committee. Although 'regarded locally as a "leading comrade" … I don't feel I have those qualities, e.g. I was not a success as tutor at national school at Hastings in 1948'. His aspiration was really 'to serve the party primarily on the historical front. I have a great deal that I want to say in the form of books, articles, lectures etc, that I believe will make some contribution to the battle of ideas … This, I know, is a smallish backwater of activity; but I think it is the one in which I can be most useful.'[49]

In July 1945 Dona Torr reported that, 'to his great delight', Hill 'turns back into a don again on Aug. 1st'.[50] By September he was actively engaged, promising John Lewis, editor of the *Modern Quarterly*, an article on the Jacobite rising in Scotland in 1745, as well as to think about another on historical materialism. He wrote animatedly about recent Soviet work on the Levellers and Diggers and made other editorial suggestions too: about translations of recent work by Soviet authors, and a substantial piece on Louis Aragon's recent poetry ('the only really great literature that has come out of this war … we ought to make a song and dance about it'). He also wondered if it would be worth 'demolishing' C.S. Lewis, who to Hill's evident distaste had 'become quite influential'.[51]

In the late 1940s, after rejoining the faculty at Oxford, Hill went on to make a number of broad theoretical and historiographical interventions in the pages of *Modern Quarterly* and other Marxist-affiliated journals. In 1946 he published a version of the paper on Marvell he had written to Shiela about, in which he argued that previous critics had missed the politics in Marvell's work because he had written hardly anything that commented directly on contemporary events beyond the 'Horatian Ode'. Marvell's poetry, he suggested, represented a new kind of lyric, not intended to be sung, but rather as a highly individual statement. Characteristically, these lyrics laid 'incompatibles' side by side, uniting 'the apparently unrelated, indeed logically contradictory' elements and so creating 'the lyric of conflict'. It was in these tensions – nature and the work of man, heart and mind, body and soul – that the politics of the poetry lay. 'If we study Marvell with a knowledge of the political background of his life', Hill wrote, 'we can discover in the great lyrics new complexities which will increase our appreciation of those very sensitive and civilised poems.' Specifically, 'To his Coy Mistress' (much on his mind of course when he wrote to Shiela) was not about the repression of the libido in favour of chastity and modesty, but a reconciliation of desire with the world we actually inhabit. It was this struggle to resolve ideal and reality that made Marvell and the other metaphysical poets so attractive to 'our generation': Marvell's 'double-heart' was echoed, for example, in Cecil Day Lewis's 'divided heart'. Both were products of 'a sensitive mind in a divided society'.[52]

An article on Hobbes took the same approach, seeing him suspended between his own bourgeois background and the aristocratic milieu in which he found himself as tutor to the Duke of Devonshire. From that position he arrived at a revolutionary view of politics, but one that was also limited by his angle of vision. Hobbes famously argued that in the state of nature life was 'solitary, poor, nasty, brutish and short', and that the construction of the state freed men from that existence. Obedience to the state was therefore based on expediency and reason, not divine ordination or morality, and political relationships were contractual and based on rational calculation. Secondly, it followed that individual rights were a product of this contract, not something that preceded it: there were no divine and no natural laws of freedom, only a contract with the state in return for protection. Finally, this made politics a matter of rational science, not the 'text swapping' of medieval scholarship, which tried to synthesise what conventionally acknowledged authorities had said about divine or natural rights in the past.

For Hill this materialism and rationality made Hobbes a bourgeois thinker, critical both of aristocratic theories of divine right and the puritan hopes of the petty bourgeoisie (who aimed to achieve a reformation of society and morals through appeal to Christian belief rather than rational calculation). Hobbes's materialism displaced puritan idealism in Restoration culture, and this rational political science was subsequently infused with hope by Marx and Engels in the nineteenth century through their analysis of the overall direction of historical development towards a state of freedom. In their hands, awareness of the material and rational basis of politics was thus yoked to the idea of progress and redemption that had featured among seventeenth-century puritans.[53] Seen this way, Hobbes's *Leviathan* was 'a theoretical revolution corresponding to the revolution which Oliver led', but limited by the absence of a theory of progress; it had been similarly overtaken by nineteenth-century developments.[54]

These pieces were characteristic of much of Hill's later work, reflecting his interest in the struggle of an individual to make sense of a society in conflict at a time of rapid change. He reviewed Toynbee's *Study of History* for the *Modern Quarterly*, finding in it a liberalism only slightly less hopeless than Fisher's: Toynbee could see patterns in history, but could not escape his racism and English exceptionalism, or his horror at democratisation and plebeian culture. It was a bourgeois view of a failing civilisation, and Toynbee took refuge in the attractions of a revived Catholic Church as a way to unite and guide that civilisation. Hill thought Toynbee had gathered the material to see a more coherent pattern in history, in successive waves of revolution leading towards a fully free society, but had recoiled from it.

Here was his clearest repudiation of liberal and modernist responses to the crisis of the 1930s. He denounced H.G. Wells for saying that 'The mind is at the end of its tether.' In this bind liberals could stop communicating with the world or take refuge in traditionalism. Those who gave up communicating with the world included Professor Tout who 'declared that the ideal history would have no readers'; modern economists (aside from Keynes) who had ceased to deal with the real world; philosophers drawn to logical positivism who refused to move 'from words to the things they represent'; James Joyce who used a private language; and

E.M. Forster who 'ceases to write at all'. The traditionalists included of course T.S. Eliot but also Bertrand Russell (who 'urges us not to seek for certainty'); Sartre who 'detaches himself from the real world in order to make romantic poses in the face of irresistible evil'; and Toynbee who 'offers us the bosom of Mother Church'. This was 'the true *trahison des clercs*, the use of reason to deny reason'.[55]

In another comment for *Modern Quarterly* he related this to the bourgeois myth of western civilisation, which had been fostered to unite a group of powers with a shared interest in colonial exploitation and a willing subservience to the United States. That civilisation was born out of a revolt against the Roman Catholic Church: western civilisation was what the bourgeoisie claimed to have recovered from Catholic autocracy.[56] Hill had returned to Toynbee, part of his longer preoccupation with Catholicism. To him it seemed the main, and most pernicious, alternative to Marxism: people responding to the crisis of bourgeois culture by trying to revive the pre-Enlightenment tradition, attempting to overcome the failure of liberalism by restoring the preceding culture. Eliot and Graham Greene were notable examples, as was Toynbee (and his lifelong friends T.S. Gregory and Richard Southern, for both of whom he clearly retained a strong personal sympathy). For Hill, however, this regressive move was politically deplorable, a view he apparently shared with Trevor-Roper, with whom he joked about 'our mutual enemies the papists'.[57]

Gregory's longest work, *The Unfinished Universe* (1935), in a way illustrates the point. It distinguished between magical approaches to the world – based on the belief that human skill could command the social and material world – and religious ones based on the idea that the world is ultimately unknowable, and faith is the thing that makes understanding whole. Gregory's book narrates the battle of these worldviews in a kind of dialectic, leading perhaps to the kind of self-realisation, and oneness with the world, that was also preoccupying Hill in the 1930s. It did so through faith, rather than a magical belief that humans can manipulate these things by their own powers. It was an elaborated version of the argument for abandoning liberal certainties in favour of faith rather than investing them with new hope. Gregory reached this position through discussions of many of the topics that interested Hill: for example, religion, science and magic, and a chapter on Pythagoras and puritanism which discussed Bodin, Hobbes, Locke and others.

Hill, by contrast, wanted to escape both liberal surrender and this retreat into tradition. Humans, he thought, could take control of the conditions of their lives; he had what Gregory would call a magical worldview, based on faith in human reason and action. In an article on Marxism and history for *Modern Quarterly* Hill argued that Marx and Engels were materialists but not determinists: they left a role for the creative power of ideas and conscious human action. According to Hill they were interested in the interaction of humans and the material world, a dialectic between the material environment and human action. The material world was modified by human action, which changed as humans developed technologies and new patterns of social relations. As these relations of production developed and the material world became more complex, humans developed diverging material interests: the origins of class conflict. The pattern of technology and its use favoured some people while requiring the exploitation of others. Economic change thus ultimately dictates the pattern of politics, but only ultimately – the pattern of thought and action is also affected by culture, belief and so on. What is possible in any given situation is shaped by the institutions and beliefs of the society built on this material foundation.[58] This was Hill's critical distinction between determinism (that the economy determines all else) and what he called 'materialism' (that politics is the outcome of a dialectic between, on the one hand, human thought and action and, on the other, the material world). It held out the possibility of changing the world through the application of reason, avoiding the retreat into faith or despair.

For many of his critics this distinction between determinism and materialism has been hard to grasp, and indeed Hill himself often seems to err towards the former; but he was at least consistent in stating his position. In an article for *University* in 1951, he made much the same case in a defence of Plekhanov against charges of determinism, quoting him to the effect that '*the economy of society* and its *psychology* represent two sides of one and the same phenomenon of the "production of life" of men'. The struggle for existence creates the economy but also their psychology: economic life and its attendant psychology are both derivative in that sense. That is 'why the economy of every progressing society *changes*: the new state of productive forces brings with it a new economic structure just as it does a new psychology, a new "spirit of the age"'.[59]

Hill thought such an approach far superior to idealism. Marxism, for him, could explain the history of ideas, but historians of ideas could not explain material history. He also had in his sights a crude determinism which he often associated with non-Marxists. Shorter pieces for *Communist Review* and *Science and Society* discussed Lenin's theory of revolution and recent work on the rise of British capitalism and the transition from feudalism to capitalism.[60] His views were also developed in his very active work as a reviewer for these and other journals.[61]

This conviction about human agency informed his work on the state and revolution. It was here that the dialectic between ideas and material life could most clearly result in improvements to the human condition, and alongside more programmatic statements stood publications specifically on the English Revolution. In an article for *Science and Society* in 1948, Hill pieced together Marx and Engels's views on the English Revolution, seeing them as heirs to a tradition of class interpretation that had begun at the time – with Hobbes, Edward Hyde and James Harrington. Modern research was making it clear how material conflicts had offered a congenial environment for the ideas that underlay civil war and revolution, and explained the differential appeal of those ideas among the English people. It was these pressures that ultimately shaped the outcome – it was the product of human action, not determined merely by economic forces; but human action is only comprehensible when set against the background of economic transformation.[62]

An article in *Modern Quarterly* argued in some detail that the seventeenth century saw a compromised revolution as the bourgeoisie first defeated the aristocracy and then made common cause with them against a more democratic revolution launched from below. In another piece for *Science and Society*, Hill reviewed in more detail the evidence that, in complex ways, a freer market for land had developed in the course of the revolution, ripe for increased commercial exploitation. The ideas that shaped this transformation of land use were underpinned by the wider intellectual transformation of the period, manifest for example in Hobbes's thinking about reason, contract and rational calculation.[63] This was the origin of bourgeois civilisation, whose crisis Hill had witnessed in the 1930s.

Hill's ambition to write Marxist history was separate from his decision to join the CPGB, and was not just a party obligation. Nonetheless, much of his programmatic Marxism was informed by discussions in the Communist Party Historians' Group.

The group had been launched at conferences held in June and September 1946, at the second of which Hill was elected chair of the group. The first meeting came soon after, in October.[64] Dorothy Thompson, the historian of Chartism and a party activist, was later sceptical about its virtues, and thought there was a tension 'between the academics and those led by Harry Pollitt who saw it as a means of celebrating the glory of the Party'.[65] Victor Kiernan, though, was adamant that Torr, a more significant influence on the group, had not insisted on strict adherence to the party line in historical writing, and that the atmosphere of the discussions was very open.[66] Rodney Hilton also thought that there was 'a genuinely free debate, as one would expect when the tone and the high scholarly level were set by Christopher Hill'. In contrast to the atmosphere in the USSR, he recalled, the leadership of the British party 'made no attempts to impose ideological purity and at one meeting (through John Gollan) stated this as conscious policy'.[67] Gollan was a working-class party activist, formerly an apprentice painter, who was to take over as party general secretary in 1957. A year older than Hill, he had also been involved in the Cultural Committee and was assistant editor of the *Daily Worker* in the early 1950s. In other words, his endorsement carried weight. For his part, Hill recalled the discussions as 'the most exciting and stimulating of any I have ever participated in, unforgettable'.[68]

One focus of discussion was the proposed revision of A.L. Morton's *People's History of England*, particularly in the light of Maurice Dobb's *Studies in the Development of Capitalism*, published in the same year as the founding of the Historians' Group.[69] The challenge posed by Dobb was twofold: he offered a much more fully worked out view of the economic change than Morton's earlier book had, and, in doing so, tended to downplay the importance of culture and custom, and of a radical tradition. It was a more hard-nosed and less romantic Marxism, laying greater emphasis on changing patterns of economic activity and comparatively less on the popular radical tradition celebrated by Morton.[70]

Although they do not seem to have been personally close, Dobb was a major intellectual influence on Hill, and this shaped his view of Morton's work.[71] When Beryl Smalley had written to Hill in October 1945 about the proposed republication of Morton's book, he said that an appendix noting revisions would not be sufficient since it would, in effect, be saying 'for black read white throughout'. Dobb's work, he thought, had shown Morton's to be fundamentally flawed.[72]

Although at the time they were very critical of Morton, Hill later thought his 'free-ranging suggestions opened up an infinity of questions to think about, explore further, discuss'. He also admired Morton's attitude to his younger critics: he was 'infinitely patient, infinitely courteous; he listened tolerantly, not necessarily taking us all too seriously though far too nice to say so'. Reflecting on it at an event to mark the eightieth anniversary of the book, he thought Morton's achievement in trying to

Maurice Dobb in 1933.

sketch out single-handedly a Marxist framework for understanding the English past a very great thing, a work the Historians' Group did not surpass.[73] Hill travelled to the USSR with Morton and others in 1954, and they maintained correspondence over several decades, though it seems Hill did not know much about him. Asked to write about Morton following his death, Hill felt ill-equipped to do so, asking John Saville: 'Have you *any* information about him – his family background, his education, his work on the Herald – *anything*? I discover that I never knew anything about his life. Part of his charm no doubt; but that should be put right.'[74]

Hill's long essay, 'The English Revolution, 1640', first published in 1940, was a second and perhaps more important focus of discussion for the Historians' Group. Hill's characterisation of the Tudor state as feudal, and the revolution as bourgeois, had caused controversy in the party. *Labour Monthly* had carried a vituperative review by 'PF' (Jürgen Kuczynski), which said that the book was un-Marxist: feudalism, wrote Kuczynski, was dead long before the sixteenth century and the civil war was caused by a monarchical reaction against a capitalism that was already triumphing. In effect, England had never had a bourgeois revolution in the true sense.[75] A member of the Communist Party of Germany

(KPD), Kuczynski had been ordered to London in 1936, where he became a leading, though not uncontroversial, figure in the exile community. He saw the German revolution of 1918–19 as a partially achieved bourgeois revolution, in which workers' councils had been turned into tools of the bourgeois parliament. In relation to the intense in-fighting in 1939–40 over how the KPD should respond to the Nazi–Soviet Pact, Kuczynski was, in a way, fighting a battle within German communism by proxy. In his view, Nazism had arisen from a compromised bourgeois revolution, and he was attracted by the view that England had not had a bourgeois revolution either: capitalism had been triumphant before 1640, and the bourgeois grandees who emerged triumphant from the crisis had failed to eradicate vestiges of feudalism, just as the German revolutionaries of 1918–19 had. His point was that Germans of the early twentieth century were no more to blame for the limitations of their democracy than the English of the seventeenth century – the explanation lay in the compromised nature of their revolutions rather than national character.[76]

The result was a furious debate in the pages of *Labour Monthly* (of which Kuczynski was an editorial board member) in which Torr, Dobb and Douglas Garman weighed in on Hill's side. In March 1941, Dutt, the editor of *Labour Monthly*, was moved to publish an apology for the review, 'which advanced several incorrect propositions [and] challenged several fundamental Marxist ideas on the subject of the State'. Kuczynski and Hill both stuck to their guns, however, when they met face-to-face in 1971.[77]

In addition to sparking a debate within Marxism, this exchange also exposed tensions between an academic sensibility and a more robust intellectual culture in the party, and in this Hill's cause was taken up by Edmund Dell. Dell had been involved in the Oxford University branch of the Communist Party before war service had interrupted his studies, and it was in that capacity that he wrote to the national secretariat protesting about the tone of the review and the discourtesy shown to Hill personally. The secretariat responded saying that *Labour Monthly*, as the theoretical organ of the party, had a responsibility to review books written by party members with care and, where necessary, with constructive criticism. Hill's book fell into the class of a controversy because the political line of the party was not involved: unvarnished and critical debate on controversial issues was essential in order to refine Marxist understanding. Dell was castigated for seeing this as a negative thing, and the Oxford University branch warned of the danger of dogmatism in resisting such controversy: that was an approach more appropriate to the Catholic Church than to Marxism, 'the most critical of all theoretical systems'. It was through such discussion that 'Marxist thought and propaganda is strengthened and deepened'. Dell evidently renewed the objection, receiving in return an even loftier dismissal.[78] It must have been galling for academics to be accused by party HQ of trying to stifle debate, but from the party point of view these were open discussions, and academic comrades (and their personal feelings) were not held in special regard when trying to arrive at a definitive view.

A central issue here, as in the discussion of Dobb and Morton, was the transition from feudalism to capitalism. Hill's view, and his claims about a bourgeois revolution, would become central to the agenda of the Historians' Group – in fact the 'real point of departure for the discussions', according to the historian David Parker. The heat generated was partly theoretical, but it was also political. Hill was reluctant to concede that capitalism pre-dated the revolution because that took away the role of active political agency in achieving the transition: if the change happened organically then the work of progressive thinkers and agitators was redundant, which would have implications for contemporary struggles across the globe. At the same time, Dutt and others felt the integrity of Marxist theory was at stake. As a result, some rather arcane and inconclusive discussions ensued about exactly how to characterise the Tudor state in Marxist terms, and Hill was later a little embarrassed by an article published at this time in the *Communist Review*, full as it was of Marxist-insider language.[79] It is important to note, however, that the discussions were in no sense shaped by a pre-existing line – these were debates among Marxist thinkers, not the rolling out of party dogma. They were deliberately robust precisely because the party wanted to work out what it should think about these issues.[80]

Hill was central to the organisation of the discussions too. In 1948 he produced a key manifesto for the Historians' Group, having found the meetings and agenda too haphazard and instead laid out some key topics for discussion: for example, the end of the Roman empire and Tudor absolutism, in place of ad hoc initiatives such as responding to the tercentenary of the execution of Charles I.[81] Certainly his personal energy was important to the group's success.

As a result of these wide-ranging discussions, and of the power of the intellects at work, the group's meetings were of fundamental importance for post-war historiography, and Hill certainly saw them as foundational for his career as a whole: nearly forty years later he said that '[e]verything that I've written since then derives from discussions in that group'. He did not associate this with the debates about the state and bourgeois revolution, however, but with 'The idea that one ought to take the radicals more seriously … The questions we were asking about the relationship of history and literature all come through in my later works.'[82] At the same time, Hill's role in organising the discussions, and the place of his work in the intellectual agenda pursued by the group, make him appear altogether more central to the history of British Marxism than some accounts have allowed.[83]

Hill was also active in the public defence of Marxism and of the Soviet regime as a test of its claims: of all his work, this is the body of publication that has aged most badly. His first full-length book, *Lenin and the Russian Revolution*, published in 1947, is best understood in this context. It was commissioned by A.L. Rowse for the English Universities Press, a series committed to the view that historical understanding is critical for understanding the world, and that authors with 'good academic standards' should write for a 'general reading public', bringing 'the best that the universities can provide' to that public. Hill's book, therefore, was not at all a party propaganda exercise, although it was dedicated to Dona Torr, and prominent acknowledgement was made to Dobb and to Rodney Hilton and Margaret Palmer, Hilton's first wife.

In it, the form of the analysis is the same as Hill's study of the English Revolution, associating the development of particular ideas with the social basis of their appeal and political effects. The Red Army, the Soviets and the Communist Party are all lauded in this latter respect, as giving force to revolutionary ideas. Hill's positive affirmation of these features of the revolutionary regime and of Lenin's role in their triumph was largely undiluted. That bias was clear in the treatment of Trotsky, who featured hardly at all except for his miscalculation about, firstly, how to conduct talks with the Central Powers at Brest-Litovsk in 1917, over the terms of Russian withdrawal from the First World War – which Hill argued cost the USSR a massive loss of territory before an agreement was finally reached – and, secondly, his naivety about the prospects of world revolution and Soviet strategy in the absence of one. Hill wrote that Trotsky was a more gifted rhetorician than Lenin but a far less substantial and serious speaker. As in *The Two Commonwealths*, Hill accepted that collective farms and distinctive forms of organisation were democratic, and appropriate to the social conditions the Bolsheviks were encountering.[84]

When the book was republished in 1994 Hill stood by it, distinguishing between the communist vision of Lenin and the October revolutionaries and the later crimes of Stalin. It was written in 1945–6, he said, before the Cold War had killed off hopes of a healthy relationship with the USSR, and before the full revelation of Stalin's crimes. Although a product of that time, he stood by the book's faith in the initial ideas of the October Revolution. High hopes for 'the equality of men, women and nations, the right of everyone to work and to have a fair share in the distribution of the wealth they produce, the undesirability of an idle leisure class', although lost in later Soviet practice, retained their 'validity'. It was important not to 'fall into the trap of blaming Lenin for Stalin, whatever links we may see between the two'.[85]

Many readers did not achieve such detachment. The difficulty was that many of the lies and perversions of Stalinism would by 1947 have been well known to anyone willing to know about them. Rowse recalled that he had invited Hill to write the book 'but never expected anything so Stalinist, so eunochized. Impersonal, communist propaganda portrait – Trotsky might never have existed'. Rowse wrote that he had only managed to prevail on Hill to put in 'a few living touches', and the book caused a long-lasting quarrel with Berlin, who 'was disgusted by such a deformation of history as to omit Trotsky's part in the Revolution – too disingenuous and lying'. This was an element in a falling out between Hill and Berlin that lasted many years, and when there was some reconciliation, in 1962, it did not include an end to differences over the book: Hill did not send him a copy of the revised edition, thinking Berlin 'would be more annoyed by what remained than gratified by what was changed'. It caused Rowse some chagrin that he was personally criticised for the contents of the book, particularly in the United States, since 'I disapproved of it more than anyone'. As he also noted, however, it 'sold more than practically every other [book] in the series'.[86]

Hill was also criticised within the party, and John Gollan complained in *Labour Monthly* that Trotsky's *History of the Russian Revolution* had been included in the bibliography. J.M. Cameron recalled this as indicative of the atmosphere in which British Marxists lived at the time. There 'could, of course, be no good reason for omitting' Trotsky from the bibliography, he wrote, but Gollan was free to criticise the inclusion of 'a work by that notorious spy for the German, Japanese, and British intelligence services'.[87]

Hill also defended Marxism and the Soviet Union in more public contexts. In 1948 the *TLS* published a leading article about the 'tragedy' of the Soviet regime, quoting a recent book by the Menshevik activist Fyodor Dan, *The Origins of Bolshevism*. In response to Dan's central claim, that the Russian Revolution had occurred in a society ill-prepared for democracy, Hill wrote that this had been no less true of the English and French Revolutions. The reality was that the USSR had experienced a revolution from below, 'whether in collective farms, the Stakhanov movement or in guerrilla bands', and it had been carried out through democratic forms appropriate to Soviet society – for example, the Moscow Soviet. 'Soviet democracy', wrote Hill, 'is democracy of a different order from parliamentary democracy in England, but then socialism is a different social order from capitalism.'[88]

In 1950 he was co-signatory of an outraged letter to the *TLS*, protesting about the use of terms like 'sub-human' and 'animality' to describe life in the USSR. Revolutionaries died, 'and those surviving live, in defence of a culture which, to take only one example, enables and encourages millions of recently illiterate people to read the works of Aristotle and Plato, of Spinoza and Descartes, of Milton and Chaucer, of Dickens and Thackeray, of Pushkin and Tolstoy' – an important context for his own sceptical reflections on the 'myth of western civilisation'.[89]

Throughout the late 1940s and early 1950s, Hill was a regular contributor to party publications, writing essays and reviews for wider audiences. His writing ranged from essays on liberty and private property for the *Daily Worker* and on the October Revolution for *World News and Views*, to a criticism of claims that the accession of the new queen would usher in a second Elizabethan Age, a view that 'shows us the pipe dreams of the ruling class today'.[90] He was also an active speaker in this vein, included in a list of party speakers and tutors for the London district on English and Russian topics.[91]

Hill's commitment to the party position clearly clouded his judgement about the USSR. In a talk given to the Reading branch on 26 March 1950, for example, he outlined how the socialist revolution in Russia signalled the beginning of the transition to communism, in the course of which capitalism would be annihilated and all industries and agriculture taken over for state purposes. Stalin had declared this preparatory work completed in 1939, he said, and the Soviets were 'forging ahead with communism'. This was harder to achieve than many people had imagined, due to the 'desolation left by the ruling classes, and in fact thousands of [Soviet citizens] died of starvation'. However, state management had made the Soviet Union the 'greatest producing country, both in agriculture and industry, in the world'. From a position far behind American and British productivity, the USSR was now in the lead, an achievement that had taken only twenty years. In the USSR there 'was no opposition to the will of the people, as [was common] in capitalist countries'; rather, he said, in the Soviet Union 'everything was done for the benefit of the State' and technology was immediately put to work for public ends. Thus, the Soviets had already harnessed the power of the atomic bomb 'to remove a mountain and divert a river, so that thousands of acres could be irrigated'.

Although the final goal was to do away with state rule, 'at present this was impossible owing to the dangers of capitalist attack'. Nonetheless, the advance of communism was inspiring. Money would eventually be unnecessary, and bread was already free for citizens, although 'the world had scoffed at the idea' when Stalin had first voiced it. Free education, pensions and medical treatment were provided, and all citizens could attend night schools and technical colleges. Recalling his own visits in 1935 and 1936, Hill described an election campaign and 'painted a very rosy picture of the Communist way of life'. All this was well received by the fifteen members of the audience.[92]

This account of Stalin's regime was unduly credulous for someone speaking in 1950, in particular that the numbers dying of starvation could be numbered only in the thousands and attributed to the desolation left by the ruling class, or that selfless devotion to the state should be described in this way without reference to the purges and gulags. All this was known in Britain at the time, although discounted by Soviet sympathisers as capitalist propaganda. While in Moscow, Hill had an operation for an ear infection which left him with damaged hearing in one ear; it is tempting to see in that a metaphor – that his experience in Soviet Russia left him unable to hear liberal criticism of the regime effectively.[93] Given the professional and public difficulties that communists faced in this period, it is unsurprising that many chose to believe the party rather than the hostile capitalist press; but that judgement made Khrushchev's revelation of Stalin's crimes later in the decade all the more devastating.

More credulous still, and the published work that has earned him most opprobrium, was his appreciation of Stalin as an historian, published in 1953. Hill's essay was a companion piece to J.D. Bernal's celebration of Stalin as a scientist in the previous issue of *Modern Quarterly*. Bernal was a pioneer of the sociology of science and an advocate for state sponsorship of technology who had brought his scientific expertise to bear on various aspects of the war effort. His championship of Stalinist science was highly divisive in the aftermath of the Lysenko affair, in which Stalin had endorsed Trofim Lysenko's theory of plant genetics. Support for Lysenko, the son of a peasant who had arrived at his views through practical attempts to breed and improve crops, was seen as an endorsement of proletarian science, and Lysenkoism became a state orthodoxy, despite the accumulating evidence against it. Support for Lysenko came to seem increasingly like a political rather than a scientific affiliation; Bernal was destined for the Stalin Peace Prize in 1953.[94]

Hill's endorsement of Stalin the historian in the next issue was hardly less political. He commended Stalin's historical materialism for its lack of determinism, the emphasis it placed on human agency, the hope it invested in the future, and for the lack of dogmatism – Marxist ideas were for use, not for 'Talmudic' analysis. He commended Stalin for his work on national liberation within the USSR and for his understanding of international affairs; collectivisation is mentioned only in connection with a speech Stalin made celebrating the power people had to make their own history. In sum, Stalin was a 'great Marxist thinker who had himself made history more effectively than any of his contemporaries':

> he was a very great and penetrating thinker, who on any subject was apt to break through the cobwebs of academic argument to the heart of the matter; … he was a highly responsible leader, who expressed a view only after mature consideration and weighing the opinions of experts in the subject. His statements therefore approximate to the highest wisdom of the collective thought of the USSR.[95]

It is hard to know what to make of this paean to Stalin. Hill certainly had a well-developed contempt for the capitalist press and the 'whoppers' it told, and a greater (but totally misplaced) confidence in the party papers. From Methodism and his time in Moscow he had a strong sense of duty and a desire to be of service to the party – in this case by taking on a commission that does not seem to have been his in the first instance.[96] In the end, though, perhaps it is also to do with the obstinacy he confessed to Shiela Grant Duff, which he worried had the potential to substitute for moral seriousness. He had been very publicly committed to a pro-Soviet posture, and to discounting capitalist misrepresentation, since the 1930s. Abandoning these commitments in the aftermath of Khrushchev's revelations about Stalin and the dishonesty of the party papers about the Soviet invasion of Hungary in 1956 was to prove deeply traumatic.

⇛

Although much of Hill's output down to the early 1950s was in the more or less direct service of the party, he did not neglect more academic writing altogether. Towards the end of the war he contributed an introduction to the writings of Gerrard Winstanley, the Digger leader, which was one of the projects to which he turned following the romantic disappointment with Shiela.[97] In response, Trevor-Roper expressed scepticism about the place of Winstanley in English history, kicking off a series of exchanges in the review pages which continued for several decades and which both seemed to relish.[98] Hill claimed significance for Winstanley in three areas: as an acute social critic of seventeenth-century English society; for the spiritual egalitarianism and communism of the Digger community he led; and for Winstanley as a literary figure. His pamphlets, said Hill, 'are written in some of the finest prose which even the seventeenth century produced'.[99]

It is worth emphasising this final point, which is in no sense simply Marxist and which reflects a persistent thread in Hill's writing. He was a consistent admirer of literary style, of Marvell's lyricism, already noted, and of Hobbes's writing:

> The style and form of *The Leviathan* were undoubtedly influenced by the new sciences: that is why the book is so important in the history of English prose. Its construction is beautifully logical. Once we have started, it is almost impossible to break the chain of Hobbes's argument without going back to the beginning.[100]

In fact the communist circles in which Hill moved were in general marked by such a literary sensibility, which again gives the lie to claims that Hill and others were, in the end, uninterested in the products of the human mind.[101]

More importantly, and once more under Dona Torr's guidance, Hill worked with Edmund Dell on a collection of documents which supported the interpretation of the revolution set out in 1940.[102] Dell had been admitted to Queen's College, Oxford in the summer of 1939. Having intermitted for war service, in which he saw action in Europe, he returned in 1945, graduating with a first in 1947. He was then appointed lecturer at Queen's on a rolling one-year basis, retaining the position until September 1949. As an undergraduate he had been active in student politics, trying, for example, to organise opposition to a ban on the *Daily Worker* in junior common rooms in 1941;[103] by the time he graduated he was writing and lecturing for the party as well as the WEA, and also served temporarily as secretary of the Historians' Group.[104]

Dell's Oxford life obviously intersected with Hill's at many points. In February 1947 Hill had commented on a paper of Dell's relating to the British war effort, commending his views on the Ministry of Supply, and Hill had taught Dell towards the end of his degree, writing a reference for him prior to graduation.[105] In it he predicted Dell's first, praising his 'wide and detailed grip of 17th century English history', noting also that he had seen a fair amount of him in university societies and study groups. He endorsed Dell in non-political terms: 'He has a passionate interest in the past for its own sake, together with admirable maturity of outlook and a real ability to sift and handle material. I have had few pupils with his capacity to absorb and master detail without losing his sense of perspective.'[106] When, as predicted, Dell got his first, Hill wrote congratulating him,[107] and later supported his application for a Fellowship at Worcester College, while noting that the Provost 'is determined at all costs to avoid anything that is not deepest blue in politics'.[108] By 1948 they were regular collaborators, and Hill wrote to Dell expressing frustration that they had not been consulted on some educational initiative either in the university or for the party: 'It is a little remarkable if we weren't consulted at all.'[109]

Hill's chosen title for the volume of documents was *The Good Old Cause*, which he thought sounded simple, not obscure or exotic, and not 'left-wing political', although it did have a 'friendly, intimate, comradely ring'. He also noted that it had 'an indefinable air of bourgeois smugness and hypocrisy', which had 'its relevance'. The introduction, he suggested, could make the point that the Good Old Cause 'always remained undefined'.[110] Much of the correspondence about the book, between Hill and Dell and with Dona Torr, was routine: concerning Torr's expectations for the overall length as well as the length of the extracts, about how to edit down their initial selection and so on. In the latter context Hill suggested cuts informed by 'what I conceive the main function of the book to be, as we discussed it: primarily to bring out class and revolutionary points, rather than to tell a narrative which can be found elsewhere'.[111]

The collection aspired to clinch the argument prompted by publication of 'The English Revolution, 1640', and to realise Hill's ambition for an academically acceptable Marxist history. Readers were referred to Hill's 1940 essay for 'a first sketch' of an analysis of the revolution, while the collection reproduced some of the evidence on which those earlier generalisations had been based. Essentially, and like Morton's book, it took established landmarks in English history and placed them in the context of economic change and class struggle – progressive social forces triumphed through human agency not simply by their own logic. In this he and Dell were echoing Hill's earlier reviews of standard textbooks and of the approach of most constitutional historians, which, he said, 'abstracts constitutional history from its social and political context, and so creates the picture of an England developing through compromises towards the democracy we know to-day'. For Hill and Dell, rather, 'advances towards democracy were the product, not of a beneficent spirit of compromise but of class struggle'. The final extract in the collection is a reflection on the seventeenth century by the radical Chartist Bronterre O'Brien – both an inheritor of a tradition and someone who developed it to a new stage of coherence. For O'Brien, history was not 'something dead, concealed in books; it was a weapon of struggle'.[112]

In 1952, George Thomson, an academic and party member, wrote with some exaggeration to Emile Burns, a key figure in the party's educational work, that the view of the crisis of the 1640s as England's bourgeois revolution, once discounted by Dutt himself, was now 'universally accepted as correct'.[113] The book was widely used in university teaching over the coming years, going into a second edition twenty years later: this was a major step towards making a Marxist interpretation of the English Revolution available for academic use.

In December 1951, Hill's watchers noted that he was 'about to found a new Marxist historical review called "History Today and Tomorrow"'.[114] That this journal, which was actually published as *Past and Present*, would become one of the most influential historical journals published in English would surely have surprised those opening Hill's mail. Hobsbawm recalled that the founders had very consciously planned it as a 'popular front' rather than Marxist journal, but that in the Cold War context of the early 1950s it was difficult to escape suspicion. The journal's foundation and aims were discussed in the Historians' Group, including its financing and the composition of the editorial board; as Hill, Hilton and Hobsbawm later acknowledged, the journal would have failed but for subscriptions from a left-wing public to which the party gave access.[115]

The founding members of the board included prominent communists – Gordon Childe, Maurice Dobb, Rodney Hilton and Hill – but also Geoffrey Barraclough, A.H.M. Jones and David Beers Quinn, who were not party members, nor easily identified as Marxists. All articles had to be read by the entire board as a defence against Marxist domination; if the non-Marxists were in the minority, any one of them was given a power of veto.[116] The editorial team had a clearer ideological complexion, though: John Morris, a driving force behind the foundation of the journal, was the editor, Hobsbawm was his assistant, and they were joined in 1955 by Brian Manning. Rudolf Wittkower was warned by his friends and advisers not to accept an invitation to join the board, while Moses Finlay, who had taken refuge in Cambridge from McCarthyism, was only prepared to write for the journal ten years later.[117]

Considered in academic rather than political terms, the founding of the journal was a symptom of a great broadening of historiographical imagination in the post-war years: Hobsbawm saw it as a reaction against history as the study of 'past politics', offering instead 'a history of the structures and changes of societies and cultures'. For him, the contrast was between 'history as narrative and history as analysis and synthesis, between those who thought it impossible to generalise about human affairs and those who thought it essential'. Although at the first International Historical Congress after the war, in Paris in 1950, economic and social history had been a small and ill-defined field, that approach was a focus for historical 'innovators' driven by this analytic view of history. The French journal *Annales* was critical to this development and remained so for decades, but it was not Marxist – this was an historiographical trend much broader than among Marxists alone.[118] In Britain, however, most of those interested in the new approaches were indeed Marxist, and that shaped the founding of *Past and Present*, resulting in persistent suspicions of sectarianism: the historian Trevor Aston, not himself a Marxist, was asked about it as late as 1979.[119]

The editorial board was keen to make a statement about this, publishing what amounted to a manifesto in the first issue. Their ambition was to answer, they wrote, 'concerns about the state of historical scholarship', and they cited a variety of non-Marxist influences: not just Marc Bloch, the great French historian and one of the founders of the *Annales* school, but Ibn Khaldun, Polybius and Friedrich Meinecke, the right-wing liberal who had just published an analytic history of *The German Catastrophe*. The journal was effectively being positioned between, on the one hand, a view that there was no pattern in the past beyond the passion and irrationality of human populations and, on the other, the idea that historical explanation could be reduced to simple causal models derived from the social sciences. The sciences on which such simple models rested were poorly developed – much less developed than the nineteenth-century biological sciences, for instance, which had informed now-discredited models of social evolution. Reason and science, the editors wrote, could explain the process of social change, as they explained changes in geology, palaeontology, ecology or meteorology, but the 'process of change among humans is immensely more complex'. As with those disciplines, though, 'history cannot logically separate the study of the past from the present and the future, for it deals with objective phenomena, which do not stop changing when we stop observing them'.[120] This was what the subtitle – 'a journal of scientific history' – really meant, although at the time it suggested to many people a Marxist project.

The journal's contents in its early years reflected the pluralist ambition of this founding vision: what counted was a view of the value of structural, generalising, comparative history. It aimed at adherence to technical not ideological desiderata: 'Articles which merely bring the results of a piece of detailed research whose interests are narrowly restricted will not normally be published; nor, on the other hand, those which deal with wider historical problems without a firm foundation of scholarly research.' The board wanted to encourage engagement with themes of contemporary relevance, 'with the object of discovering rather than of confirming the answers', and there would be a consistent attempt to broaden geographical horizons: 'The serious student in the mid-twentieth-century can no longer rest content in ignorance of the history and the historical thought of the greater part of the world.'[121]

That first issue did have more than its fair share of party members among the contributors – Hilton, Kiernan and Hobsbawm, as well as the Chinese Marxist economic historian Wu Ta-K'un – but this was offset by publication of the last wishes of Theodore Mommsen, the great German historian, which had been published by prominent historical journals in other countries. The range of interests is as striking as the ideological complexion of the early contributors here: Chinese economic history over the long run, Athenian democracy, the French Revolution, and nineteenth-century machine breakers.

An indication of the distinctiveness of the new journal is the contrast with the contents pages of the leading journals at the same period. The January 1952 issue of the *English Historical Review*, then the most prominent English journal, consisted of three principal articles: Richard Glover on 'English warfare in 1066', F.R.H. du Boulay on 'Archbishop Cranmer and the Canterbury Temporalities' and P.M. Williams on 'Public opinion and the railway rates question in 1886'. There was also a short note by E.B. Fryde, the great medievalist, on the 'Dismissal of Robert de Wodehouse from the Office of Treasurer, December 1338'.[122] Readers did not have to look far for a view of history as 'past politics'. The *Cambridge*

Historical Journal, founded in 1923 and the principal rival to the Oxford-based *EHR*, had published A.G. Woodhead on 'The state health service in Ancient Greece', D.J.B. Fisher on 'The anti-monastic reaction in the reign of Edward the martyr', Lady Stenton on 'The Pipe Rolls and the historians, 1600–1883' and Asa Briggs on 'The background of the Parliamentary reform movement in three English cities (1830–2)'.[123] These are more obviously analytic concerns, but still the historiographical space that *Past and Present* sought to occupy is clear.

Political concerns did occasionally affect editorial policy. In May 1953 Hobsbawm advised against publishing Arthur Schlesinger for fear of getting 'mixed up in the politics of the Democratic party, the polemics between communists, pro- and anti-communist liberals ... etc. This is not P&P's business.'[124] Nonetheless, despite this Cold War uncertainty, by 1953 the board felt justified confidence in the new journal. The 'imputations of sectarianism and tendentious bias' had been proven false, and the first two years had seen the pages 'open to and filled by writers of all schools who have something new to say and a fresh approach'. The journal was now going to expand, to accommodate more papers.[125] Yet the connection with the party persisted, and in 1956 when there were further financial difficulties, they were once again discussed in the Historians' Group.[126]

A fundamental break was made in 1958, however, when the editorial board was reshaped. Gordon Childe, the Marxist archaeologist, had died the previous year and R.R. Betts, the historian of central Europe, was seriously ill. In their place came Trevor Aston, Norman Birnbaum, John Elliott, S.S. Frere, Lawrence Stone and Peter Worsley. At a special meeting in July 1958, some of those being approached to join the board laid out their conditions: notably that the banner 'scientific history' should be dropped. This was a concession to Stone's view that 'you underestimate the degree of suspicion that surrounds the board as at present constituted', something Stone felt had led to many refusals to join the board. Writing much later, Hobsbawm said that dropping the banner had implied no change in the editorial direction of the journal, although at the time he, Dobb and Birnbaum argued 'that it provided a token flag and that a magazine should not be quite flagless'. Aston said he 'had not been struck by political bias in the articles printed', but he did think that 'the names in the "shop-window" were possibly misleading', while Worsley and Joan Thirsk thought it was the policy not the flag that mattered. They and others spoke for the value of a broad-based board acting as a ginger group for this kind of history. At the end of the meeting the invitations to Aston, Stone and Elliott were confirmed.[127]

Stone also wanted to safeguard the integrity of the journal by enlarging the board through the addition of 'a group of non-Marxists' and by 'the appointment of an editor or additional editor in whose judgement and political neutrality the existing board and ourselves and the outside world will have confidence'. Elliott agreed that 'the magazine should aim for political respectability', and among the new appointments Elliott and Stone were to be particularly influential – neither of them from a Marxist perspective – while Aston, the non-Marxist editor, transformed the management of the journal. Reaffirming the founding vision, however, a note restated its essence: '*Past and Present* is not a vehicle for the expression of any single philosophical approach, but a forum for the debate of significant historical issues.'[128]

Around the time of the founding of *Past and Present*, Hill had begun to publish more frequently in mainstream academic journals and in a more academic voice. During a sabbatical leave in 1951 he did much of the writing of what became one of his most important academic books, *The Economic Problems of the Church* (although it was not published until 1956).[129] Meanwhile, in *Past and Present* he examined the attitudes of a prominent puritan, William Perkins, to the poor – a case study of the effect of environment on ideas, in this case how 'Calvinism' was shaped by the social conditions in which its principles were applied[130] – and wrote an article on Edward Benlowes, for *Essays in Criticism*, which also explored the interrelationship of personal circumstances with personal belief, and how that was expressed in thought and action.[131]

Against the background of his writing about the Soviet regime that now seems at very best credulous and naive, these more academic studies offer a better guide to the long-term expression of Hill's Marxism. He was exploring the complex relationship between thought, culture, politics and material conditions in which, ultimately, economics explained development, but when dealing with individual thinkers the analysis was more complex. The response to work in this vein also seems freer of Cold War concerns: one reviewer of Hill's account of Benlowes wrote that he described 'with something like relish both Benlowes's derivative dullness as a poet and his pitiable incompetence as a small landowner'. While he did so 'without arousing any eagerness in the reviewer to look at Benlowes's work', he did succeed in making Benlowes 'sympathetically real as a man'.[132]

When the Third Programme (a radio station, a forerunner of BBC Radio 3) planned to broadcast a talk by Hill on the tercentenary of the Barebones Parliament in 1953, the secret services got in touch with the BBC to warn them 'that this man has a Communist history in this office dating from 1935, and is known to us as a current member'. To its credit, the BBC replied that 'The information you have given to us will be most useful but we have decided to allow the talk to stand on its merits.'[133] A text of the talk appeared in the BBC magazine the *Listener*, a typescript of which was kept by the secret services.[134]

It was not notably subversive. The Barebones Parliament was summoned in 1653 and made up of nominated rather than freely elected MPs; it is often dismissed as a doomed body reflecting the weak public support for the republican regimes after 1649. Hill argued by contrast that it represented a kind of high point of revolution, a moment at which a radical but workable constitution was possible. Its members were drawn from the ranks of the respectable middling sort, and it proposed relatively moderate administrative reforms that would have made good the effects of the revolution. The Parliament failed because it ran up against the conservatism of the army leadership, particularly Oliver Cromwell. It represented the failure of the programme of 'nineteenth-century reformers in seventeenth-century circumstances'. Hill emphasised contemporary resonances, arguing that the terms in which Barebones was denounced pre-echoed later arguments against radical social policy, but this was hardly a call to revolution.[135] In fact, Sir Reader Bullard, commenting on the text in the supplement to his report for the secret services on Soviet studies in UK universities, found here no subversion, and thought the talk 'interesting' in its own terms.[136]

This was the first sign of what would become a higher public profile for Hill as an interpreter of the English Revolution. Up to this point, he had been a regular correspondent in the liberal press mainly as a defender of communist political positions or the honour of the USSR, while his work popularising history had been primarily done through the *Daily Worker* and other party publications. Now, through the Third Programme and the *Listener*, he was beginning to acquire a different kind of public presence. His first article in *History Today* also appeared that year.[137] The BBC talk was an occasion too for conventional, even bourgeois, family pride, prompting a warm and familiar letter from a proud parent, duly intercepted and filed by the secret services.[138]

In the post-war years Hill had several formal roles in the party, including in its cultural work and as secretary of the Oxford University branch.[139] He also had a broader profile as an advocate of the cause, reflecting his ambition to assist in the battle of ideas and to promote an academically respectable Marxist history of Britain. In fact, there are at least four strands in Hill's writing up to the mid-1950s: the explicit defence of the USSR; the desire to recast the established narrative of British history in Marxist terms; an interest in the struggle of individuals in the seventeenth century to make sense of a world in transition; and an interest in a native radical tradition, both as an expression of class interests and as a way of legitimising contemporary struggle. These complexities were played out in work that is inconsistent and hard to characterise as a unified and coherent Marxism.[140] Dutt's view of party intellectuals was perhaps quite accurate in Hill's case: his Marxism was a product of bourgeois liberal reflection and was held in critical tension with respect for the scholarly work of non-Marxists. Indeed, throughout this period he was working as a blameless (and much-admired) history tutor at Balliol in exactly that way.

There were potential tensions in this life – between party intellectuals and the working-class core, between party discipline and a liberal commitment to unconstrained expression and free enquiry, and between an economistic view of constitutional development and the struggle for individual authenticity as the objects of his analysis. Until the mid-1950s, however, these tensions do not appear to have caused Hill particular difficulties. Writing academically respectable Marxist history was a task endorsed by Pollitt himself, and there was no conflict between a commitment to that as a vocation and membership of the CPGB as a political strategy for achieving progressive change in Britain. The party was happy to be a home for discussion among Marxists about historical questions, hoping eventually to arrive at a definitive view, albeit in what seemed to academics like Dell an unduly bruising environment.

There was a Cold War context for Hill's work, in particular for his writings in defence of Lenin, Stalin and the October Revolution, which have aged badly and subsequently brought him little credit. For Hill, though, it seems that the commitments he had reached in 1936 coexisted reasonably comfortably down to the mid-1950s – to Marxism as an intellectual framework, to the USSR as a distinctive and hopeful form of state, and to membership of the CPGB as a progressive political strategy. He was to be driven out of the party following Khrushchev's revelations about Stalin and the invasion of Hungary soon after, when the party's apparently blind defence of Soviet policies seemed increasingly implausible and actively dishonest. Prior to that, however, the tensions had been manageable, and free discussion in the Historians' Group stimulated Hill to pursue questions that would engage him for the rest of his career.

5

Personal and Political Crises: 1953–57

We speak, correctly, of the 'lies and slanders' of the capitalist Press; but unless we can be sure of the accuracy and truthfulness of our own paper, on what basis can we refute and condemn them? And what basis have we for our own Marxist appraisal?

Bridget Hill and Christopher Hill, letter to
the Daily Worker, November 1956

With hindsight it seems odd that Hill, committed as he was to individual flourishing, should have stuck for so long with a partisan defence of Stalinism, even after the crimes of that regime were becoming known. During this period, however, there was more at stake in his historical work than the ideological needs of the party; and of course there was more to his flourishing than professional and party work. His marriage to Inez Waugh, and his conduct as an academic tutor, place him in a very different light than does his defence of Stalin, revealing a variety of Marxist humanism of enduring significance for his writing. It was his commitment to membership of the CPGB as a political strategy that gave way in 1957, not his conviction that Marxist analysis could help chart a route to social improvement and liberation.

Inez Waugh was the daughter of Gordon Bartlett, an army officer. In the summer of 1940, when she first met Hill, she was already divorced from her first husband, Ian Anthony Waugh. A party member – as Abe Lazarus was later overheard saying, 'she had been "around" the movement since she was twenty … [and] knew a lot of Party people' – in 1942 she had worked for *Soviet War News*.[1] It was through 'Roger', a mutual acquaintance of Hill and Shiela, that Inez and Christopher first met, a meeting which caused some jealousy on Shiela's part. 'It isn't me who is after Inez', Hill wrote to her, 'but she who thinks me wonderful, so aren't I loyal not to respond much except with Roger safely there? (And then only out of courtesy).'[2] In March 1941 he teasingly referred to her as his 'girl friend', reporting that Inez was considering settling for marriage to a man she had been rejecting for five years.[3]

Hill and Inez evidently picked up on that initial frisson following the failure of his relationship with Shiela. If political differences had been a problem in the relationship with Shiela, he could reasonably hope that politics would bind him and Inez together. It wasn't long before the two were married, in January 1944, when Inez was twenty-three and Hill thirty-one. Marriage may have been a rushed decision: their daughter Fanny was born the following month.

Inez seems to have encapsulated the free expression, the absence of bourgeois restraint and the authenticity of feeling that Hill had craved in the 1930s. Her godson, Mike Daunt, describes her as 'a true Bohemian in that she totally ignored all convention and was just herself. … [S]he was small and ridiculously beautiful with an elfin face and a cigarettes-and-gin voice. She also had a wicked sense of humour. She loved people and everyone loved her. … Above all, she had an extraordinary knowledge of poetry …'.[4] Corfield got to know Inez better in later life, and remembered that 'Her charm, vitality, generosity and sensuality' made her 'unmistakeably magnetic'; it was easily 'apparent why Christopher had loved her'.[5] Anne Connolly Manduit met 'the exquisite Inez' in a bus shelter in Oxford, where Inez smiled and asked if she knew anyone looking for lodgings, from which moment Manduit was swept up into 'three hilarious years' in Northmoor Road as the Hills' lodger.[6] Although politically engaged, Inez was capable of a teasing scepticism: Hill recalled fondly that she referred to the key players in his account of the revolution as the 'buggerwazzies'.[7]

Mail and phone intercepts at the end of the war revealed a life divided between London and Oxford, in which the Hills' social life centred on a group of largely left-wing intellectuals, among them many party members.[8] Inez was also a close friend of Beryl Smalley, and clearly a kindred spirit in some ways. Hill later recalled Smalley very warmly, but primarily for the glamour she brought to communist circles. She clearly shared a scepticism about bourgeois sexual mores too: Hill thought she might have been brought to the party by the poet Hugh Sykes Davies, 'via bed'. During the 1960s, when she and Hill's second wife Bridget were both at St Hilda's, they made common cause in defence of a student threatened with being sent down after having become pregnant. Hill then remembered Beryl 'after victory tinkling with girlish laughter and saying "The trouble with most of our colleagues is that they have never known what it is to have an overwhelming sexual urge."'[9] The correspondence between Inez and Smalley was warm, and even the political content had a playful tone: in 1945 Inez wrote that a visiting American on sabbatical leave in Blackpool had become an Anglophile, seeing Christopher as equivalent to Stratford-upon-Avon and Maurice Dobb to Westminster Abbey.[10] On the Hills' return to Oxford after the war, Inez brought with them a dash of metropolitan glamour.

Although it started happily, the marriage did not last. Inez confessed to finding Oxford 'a bit lost-making but perhaps it is only the decaying atmosphere of [their house at] Norham Gardens and the red plush'. The friendship with Smalley seemed to offer some hope of a happier Oxford, but their correspondence contains frequent references to the constraints placed on the couple's sociability by Hill's work.[11] As early as May 1945 Inez complained that Hill's work commitments had prevented them from using theatre tickets Smalley had got for them, and the intelligence services' intercepts reveal increasing tensions in the marriage. At root they were contrasting personalities: 'Inez enjoyed crowds, attention, mischief and improvisation', Corfield remembered, 'while Christopher liked those things but only up to a point, also seeking order and calm to conduct his academic career and solitude to write'.[12]

A crisis came in September 1948 when it emerged that Inez had been having an affair with Abe Lazarus. Lazarus's own marriage had been in difficulties in the past, but he had always put the party first. However, he had now 'gone "bats" over' Inez and even said he might leave the party and give up political work. Hill went to London to try to 'get away from things', and was 'very upset', telling the party that Inez was 'a "go-getter" and once she wanted a thing she went on until she got it'; she 'was prepared to try to make a fight'. He and Lazarus talked, Hill warning him that 'he would not be able to keep her in the way she was accustomed to living': she was a bourgeois. Lazarus too worried about the money,[13] and became ill, at least partly due to the affair, suffering something akin to a breakdown, forcing him to take temporary leave as secretary of the South Midlands District branch of the party.[14]

Two years later, as the Hills' marriage continued to unravel, a source told the secret services that Inez was 'a somewhat neurotic, rather emotional and unstable person'. She had recently announced that 'she is sick to death of the Party and of Communism and no longer wishes to belong', possibly not just a political decision but one driven by 'boredom with her husband's political activities or merely the result of a gush of emotionalism'. Behind the misogyny we can glimpse Inez's desire for a fuller life: 'she is in fact much bored with her husband's activities, especially since his political sympathies lead him, according to her, to give a considerable amount of his money to the Party'. He is reputed to give her very little 'pin money', so she might well have resented the funds going to the party, 'absorbing what would otherwise go towards a new Summer dress for herself'. Another source noted that she 'is not only fed up with her husband's politics, but also with her husband'. Neither she nor Christopher 'took any pains to hide their politics, and in fact upheld their adherence to Communism', so it was unlikely to be simply a result of the increasingly difficult atmosphere encountered by communists. Christopher, according to these sources, had been described in the past as 'mean-minded, pompous and tiresome' – not the view of many of his friends, for sure, but perhaps those of someone wearied by the atmosphere of earnestness in the party and the stifled manners of Oxford.[15]

By June 1953 they were apart. Inez wrote from Lyme on a trip through the south with 'Gwyneth', a letter full of concern and some warmth.[16] She was worried about Christopher's health (he had flu) and knew that Fanny was due home from boarding school soon, and there is more than a hint of regret about the state of their marriage. She and Gwyneth had argued over the American couple Ethel and Julius Rosenberg, recently executed for spying on behalf of the USSR, and it had made her want to see him:

> when will these terrible things cease happening? I feel very militant and politically conscious – G at least does that for me – and I am determined when I return to discuss with you more seriously what I can do. Somehow Oxford, our house, the daily routine, tends to obscure the more serious issues of life, and it is only when I find myself isolated from all that cosiness that I begin to think. Perhaps Oxford itself is a kind of drug against thought – my thinking anyway.[17]

A note recording the redirection of mail from Northmoor Road is a melancholy indication of the end of the marriage, as Christopher moved back into college.[18] A secret service report, possibly from January 1954, notes that Inez had left Fanny in Hill's care while she had gone to live with Robert Nimmo Smith, another academic, who had six children already. He in turn had 'abandoned his wife'. That connection may also have come through left-wing circles, as Smith was active in the North

Oxford Labour Party, which continued 'apparently still under the spell of the Left Book Club as a sort of hangover from the thirties.'[19]

Following the end of his marriage, Hill may have had a brief affair with Muriel Collier, who was leaving her husband at the same time, and whose love letters to Hill were intercepted. Her husband William had studied history at Balliol, and in March 1954 the secret services thought Muriel was on the verge of leaving her husband for Hill, although another note discounts the report that they were cohabiting.[20]

The overall verdict of the watchers was that 'Christopher seems to be getting himself into a thorough mess.'[21] These events had certainly hit him hard. 'Divorce was sufficiently rare in those days for the situation to be very tense and difficult for all the parties involved, including the children', Corfield noted. 'Christopher's parents were aghast and distressed too, as they believed in marriage as a sacrament.'[22] In reply to a letter from Shiela following the end of the marriage, he wrote: 'Yes, I am sad, and it is very sweet of you to register solidarity. Even when one knows positions have become untenable, there is a great emptiness when driven out of them: and the knowledge that in a year's time one will no doubt think it has all been for the best is pretty irrelevant here and now.'[23]

A secret service informant – apparently someone who had known Hill well in the early 1930s but was no longer a close friend – thought there might be a more general crisis afoot. 'Hill is probably not as convinced a Marxist now as he used to be', the source claimed, but 'is so publicly identified with his Communist role that he would find it [very?] difficult to renounce the party, especially as he is one of the few avowed Communist dons at Oxford, and much of his celebrity rests on his professi[on of?] Communism.'[24] This was the period when Hill began to publish in more conventional academic ways, and he was involved in founding *Past and Present*, but the report may well have been wishful thinking. He was to stay with the party for three more years, and with Marxism for the rest of his life. It was at this point, however, that he declined an invitation to join the board of *Marxist Quarterly*, the Communist Party journal and successor to *Modern Quarterly*. Instead, he suggested that they approach Rodney Hilton: 'a more forceful chap, [who] was more productive of ideas on the *M[odern] Q[uarterly]* board, and is in close touch with the Historians Committee.'[25]

By this time, the Historians' Group had passed through its heroic stage. Attendances were falling along with, so it seems, Hill's commitment. Many of the early members had got jobs, and so found it hard to attend, or recognised that they would not get jobs in the prevailing climate and dropped out. Moreover, Hill later recalled, 'we were, without being aware of it, becoming unhappy about the inflexible line of the Communist Party then.'[26] From 1951 the minutes of the group reveal a greater focus on party education than on academic research and debate, including cooperation in the publication of the *Amateur Historian* journal. Although Hill contributed an article suggesting that recent work had debunked accounts of national ideological rivalries in favour of social and economic conflicts that could only be understood in their local context,[27] he stopped attending the group in 1953 and wrote in June that year suggesting that there be a special group convened for professional historians, to consider their particular interests and challenges. Among them was the issue of victimisation. By 1955–6 the minutes reveal weakening attendance and discussions about the purpose, value and future of the group. Even the Working Committee meetings were poorly attended.[28]

Tension between Hill's party membership and his inner liberal was already evident in 1947, when he was supposed to vet an article written by Dell, but thought it 'will hardly be necessary'. Emile Burns, by contrast, as well as making a few suggestions, also confirmed that 'the line is OK'.[29] Dell's tense relationship with the party evidently continued, and the orthodoxy of his Marxism and commitment to the party came under close scrutiny in 1949/50.[30]

Around the same time, Thomas Hodgkin told Hill he was leaving the party. Although, he said, he 'tried to be a good Communist … liberalism was constantly breaking in'. In response Hill had 'very decently admitted that he had the same problem'.[31] As early as 1948, Hobsbawm had reported unease about the requirement that people show party cards at meetings of the Historians' Group, arguing that it 'would discourage comrades from inviting sympathetic non-Party people to attend'. In response the Historians' Group Committee 'repudiated the suggestion that the group was not a Party organization and re-affirmed its decision on Party cards, but added to this a resolution that comrades should certainly encourage sympathizers outside to attend meetings to take part in discussion'.[32] The issue was raised again in 1954.[33] The impression is that in the first half of the 1950s the group had come more and more to resemble a party committee rather than a forum for academic debate, and that the academics were unhappy with the direction it was taking: a symptom of the broader tension between an academic sensibility and party loyalty.

Stalin's death in March 1953, however, signalled an opening up of Soviet intellectual life, and Hill was one of four historians who joined

Christopher Hill in the Soviet Union in 1954 with A.L.
Morton (3rd left) and Eric Hobsbawm (on the right).

a cultural visit to Moscow and Leningrad at the end of 1954, along with Robert Browning, Eric Hobsbawm and A.L. Morton. The visit had a high profile in the USSR, and was covered by the home service broadcasts as well as transmissions in English there. They were treated in some style, as Hobsbawm recalled, hosted by scientific institutions in Moscow and the Praesidium of the Soviet Academy of Sciences. Hill and Morton gave well-received papers at the Department of Historical Studies, part of the Academy's Historical Institute: Hill on the theory of the Norman Yoke, Morton on martyrs in English history.[34] Hill had visited old friends in Moscow, including perhaps Tanya and Kostya, 'but he did not pass on impressions to us', Hobsbawm remembered, 'except through that osmosis that operated without words in those days between party members who shared a sceptical, but not quite illusionless loyalty to the cause'. In part this reflected the difficulty of knowing Hill: 'I remember him vividly, with a long dark winter coat reaching almost to his feet and a round fur hat, as usual saying little and looking reflective and always friendly.'[35] For Hobsbawm the visit 'helped prepare me for the crucial turning point in the lives of all communist intellectuals … the crisis of 1956'; he recalled the high-powered entertainment, which was something of an embarrassment in a 'visibly impoverished country', and the absence of 'serious discussion'. He returned 'depressed'.[36]

Hill, by contrast, seems to have found the visit, and the more open political culture, invigorating, at least initially: just as a visit to South Wales had restored his certainties in 1939, so this visit seems to have given him a renewed commitment to party work. On his return to Britain he seemed to step up his involvement with the SocCR as well as the British Soviet Friendship Society and the Russia Today book club. The secret services noted 'his new commitment' (although they may have been mistaken in thinking he was joining the SocCR, or at least joining for the first time, since he had been branch secretary in Cardiff in 1937–8).[37] The main evidence of renewed commitment, though, was in his educational and intellectual work. Writing to Andrew Rothstein soon after his return, he complained of the backlog of regular work that had accumulated while he was away, but also of 'lots of commitments taken on in Moscow and piling up since we got back'. He was committed to writing about 'Moscow after 20 years' and 'The teaching of British history in Soviet Universities', and he was offering articles and broadcasts on these subjects to 'all who may be interested and – I fear – to many who may not'.[38]

One of these commitments was a review of Mikhail Barg's recently published two-volume history of the English bourgeois revolution, which he felt 'morally committed' to write. A relatively full review was published in *World News* in July, which signalled the value Hill could see in engagement with Soviet intellectual life. 'At a time when English scholars, busy getting to know more and more about less and less, are quite unable to agree what the English revolution was about', he wrote, 'Soviet Marxist historians have put our revolution in its proper place in World history.' That place was, of course, prominent: 'one of the most important turning points not only in the history of England and of Europe, but also in world history'.[39]

He also published an article in *Universities Quarterly* on the teaching of history in the USSR, which, although primarily descriptive, celebrated the prominence of English history in the curriculum and the roll call of distinguished historians of England. He thought the standard of teaching was high, and was sure that there was no 'party line'. Sitting in on a discussion among historians in Leningrad, Hill was struck by how resistant the participants were to orthodoxy and dogmatism. The comparison favoured the USSR in some ways: 'I wonder ... how many

English students get degrees in history, as I did, without ever having studied Russian history at all?', he wrote. 'Can we be altogether proud of the comparison?'[40]

This may have informed his thinking about a comprehensive programme for teaching history in the UK, itself a response to a proposal for a book 'on history' from Emile Burns.[41] Although he later back-tracked, thinking it was undeliverable, Hill's enthusiasm for the ambition remained, as well as for a programme of communist schools being organised by the Durham District branch of the party.[42] He also kept notes on the Marxist art historian Francis Klingender's analysis of the effects of the 1945 Education Act on the university student population, in particular how recruitment of students from a wider range of family and social backgrounds posed new challenges which university teachers needed to understand in order to remain effective.[43] Hill was clearly committed to progressive educational values, despite his career in the relatively conservative educational environment of Oxford University. For example, after their divorce, Inez and Hill sent their daughter Fanny to St Christopher School in Letchworth, a co-educational, non-denominational boarding school run according to progressive educational values. There seems to have been a communist connection: A.L. Morton's brother Max had taught at the school in the early 1930s, and sent his sons there in the 1950s; Doris Lessing's son arrived soon after Fanny left.[44] This was of a piece with Hill's cultural and educational views more broadly.

The trip to the USSR seems to have been rejuvenating for Hill, coming after a personal crisis and lending energy to his cultural efforts on behalf of the party. Within a year, he had found domestic happiness too. He and Bridget Sutton announced their intention to marry in September 1955, soon after Hill's divorce had been granted. The secret services had had no prior inkling of the relationship, although Bridget's first husband, Stephen Mason, was a member of the Historians' Group. Christopher and Bridget married on 2 January 1956; the marriage was to last until her death nearly fifty years later.[45]

Bridget was the youngest daughter of H.H. Sutton, a progressive Baptist minister. Like Christopher, she retained some of her nonconformist values for the rest of her life. She had been raised very plainly; for example, when the family was holidaying in the West Country and it was not possible to fit all the children and the luggage in the family car, the children were given a small amount of money and put on bicycles, riding down from London and sleeping in barns along the way. Raised this way, Bridget was undemonstrative, making no fuss, just like Hill.[46]

Ten years his junior, she went to Godolphin and Latymer School in west London and then to the LSE. During the war years the LSE relocated to Cambridge where, it was claimed, she was 'Tawney's favourite pupil'. While there she renounced Baptism and joined the Communist Party. Thomas Hodgkin, of the Oxford delegacy of extra-mural studies, recruited her as a staff tutor in Staffordshire. She was involved in an international trades union school run by the delegacy in 1947–8, and won a scholarship to Prague the following year. She married Stephen Mason in 1949 and moved to Oxford, where she became an extra-mural tutor. Christopher knew Mason well: they were colleagues in the Historians' Group, and Hill later acknowledged his influence in his own work on seventeenth-century science (Mason was a distinguished historian of science as well as a chemist). Bridget and Stephen divorced amicably in 1953.[47]

Like Inez, Bridget exuded an intellectual liveliness and emotional openness, but she shared more of Hill's personal restraint. With her 'bright eyes, springing gait and open, hospitable manner, [she] radiated an intense engagement with life'. Eager in discussion, shrewd, witty and knowledgeable, she was, Mary Prior recalled, 'a good friend, and a vivacious conversationalist [who] ranged over history, politics, literature, theatre and gardening'. Sheila Rowbotham saw her as an embodiment of 'concentrated energy, bobbing a head of short brown wavy hair to emphasise political points and speaking with an undonnish directness'. She had an artist's eye for colour, relaxing by gardening as well as painting in oils and watercolour.[48] But she was also 'a deeply private person, who kept her innermost feelings to herself' – another trait she shared with Christopher.[49]

Bridget and Christopher had first met in the late 1940s when Hill had spoken at a WEA class in London she organised. There she had been attracted by his mixture of 'informality and erudition' and they met again as Oxford neighbours, both nursing the wounds of divorce, they began a cautious courtship. Hill was in fact too cautious, and eventually Bridget, 'distressed at the uncertainty', moved back to London: she had other admirers. Hill suddenly 'saw the light' one day, called her unexpectedly and told her to meet him at Paddington Station. She did and they remained together for the rest of their lives. He once told Corfield that 'His major regret ... was his own delay, after his divorce, in deciding to marry Bridget Sutton, his "beloved fellow pilgrim" and deeply kindred spirit.'[50]

Christopher and Bridget.

If Inez had promised Hill the kind of free emotional expression he had valued from afar during the 1930s, Bridget offered him a more conventional, bourgeois, domestic warmth and affection that proved crucial to his happiness. It was perhaps the haven of which he had once written to Shiela Grant Duff, a place where 'one can take one's armour off and be a real person', away from the demands of one's public role.[51] To start with, they lived in Bridget's London flat during vacations, but soon moved to a house in Rawlinson Road, Oxford.[52]

Although the new marriage brought domestic happiness, Bridget and Christopher already shared a well-developed discontent with the party. In January 1956 Hill had written to Emile Burns, expressing clear signs of a critical post-Stalin dissatisfaction. Apologising for not having been at a meeting of the Cultural Committee, he confessed that he had been 'rather appalled by the utter inadequacy of the statement circulated for discussion', which seemed 'merely to repeat all the platitudes we have been mouthing for years without a single concrete or new idea in it. I hope it was torn to pieces?' The fresh ideas he was pursuing were those of Gramsci and John Eaton's analysis of socialist realism. He had long thought that Gramsci in particular 'could help us to find a fresh approach to our cultural allies, as he has helped the Italian comrades in their very successful work in this field'. Could Eaton, a prominent Marxist intellectual, perhaps be invited to lead a discussion on Gramsci, he wondered: on that basis 'we might get somewhere'.[53]

Hill had a life-long aversion to explicit theoretical reflection, and so it is difficult to know exactly what he saw in Gramsci, theoretically or politically, but it is plausible to think that it was Gramsci's emphasis on the importance of cultural critique. For Gramsci, the ruling class achieves dominance partly through cultural hegemony, not simply by direct coercion, and so challenges to its position require critique of that hegemony. While communist parties needed to lead the struggle, they should do so in alliance with all those who were critical of ruling class hegemony – often those Gramsci called 'organic intellectuals', thinkers outside hegemonic institutions who were thus free from their constraints, and whose opinions provided ammunition against class domination. Gramsci was, like Hill, strongly opposed to determinism – class domination has to be understood in the total context of cultural hegemony not simply in economic terms – and this opposition also implied a critique of Marxist fatalism, of the idea that only changes in the mode of production would allow political and social change. In Italy, Gramsci was associated with the achievement of cooperation among a range of progressive groups, and he was seen as a godfather of the later 'Eurocommunism' aiming to foster social coalitions to achieve a hegemonic support for social reform. It is easy to see the appeal of this for Hill, although characteristically there is no obvious record of his position on these issues.

Hill's discontents with the CPGB and its intellectual posture were soon to crystallise into a concerted attempt to reform the party. This was prompted in part by the secret session of the Twentieth Congress of the Communist Party of the Soviet Union in February 1956, in which Nikita Khrushchev revealed the crimes of Stalin's regime and called for a new approach to domestic and foreign policy. Hill had been asked to lead a discussion of the implications of the Congress with James Klugmann in April 1956, but before that he and Bridget had already written to the *Daily Worker* expressing their unhappiness at the response of the British party to the revelations. While the new attitude of the Soviet leadership was 'excellent', they wrote, the party could have been more critical of its own failings and not just of Stalin's. More immediately, though, 'The historical facts which help to explain lack of democracy in the Soviet Communist Party do not apply here. We had no cult of the individual. Can we be satisfied with our attitude as Communists over the past 20 years?' The party had either been ignorant of what was going on or had known and chosen to remain silent. If the latter was true, were they not guilty of 'that loyalty to Party rather than Socialist principle which we sometimes criticise in our Labour Party comrades'. They called for a full and frank discussion at the CPGB Congress: 'If we do not discuss [the revelations] fully and frankly, how can we claim to be heirs to the great tradition of British democracy?'[54] This was to be the theme of Hill's terminal disagreement with the party, and also a line of criticism against him – that he was serving a wider ideological constituency more faithfully than he was serving the party.

In May he was still serving as branch secretary but asked to be excused service on a Working Committee of the Cultural Committee, supposedly on the grounds that he was not in London at the weekend, and that he should not be on the latter committee as a delegate of the Historians' Group, since he had 'been a very bad attender recently'. He did, however, accept with alacrity an invitation to join a Commission on Inner Party Democracy, formed to review the internal processes of the British party; he was, he said, 'very flattered'.[55]

In August, Bridget and Christopher wrote another powerful denunciation of the control exercised by the party leadership, published in *World News*, and Hill's own discussions with party officials became increasingly blunt. Asked to write about the British struggle for parliamentary democracy, he told Edwin Payne (one-time secretary of the Historians' Group) that 'I find the qualification "providing they do not raise questions which should more properly be posed in the current discussion" rather sinister'. He did, though, write the piece, which made the familiar (and plainly correct) case that Parliament was not a naturally democratic institution, that it had only become so through the struggles of ordinary people, and that the work was not yet complete.[56]

From early on he was pessimistic about the Commission on Inner Party Democracy, writing to Betty Lewis that the terms of reference, and the Commission's working practices, meant that it would fail to achieve any substantive change. The acid test was whether the grassroots could ever achieve a change of party leadership given that all the internal processes seemed to create a self-perpetuating cadre of party officers, and all discussion had to be channelled through the branch structure. To make common cause with members of other branches was to be judged guilty of factionalism – creating a lobby group within the party for a particular political view, rather than fostering appropriate discussion within the branch structures. That seemed to make such a change impossible. However, the experience of 1928–9 and 1939 showed that it was sometimes a good thing to allow the grassroots to change the leadership.[57] Tense relations had not prevented Hill being named as a member of a delegation due to visit the USSR in late October and November, but by early November his name had been removed and Morton's had been added.[58]

In the meantime, the Hungary crisis had erupted. Hill was a prominent figure in the subsequent controversy, a key cause of which was the 'enormous disgust' at the party leadership's repudiation of Peter Fryer's on-the-spot reporting of the Soviet invasion for the *Daily Worker*, which was favourable to the Hungarian anti-Stalinists. There was widespread anger and disapproval of the Soviet action, but also of the response of the CPGB bureaucracy, which at that time, as Rodney Hilton later wrote, 'seemed incapable of … independent political judgement'.[59]

At the heart of the issue was the importance, and meaning, of 'democratic centralism'. Discussion within the party was allowed in order to develop a line, but once the line had been adopted party members were expected to follow it. There was, in effect, a democratic stage but also a centralist phase as the party decided on political issues. For Malcolm MacEwen, the *Daily Worker*'s House of Commons correspondent at the time, democratic centralism had come to stifle discussion: 'The party principle was that all discussion must be controlled by the party', wrote MacEwen, 'and party policy could only be discussed in the party press, where the party leadership would decide on what was to be published, and what not.' His own reporting on Hungary for the *Daily Worker* had been suppressed along with Fryer's, and in his view mistaken party loyalty had led people to suppress their own thoughts. Harry Pollitt exemplified the personal costs: although he had disagreed with the Moscow line opposing war in 1939, he had never uttered a word against it. MacEwen thought that accepting the Khrushchev revelations, which Pollitt declared in the *Daily Worker* a closed issue, had made Pollitt ill, leading to his resignation as leader. Having spent sixteen years at the *Daily Worker*, MacEwen walked out when a petition from about half the staff calling for public criticism of Soviet policy in Hungary fell on deaf ears.[60]

Democratic centralism was intended to maintain party discipline, but it made discussion, in effect, a scarce resource. The obligation placed on party members to stick to the agreed line applied to practical questions, such as whether to contest a particular election, but also to 'political and theoretical questions on which people held passionate views'. Discussion of principle was akin to a stage in policy-making, rather than something ongoing; it was a view difficult to reconcile with an academic or historical sensibility, and party members were right to suspect that intellectuals would find it hard to submit to such discipline.[61]

After an initial attempt to ignore the revelations, the party had allowed discussion, which was led by Hill, Hobsbawm, E.P. Thompson and other members of the Historians' Group. However, after the leadership visited Khrushchev in Moscow in July 1956, it became more reluctant to countenance demands for change.[62] Thompson, along with fellow historian John Saville, became frustrated at the difficulty of airing basic criticisms of Stalinist theory and Soviet policy, and responded by launching a new journal, the *Reasoner*, in July. In their eyes, they were preserving party discipline by keeping dissent within it, but they were 'instructed by the executive to stop publication because, it was said, they were setting themselves up as the controllers of discussion, and, what is more, organising a faction'. Having been summoned to a special meeting of the central Political Committee on 31 August, in early September they were instructed to cease publication. They refused and produced the second issue. A third issue followed, with news of the Hungarian rising, after which Saville and Thompson were suspended. Both immediately resigned from the party and relaunched the journal as the *New Reasoner*, along with MacEwen.[63]

Hill stayed on. There was, however, no doubt about the sincerity of his objections to the party's approach to policy-making and internal debate, nor that he was willing to abandon party discipline in order to make them. Raphael Samuel, a former student of Hill's and a rising left activist, told Saville that five party members in Oxford had resigned over the Executive Committee's statement on Hungary, and two more were about to. Christopher, he said, 'seems undecided on principle of intervention but decidedly against EC statement'.[64] Ernie Keeling, the branch secretary of the South Midlands district, agreed that Hill was 'more deeply concerned over events from/after the 20th Congress and not so much Hungary'. He had met Hill and attended a branch meeting where he found members, including Hill, 'intensely cynical – even bordering on demoralisation'.[65] Others who stayed on initially were equally outraged by the party leadership. According to Victor Kiernan, the Edinburgh branch was in uproar, and its organiser, a veteran of the International Brigade, was very upset by the revelation that Fryer's reports from Hungary had been suppressed. Kiernan himself was entirely hostile to the Soviet intervention, and he celebrated the fact that 'we are at last trying to think independently and objectively, instead of just repeating tunes on a hurdy-gurdy made in Moscow'. He favoured junking the party line and removing all those who had supported it from the Executive.[66]

This became as much a tactical question as one of principle: whether to try to reform the party or to abandon it to the current leadership and try something else. The launch of the *Reasoner* had come to seem like the latter, and Hobsbawm tried to mediate, sympathetic to the new journal but unsure whether 'one should now give up hope in a change of policy and leadership'. He thought the only alternative to the CPGB would be to join Labour but maintain some sort of Marxist organisation, for example around the *Reasoner*. For him, talk of a new party was utopian and would simply fragment the left: 'If we have to give up hope in the Party for the foreseeable future, we shall also, I am afraid, have to give up hope of getting Socialism in Britain. I expect it'll mean dropping out of politics for some of us, though old habits are hard to get rid of.'[67] Dorothy Thompson, by contrast, had apparently suggested that Thompson and Saville should wait to be expelled, in order to increase the force of their protest.[68]

For the time being, Hill tried to reform the party rather than resign. Part of the Executive's response to Saville and Thompson was to point out that the party had already responded to its political problem with Commissions on the British Road to Socialism and on Inner Party Democracy.[69] Hill was a member of the latter Commission, and in April 1957, when the party discussed establishing its own theoretical journal in light of the upheavals of the mid-1950s, he was mentioned as a potential member of the editorial board. In the event he was rejected because he was at that point vacillating about his membership of the party.[70] This suggests, though, that he retained some influence and that it was not an altogether forlorn hope that he could mobilise support for reform.

On these questions of tactics Dorothy Thompson felt there was a generational difference. 'We had after all, been 15 when the war broke out', she wrote, 'and … none of us [had] been to the S[oviet] U[nion] or had much to do with the CP in the thirties'. She recalled being flummoxed by Klugmann, a prominent party intellectual and member of the Executive Committee, who later edited *Marxism Today*. They were on very good terms, but a gulf of understanding opened up when he told her he was puzzled as to why 'this Joe business' had upset her so much or what she thought the CP could do about it.[71] Hill agreed about that:

> Those of us who had known the great days when the CP had given a lead to the left – Spanish civil war, World War II – were aware of a staunch rank and file of members devoted to good causes, who wanted to change the leadership, or reduce it to rank-and-file control, but who still desperately wanted to keep an effective organ of the left.[72]

Although supportive in the long run, Hill was hesitant about the political wisdom of launching the *Reasoner*, and sent a lengthy letter to Saville and Thompson explaining why he would not subscribe.[73] He had softened by November, however, when he sent money for the journal's third edition: 'Without prejudice to our former point of view, Bridget and I would feel in agreement now with many of your arguments.' They remained in the party but, he wrote, 'it is terribly late and terribly difficult to organize movements for change from within now. We still want to try though. God help us all.'[74] He was apparently supportive of Thompson's and Saville's intellectual position if not their political tactics, publishing a review of a translation of Gramsci's writings and Cornu's study of Marx and Engels for the *New Reasoner* in 1957. Among other things, he commended Gramsci for offering the basis of a critique of 'those Marxists who have fallen back on liberal standards for their critique of the crudities of Stalinism'. His reading of Cornu's study was a thinly veiled critique of dogmatism and illusions in the recent history of the CPGB, seeing them as betrayals of the early hopes of Marx and Engels.[75]

Christopher and Bridget were ultimately correct that the New Left would not be a vehicle of mass mobilisation for the achievement of socialism. Fears of fragmentation were not too wide of the mark either. As early as May 1957, Hill wrote to Saville suggesting there should be some coordination among the proliferating left-wing periodicals.[76] In particular, the *New Reasoner* had a sister magazine with a slightly different political agenda, the *Universities and Left Review*, originating in Oxford University rather than the communist networks of the industrial north. Both struggled in different ways over the next two years, leading to a merger in 1960 as the *New Left Review*. These and later initiatives were tremendously fruitful intellectually, and gave rise to currents of Marxist humanism that Hill could only have applauded, but as a political strategy his fears would be realised. The New Left was divided and never acquired a mass base of support; in fact, debates about what relationship to have with the Labour Party revived a key problem of political organisation, a problem with which the CPGB had also grappled.[77]

More than twenty-five years later, Hill still felt it had been right to continue to try to reform the party, however futile that effort proved: 'if we had been defeated after a united fight against the leadership we could perhaps then have formed a viable alternative party'. It was this that he 'most bitterly regret[ted]' about the events of 1956 and '57: the New Left, he wrote, 'contained many powerful personalities but never amounted to a coherent party which could attract a mass backing to do the sort of job which the CP did in the 30s and 40s and which still desperately needs doing'.[78]

Hill was therefore one of the key figures championing party reform in the autumn of 1956, not as a Stalinist but as an anti-Stalinist who wanted to save the CPGB, in part at least from itself. On 22 November Bridget and Christopher wrote to the *Daily Worker* calling for a 'highly critical assessment of [its] presentation of news from Socialist countries over the past 11 years, and analysis of the reasons which made it lead its readers so badly astray'. They wanted assurances that future reporting would be accurate and independent, as the only way to rebuild shattered confidence. The movement continually referred to the 'lies and slanders' of the capitalist press, 'but unless we can be sure of the accuracy and truthfulness of our own paper, on what basis can we refute and condemn them? And what basis have we for our own Marxist appraisal?'[79]

This developed into a more direct challenge to the party leadership when fourteen members signed a draft letter expressing dismay at the party's approach to internal debate. Critically, they were not members of the same branch, leading the Executive to say that this was incipient factionalism – comrades making a controversial case in alliance with members of other branches, rather than arguing within the branch structure for a change in party policy. This was therefore, in effect, a direct challenge to democratic centralism. Moreover, when the *Daily Worker* refused to publish the letter, the reformers sent it to the *New Statesman*, taking a party controversy to the pages of a non-party paper. Hill was seen, quite rightly, as the ringleader in this.[80]

The background was a heated debate about the fitness of the current leadership and the related issue of party processes. Just as there were tactical differences between those who left and those who stayed, so there were also among the reformers. Peter Trent, another reformer, had drafted a letter that Hill felt did not go far enough. Hobsbawm, on the other hand, wanted to call directly for a change of leadership, which Hill had felt went too far: it would fail and along with it so would the more general cause of reform. Nonetheless, Hill clearly thought that the Executive Committee had reached a 'hasty estimation' on Hungary, one which now overshadowed the work of the Commission on Inner Party Democracy. For him, it seems, the failures over Hungary were symptoms of the deeper malaise already revealed by the Khrushchev revelations. Returning comments on a draft of the Commission's report on 20 November, Hill wrote 'It all seems a little beside the point now.'[81]

Gollan heard about the potentially factional letter to the *Daily Worker* a week later.[82] Johnnie Campbell, another senior party official, tried to persuade Hill to fall into line: the issue was not criticism of the leadership, but factionalism.[83] A critical letter on a controversial matter signed by a single author, or by members of the same branch, would have been fine. The key issue, therefore, in deciding how a letter could be put together was to know whether the matter it discussed was 'controversial' in this technical sense. Hill picked this out, asking the Executive Committee to provide members with guidance on the issue, without which they 'ran the risk of engaging in some factious activity unawares, or they would think the only safe weapon to use was to avoid the use of faction and never to criticise at all'.[84] Betty Reid, another prominent comrade, found Hill hard to deal with: whereas MacEwen was willing to argue, 'Christopher, he just puts up a hostile barrier, doesn't he? and that's it.'[85]

With due warning to the Executive Committee, the letter appeared in the *New Statesman and Nation* on 1 December 1956. The signatories explained that the *Daily Worker* had received it on 18 November but, as 'it appears it will not be published there', they hoped the *New Statesman* would find space for it. They made no bones about the fact that they were writing as intellectuals, feeling 'a responsibility to express our views as Marxists in the present crisis of international Socialism'. The uncritical support of the party Executive Committee for the Soviet invasion of Hungary 'is the undesirable culmination of years of distortion of fact, and failure by British Communists to think out political problems for themselves'. The reformers had hoped that the revelations of the 20th Congress would have made the leadership 'realise that Marxist ideas will only be acceptable in the British Labour movement if they arise from the truth about the world we live in'. Recent events demonstrated that 'for the past twelve years we have based our political analyses on a false presentation of facts'. It was the falsity of the facts, however, not the theory, that had led them astray. If the party wanted to win support for the left-wing and Marxist trend in Labour, 'this past must be utterly repudiated', including 'the Executive Committee's underwriting of the current errors of Soviet policy'.[86]

Among the signatories was Chimen Abramsky. Son of a Lithuanian rabbi, he had graduated from the Hebrew University of Jerusalem and was a leading scholar of Jewish history. He had wanted to add a clause appealing 'to all Comrades at the present moment not to leave the Communist Party and to fight for a reversal of the line'. Although the clause was not included, the general unease about proceeding in this way was reflected in the rider at the end of the letter: 'Not all the signatories agree with everything in this letter', it said, 'but all are in sufficient sympathy with its general intention to sign with this reservation.'[87]

Hill was a leading figure in the circulation and publication of the letter, and the secret service files suggest that it was he who took the key decision not to accept an offer to publish the criticism over a single name, or the names of members of the same branch. Hyman Levy, son of an Edinburgh Jewish family and later a distinguished physicist, was another of the rebels. He later admitted that he had not known that Hill had received this offer, and thought Hill had made a mistake in not accepting it. Nor had he known that the Political Committee had offered to meet the signatories.[88] Hill clearly had a key role in managing the expression of dissent and his preferences were clear: after chairing a branch meeting, he wrote asking for an early party Congress to discuss all these matters. However, relations with the Executive were obviously very strained, and Abramsky and Hill agreed that if one of them was ousted from their committee positions the other would resign, although the tone suggests they both intended to try to stay in the party.[89]

In response, the Executive set out its position in the *Daily Worker*, essentially stating its concern about 'the danger of factionalism'. Hill subsequently expressed mild annoyance that the paper had published a letter from him to the Executive without asking him first.[90] Much more confrontational was an article by Joan Simon in *World News* which denounced the intellectuals. The signatories of the *New Statesman* letter, she wrote, 'have no idea how to work within the Party for the necessary changes'. Lacking real experience of class solidarity, they tended to express 'anger with the Party if it does not immediately meet their individual demands'. She pointed out that they had all expressed their views before, and since they knew very well that the *Daily Worker* would not publish their letter, it was not clear what they thought they would achieve by publishing it in the *New Statesman and Nation*. Saville and Thompson had done a similar thing following the 20th Congress, with the result that the party had been distracted from the real issues.[91]

The principal charge, though, was that the intellectuals were blinded by arrogance: 'these comrades take their stand pre-eminently because they believe themselves to be leading Marxist thinkers. Some ... are somewhat contemptuous of working class leaders of the Party, who, in their view, are incapable of understanding and applying Marxism adequately'. This, she wrote, was far from the truth, for 'active participation in the struggle [is] the essential guarantee of a revolutionary theory'.

Upholding Marxism 'in words' was not only insufficient, but in fact a major error.[92]

In January 1957, after years of ill health, Dona Torr died. It was hard to think of a figure of equal stature who could now serve as a similarly powerful advocate within the party for Marxist historical inquiry conducted according to academic values. There was an attempt to keep the Historians' Group going by opening it up to non-party members.[93] It failed though, and Hill was described as the leader of a 'right faction' which was suggesting that the Group be 'dissolved into a broad organisation'. Betty Grant and others were insistent that it should be a group for party members, although there was a concern that the party would lose all its historians.[94] The tension between academic values and democratic centralism was now out in the open.

The Commission on Inner Party Democracy reported in January 1957. The majority report gave few concessions, and Peter Cadogan, Hill and MacEwen put their names to a dissenting minority report. Many years later, Hill said that the minority would actually have been the majority but for pressure exerted by the Executive on 'a very good working-class comrade who had been with us all the way up till then'.[95] It was in any case quickly in the news. Reporting for the *Observer* in late January, Edward Crankshaw concluded that 'It is all the more damaging because the report is written by men in the grip of a crisis of conscience and desperately anxious to save their party from disaster.' He thought that, in effect, 'the leadership have decided to turn their backs on experience, to learn nothing from Yugoslavia, Poland and Hungary, and to take their stand on the reassertion of a bleak and rigid conception of party organisation that would have done credit to Stalin's most trusted bureaucrats'. The results, he said, were startling: the circulation of the *Daily Worker* at the end of 1956 was 43 per cent lower than its peak in 1949. By contrast, he commended the minority report: unless the party became 'fully independent [and] thoroughly democratic in its inner-party life, and stands for the development of democratic Socialism, [it] will be unable to exert political influence on the British labour movement'.[96]

The mood among reformers, intellectuals in particular, was gloomy. Although John Gollan had succeeded Pollitt as general secretary, it did not seem to make much difference: there was a 'desperate mood of disillusion'.[97] In February, Joan Simon told Klugmann she had been trying to meet Hill, 'but am afraid he is intentionally avoiding us'.[98] Daphne Simon told Betty Grant that she thought Hill 'was on his way out'. Grant agreed and said she could not really blame him 'after getting into that position. He had been attacked far too much.'[99]

A special party Congress was held in April 1957 in Hammersmith, giving reformers their last chance.[100] Theirs proved to be a doomed enterprise. Ernie Keeling had reported to the Executive that voting in his South Midlands district was 'solid', although 'Chris' was 'invariably against'. There had been an attempt to ensure that supporters of the majority report were nominated to attend the conference, although Hill had secured a nomination.[101] Nationally, however, the delegate list was effectively managed: although some critics were elected to the Congress they were not in proportion to what seemed to be the scale of the opposition.

The agenda was managed too. Three documents would be discussed: the results of the Commission on the British Road to Socialism; a political resolution; and the majority report on inner party democracy. Fifty-seven branch resolutions were remitted to the Executive but not discussed at the Congress because it was felt they had been dealt with in other documents.[102] A branch resolution calling for an end to H-bomb testing by the USSR was allowed, and the discussion was largely 'amiable';[103] this was not an issue that drove a wedge between the Executive and its critics. The real division was caused by a resolution put forward by two branches to substitute the minority report on inner party democracy for the majority one.[104] There was also discussion of the expulsion of Peter Fryer from the party and the consideration of his appeal; the notes of one delegate included a copy of a speech Fryer would have delivered to Congress if allowed.[105]

The speech that got the most attention in the press was Hyman Levy's. In January 1957, he had had a heated two-hour meeting with Gollan and George Matthews, acting editor of the *Daily Worker*, after which the latter two had agreed between themselves that if Levy spoke to too many branches they would have to kick him out of the party; but if he left it as it was after sending a letter to the press, then they 'should just let him "stew in his own juice"'.[106] At the Congress Levy launched an excoriating attack, recalling how he had been profoundly shaken by a trip to the USSR, during which he had been appalled to learn about the persecution of Jewish writers and intellectuals between 1948 and 1952, including torture and killings. The Lenin Library had stopped acquiring work in Yiddish in 1948, and Soviet Jews referred to the period as the Black Years, when many Jewish poets and writers had been arrested, charged with treason and executed. Levy had said to Gollan and Matthews that the

Soviet authorities 'had nothing at all to learn from the NAZIS, *nothing at all*'. The revelations fitted with the wider pattern of lies on behalf of the USSR – about this matter, but also about the faking of production figures, for example. He found the stifling of discussion unacceptable: it was ludicrous that Crankshaw could use information from *World News* to write in the *Observer* while members were told not to publish in the *New Statesman and Nation*.[107]

In an earlier speech, the literary critic Arnold Kettle had tried to draw a distinction between subjective honesty and objective truth, as a way of navigating these problems. Kettle had previously prepared a memo for the Political Committee on the position of party intellectuals. In it he said that middle-class activists had a distinct relationship to the cause because of their social formation and situation, but that they could not claim moral superiority, as the editors of the *Reasoner* had seemed to do. While he urged the conference to be understanding about the distinct position of intellectuals and the role they played, he gave no support to the idea that they were the conscience of the party. Their concern for their subjective honesty prioritised petty bourgeois rather than communist morality, as exemplified in the minority report. They needed to understand that 'the doing of the necessary right thing at each particular moment of struggle … is a higher principle than that of subjective sincerity'. Accepting working-class leadership, and the truth of this point, was essential 'before they are entitled to the ear of the working class movement'.[108]

Levy was utterly dismissive of this line, as well as of the denigration of 'intellectuals'. 'The working class of this country have consistently repudiated the Communist Party', Levy said, 'and Arnold Kettle can draw his own conclusions from that.' Having been born into the Russian working class, 'I refuse to make any distinction between a worker and an intellectual.' In conversation with Gollan, Levy had referred to this as the equivalent of a colour bar: everyone in the party was an intellectual regardless of their occupation. Seven thousand members had left, he said; 'isn't it time you looked at the reasons objectively, with "subjective honesty", for this colossal failure, instead of letting yourselves be bamboozled by enthusiastic speeches?' The October Revolution had achieved great things but also created 'a cast-iron bureaucracy, a terror and a fear – a form of gangsterism that battened on a sound social and economic basis'. This was not simply a product of Stalin's character, but something within the history of socialism that Marxists should understand. 'Without this understanding our Marxist education is incomplete.'[109]

For Congress, though, the key question was whether the leadership had known of the crimes of the Stalin regime. 'If they knew and kept quiet', said Levy, 'then they were misleading you as regards your Marxist education.' 'I am not standing by while the working class is deluded. I have spent my life on this matter. Isn't it the truth that the leadership knew what was going on, didn't trust you, didn't trust the working class, thought you couldn't take it? Is this what you call Marxism?'[110]

The main response in Congress came from Andrew Rothstein, himself a former academic and Balliol man, who Hill had supported when he lost his job at SOAS. Denouncing 'Backboneless and spineless intellectuals', Rothstein now accused Levy of opportunism, sectarianism and revisionism. Bourgeois conceptions of democracy should not be allowed to distort the party organisation, he said. By acting this way, the rebels were offering comfort to the capitalist press, which was always ready to 'give hospitality to the enemies of the party, to dissenting members'. 'How can a Party of Marxist principles accept the idea voiced in Congress of becoming a bundle of differing trends on questions of national and international policy[?]' His intervention goaded one delegate, John McLoughlin, beyond endurance. He was well known in the press for prompting an unofficial strike at Briggs Motor Bodies by ringing a hand bell. Now he shouted Rothstein down: 'You lying old swine; you filthy stinker'; 'take your medicine', Rothstein retorted.[111]

Rothstein had better captured the mood of the delegates. Bill Lauchlan, a prominent party official, answered Levy's questions, saying that the Executive had 'told what we knew', adding that 'If we didn't know what had happened in the Soviet Union it was because our eyes were fixed on the sweeping advance of fascism.' He supported the view that challenges to party policies by those who did not like them threatened permanent controversy. Many agreed with him that Levy's speech was a 'cry of desperation not dealing with the facts'.[112] Levy stayed away from the Congress the next day but gave an interview to the *Telegraph* in which he chuckled about the explosion he had caused, predicting that there might be another soon. Many delegates seem to have agreed, however, that he had made a gift to anti-communists.[113]

Hill also spoke, commending Levy's speech as the most important of the Congress and discounting Gollan's view that good comrades would not leave, or that only a handful would do so. Where Gollan talked of international revisionism, Hill spoke of a trend towards authoritarianism, equally obvious in socialism, and present in the top-down world of the British party. 'We have been living for too long in a world of illusions',

Hill said. 'It was a snug, cosy little world. One could feel the resentment of some comrades when Comrade Levy let the fresh air in.' It was not just the fault of the leadership: 'We are all responsible for the bad state the Party has got into, for taking lines from the top.' There had been a failure of leadership, however, and the majority report offered no proper remedy. He urged Congress to adopt the minority report, even if they did not agree with everything in it ('I don't myself'). It was the only way to get a more effective response to the crisis.[114] One delegate thought that although Hill had explained why they should not support the majority report, he had not explained why they should support the minority report instead.[115]

The Times contrasted Hill's tone with that of the defenders of the leadership, who it claimed showed little humility or self-criticism. Margaret Hunter, a Scottish delegate, argued that indulging the views of minorities in the party 'would lead us back to the creation of some liberal kind of association for the expression of views by experienced individuals', and that this would prioritise 'protection of people's consciences' over the needs of the party. According to *The Times*, 'Delegates laughed intellectual consciences to scorn'. Hunter claimed that 'The leadership of our party precisely represents the best defenders of democracy in this country.'[116] The final vote was utterly decisive: the majority report won by 423 to 23 with 15 abstentions.

Those who feared that this controversy would provide fodder to the capitalist press were proved right. Liberal commentators denounced what they saw as a 'parade of democracy', while the *Herald Tribune* commentator, writing under the headline 'U.K. reds are under freer speech', argued that tightly licensed freedom of discussion was balanced by the use of new terms to silence dissenters: 'intellectual' and 'revisionist'. *The Times* compared it to the use of 'scab' and 'blackleg' to silence dissent on the shop floor and attributed the failure of reform in part to the timidity of the reformers in the face of this hostility: they withdrew motions, admitted fault and self-doubt (as Hill had done), or fell ill when due to recommend their motion to Congress.[117] The reporting is quite accurate, but consistently unsympathetic to speeches that supported the party leadership. In his own summary of the conference Harry Pollitt was, by contrast, able to celebrate a show of party unity which represented a rebuke to the capitalist press, a line promoted by the party press in the weeks after the Congress.[118]

The subsequent history of the party suggests that the critics were right that this would prove a pyrrhic victory. *The Times* thought that

'By their attitude … they have made it almost impossible for normal, humane, people to enter or stay in the party', which would forever remain 'the small, narrow sect that it now is'. For liberal commentators this had been a missed opportunity to free the party from the Soviet line, reform its internal structures and make it 'less intolerable' for British people.[119] However, following the Congress, Matthews thought there had only been another ten resignations.[120]

For Hill, these questions about truthfulness and the role of intellectuals were obviously critical: he had been attracted to Marxism by the possibility that a post-bourgeois world would offer means to a fuller and more authentic self-expression. This concern for authenticity pre-dated his Marxism and was central to it. At the back of his mind too will have been the reactions in the wider academic world, of the kind articulated by Rowse: '[Hill's] conversion from years of nonsense and lying came, very belatedly, with the Russian suppression of Hungarian liberty in 1957 [*sic*]. Fancy waiting til then for one's eyes to be opened!'[121] Hill had built a career in opposition to an academic mainstream that denounced both Marxism and the Soviet Union; he must now have felt both betrayed and terribly exposed. Corfield records Hill's personal anguish – a second loss of faith, akin to his departure from Methodism, as an established truth became a lie.[122] The humiliation of being found to have been working in the service of falsehoods must have been particularly acute. Rowse remembered seeing him at Oxford station around this time: 'with his little girl … sitting crouched down on a truck, utterly abject'.[123]

The failure of the minority report at Congress confirmed what had seemed inevitable for Hill and he resigned from the party on 1 May 1957. Thompson had written angrily to Hill about his failure to offer leadership during the crisis; Hill felt the outcome might have been different but the premature departure of people who might have helped lead reform had 'ensured that the Party would decline into insignificance'.[124] He remained proud of the minority report, though, later recalling that the vice-chancellor of Glasgow University had called it 'an impeccably liberal document' (in the course of an interview which ended in a refusal to give Hill a job because of his political opinions).[125]

This was more than a crisis of political tactics for Hill, however, as his reported mood at Oxford station suggests. Having left the party, he did not immediately commit to a new path. He wrote to Saville that month saying he had nothing to offer the *Reasoner*: 'frankly at the moment I want to sort myself out first before starting to tell other chaps what to think: I feel I have done a bit too much of that over the last 20 years.'[126] When Margot Heinemann met Hill at Dona Torr's funeral, he spoke of the crisis as liberating: her death 'ended his strongest emotional tie within the Party and left him feeling freer to exercise his moral and political judgements'. Reporting the conversation to Saville, she went on:

> I thought you would also like to know how warmly he spoke of you and Edward. He said that the only thing that gave him comfort was that all those whose companionship he had enjoyed were moving in the same direction although at different paces. I quote him 'I am only ashamed I didn't move as fast and see as clearly as John and Edward.'

Others who had been doubtful about the wisdom of launching the *Reasoner* also now felt that Saville and Thompson had been 'dead right'. Pollitt had spoken at the funeral to the effect that Torr would have been against the faint-hearts and dupes of the capitalist class, but Heinemann reported that 'Christopher Hill said to me, it was good that she wasn't able to take in all that had passed since the 20th Congress.'[127]

Although profoundly disillusioned with the party, Hill avoided giving any comfort to the capitalist press. Keeling reported that he had announced his resignation to the branch meeting on 30 April, telling them that 'he will just drop out but nothing publicly'. The resignation was reported in the *Telegraph* the following day, but Hill had refused either to comment or to confirm or deny that he had resigned. He took the same line with the *Oxford Mail*.[128] He made no public statements afterwards either.

Over the long term this was another source of reserve, overlaying his own temperament: a refusal to give comfort to the enemies of those with whom he had suffered. He could not stay in the party, but he did not want to offer any ammunition to those who wished to discredit the comrades who had stayed on – I have found no evidence that he ever repeated to a non-party audience the criticisms he had made at the Congress. This was a broader feature of these radical circles. Heinemann, for example, ducked public scholarly controversy with John Saville decades later – despite an evident personal antipathy at that point – exactly because he had predicted there would be a political reaction to his views. She also refused to renew acquaintance with an old friend, Michael Straight, despite initially welcoming contact. Having read his memoirs she could not forgive him for public attacks on the reputations of people who were not around to defend themselves.[129] Hill had quite clearly renounced

Stalin and his regime, as Rowse noted, and left the party over its refusal to acknowledge its mistakes and attempt to reform; but his failure to make very public statements about that allowed later critics to claim that he had not truly repented.

Hill's Marxism was closely tied to his experience of the Soviet Union, and the ease with which he could be himself in that society. The behaviour of the USSR was perhaps therefore a more challenging issue for his political beliefs than it was, say, for Eric Hobsbawm, whose Marxism came from a Germanic and philosophical context, and had been anti-Nazi in its first practical application.[130] Hobsbawm stayed in the party after the crisis of 1956, saying later that 'Some of us … still wish to bear witness to what we believe to be a great cause, even if it has been distorted in practice.' 'What we had done was not something to be ashamed of. That we happened to be associated with people who had a lot of be ashamed of is another question.'[131] For Hill, author of a lavish paean to Stalin following his death, it was not so easy to distance himself: in several ways Hobsbawm's communism was more easily separable from commitment to the USSR.

Levy too, had a different route into the party, and so perhaps made a different accommodation to the crisis, expressing disappointment that Hill had mishandled things and ended up leaving the party.[132] He stayed, as did Cadogan, although they were both subsequently expelled. Heinemann, who also stayed, was tight-lipped about the conflicts, although she remembered the frustrations and disappointments. There had been few expulsions and nearly all those who left had seceded, in her memory, prompted by Khrushchev more than Hungary. Her own feeling was that they wouldn't have been expelled either, 'but they didn't *try* to stay in or fight to turn minority into majority'. She named Thompson and Saville but also Hill and Hilton, remembering that 'For those of us who were deeply and publicly critical and did *not* resign, these secessions were a great blow though one fully understood why people felt they had to leave.'[133]

There were attempts by the party to keep channels open to Hill after his resignation, but he seems to have been unreceptive, and opinion among party leaders was in any case divided. In his resignation letter to Keeling, Hill thanked him for considerate treatment and hoped 'to maintain the contact of friendship despite what has happened'. Gollan was hurt that he heard about the resignation in the press and not directly, but he said that Hill was the only one of those who resigned after the Congress that he would have tried to dissuade. Lauchlan had approved Keeling's proposal to try to maintain friendly relations with former members if at all possible, in the hope that they might eventually be tempted back. G.C.T. Giles, however, a seasoned campaigner who had suffered persistent public denunciations, felt that Christopher and Bridget had not been straight with him.[134]

In August 1957 the Hills were involved in a tragic car accident near Doncaster, in which their eleven-month-old daughter Kate was killed. Bridget was 'pretty badly knocked about, but there is nothing wrong with her that a few weeks rest won't put right'.[135] The party leadership sent messages of condolence, and Hill responded with varying degrees of warmth to the consideration, revealing perhaps differing degrees of friendship with erstwhile colleagues: his letter to Gollan was handwritten, headed 'Dear Johnnie' and signed off 'Thank you very much for writing, best wishes from both of us'. The letter to Pollitt was typed, headed 'Dear Harry Pollitt' and signed off 'Yours sincerely'. Hobsbawm had not known about the accident until told by an official – he got the news from Betty Grant.[136]

In all, it seems, Hill made a clean break with the party. He had 'lain low and said nothing' about a proposed meeting in July 1957 with former party members.[137] In 1958 Hobsbawm told party officials he had seen Hilton and Hill at meetings of the editorial board of *Past and Present*, but 'he did not know what they were doing other than this', although he had heard Hilton had joined a Worcester branch of the Labour Party. Abramsky bumped into Hill in June, reporting that 'he is not doing anything politically' and was instead concentrating on his research for a year.[138] Although Hill responded courteously to a letter from Joan Simon about her son's application to Balliol, he did not reply at all to an invitation in March 1962 to join a discussion of the 'Stages of History' at Marx House. On the other hand, he did agree to speak to the Oxford Young Communist League on Marxist History that year, suggesting that it was party business he was avoiding, not other Marxists.[139] He rejoined the Labour Party, as Hilton and as Hobsbawm had predicted exiles would do, but he was not an activist.

Instead, he seems to have committed to a broader range of left-wing and liberal causes. On the anniversary of the Hungarian rising, he co-signed a letter condemning the treatment of political opponents by the new regime led by Kádár, which seemed at least as tyrannous as the previous Rákosi regime had been. The co-signatories included a number of Oxford luminaries, among them Arthur Norrington (president of Trinity

College), Maurice Bowra (warden of Wadham) and, rather remarkably, R.N. Carew Hunt, author of the hugely influential *Theory and Practice of Communism* – almost a handbook for those who wanted to show that the failures of communist regimes were not aberrations but an expression of essential elements of Marxist thought.[140] Hill again joined with figures of quite different political views (including Berlin, as well as Norrington and Bowra) in signing a letter to the *Telegraph* decrying the political use of the courts in Hungary, and in 1959 he joined in the organisation of a CND march on Brize Norton.[141] That same year, he gave financial and moral support to Lawrence Daly's campaign as an independent socialist candidate in West Fife, a candidature somewhat controversially supported by key figures in the New Left. Significantly though, Thompson had thought Hill might not want to sign a letter of support, 'since he has very much retired from active politics, and dislikes signing things unless he knows all the ins and outs'.[142]

At this stage the secret services concluded that Hill had 'remained very quiet' since leaving the party, and that 'it is not possible to say for certain exactly where his sympathies lie', although they noted his strong support of CND.[143] This engagement with the broader left perhaps contributed to the view of Soviet historians in 1960 that Hill could no longer be regarded as progressive, by which they meant Marxist and only Marxist.[144] Rothstein applied a different measure in 1962: Hill had been 'Marxist enough to have left the party before 1958'.[145] By that time the security services had lost interest in him.

Criticism of liberal intellectuals in the party press and at the special Congress missed an important point. Hill was not interested in protecting only his own autonomy, nor did he want to dictate opinion; he believed that it was through free discussion (not democratic centralism) that advances in understanding came and new ideas were born. In March 1947, writing to Kenneth Andrews about a proposed National Student Cadres School of the Party, he said he would not participate in the organisation, thinking it 'better that the students themselves should deal with it'.[146] This was entirely consistent with his teaching practice in Oxford and his own view of his weakness as an army officer: 'the basis of all my educational theory is to let people do as they like and learn by their own mistakes (that's why I'm not a good officer, because the army can't let people learn by their own mistakes as they would always be finding better ways of doing things than the army way).'[147]

In 1950 Hill had said that he could be most useful to the party by working towards the birth of ideas through his historical writing; in 1936 it had been to this that he had committed himself on returning from Moscow, not preaching bloody revolution. In an obituary for Richard Pares he commended the latter for taking Marxism seriously although he was not Marxist, but this cut the other way too: scholarly standards should also be applied to Marxism by Marxists.[148]

Hill was by temperament dutiful, an inheritance no doubt from his Methodist background, and he seems to have worked diligently for the party even in roles in which he felt ineffective. However, there was always a slightly uncomfortable fit, much more evident with hindsight, between his intellectual commitment to Marxism and his duty to the party. For the party, controversy was important for the development of Marxism, and the approach to the work of the Historians' Group was not restrictive; but the demands of democratic centralism were potentially difficult for an advocate of these values, and the experience of Lysenkoism was a potential warning. For Hill, Dona Torr was the key intellectual figure in British Marxism, not Palme Dutt or Harry Pollitt, and in the end his loyalty was to Marxist analysis, not the strategy of the British party. Marxism was an intellectual commitment that lasted a lifetime; membership of the CPGB a political strategy that lasted twenty years.

Writing to Gollan after Kate's tragic death, he had said that once Bridget was rested and recovered 'we shall have to start again'. Following their resignations from the party they were also, in a way, starting again politically. An element of this new start was buying the cottage he had once fantasised about with Shiela Grant Duff, albeit without the pigs. In September 1958 he wrote an excited and chatty letter to Ivy Gwenda Coslett, a comrade still in the party, celebrating the fact that, although they had not got the cottage they had been hoping for, they had found 'a ghastly old one which we bought for £200', in a lovely village twenty-five miles from Oxford. It was thatched and lacked water, gas and electricity, but with the help of a development grant it would be habitable by the following summer.[149] They later acquired a house in France too, near Verteillac in Perigord, at which they entertained, and which they also offered to their neighbours in Oxfordshire and to students who needed a cheap holiday.[150] Their son, Andrew, was born in 1960, and their daughter, Dinah, two years later. They did not escape further loss: Fanny died young in 1986, drowned while on holiday in Spain;[151] but, after the crises of the mid and later 1950s, married life with Bridget, his career as an Oxford don, and his open and undogmatic engagement with a broad left became the pillars of his life.

6

Science, Radicalism, Revolution and Progress: 1957–65

Christopher was singular among dons for being so egalitarian and fair-minded that all distinctions of degree, rank, and age were repugnant to him. He was devoid of race prejudice of any kind, and so far ahead of his time that he treated women no differently from men, without a hint of condescension.

Ved Mehta, *Up at Oxford*, 1993

Balliol is not just an Oxford college but a renowned one. In college memory, Benjamin Jowett, Master from 1870 to 1893, transformed it, establishing a commitment to excellence in all its varieties that became, and remains, a defining feature of the college's self-image. To outsiders, that has often seemed smug: in the mid-1960s the *Sunday Telegraph* noted that critics are 'seldom backward about complaining that Balliol lives both in, and on, its past'. At that point, though, its success was unquestionable – top of the academic table, with the highest number of firsts in the university; home to the editors of both leading student magazines, *Isis* and *Cherwell*, and the captain of the Blues rugby team. The success, and the self-image, lent itself to satire: 'To its members Balliol remains the country's leading university.' Harold Macmillan, an old member of the college, was a butt for this kind of joke, saying '"The sun rises on Wadham and sets on Worcester." Which is a Balliol way of saying that Balliol is where it shines.'[1]

It was an intimate community, governed inclusively and inculcating a strong collective identity. Down to the 1960s student numbers were small, and the number of Fellows likewise. Most college business was discussed and approved by the College Meeting, consisting of all the Fellows. Among the members of the Meeting, however, the Master was of particular importance, able to significantly affect all aspects of college life. A.D. Lindsay, the Master during Hill's time as an undergraduate, had been an admirer of the Balliol ethos, which he associated with aristocratic values of independence and leisured reflection; but he was keen to open up the community to a wider pool of talent. He wanted to dilute the influence of actual aristocrats and to focus on the already established atmosphere of serious academic enterprise. In the late 1940s, Lindsay left Balliol for the University College of North Staffordshire – soon to become Keele University with Lindsay as its first vice-chancellor. In his final Master's Letter he had expressed faith in the ambition to create a classless Balliol, although Hill noted the pathos in Lindsay's recognition that the ambition was not yet fully realised.[2]

Lindsay's successor, Sir David Lindsay Keir, lacked his reforming ambition. Despite the change of tone, however, Balliol retained its reputation for academic excellence and relatively relaxed manners. Hill, as the senior History tutor for much of the 1950s, played an important part in that. When Robin Briggs arrived as a first-year undergraduate in October 1961, Hill greeted him at their first meeting with: 'Hullo Robin, I'm Christopher. Never dare call me anything else.' For Briggs, 'it came as quite a shock … I had never called anyone so senior to me by their first name in my life up to then. Somehow he made it both gruff and friendly at the same time.'[3]

It was not just undergraduates either. On his first day at the college as a new Fellow, John Carey was approached after lunch by 'a square-jawed man with a lively face, pointed eyebrows and dark curly hair', who said 'Hello, I am Christopher Hill. Can I get you some coffee?' Carey was shocked since Hill was 'one of my gods', in his view one of the few historians who wrote intelligently about seventeenth-century literature. He was immediately struck by Hill's friendliness and informality, an experience recalled by many others.[4] Maurice Keen thought Hill particularly approachable and that this was a key factor in Hill's own election as Master. Following that election his 'first request was that he would continue to be known, except on the most formal occasions, as Christopher'.[5]

Although Balliol was committed to academic excellence it was openly acknowledged that this was not the sole criterion governing the admission of students. In 1945 the College Meeting had formally approved a statement that for scholarships and exhibitions (a slightly less generous

Christopher Hill in middle age.

form of scholarship), 'we judge solely by intellectual performance and promise'. In the broader run of admissions, though, it was agreed to be entirely appropriate to think about other qualities, since admissions had become 'pretty savagely competitive'. Essentially,

> we would far rather have a boy here who is likely to cut some ice, and so far as one can forecast, some more after he graduates, even if he only gets a decent third, than a boy who drifts blamelessly through his three years, gets some kind of middle second, and leaves without having made any mark here and apparently having no prospect of making a mark anywhere else later.[6]

This attitude was not uncommon of course, no matter how outdated it may now seem. What commends it is that admission to a college is a way of sustaining a community through time. Until recently it was conventional for colleges to refer to junior members and old members, rather than students and alumni. Fellows, as senior members, are stewards of a charitable trust as well as employees, responsible for nurturing the health of a community with a life counted in decades or even hundreds of years, through which the current generation is passing with a conscious responsibility for future generations. These are high ideals, and they exert a serious influence on the way colleges approach their business.

They are not exactly principles we would associate with a prominent Marxist intellectual, but they were important to Hill: he was very loyal to Balliol and to the college ideal more broadly. This was manifest in his choice of portraits: his pupils recall that as well as Cromwell, there were two famous college men in his room, Lindsay and Kenneth Bell.

Hill acknowledged his students in the preface to *The Century of Revolution* (1961): 'I am conscious that my ideas are at least less half-baked than they would have been if I had not had to defend them in tutorial discussions with pupils, extending now over twenty-five years.' Robin Briggs thought this would have startled many of his pupils, reeling from the pressure of interrogation punctuated by silences of apparently open-ended length. Hill thought students should make their own mistakes rather than receive a lecture, and the silences were allowed to draw out while they found something to say. Hill's informality of manner and self-deprecation could be disarming, but many of his former pupils also recall the terror of presenting ideas to him as he sat curled in a 'curious hammock-like chair, beneath a picture of Cromwell'.[7]

According to Maurice Keen, Hill's gift was to know where to send students for the topic and the book 'that would make the past come alive to them'. The experience of the brightest and most committed students was that they were 'being encouraged to look for … new ways of looking at things'. History was a subject on the move, 'where everything was open to reassessment if one could meet the standards required'.[8] Hugh Stretton characterised Hill's tutorial teaching as 'reserved, attentive prodding and direction-finding'; Donald Pennington thought Hill 'could seem interested even in the most tedious essays and would rather have an argument between a pair of pupils than one with him'. The long silences might lead students to 'babble nonsense', but Hill was convinced that 'these were occasions for students to talk rather than for tutors to soliloquize'.[9]

If the silences could be terrifying, Hill's tutorials were on the whole (at least according to his admirers) 'cheerful rather than formidable occasions'.[10] Speaking at an Exeter University graduation ceremony in 1979, where he had been awarded an honorary degree, he recalled that a student had once requested a tutorial on music in Tudor and Stuart England. Hill had gamely responded, in what he characterised as more or less total ignorance of the subject, only to discover that it had been a prank, his floundering performance reported widely for the entertainment of the student body. That he could be the butt of such a joke, and also recount it with such self-deprecating humour, reflected the warmth that many of his students remembered.[11]

Although, as the secret service noted, he 'apparently makes no secret of his political sympathies', Hill was, therefore, far from ideological as a tutor.[12]

> Anyone who supposed that he inculcated Marxist dogma into his cred-ulous pupils was hopelessly wide of the mark, since in his tutorials he relied almost entirely on abrupt questions, then displayed steely resolve in sitting through the longest silences until someone had to offer at least a feeble guess in response.[13]

He made few interventions of any directive kind, particularly not polit-ical: 'If one said something very Royalist ... he might suddenly become animated; more often he seemed laconic, and rather withdrawn.'[14] He was eventually to train a number of people who went on to successful academic careers, of whom few could be identified as Marxists. Brian Manning pointed out that while he was habitually identified as 'a Hill student' as a code for 'Marxist', non-Marxist students were not routinely identified as former Hill students – Gerald Aylmer was the example he gave. In fact, most of Hill's most loyal, successful and grateful students were not Marxist – Keith Thomas or Hugh Stretton, to take the two most eminent.

Moreover, the direction his undergraduate students found did not have to be academic, and he was willing to see students fail. He could be wry about them, as many academics are when off duty. For Shiela Grant Duff he recalled the embarrassment of being asked by one earnest but not particularly gifted student how she might get a first: 'we both came through it with credit and she will get a reasonable second god help us'. He also apologised to Shiela that he had to attend an admissions exam-ination, not least 'because the man to be examined is an evil man being an Etonian and ought to be kept out of the college if possible or at least let in only under protest'.[15] In reality though, he was a highly conscientious tutor who took his academic responsibilities seriously. At one point in the late 1940s, house-bound and unable to meet or talk to his students due to illness, he apologised to Edmund Dell: 'So sorry you aren't getting your money's worth out of me.'[16]

Certainly his professional gallows humour did not reflect any lack of pastoral concern or personal encouragement. Raphael Samuel, a brilliant but wayward student, enjoyed honest but firm support from Hill while at Balliol and in his subsequent pursuit of an academic job. The help he gave Samuel in a personal crisis in the early 1960s moved Samuel's mother to write to Hill:

Had Raphael not felt able to turn to you for help when he was quite desperate, I shudder to think what may have happened. And when, after you had gone to so much trouble to help him he suddenly threw everything up, you could so easily have washed your hands of him, but again you were incredibly kind and deeply human and understanding about the situation.

As Samuel himself put it, 'there is only one person as fine and good', 'Christopher Hill saved my life!'[17]

This pastoral concern was not dependent on political fellowship either. The eminent military historian John Keegan, who was at Balliol in the mid-1950s, remembered Hill 'as a tutor of unusual kindness who extended unaffected friendship to those he taught. Christopher was genuinely loved by the history undergraduates, whatever their political outlook, which he never attempted to influence.' As a Roman Catholic with sceptical views about politics, Keegan was a case in point: 'I got nothing but affection and encouragement from Christopher.' When a serious childhood illness (orthopaedic tuberculosis) recurred, it was Hill who took Keegan to the college doctor and escorted him to hospital; and when he returned to college after a year, Christopher and Bridget made him welcome at their house. 'Unbeliever he may have been, but there was something Christian about the way he lived his life.'[18] James Douglas-Hamilton, later Lord Selkirk, QC, and a Scottish MSP, was president of the Conservative Association while at Balliol in the early 1960s. He recalled that all the Balliol historians in his time respected Hill's scholarship, 'admired his professionalism and … liked him as a man'. Divided by politics, he and Hill were 'united in our support for Balliol and the pursuit of educational excellence'.[19]

Keen remembered 'the infinite trouble that he was prepared to take for people in difficulties' and his capacity to 'stand apart, when dealing with people, from all his own prejudices'. This human concern is what really lay behind Hill's informality of manner and what was communicated by it – a concern with the essence of human interaction, perhaps, rather than its forms. As Stretton put it, 'Hill seemed to be a man for all seasons, a helpful human without any barriers whatever'.[20]

These were non-partisan academic values and standards, the conventions of Oxford academic life, and commitment to them was a feature of Hill's professional conduct more generally: 'whether in College meeting, or when one was examining candidates for entrance, or when this or that problem arose in the faculty, [Hill] seemed always to be completely independent, firm, and fair'.[21] He had an essential respect for Balliol men, whatever their political views; a consciousness of the traditions and the people who carried them. This came across in his appreciations of major college figures, like the history tutor A.B. Rodger and, of course, Lindsay.[22]

His informality of manner and approachability were reflected in the parties remembered by so many of his pupils. Once a week Hill had an open house for his students in his room. There was no need to answer an invitation, 'we simply knew that Christopher and Bridget, a barrel of beer, and a large number of people would be in his college room'. It was an opportunity to meet other students, including female students from other colleges – a 'radical and popular move'. Hill, 'smiling quizzically, would spar verbally with his fellow historians … greatly entertaining the students who were encouraged to join the banter'. Critically, though, this was an opportunity to meet tutors informally, and it ensured that students 'did not think of this tutor at any rate as someone on the other side of a barrier of status. No other tutor, then or since, has ever done anything like it', thought Keen. There was, however, one odd status distinction – only third-year students could drink from pint glasses, those in earlier years had to use half pints. It was not a limit on how much they could drink overall, only of the vessel they drank from.[23] Nonetheless, despite all this evidence of warmth, concern and engagement with his students, everyone who knew Hill commented on his shyness and reserve. Mehta was not the only one to note his habitual nervous sniff, and Alex Callinicos found him 'sphinx-like'.[24] There was always a part of Hill held in reserve – the product both of personal temperament and political caution.

It hardly needs to be said that this intellectual culture was very different from that of the CPGB, some of whose leaders regarded such radical individualism with deep suspicion, and not without reason: as Lindsay noted, it had aristocratic origins, associated with the leisure of a moneyed class. Nonetheless, this ethos was critical to Hill's formation. It had been in this environment that he thought about the crisis of bourgeois culture during the 1930s and had reacted against the hyper-intellectualism of All Souls. In a way that is hard to understand for those outside the collegiate world, Hill was a Balliol man – a term used very freely, but in this way very apt for Hill. It shaped how he came of age: to write academically acceptable Marxist history, the stated ambition of the Moscow narrator, really meant writing it in this atmosphere, and in this spirit.

҂

In 1954 the secret service recorded a hostile opinion that Hill depended on the party for his profile, and that he could not officially drop the party even if he had wanted to. This was exaggerated, but not entirely groundless.[25] *The English Revolution* and *The Good Old Cause* had laid out the general case and were to prove very influential in the teaching of the period. Hill had also continued to build his academic profile through regular book reviewing: alongside reviews for *Science and Society* and *Oxford Left* were numerous reviews for the *English Historical Review* as well as for other leading academic journals such as *Economic History Review*, *History* and *Sociological Review*.[26] He reviewed for the *Daily Worker* and made a brief contribution to a discussion in *Science and Society* of Paul Sweezy's account of the absolutist state, defending the line that had been developed in the Historians' Group.[27] He continued to build a public profile beyond the party too. Following the success of his broadcast talk on the Barebones Parliament in 1953, he appeared on the Third Programme again, speaking alongside Trevor-Roper, C.V. Wedgwood and D.H. Pennington in a discussion of the causes of the English Civil War, and giving a short talk of his own on James Harrington's political treatise *The Commonwealth of Oceana*.[28] He marked the tercentenary of the restoration of Charles II in 1660 in both the *Guardian* and the *New Left Review*.[29] By the mid-1950s though, he had not published a really substantial research monograph.

From around the time of the foundation of *Past and Present* he had been publishing more often in mainstream academic journals and in a more conventional academic idiom. Editorial notes appeared in *Past and Present* with greater frequency from 1960 onwards, as the journal proclaimed its reforming role more confidently, and Hill appeared regularly as a rapporteur on emerging historiographical developments. In 1956 he wrote an article on recent interpretations of the English Civil War for *History*, a mainstream academic journal. It was a contribution to the key debate of the period, which developed into the academically notorious 'storm over the gentry'. (The argument, broadly, was whether the civil war had been caused by gentlemen whose fortunes were failing, who resorted to political radicalism to protect themselves, or by gentlemen whose fortunes were rising, and wanted a political influence to match; and whether the evidence for either position stacked up.) Hill in fact denounced the whole controversy as naively determinist – reading off the politics of individuals from their own material interests, as if the ideas were, in Marxist jargon, simply epiphenomenal. His own views would have been familiar to readers of his earlier articles; what was new here was the way he explicitly positioned them against the dominant lines of academic argument.[30]

The real breakthrough in his academic publishing profile came the same year, as the party crisis was looming, with the publication of *Economic Problems of the Church*. It was an attempt to work out in detail the role of religion in the revolution, and 'by implication' the link between Protestantism and capitalism. Rather than the simplifications of the gentry debate, he offered a view of the economic and political context in which hostility towards the bishops drove political radicalisation: 'There might be many reasons, over and above the purely religious, why men should wish to overthrow the ecclesiastical hierarchy in 1640.'[31]

These various grievances reflected the many political and judicial functions of the church, but Hill's focus was on how the church was financed, tracing the complex changes in the income and fees that it could collect in the aftermath of the Reformation. Church lands had been sold off, and with them rights to fees and patronage, including appointments to church livings. This tended to favour lay interests: those buying church lands were also buying a role in the government of the church. Reformation thought tended to increase the demands placed on the clergy, which they were less and less able to meet as their income and influence was eroded by these land sales and the associated loss of control over patronage. At the same time, religious reformers among the laity who bought up lands could use the associated powers to promote puritan views, sometimes in opposition to the ecclesiastical establishment. Behind that lay the rise of capitalist attitudes to the resources freed up by the spoliation of the church – the new owners made better profits than the more traditional and paternal ecclesiastical hierarchy – producing a confluence of pressures behind the puritan cause. Church and crown responded by trying to re-endow the church, to reassert its rights and to reaffirm the special role of the clergy in religious life. It is a densely argued book, and the only work in which Hill paid close attention to local government and administration, drawing generously on the DPhil thesis and advice of Miss D.M. Barratt, which threw light on these local realities.[32] Hill's arguments in these areas stimulated a lot of work in the next generation on the institutional structures and economic interests of the church, and how that affected its religious mission.

At its core, though, *Economic Problems of the Church* was an engagement with Tawney and Weber on the links between Protestantism and capitalism. Hill's argument is grounded not in the psychology of particular individuals but in the life of an institution, the sources of opposition to it, and the political implications of that opposition. In the conclusion Hill suggested that historians who do not make those connections are shaped by a modern 'departmentalisation' of thinking that separates economics, politics, science and religion in ways that seventeenth-century people did not.[33]

Equally importantly, Hill rejected the idealism of the 'Puritan revolution'. For him, to understand the appeal and triumph of puritan ideas it is necessary to understand the environment in which they were working: 'the way a man thinks about religion', he wrote, 'cannot be separated from his religious or philosophical beliefs, his relations with his wife and family, the way he earns his living'. Puritanism embraced nobler ideals than simply capitalism, but its triumph was unthinkable without a bourgeoisie: 'In the history of ideas … environment is more important than heredity.' But he also opposed what he saw as the reductivism of Trevor-Roper and others in the gentry controversy – that ideas can *simply* be mapped onto rising or falling economic fortunes, or degrees of access to the spoils of government office. This was the 'more modern heresy' that such factors 'sufficiently' explain the English Revolution (that is, without having to consider religious ideas in detail or with sympathy).[34]

Another publication of abiding importance from this period was Hill's article on the 'Norman Yoke' for Dona Torr's festschrift, the topic on which he had spoken in Moscow. There was, he wrote, a long history of popular belief in the possibility of restoring lost liberties; myths of a lost golden age long persisted, as did the hope that through political struggle those rights could be recovered. English people had long remembered the Anglo-Saxon freedoms which had been extinguished by the Norman Conquest, when the 'Norman Yoke' had been put on the backs of a people who had previously been free. Hill traced how this had been interpreted and reinterpreted from the sixteenth to the nineteenth centuries, but with a particular interest in the way it was connected to a veneration of the common law by seventeenth-century thinkers, chief among them Edward Coke. That tradition saw the common law as prior to the Norman Yoke, and superior to it; royal prerogatives and other powers impinging on the law were later impositions on a native freedom. The article is not notably Marxist, however, even though Anthony Crosland noted in the *TLS* how an otherwise unexceptionable piece of historical work had been slightly 'marred' by the addition of an ideological envoi.[35] The essay in fact belongs much more with Hill's interest in struggle and a native radical tradition than with the attempt to connect Dobb's analysis of changing modes of production to the history of constitutional development in England; it is in that sense related to a nativist socialist tradition that is more eclectic than formal Marxism, more A.L. Morton than Maurice Dobb, we might say.[36]

Other work reflected the literary sensibility of Hill's youth and his interest in the struggles of individuals to make sense of their world. An essay on Clarissa Harlowe, for example, explored the interaction of ideas and their environment in Samuel Richardson's novel of 1748. Her story reflected the tensions between marriage as a political and economic strategy and as the expression of individual choice and desire. Commentators in later eighteenth-century France drew radical implications from the book which Richardson himself seems not to have perceived. He was clearly unconvinced by the virtues of aristocratic values in relation to marriage (politics, family and lineage), but he was not able to embrace bourgeois freedom (choice and desire): Richardson's was another divided heart.[37]

This biographical approach lent itself to publication aimed at a wider audience too, and studies by Hill of Roger Crab, 'the mad hatter', and John Mason, otherwise very obscure figures, appeared in *History Today*, a large circulation magazine for history teachers and enthusiasts. He followed Crab through civil war service to life as a vegan hermit who had been condemned to death by Cromwell before becoming a quaker and giving up on politics. Drawing on traditions of Christian ascetism, Crab was willing now to wait for the transformation of the world. John Mason, a more educated figure, had an MA from Cambridge and a benefice in Buckinghamshire. Largely orthodox until 1690, he became convinced that Christ would raise his standard at Water Stratford in Buckinghamshire at the end of the world in 1694. He attracted followers there, who engaged in 'antick' dancing and music among other things. When he survived past 1694 he came to believe that the world had indeed ended, but without anyone noticing. Hill's interest was in how millenarian beliefs like this had ceased to be a social threat. What had been terrifying to elites for more than a century was now an amusement and a commercial opportunity. 'The Royal Society had done its work. The age of reason had arrived. The age of revolutionary Puritanism, with its heroes, its passions, its eccentricities, was over.' When the lower classes raised the spectre of revolution again a century later, it was in a secular mode, not a millenarian Christian one. 'So the end of the world ended with John Mason – not with a bang, not even with a whimper, but with a sympathetic clinical analysis.'[38]

Again, this is a quite different expression of Hill's Marxism than his work on the causes and consequences of the English Revolution, in fact perhaps not obviously Marxist at all, although clearly engaged with long-term change in politics and mentality. He was here concerned with the birth of new ideas and individual experience: how people made sense of a changing world and the contradictions that created, as opposed to the analysis of the relationship between economic forces and constitutional change.

By the time Hill left the party, aged forty-five, he had gone some way to cementing his academic reputation. There followed a period of extraordinarily fruitful publication which would eventually help to win him one of the most prestigious academic posts in the country at the time: the Mastership of Balliol College. Some have wanted to see his resignation from the CPGB as the liberation that allowed this. Others who knew him well, like Rodney Hilton, did not see such a straightforward causal connection, not least because in later life Hill so generously acknowledged the stimulus of the Historians' Group. Neither had his political work ever been forced.[39] In any case, much of the writing of *Economic Problems* was complete after a sabbatical in 1951, and the book had appeared in 1956.[40] He had been building his conventional academic profile since 1952; certainly before he left the party.

A more plausible explanation seems to lie in the support he enjoyed from Bridget, who organised his domestic life, creating the conditions for his prolific subsequent publishing career. *Society and Puritanism*, published in 1964, carries the dedication 'for Bridget, but for whom …'. This is not to suggest that their marriage was anything but a partnership: Bridget was herself making a career, becoming treasurer at St Hilda's in 1960 and a Fellow in 1961. Her working life was interrupted by child-rearing, as well as by supporting Hill during his tenure as Master of Balliol, but she was a dedicated and assiduous tutor, even if her own publishing career was largely deferred until retirement. Sheila Rowbotham, a student at St Hilda's who had a less than successful first year, remembered Bridget as a powerful and effective advocate on her behalf. 'It is remarkable how Bridget', Rowbotham recalled, 'then a working mother with many interests, found time to relate to individual students.'[41] From Hill's perspective, though, it was a much more settled domestic regime than he had enjoyed with Inez, and it allowed him an academic flourishing.

Puritanism and Revolution, published in 1958, offered perspectives on the relationship that had been at the heart of much of his work up to that time. There was no interpretive essay about the revolution, and none of his essays on Marxism and Marxist thinkers from *Modern Quarterly* or other partisan journals were included. Two new essays were added, one of them based on his broadcast on James Harrington for the Third Programme. Five were thematic essays and nine considered the thought of particular individuals, offering a variety of windows onto the connections between puritanism and politics, including in the period when puritanism had lost its political charge.[42]

Puritanism and Revolution collected essays that threw light on the subtle relationship between ideas and context but without any underlying model, except a Marxist history that is interested in connection and totality, not 'departmentalisation'. This approach was the preference of most of those involved in the Historians' Group, who all avoided programmatic statements of Marxist theory or model-building in favour of exercises in substantive historical writing. In a later interview Hill said that a party member had told him she found *The English Revolution* hard to follow because of its technical language. After that he avoided Marxist jargon: 'it was no bloody good being technically right in our Marxist jargon if nobody was going to read us. The important thing was to communicate.'[43] He had also been alarmed by Tawney's reaction to *Lenin and the Russian Revolution*: 'Hill is good, but I wish he wouldn't sing the doxology at the end of every chapter.' If Tawney found it off-putting, 'what must others think?', he wondered.[44] Hobsbawm thought that 'Marx's statements about history were of more value to historians than his statements about society in general, and that Marxist history in its most fruitful versions uses Marx's methods rather than commenting on its texts.'[45] That certainly fits for Hill: *Puritanism and Revolution* demonstrated the power of Marx's methods in understanding the complex relations between puritan ideas and their economic, social and political environment; it did not apply a ready-made analysis of the relationship between puritanism, the transition from feudalism to capitalism, and the English Revolution.

Given this approach, it is not surprising that so much of Hill's work took a biographical form. In *Economic Problems* he had characterised determinism partly as the view that 'the ideas and aspirations of a Cromwell or a Milton are to be seen as no more than epiphenomena of economic decline (or rise)'.[46] He was eventually to write book length studies of both, but the roots of those later books can clearly be seen in his writing in the late 1950s. He also published an Historical Association pamphlet on Cromwell to mark the tercentenary of his death; a mark of his standing was that it was discussed in the *Listener*.[47]

⁂

The really key publication of the early 1960s, however, was in fact highly schematic: *The Century of Revolution*. Hill's target during the 1930s and after had been 'textbook accounts' of the seventeenth century, which rested on Gardiner's interpretation. Here was his answer: a textbook taking account of modern research and trying to treat the interaction of ideas and environment in a more sophisticated way.

Hill divided the century into four chronological phases. For each, he offered a short narrative of events followed by analytic chapters on economics, 'politics and the constitution', and 'religion and ideas', before a conclusion to each chapter and an epilogue to the whole book. This splitting of the subject was an attempt to capture a complex and interlocking whole: 'The transformation that took place in the seventeenth century is … far more than merely a constitutional or political revolution, or a revolution in economics, religion, or taste. It embraces the whole of life.' Out of this complex intellectual and political crisis came progressive ideas – across the century as a whole, progressive social forces had underpinned the triumph of such ideas. The freedoms that won out were bourgeois freedoms, those that favoured the increasingly dominant social class, but they were not fully democratic. In fact the bourgeoisie had closed ranks against democratic claims in 1649, 1660 and thereafter. Those limits on freedom, Hill implied, should be the focus for progressive change now: freedoms had been won, but 'Freedom is not something abstract. It is the right of certain men to do certain things.' The seventeenth-century settlements that had set limits on who enjoyed what freedoms were now ripe for challenge.[48]

This structure contrasted with 'The English Revolution, 1640', which had started with economic change and only then discussed political conflict. Despite Hill's methodological statements, the effect on the reader of that earlier book is to ground political conflict fairly directly on the working out of clashing economic interests and their associated worldviews. In some ways the difference is one of focus: in *Century of Revolution* Hill was capturing a century of social, economic, political and intellectual change, not making the case that England had a bourgeois revolution. That gave the book a different structure, and perhaps also allowed freer play to his methodological hostility to economic determinism. Although the focus was narrowly on England, Hill was keen to make connections with a wider European history and historiography, resisting English exceptionalism and placing English experience in the context of the European Reformation and European capitalism.[49] A number of commentators have seen here a move away from economist Marxism towards a freer engagement with the left, but many of the preoccupations and examples were familiar from the 1930s, from his notes and the Cardiff and Balliol lectures, for example the commendation of Eliot's view of the metaphysical poets, comments about Halifax and Baxter and remarks on censorship and freedom.

The result was a very successful teaching book. It was used in A-level teaching through to the 1980s – particularly after the paperback publication in 1969, which made it, for example, the 'unofficial textbook' of Michael Roberts's sixth-form[50] – and a new edition published in 1979 was an Open University set text.

As was often the case with Hill's work, the book's conclusion marked the beginning of another subject as much as the summation of the current one. The final pages of part four note how recorded history reveals the tip of an iceberg consisting of the now-anonymous and unrecorded lives of ordinary people: 'let us also remember how much of the lives of how many men and women is utterly unknown to us'.[51] An essay from around this time was a first effort to remedy this defect, exploring how the fear of the lower classes shaped the political attitudes of elites.[52]

At the same time, Hill had edited and prepared for the posthumous publication H.N. Brailsford's study of the Levellers. Brailsford was a prominent journalist and man of the left, neither a communist nor a Marxist but rather a 'devoted worker for women's suffrage, for the emancipation of Balkan, Irish and Indian peoples, the steadfast advocate of internationalism and socialism'. Hill's affirmation therefore sealed an association with a broad left beyond the CPGB, making a case for the progressive potential of such an alliance. 'One can see why Brailsford devoted to the Levellers the last year of his dedicated life', wrote Hill in the introduction to the book. 'He thought of this book not as a mere history, but as a profoundly political study, which would convey a message from him to the younger generation.' It too attracted attention so that Hill's name was in all the main literary pages, often alongside reviews of *Century of Revolution*.[53]

Hill's star was clearly in the ascendant in the early 1960s and, as he featured across all the literary pages in the summer of 1961, news of another major career break came: the invitation to deliver the Ford Lectures.[54] This is an annual series of lectures at the University of Oxford which gives leading historians the opportunity to make a major statement about their subject; the lectures are normally published soon after they are delivered. How Hill used that opportunity says more about the future direction of his interests than *Century of Revolution*. The theme was the role of ideas in prompting the English Revolution. Class analysis was less visible than his interest in how innovative thought arose from outside established political and professional institutions, offering challenges to intellectual orthodoxy as well as to the cultural hegemony of those institutions: it was more Gramscian, with its interest in challenges to hegemony, than the Marx of Dobb and *Capital*.

A central theme of the lectures was science – natural, social and political. Many people found the claims of science during the 1950s and early 1960s bewitching. On the one hand, *Past and Present* had originally been a journal of scientific history: the claims of 'modern' historiography went alongside claims to scientific rigour. On the other hand, the progressive possibility of science led to academic study of science as a system of thought: many scholars in the humanities were interested in its logic and origins. Hill had thought it a serious omission that the proposed board members for *Marxist Quarterly* in 1954 had not included a natural scientist.[55] This was a two-way street, and some leading scientists had become interested in the social, cultural and political history of science, treating its development not simply as the progressive discovery of more and more truths but as a system of thought to be understood in social, political and cultural context. Fellow party member and eminent scientist J.D. Bernal was one influential example, as was Joseph Needham, the famous historian of science, whose first publication in the 1940s had been about the Levellers. Stephen Mason, Bridget's first husband, was another.[56]

The cultural claims of 'science' could be seen everywhere in mid-century Britain. As Ernest Marples, the minister of transport, said in his speech at the opening of the M1 in November 1959, the new road was 'in keeping with the bold, exciting and scientific age in which we life'. My father shared this view, recalling the feeling when he first drove on it that he had encountered the future. Hill's collaborator on *The Good Old Cause*, Edmund Dell, now a centrist Labour politician, was soon to become parliamentary secretary at the newly established ministry of technology in the Wilson government – Wilson of course having promised to harness the white heat of technology to improve society. To some extent this took advantage of the unifying faith in science and technology as a way of healing the rifts on the left caused by Gaitskell's efforts during the 1950s to ditch Labour's formal commitment to state ownership as a route to socialism.[57] It had also been an important current in Soviet thinking during the 1950s and early 1960s – the belief that the new socialist state built on reason would eventually vanquish religious beliefs.[58]

J.G. Crowther's book on Francis Bacon (1561–1626), which Hill reviewed for the *Listener*, captures something of the mood in academic circles. Crowther's argument was essentially that Bacon had been both a courtier and a scientist, and that he had tried to gain court sponsorship for his vision of social improvement through the systematic application of the scientific method. For Hill, the lesson of Crowther's book was that

> Bacon was not 'primarily concerned in making scientific discoveries, but with the organization and utilization of science, and its proper integration in the rest of human life'. He wanted an advance on the whole front, a total planning of science, including the sciences of history, politics, and ethics.

For Bacon, according to this 'tract for the times', 'the matter in hand is no mere felicity in speculation but the real business and fortunes of the human race'. His failure, and the subsequent divergence of natural science and practical politics, posed a problem for the modern world: 'If scientists do not turn statesmen, the politicians may destroy the world.'[59]

Despite fears of what it might destroy, and the strength of disarmament movements in western Europe, for many of this generation modern science was the progressive idea par excellence. It had been an abiding interest of Hill's too. The rise of natural, social and political science had featured in his lectures at Cardiff – framing how in the seventeenth century understandings of the world had shifted so dramatically. The loosening grip of the church had created the space for Hobbes's political science, and from that, eventually, had flowed Marxist political science.[60] Hill's brief article on John Mason had attributed the loss of the political charge of millenarianism to the rise of the Royal Society – it became a matter of intellectual curiosity where once it had been an apocalyptic belief about the end of times. In the early 1960s he was involved in debate about the relationship between science, religion and economic change in seventeenth-century England in, appropriately enough, *Past and Present*.[61]

However, there was more to his Ford Lectures than excitement about the application of reason to social improvement. Hill was in effect emphasising the role of ideas in the origins of the revolution, taking that interest beyond simply the ideas and practice of puritanism. The resulting book, the *Intellectual Origins of the English Revolution*, made a big impact.

It is a difficult book to summarise, making easy reference to thinkers and currents of thought of the most diverse kinds, and pan-European in its scope. In essence though, Hill was addressing the assumption that the English Revolution had no intellectual causes. The comparison with the French Revolution now being accepted (so he claimed), it was reasonable to look for the English equivalents of Voltaire, Rousseau, Montesquieu and Diderot, something English historians so far had been reluctant to do. The origins of the revolution were not simply religious: he looked for them in new views of science (primarily through the thought of Francis Bacon), history (in Walter Raleigh) and law (Edward Coke). Baconian science dethroned precedent and authority, prioritising reason and evidence: the world was to be understood not by interpreting ancient texts but by testing hypotheses against observation. The text-swapping that had been the basis of political science had been disposed of by Hobbes; Bacon had done the same for natural science and its application to social improvement in the previous generation. Raleigh accepted that God was the first cause of historical developments, but concentrated on secondary causes, and in so doing demonstrated the radical potential of historical study, undermining the easy patriotism of his Elizabethan predecessors.

There was a ferment of ideas but the successful ones acquired their force from particular social and political conditions. 'Ideas do not advance merely by their own logic', Hill wrote. He did not explain this in simple class terms, however. Rather, he saw a failure of nerve and creative power among established intellectuals, with the advances being made from the margins, among those denied preferment or who were casualties of court politics. Controversially, he made a case that scientific advance came from outside the ancient universities, driven by men who took technical skills seriously and who learned through providing 'adult education'. The key institutions were Gresham College in London and the Royal College of Physicians; their rivals were institutions enjoying royal privilege and protection. Innovative thinking ran up against royal power in numerous ways.

Overall, Hill aimed a blow at economic determinism by showing how ideas had fuelled a revolution: echoing Orwell's hostile review of 'The English Revolution, 1640', he wrote 'Most men have to believe quite strongly in some ideal before they will kill or be killed.' He managed to pursue a coherent thread through these thickets of complicated and often unfamiliar ideas, acknowledging the much longer heritage of many, and also the complexity of their interaction: 'wisdom lies', he wrote, 'in recognizing the complicated interconnexions and not allowing ourselves to be unduly influenced by the categories of analysis which we invent for our own convenience'.[62]

Hill's interest in radical ideas seemed to strike a powerful chord. T.S. Gregory, who had inspired Hill with his lectures to the York Methodists in the 1920s, and to whom *Intellectual Origins* was later dedicated, was by the early 1960s a producer at the BBC, and it may have been thanks to his influence that versions of Hill's lectures were broadcast on the Third Programme. In 1962 the *Listener* carried a serialisation, and they became a point of reference when discussing the work of other historians. In a wholly enviable way, Hill's academic interests intersected with his life as a public intellectual.[63] The following year the *Listener* carried a long piece on the politics of John Milton,[64] and in January 1963 Goldsmith's College hosted two lectures by Hill for paying customers on a Saturday afternoon and early evening on the themes 'What was puritanism?' and 'Puritanism and politics'.[65]

In 1964, before the publication of the Ford Lectures, Hill had published a companion book to *Economic Problems of the Church*, on *Society and Puritanism*, which took a sociological approach to puritanism with a familiar core emphasis: that 'religion' was not a free-floating social phenomenon that worked its effects due simply to the content of the thought, but something to be understood through its interactions with social structures. Again he apologised for the book's English focus, which was not intended to suggest that the English experience was not part of a wider European Reformation. The book covered aspects of religious practice – the importance of preaching and the practice of endowing lectureships for that purpose – but also the exercise of power by and against puritans, in discipline over the poor or persecution by the courts of the established church. It also considered how the impact of puritanism contributed to a transformation of the parish from a spiritual community into a unit of secular administration, and how spiritual individualism was expressed too in the 'spiritualisation of the household'.[66] Two related essays published around this time also explored puritanism in that non-theological context: in the 'dark corners' of the land, the propagation of the gospel amounted to a programme of social improvement as well as an attempt to save souls.[67] This is really a very broad vision of puritanism as a movement, going far beyond the outworkings of Luther's theological objections to medieval Christianity, and developing into an ambitious sociology of religion intent on making connections between ideas and the environment in which they operated in practice.

In May 1964, Gregory wrote to Hill asking who might review his books for the Third Programme, while ruling out Trevor-Roper. The answer, it seems, was Veronica Wedgwood, one of the most prominent public historians of her generation, and the result was an entire programme devoted to discussion of Hill's views of the English Revolution.[68]

Hill had arrived as an influential public writer, publicising perspectives on particular issues that derived from a broadly Marxist analysis. He was not perhaps reaching the 'drawn faces on street corners' that had haunted his imagination in the 1930s, but through the pages of the *Listener* he was introducing a wide reading public to an academically respectable if not universally accepted Marxist analysis. The literary pages of the main broadsheets and influential magazines routinely carried reviews of his work. Here was what, on his return to England, Hill's Moscow narrator had thought he could do. By 1965 Hill was perhaps the major figure in the field, described as 'the leading historian of seventeenth-century England' in the advertisement for Wedgwood's 1965 radio programme.[69]

He was also by now a prolific reviewer, particularly for the leading English journals (*English Historical Review*, *Economic History Review* and *Past and Present*) but also *Science and Society*, and he clearly had contacts at the *Welsh History Review* and in Durham too. Between them there are at least forty-eight reviews between 1958 and 1965, one every other month.[70] On top of this, there was an even more prolific output for a general readership. From 1956 onwards Hill was a regular correspondent for the *Spectator*, perhaps as a result of his connection with the owner and editor, Ian Gilmour, a former student.[71] Between November 1956 and September 1962 he published 110 *Spectator* reviews. Following this, he switched to the *New Statesman*, where his output was only slightly more modest: twenty reviews between May 1963 and September 1965. In just seven years, Hill published around 170 reviews: around two per month, sustained over a long period. They reveal a consistent range of academic interests and a generally open-minded reviewing style: he was rarely guilty of accusing the author of not having written the book that he, Hill, would have written, even if he did often draw from the book the material that was most interesting to someone with Hill's outlook.

Criticism of Hill's work has often amounted to a rejection of his Marxism, but there has also been a more technical objection to his working methods, the limitations of which were being pointed out as his star was rising. His working papers reveal eclectic reading but also selective note-taking. In the very earliest notebooks, he records the arguments of some key books – for example Angell on capitalist states and international relations – although even at that point there is no real sign of his reaction to the arguments. As time went on his notes became much more sparse and restricted to particular details. To take a more or less random example, one book contains notes on Hobbes's *Behemoth*: there is no summary of what he thinks Hobbes is really arguing, simply two notes, one from page 259 and one from pages 759–60. The notebooks are really a series of notecards in book form. Another one has eleven notes from *Calendar of State Papers* volume covering 1636–7 (a 500-page volume). Around 1960 the numbering of the notebooks switches from Roman to Arabic, and by the mid-1970s he was writing in biro, but there is little else to be gleaned about his personal tastes from them. His research files are similar – slips of paper with particular facts or sources, or quotations relating to a particular topic or theme, are interspersed with occasional substantive correspondence on that topic, and with successive drafts of related talks and lectures. He treated the work of other historians in the same way, filleting books before selling them to Thornton's, the second-hand bookseller across the road from Balliol. The endpapers of his books were covered in scrawled 'references to the contents', a kind of index of key points, rather than a summary of the argument.[72]

This method allowed him to process a huge and diverse body of material – the enormous and genuine erudition on which many commented could be disciplined through this cross-referencing system, the key to which seems to have been carried in his head. It created the dizzying effect, evident in *Intellectual Origins*, of easy reference to a huge range of sixteenth- and seventeenth-century thinkers. But there is a risk in this way of working, too. The material could be decontextualised and its intended meaning lost. Later scholarship spent much energy on demonstrating that Hill escaped the complexity by imposing external categories of his own devising.

This problem was identified as early as 1961 by Jacob Viner, in response to Hill's contribution to a festschrift volume for R.H. Tawney.[73] Tawney had been a major intellectual influence on Hill, particularly in his approach to the relationship between puritanism and capitalism, and they shared connections in Fabian and LSE circles, including with Margaret James and Bridget. They had corresponded in fairly formal terms during the war, about the future of Russian education once the war was over, and Steven Lukes recalls Hill's admiration and fondness for Tawney, although they do not seem to have been personally close.[74]

To the festschrift Hill contributed one of his major statements on puritanism and capitalism. It is a subtle and nuanced essay, sensitive to the meanings of sixteenth- and seventeenth-century religious writings, and it is persuasive. He starts from the fundamental principle of the Reformation, that faith rather than good works was the route to salvation. From this he draws out a central implication: that it was the motive of an action rather than the action itself that mattered; the key to godly behaviour was faith, the prompting of the conscience to act in a godly way, rather than dutifully meeting demands of the church to do good works. Those acting in line with their consciences would of course do good works, but for the right reason, as a manifestation of their faith; the work did not in itself secure salvation but the faith that prompted it. The emphasis on the individual conscience as the only sure guide to salvation gave 'protestantism its fundamentally individualist bias', wrote Hill. He argued that this theology appealed to those 'whom it helped to trust the dictates of their own hearts as their standard of conduct'. In this case, Hill suggested, that meant artisans and small merchants. Here is where the imprint of his Marxism lay: in understanding the social contexts in which ideas for the structuring of society prosper. Although this theology was rooted in early Christianity and medieval heresies – 'there is nothing in protestantism which leads automatically to capitalism' – the appeal of Calvinism was socially slanted, just as 'that of Marxism has been limited to the urban working class in our own day'.[75]

Hill sent a copy of the essay to Viner, an eminent economist, and received a sharply critical response in return. Viner was a prominent critic of Keynes and a champion of the Chicago School of what became monetarism. He might therefore have been expected to believe in a timeless economic rationality rather than the impact of culturally variable values on economic behaviour (although he was at work on a book titled *Religious Thought and Economic Society*). His objection to Hill, however, was methodological, not political – that by lumping texts together he had lost sight of their real meaning. It is a stringent critique, pointing out that Hill offered no comparative evidence that the attitudes of lower-middle-class Calvinist businessmen differed from those of other religious groups, and expressing extreme scepticism about the 'proofs' of connection between distinct ethical views and particular business practices. This was partly a matter of technical discussion – what Calvin meant by 'merit', 'value' or 'worthiness', or the supposedly distinctive centrality of the idea of a 'calling' to Calvinism. But the central charge was methodological. If 'citing short passages' passed for historical argument, Viner wrote, 'I could "demonstrate" that all the leading religions taught the most extraordinary things in the field of social ethics'. He had learned, though, that checking 'apparently extraordinary propositions' almost always revealed that they 'had been wrenched violently from their contexts'. Back in context they 'ceased to be exciting or even interesting', or proved to be badly misinterpreted as a result of the translation of technical theological terms into modern usage, or had simply been misquoted or inaccurately paraphrased.[76]

Hill faced criticism of this kind throughout his career but was generally unrepentant. To his mind, he accumulated files of references relating to a particular subject, and wrote it up when he thought it might amount to something. His notetaking appears from this perspective like an extraction of data to which he then applied his ideas, as Kenneth Bell had promised to do for his Balliol undergraduates in the 1920s and 1930s. In *Intellectual Origins* he commended recent work which had 'revealed new facts which will transform our understanding even of political history when they have been assimilated', and he started his lecture on that subject by laying out 'some of the facts'.[77]

For Hill, here and elsewhere, facts acquired their meaning from an interpretive framework. The ideas he applied were those of Marx about the interrelationship of belief and its social context. He was dismissive of rival frameworks, such as Fisher's view that history was a stream of events which sometimes turned out well, or Toynbee's that the facts revealed the hopelessness of human action, leaving us to hope for God's mercy, which might be granted 'if we ask for it again in a humble spirit and with a contrite heart'.[78] Hill was shortly to launch a major attack on the historian Peter Laslett, author of *The World We Have Lost*, for what he saw as the lazy sentimentality of his interpretive framework.[79] To the objection that his own ideas were predetermined and that he got stuck in files he had started compiling long ago, he declared simply: 'I do not think I have. That is all I can say to you about that.' He thought his ideas were constantly challenged by what he read, and that discovering new things led him to change his mind, as did the work of other historians. He acknowledged that he had an overall thesis and that the evidence he collected was what related to the thesis, but many historians do that without ever examining their core thesis as Hill examined his. In any case, he believed of his own work that 'the thesis keeps changing … It has to.'[80]

The fact that Hill kept Viner's letter reflects another general point about his practice – that he was interested in alternative views and criticism. Although Hill would defend himself vigorously on essentials,

Briggs later observed that he could be 'disarmingly ready to admit lapses' of a more minor kind, while emphasising 'the provisional nature of all historical arguments'. Setting aside his broad commitment to Marxist analysis, what strikes many professional historians about Hill's practice was a 'passionate conviction that the historian should seek to connect up as many aspects of the past as possible, and must be free to speculate about links even when they could not be proved'. This led him to take intellectual risks – 'it seems unlikely that he ever chose the prudent course in preference to the bold one' – but also laid him open to the charge of lumping.[81]

Hill's stylistic preference for avoiding the use of Marxist terms of analysis, coupled with a suspicion of theoretical discussion, means that it is hard to trace the development of his Marxism. However, there are signs in his work in the late 1950s and 1960s of an interest in the ideas of Gramsci and the Marxist humanism that became a central element of New Left thinking. He had been interested in Gramsci during the crisis of British Stalinism in 1956 and 1957, and his work thereafter seems to bear that stamp.[82] The new ideas he traced in *Intellectual Origins* were located in particular social environments, but not in a class identity as such: we might think of it as concerned with the contribution of 'organic intellectuals', those outside the established institutions that perpetuate the hegemonic ideas of a given society. That book is criticised more often for associating progressive scientific ideas with parliamentarianism, and with London not Oxford, than for deriving them from class interest – an oblique recognition perhaps that the explanatory model was not quite the same as that in *The English Revolution*.

Yet it is striking how little associated Hill is with the New Left, even though his interests were moving (and were to move further) in the direction of the broader history of radicalism, both cultural and intellectual. Rather, leaving the CPGB had revealed the Oxford historian in him. Having left first Methodism and then the party, it is easy to see how his temperamental intellectual individualism, and commitment to an Oxford model of scholarly practice, led him to plough a more independent furrow. It was rooted in a democratic view that we should all be able to do that, to be ourselves; and it shaped his tutorial teaching. But he also had a strong social ethic, a desire to be of use in the world, and an aversion to self-indulgence. To the extent that he perhaps also needed a congregation as a focus of belonging, purpose and loyalty, it seems that that need was now met to a significant degree, if not entirely, by his teaching at Balliol and by the collegiate ideal.

By the time his Ford Lectures were published in 1965, Hill was both a public intellectual and a senior figure in Oxford. That year also saw his election as Master of Balliol College, a consummation of his academic work and a testament to his academic standing.

7

Master of Balliol and Modernisation in British Universities: 1965–69

> *It [is] high time that Oxford took stock of itself. We are going to face, perhaps for the first time, fierce competition from other Universities with an outlook more aggressively modern than ours, and offering facilities with which, at the moment, we do not compete ... The next few years are likely to be an exciting period of change. I hope and believe that Balliol will continue to give a lead in the process of fitting Oxford for the modern world.*
>
> Hill, *Balliol Annual Record, 1966*

The election of a new Master of Balliol was 'supposedly secret',[1] but in Oxford, as the saying goes, 'a secret is a thing you tell one person at a time'. Gossip about the election circulated quite freely in the national press and, where verifiable, it seems to have been well informed.

It was widely assumed by outsiders that Hill's Marxism would be a problem: 'Everyone felt that Christopher was a marvellous man', said Atticus in the *Sunday Times*, 'but, well, his Marxist bent would inevitably disbar him from anything as orthodox as a Mastership, even a Balliol Mastership.'[2] This was not quite right: within the college his political commitments (and his divorce) were not the issue. There was no simple political division in the college, nor a corporate view, but opinion did tend to line up along roughly predictable lines over such issues as college admissions policy, elections to the Fellowship and other regular academic business. This was a matter of emphasis rather than principle, but tended to divide progressives and traditionalists. Everyone agreed that academic excellence was the pre-eminent concern, but after that people differed, for example, between being more committed to broadening participation or to recruiting talented people who would enrich college life in other ways. At stake in coping with change were often divergent views of the appropriate balance between tradition and innovation.[3] In a close election it was important that Hill was able to promise moderate change while reassuring the traditionalists.

The election was indeed close. His chief rival was R.P. Bell, a science tutor;[4] Russell Meiggs, another long-serving tutor, with a reputation as a larger-than-life college character, had also been mentioned as a potential candidate.[5] In the months before the election the papers named others including Roger Mynors, who had been close to election in 1949. In May the *Telegraph* suggested that internal deadlock might lead the college to look outside, and the *Financial Times* reported in January 1965 that Isaiah Berlin was being touted, although both Berlin and the report discounted the possibility.[6] Robert Birley was also mentioned. Like Mynors he had been a candidate before, and by the 1960s was at Witwatersrand, in South Africa. As the election loomed, he was hosted in the college by the outgoing Master, David Keir, who was quoted in the national press as saying that the visit had nothing to do with the election; obviously this denial aroused further suspicion.[7]

According to Atticus, in the *Sunday Times*, by election day Bell's candidacy was waning and Birley's candidacy had split the opposition to Hill: those opposing Hill spent too much time criticising him and not enough promoting their own candidate. On the first round of voting Hill was short of a majority: twenty out of forty-two. In a second round he secured election with twenty-six votes.[8] Although the *Sunday Times* subsequently apologised to one of the Fellows for claiming to know how he had voted (it was a secret ballot so they could not have), it does seem that the paper gave an accurate account. Richard Cobb, a Fellow who had participated in the election, later confirmed it: in fact he was more interested in the source of the leaks than contesting the accuracy of the report.[9]

The election provoked 'some predictable outrage in the conservative press'.[10] The *Daily Mail* expressed shock that 'A former communist has been appointed to one of Britain's foremost academic posts – Master of Balliol, Oxford's top academic college.' Mr Hill, fifty-two, it noted, 'has written books on political history'.[11] On the whole, though, even the negative coverage was more nuanced. The *Telegraph* reported the news on the front page, mentioning Hill's membership of the Communist Party (and more accurately noting the reasons for his resignation), but giving much more prominence to his actual qualifications for the job. On the inside pages, however, it was more disapproving: the choice might show Balliol Fellows were 'living in a smug little world of [their] own illusions', the terms in which Hill had characterised party members in 1957.[12]

But there was plenty of positive press too. Both the *Guardian* and the *Financial Times* put the story on the front page, and on its inside pages it celebrated the election of 'a brilliant scholar and a Balliol man', 'an exciting historian [who] should be a magnet for new talent'.[13] The *Sunday Times* called him the country's most distinguished scholar of the seventeenth century, and reported that the 'brighter young historians and the undergraduates worship him'. For his part, Keir sought to downplay any controversy: 'Although I agree he is more to the Left politically than I am, I think we share a dedication to the college.'[14] Some Cold War hardliners in the college are said to have remained suspicious of Hill's politics, but his Balliol colleagues had recognised a capacity for pragmatic and consensual action, and the qualities of a Balliol man.[15]

The College memory of Hill's predecessor, David Keir, was 'somewhere between lukewarm and adverse'.[16] Although he had had an academic career prior to 1939, he had since devoted himself to administration and was not regarded in Balliol as a major intellect. He had been vice-chancellor of Queen's University, Belfast during the war and commanded respect, but insisted on a kind of formality that was not fondly recalled: the students nicknamed him the Silver King, a reference to his greying hair and ponderously regal bearing. His preoccupations seemed eccentric and oddly dated, and he was much impersonated by the students in unflattering ways.[17]

He also used the formal powers of the Master to intervene directly in the academic life of the college. In 1953, E.H. Carr, a very talented historian who would have brought lustre to an already glittering Fellowship, was put forward as a candidate. Keir refused to nominate him for more than a lectureship, a position of lower status that did not confer, for example, membership of Governing Body. This was because of Carr's Marxism and the fact that he was 'living in a state of adultery, albeit stable and respectable'. This kind of intervention, by a man not himself regarded as a particularly distinguished scholar, was widely resented; it was in fact 'the last occasion when the Master was able to obstruct the Fellows in a matter of any substance'.[18] Keir also made use of his right to nominate to two Commoner places (non-scholarship admissions to the college) at his sole discretion – something that by 1960 was causing a lot of ill feeling.[19] He had been judgemental about Hill's divorce too, something Hill saw as 'a symptom of narrow-minded repression and an excessive reverence for outward forms with which he fundamentally disagreed'.[20]

Although Hill's election was not a simple reaction to frustrations with Keir, he was, in most ways, a contrast with his predecessor, cooperating with the forces of change and in particular in a diminution of the role of the Master. A Balliol man as well as a man of the left, his personal manner was informal and unlike most Oxford college heads. As the *Financial Times* put it, he was 'A shy, intensely informal man, ... likely to cut an unusual figure in the Master's Lodge', while the *Sunday Times* noted that 'his parties tend to be proletarian beer and cider thrashes'.[21] During Keir's tenure, wearing academic gowns had been compulsory for dinner, Chapel and interviews with the Master or Dean. Dining in Hall, however, began to suffer competition from the Junior Common Room (JCR: the name for the undergraduates' organisation as well as an actual room), which was offering informal meals familiar to students at other universities.[22] Keir's was a world increasingly remote from the lives of new undergraduates.

In the period before he took up office, Hill's public statements signalled a change of tone, in one case in direct contradiction to Keir. In 1965, the Oxford Union, prompted by its president Tariq Ali, decided to re-run the famous King and Country debate of 1933, debating whether members would fight for Queen and Country. This provoked outrage, including among some of the Union's trustees, two of whom resigned over the matter, and Ali received threatening letters purporting to come from the Ku Klux Klan. Keir, another trustee, voiced his outrage at the proposed debate: 'a most unhappy and disgraceful episode in the Union's history'.[23]

The most prominent counter-voice was Hill's. He had no formal position in relation to the Union, but he wrote to Ali defending the Union's right to hold the debate, recalling how in 1933 the Union had refused 'to be told by its elders what it ought to think and discuss'. He hoped the current generation would be equally independent-minded, having always thought that 'was one of the things one was supposed to acquire at University'.[24] This final point proved a red rag to one commentator in the *Telegraph*, who claimed that since Ali's views, in varying shades, were conventional among the young, voicing them was in fact an act of 'a positively slavish love of conformity'.[25] In the event the controversy was good for business: it was reported that 800 tickets had been taken several days before the debate leaving no space for visitors, and the BBC televised the debate.[26]

Less controversial but equally significant was Hill's support for the UK's first teach-in, to discuss American intervention in Vietnam. The event figured quite prominently in the press, making the front pages of several papers. The model – of lengthy academic debate on a controversial political issue – was seen as an interesting innovation, and largely welcomed. As the *Mail* put it: 'It is not an occasion on which people sit down, shout slogans or smash Embassy windows.'[27] A portion of the discussion was broadcast live on the Third Programme, which cleared its schedule in order to do so, although *The Times* subsequently reported rather wearily on the 'interminable' proceedings which stretched into the night.[28]

In the months before becoming Master, Hill gave public support to a variety of progressive causes: signing a declaration in December calling for a de-escalation of US policy in Vietnam;[29] serving as patron of a new organisation launched by Joseph Needham to promote Anglo-Chinese understanding, which replaced the Britain–China Friendship Association, an organisation associated with the Communist Party;[30] and signing a memorandum calling on Harold Wilson to implement the Wolfenden Committee report.[31] A motion to implement the report's findings had been defeated in parliament in 1960 and progress stalled. The renewed pressure in 1966 contributed to the successful legislation of 1967, the Sexual Offences Act, which legalised male homosexuality.

Hill was, however, also serious about Balliol and its community, and had this in common with people whose politics he did not share, including his predecessor. When Keir died, Hill wrote appreciatively about how he had gone 'out of his way to make my succession of him in the Mastership as easy as possible. He was invariably loyal and helpful, in public and in private.' He was to be equally supportive of his successor, Tony Kenny, a former Catholic priest whose instincts were sometimes very different from Hill's. Nonetheless, he welcomed the election of a man who, 'in the thirteen years since we elected him has become a personal friend and ally in many good causes'.[32]

This sense of corporate fellowship was echoed by Richard Southern in his appreciation of Hill at Hill's retirement. They had been undergraduates together in the 1930s, and tutors together in the 1950s. Southern was now president of St John's College and again a person with quite different instincts than Hill. Despite their very different principles, though, 'It would be hard to think of a more harmonious relationship; and it was harmonious because Christopher's wit is without rancour, and his doubtless deplorable principles betray no sign of dogmatism or intolerance for others, firm and fixed though they are for him.' In fact Southern remembered only two occasions on which they had been on different sides on a major college issue, and in one case he recognised that Hill had been right.[33] The collegiate ideal was powerfully important for these men, whatever their differences on other issues.

Hill inherited a strong financial position: under Keir the college had run a 700th anniversary appeal which by December 1963 had raised £700,000, then regarded as a staggering success, and eventually raised over £1,000,000.[34] That investment was critical in helping Balliol cope with the changes that were coming to Oxford, which had been outlined in the Report of the Franks Commission in 1965. That Commission was in turn a response to the Robbins Report of 1963, which had called for, among other things, an expansion of UK higher education both at undergraduate and postgraduate level, and an integrated higher education system in place of the existing conglomeration of largely autonomous institutions. It explicitly posed the question of the place of Oxford and Cambridge in that system, and in the ensuing debate Oxbridge often appeared old-fashioned, offering an outdated, gentlemanly education delivered by a self-perpetuating group. The specific challenges for Oxford were to define its place in the national system, to expand its scientific and technical education, to be open to the world and to show that it could make coherent plans for its future. This last point was particularly important: developing a university plan entailed coordination of the activities of autonomous colleges, each of which was self-governing. There was a profound suspicion, among the generation basking in the white heat of technology, that Oxford lacked the capacity to move with the times.[35]

Keir's final Master's Letter in the *Balliol Annual Record* expressed justified pride that the fundraising campaign had put the college in a position to begin to rise to these challenges, but also his profound suspicion of this new world. Funds had been raised for building works that would accommodate increased numbers of students, including greatly increased graduate numbers. He thought that 'the College has accepted new responsibilities; but also made certain that its response is its own and not one imposed on it.' This last point was fundamental: 'for otherwise the College life which lies at the heart of Oxford life risks becoming engulfed in the tidal wave which has swept over universities all over the world'.[36]

The tone of regret was unmistakeable. Loss of the college system as Keir had known it would be significant for the global republic of letters: 'the uniqueness of the College system, its weaving together of education and life in a community which is more than just a teaching and research institute, must be conserved and defended, because without it the cause of learning everywhere would suffer irremediable harm'. He referred directly to his opposition to the college's plan to establish a joint graduate institution with St Anne's, a women's college, at Holywell Manor: an experiment in co-education as well as an attempt to fit Oxford for a more coherent approach to postgraduate education.[37]

On these academic matters Hill's approach contrasted with Keir's: it was here that the distinction between a progressive and a traditionalist in university politics lay. Hill's first letter as Master took a more positive view of the challenges posed by the Franks Commission, calling for Oxford to take stock of itself and prepare for competition from other universities. He thought reform was well overdue and that there were other nettles to grasp which Franks had avoided. His hope was that 'Balliol will continue to give a lead in the process of fitting Oxford for the modern world'. There were more direct contrasts too: Hill explicitly welcomed the initiative at Holywell Manor, and reported that E.H. Carr – who ten years earlier had been refused election to the Fellowship due to Keir's intervention – had been elected an honorary Fellow.[38] In 1967 Hill wrote to *The Times*, along with a number of vice-chancellors and other prominent academics, welcoming the education reforms proposed by the Robbins Report as well as the 1959 Crowther Report on post-compulsory education. They were writing in opposition to concerns expressed by other vice-chancellors that the reorganisation of secondary education would lead to a decline in academic standards.[39]

One symptom of modernity was the growth of education in natural and medical sciences. Its expansion at Balliol cannot be attributed to Hill, but given his interest in science as a progressive intellectual force it is no surprise that he celebrated it. In December 1966 the Fellowship was divided 22:29 between 'science' and 'arts', a dramatic change from the 1930s when the split had been 4:14. Similarly, the balance of the undergraduate population had shifted from 40:183 to 132:179, figures that also reveal a considerable increase in the size of the college population. Hill also welcomed the fact that ten nationalities were now represented among the Fellowship, and that half of the Fellows were under forty.[40] The Franks Report had recommended a ratio of graduates to undergraduates of 1:2, which Balliol had achieved by 1970, the first college to do so.[41]

Balliol was also leading the way in co-education at postgraduate level, and it was in Hill's time that the partnership with St Anne's came fully into being. He was a strong public advocate on its behalf, careful to emphasise that the benefit was mutual, allowing Balliol to enlarge the scope and sustain the quality of its graduate work.[42]

The Times hailed the initiative as the beginning of the end for 'Oxbridge segregation' and a solution to problems of academic and social isolation faced by graduates. By providing 'a sensible adult framework of social life where the other sex is admitted on an everyday basis of normal acceptance' it would also be a laboratory for a more relaxed, less monastic, approach to student discipline. Russell Meiggs, who was to oversee the new centre, hoped there would not be many rules, and that any such rules would be worked out with a committee of graduates. The college was rightly proud that it would include a morning crèche facility for graduates and Fellows.[43] Although it was ultimately superseded by wider developments in graduate education and co-education, it was a significant initiative in both respects, strongly supported by Hill in contrast with his predecessor, even though it was partly the fruit of the very successful fundraising effort that Keir had led.[44]

Hill also introduced modest steps to broaden participation. In 1968 he announced that the college would host a summer school for bright sixth-form boys from under-privileged backgrounds who were not currently intending to go to university. The *Guardian* reported that sixth-formers from Northumberland, Leicestershire and Monmouthshire had been invited, twelve Fellows gave up their time, and undergraduates were employed as tutors and guides for £8 per week. The counties paid some expenses and Robert Maxwell gave further financial support. Hill had chosen to talk to the boys about the politics of the 1930s, but finding 'himself faced with a demand for "real history" [was] compelled to return to his vineyards of the seventeenth century'. The overall results were positive: Fellows appreciated the challenge of non-specialist teaching, while the pupils, given a taste of both general topics and of tutorial-style teaching in a specialist area that interested them, were generally impressed. Less successful had been the opening address by Thomas Balogh, a Fellow in economics: 'It was awful. He went on for an hour and three quarters', said one sixth-former. 'He wouldn't stop talking and I didn't understand a word he was saying.'[45]

Hill had hoped that it would be a model for other colleges and universities to follow. There was clearly greater potential here and he celebrated the fact that four-fifths of the boys had changed their minds about the desirability of a university education. Success owed a lot in particular 'to the energy and devotion of undergraduate and graduate tutors … some of whom revealed remarkable talents'.[46] Among them was Howard Marks, a bright but maverick student, who had been involved in some serious disciplinary issues. Hill had warmed to 'the young Welsh proletarian with the wicked sense of humour and the obvious lack of an aim in life'. By employing him he hoped to give some direction to his undoubted creativity and to tap into some altruism in him. In that he failed, but Marks was a success in the role, not just as a teacher but in demonstrating 'that university men were not all stuffed shirts. This was easily achieved by a pub crawl followed by the viewing of a pornographic film at the Scala cinema in Walton Street.'[47]

These changes all raised, in one way or another, the question of how the college was governed: the increasing size and shifting academic balance of the Fellowship and the student body; the possibility of co-education; the content of college rules and the process by which they were made and policed. Prior to 1960, all decisions had been taken by the Master and Fellows as the Governing Body. Formal meetings of Governing Body heard reports from eight or nine committees and made the final decisions. There were other, informal meetings, called consilia, at which no record was made, where matters of policy or controversy were discussed; any decision proposed in a consilium had to be formally ratified at the next College Meeting.

By the 1960s the increasing size of the Fellowship had created an appetite for more executive efficiency in routine matters. In 1963 a tutorial board was created with power to deal with all tutorial and student matters. Under Hill's Mastership this was taken further in the creation of an Executive Committee which would meet frequently to deal with all non-academic business, although it was subject to oversight and control by the Governing Body. Hill supported these changes, overseeing also the creation of the office of Vice-Master and measures limiting the personal powers of the Master. His support for such reforms had been an important argument in his favour as a potential Master, and his mantra once in post, whenever a contested proposal came up, was 'I am in the hands of the Fellows.' Some saw that as a weakness or covert support for radical ideas, but in Oswyn Murray's view it reflected Hill's genuine commitment to consensus and reluctance to use his vestigial powers.[48]

A related issue in the running of the college was student representation. By the later 1960s relations between Fellows and students were becoming strained and Hill signalled this as a major challenge very early in his tenure. 'With the disturbing example of the London School of Economics before us', he wrote in 1967, 'we sometimes wonder about relations between undergraduates and dons.' He identified increasing numbers of students and the decreasing number of Fellows living in college as the core problem. There was regular discussion between the JCR and the Domestic Committee, marked by 'frank speaking and hard hitting'. This helped to maintain good relations, but it was hard for students to meet Fellows outside their own subject, and establishing an effective non-academic 'moral tutor' relationship with a Fellow was challenging. Increasing graduate numbers and the pressure to become a graduate university would make it hard for colleges to attract and retain leading research staff to primarily undergraduate teaching posts: 'we shall have to fight hard … to keep undergraduates, graduates and dons in an integrated community'. At the same time, integrating graduate students into college life was also a challenge: 'A lot of effort is needed on all sides if Balliol is to continue to be a community of learning in friendship.'[49]

As these informal relationships weakened, student radicals became more vocal. As a result, the Senior Common Room (SCR: again used to mean both an actual room and the people entitled to use it, the Fellows) faced continuous pressure to take more formal account of student opinion in college governance. In 1967 Hill had written 'Fortunately the J.C.R. is watching this no less intently than we are.' Two years later he reported that the main university development had been the Hart Committee Report considering 'relations between Junior and Senior members'. In Balliol a Joint Disciplinary Committee had been established to revise college rules, although 'its functions are still not completely defined'. Nonetheless, despite 'ups and downs in relations between the two Common Rooms, and divisions within each body on how those relations should develop in this year of student revolt … we still manage to remain friends.'[50]

Hill had also been willing to give (relative) youth its opportunity at *Past and Present*. In 1967, in his mid-fifties, he stepped back from the board. The journal had enjoyed great success in the years since the expansion of the board in 1958. By 1960 it was in a strong financial position and well established as a place where academics wanted their writing to appear. That year Hill and Rodney Hilton led reform of the back office, putting the running of the journal on an altogether more effective footing, and from this point, following the appointment of Trevor Aston as managing editor, a *Past and Present* archive can be said to exist. Thereafter, Lawrence

Stone and Eric Hobsbawm in particular were keen for the journal to pursue its mission with greater ambition, and in 1963 an extraordinary meeting considered the aims and achievements of the journal in a very wide-ranging taking of stock. Stone was on his way to the United States, to take up a chair at Princeton, and offered to resign, an offer that was unanimously rejected.

In 1967 Stone and Tim Mason produced memos setting out a coherent and ambitious vision for the journal. At the regular meeting in April there was an extended discussion of the most recent issue, much of it negative and to the effect that the journal was not delivering on its founding ambition. In what looks like a related decision, an extraordinary meeting was called for July to discuss general policies, although it was cancelled. In 1968, however, discussion led to a broad restatement of the purpose of *Past and Present*, affirming a commitment to its 'distinctive character as a journal devoted to the study of social change, intellectual and other change in relation to social context etc.', noting the need to actively seek out the best work, and making a number of other practical suggestions to maintain its position.[51] It was Hill's last meeting as an active board member. He stepped down from the chair, and more fresh blood was brought in. According to an editorial note, 'throughout his sixteen years on the Board' Hill had 'been one of its most active members'.[52]

On one view this was a coup, as a younger generation took control of the journal. But historians are not always good at giving way to younger people and fresh ideas; it is to his credit that Hill stepped back at a point that is now regarded as mid-career. His willingness may partly have reflected the pressure of work as much as his principles: Paul Slack, who joined the board in 1978, remembers that at that point Hill did not want any responsibility in running the journal but did want to retain a powerful voice on the board. It was a little like his view of the role of Master in Balliol, where he withdrew a little from the day-to-day business, ceding influence to sub-committees and other college officers, while wanting to retain a powerful voice on the Governing Body on critical matters.

Hill's willingness to relinquish responsibilities probably reflected, at least in part, the weight of his other commitments. Certainly, in the first years of Mastership, his rate of publication slowed. Reprints of *Lenin and the Russian Revolution* (in 1967) and *The Good Old Cause* (in 1969) kept him in the public eye and on the review pages, but he produced relatively little new work in the later 1960s. He published only an article or two per year, including some fairly slight pieces, and introductions to collected volumes. It was a steady and still impressive rate of publication but much slower than in the five years before he was Master.

He was also doing less reviewing. This was partly due to a falling out at the *New Statesman* that led to the departure of Karl Miller to the *Listener*. Hill was one of twenty-four reviewers who wrote to the *New Statesman* in protest, and, as the *Sunday Telegraph* reported in June 1967, only two – Hill and Asa Briggs – had subsequently published reviews there. Hill had been reviewing less frequently for the magazine in any case, but only published nine reviews there over the next seven years. This was partially offset by occasional reviews for the *Guardian* and the *New York Review of Books* and one for the *Spectator*. His reviews were almost entirely now in mainstream academic or broadsheet publications, not specialist or campaigning Marxist journals, although he continued to bring the work of Soviet historians to the attention of the English-speaking world. He also met his professional obligations, for example by publishing warm appreciations of Lindsay and John Morris, both of whom had been important figures in his professional development.[53]

The major publication of his first years as Master, *Reformation to Industrial Revolution: A Social and Economic History of Britain, 1530–1780* (1967), was the fruit of earlier work. It was a kind of counterpoint to *The Century of Revolution*, analysing the course of English economic and social development from a position of relative backwardness in the 1530s to the brink of industrial revolution in the 1780s. This transformation could not be attributed simply to material forces – inflation, population growth, the opening of the Atlantic trades and so on, which were common to much of Europe. It was the social forces at work in England that shaped what people made of those material conditions. Rather than the economic roots of revolution, then, it was a book about how material change interacted with politics to produce distinctive economic, social and intellectual changes. To that extent it exemplified the version of Marx that Hill championed in the *Listener* in 1967: the historian concerned with dialectics and total history, not with either idealism or determinism. Hill had wanted to be clear that it was not an economic history as normally understood, writing to Hobsbawm (at work on a book in the same series) 'What are you going to call your Penguin? I am toying with the idea of "English society from Ref. to Ind. Rev." rather than anything that would suggest I have done a straight economic history.'[54]

Although the book was well reviewed there are signs that economic history was leaving Hill behind as academic practice changed. In 1965 Peter Laslett published *The World We Have Lost*, a work which became hugely influential. Laslett had been interested in ideas too, and particularly in patriarchal political theory – the idea that power naturally resided in fathers, and that the king was like a father to the kingdom, responsible for its welfare but not answerable to its members. That had led him to explore the actual social arrangements of Tudor and Stuart society, particularly the place of households therein. He pioneered the use of parish registers of births, deaths and marriages to study household and social structures in the past, establishing the Cambridge Group for the History of Population and Social Structure. The group became the most important single influence on the development of early modern English economic and social history over the following decades, and Laslett's book was something of an inspiration for that.[55]

At the heart of the book was the correction of a series of 'misbeliefs about our ancestors'. Laslett demonstrated that the predominant form of household in the early modern period had been nuclear, not extended households of several generations. Marriage had been late (mid-twenties for women and a little later for men), delayed until the new couple were able to establish an independent household. In the interim, below the level of the aristocracy and gentry, young people spent the time between leaving the family home and setting up on their own in service or apprenticeships in other households, under the government of a master. Laslett painted a picture of a deferential world, in which the lives of the poor were tightly circumscribed and held within powerful bonds of deference and social discipline. There was only one class in this society – the gentry – whose social formation and experience connected them with each other, and equipped them with an awareness of their collective interest.

The World We Have Lost might have been the sort of study to which Hill warmed – contextualising political thought in an understanding of social practices – but this argument about a one-class society proved a red rag to him. He wrote a lengthy and withering review, later republished in a collection of his essays. He emphasised the limitations of the parish registers as statistical sources: the level of under-registration varied over the centuries (as nonconformists withdrew from the parish church), between parishes (reflecting the relative diligence of different clerks) and between classes (it is likely that the poor and mobile were less easily recorded). More than that, though, Laslett had argued from the church court records that the ideal of the nuclear family was hegemonic. But these courts were intended, at least partly, to impose the monogamous ideal on the population; if that was so, wrote Hill, it is no surprise that church court witness statements record widespread commitment to that ideal. When the courts and ecclesiastical censorship broke down in the revolution, very different views were expressed, which had perhaps been widespread before that.[56] Laslett's argument that there was no class conflict (because there was only one class) was also, obviously, a fundamental challenge to Hill's explanation for the development of capitalism in England, and was a core reason for his hostility to the book. In fact it has been suggested that the shift of perspective instigated by Laslett was the catalyst for the sustained criticism of Hill's work that took off in the later 1970s.[57]

Hill and Laslett had at one time been on friendly terms, and Laslett had sent warm acknowledgement of a copy of *Economic Problems* in 1956. Now, though, they became hostile. On a number of occasions Hill opened lectures with denunciations of Laslett: he greeted a WEA audience following the broadcast of a series of Laslett's lectures with the confession that he had decided against hanging his lecture on them, 'since I didn't believe anyone c[oul]d take them seriously: Must be clear that anyone in this r[oo]m knows more ab[ou]t 17th c[entury] hist[ory] than PL, guilty of Form IV howlers.'[58] His antipathy to the book certainly persisted. In 1970, for example, advising Sheila Rowbotham about the literature on seventeenth-century women, Hill had added, more or less as an afterthought: 'And – though don't believe it – Peter Laslett, The World We Have Lost.'[59] Although they had reviewed one another quite favourably in the past, and exchanged academic courtesies, the antipathy became mutual. When Laslett reviewed Hill's book *The World Turned Upside Down* a few years later he was unimpressed (and, it seems, equally wrong about the impact it would have).[60]

As a strictly academic issue, Laslett's approach (if not all his conclusions) have won out. Hill did not work on the records of actual enterprises or the official records relating to them, but he was dependent on contemporary social comment. In effect, he relied on the 'journalism of the age', rather than direct evidence of economic life contained in personal and business records, and few economic historians would now turn to Hill for an understanding of the origins of the industrial revolution. In the later 1980s Hill acknowledged he had never been much of an economic historian, despite his early view that that is what Marxism required of him: 'It was never very congenial, and it did not get very far apart from having a large stack of cards with things about English agrarian history on them which have remained untouched from that date [the 1930s] until now.'[61] He never matched the work of Arkhangelsky, for example, on manorial records, which he had brought to the attention of an English audience in the early years of his career, and *Reformation to Industrial Revolution* was to be his last excursion into economic history.

In truth, Hill's interests had always been primarily the history of ideas understood in their material context rather than economic history as a subject in itself. The relative lull in publication in the later 1960s was the prelude to a change of direction, away from political economy and the history of capitalism and towards a more consistent concentration on radicalism, the radical tradition and history from below. For the first time, he published with Bridget – an article on Catherine Macaulay, author of an eight-volume history of the seventeenth century published in the 1760s and 1770s.[62] The themes of his other publications in the late 1960s were familiar: the history of dissent understood in its contemporary context rather than as part of the genealogy of ideas;[63] the history of science (restating his view that scientific advance had its centre in London not the universities);[64] and the history of economic attitudes (specifically hostility among the lower order to the status of wage-labourer in the eighteenth century, published in a festschrift for Maurice Dobb).[65] This was now the core of his academic writing.

8

Youth Culture and Student Rebellion: 1969–78

> *Counter-culture radicalism is in some respects more personal and intro-*
> *spective than past radicalisms normally have been … This … reflects the*
> *perception that the revolutionary theory and practice of the past have*
> *placed too much faith in economic and institutional changes, and have*
> *neglected the need to change people's way of thought and modes of personal*
> *behaviour.*
>
> Christopher Hill, *Milton and the English Revolution*, 1977,
> quoting Anthony Arblaster

By the late 1960s Hill had overseen modest change at Balliol, supporting modernising tendencies in relation to the admission of graduates and broadening participation, reducing the dominance of arts and humanities, and the reform of college governance.

The latter part of his term of office was the era of flower power and student rebellion, which posed significant challenges for all Oxford colleges. Hill was perhaps inevitably criticised for his handling of these difficulties. Balliol quickly acquired quite a reputation for radicalism, its students taking a lead, for example, in the occupation of the Clarendon building in 1969/70 and the Indian Institute in 1974, as well as in the NUS rent strike that year. It was rather tame as student rebellion went – no cobblestones were thrown at the police and Alan Knight, who moved from Balliol to the University of Essex at the time, found Balliol very tame by comparison. Nonetheless, much of this Oxford radicalism was reported in the national press, and it added to tensions between the SCR and the JCR.[1] The drama was presented satirically for a national audience by Trevor-Roper (pseudonymously) in his 'Letters of Mercurius', published between 1968 and 1970.[2] While dealing with these tensions, however, Hill was able to cement his place as a figure in the English radical tradition and as one of its leading historians.

There was a rapid change in student manners in the late 1960s, leading to impatience with many aspects of college discipline, while student political radicalism also made life in the college less comfortable. Sexual behaviour was one area in which a generational gap became obvious. Archaic rules about overnight guests and curfews had survived until the late 1960s largely because they were not enforced: there was by then 'much breach' of the rules, 'with the connivance of cheerfully and cheaply corruptible domestic staff', and routes into and out of the locked college were well known to Fellows, staff and students. However, if breaches became public the formal position was publicly maintained. British life had come a long way since Hill had complained that sex was a matter of sniggering and jokes about rubbers; the college had come a long way since it had refused to put locks on college rooms for fear it would allow or even encourage fornication.[3] However these rules and attitudes were coming to be seen as an invitation not just to satire but to charges of hypocrisy.

There can be little doubt about where Hill stood on such issues given the record of his thinking during the 1930s. One of the two college portraits in his office was of Kenneth Bell, a man of many virtues and much integrity who left the college as a result of marital problems during the war. That his marital difficulties forced him out of Balliol, despite the transparent virtues expressed in his public service, family life and educational and pastoral work, seems now a powerful indictment of the then-orthodox college morality.[4]

Hill, however, was also bound to respect more conservative opinion among members of the Governing Body. This led him to defend positions that he did not believe in. For example, in 1969 a JCR proposal to install a condom machine was refused by the SCR, leading Martin Kettle, the JCR president (and son of Hill's former comrade Arnold), to write to Hill asking why. Hill replied 'we voted only on whether to agree to the proposal or not, so the College as such stated no reasons'. He did though, in a very neutral tone, report the main points made: that although avoiding unwanted pregnancies was a good thing, there was no urgency about installing the machine because condoms could be readily acquired elsewhere. Given that, 'it would be unpalatable to the moral feelings of some under-graduates, Fellows and visitors to the JCR' to install a machine. The JCR went ahead anyway, forcing Governing Body to order that it be returned to the London Rubber Company, and in the meantime be removed and taken into the physical possession of the Dean. The JCR immediately passed a motion affirming 'its desire that contraceptive machines be reinstalled with all due celeritude'.[5]

The traditionalists were swimming against a very strong tide. Writing in the *Guardian* in 1970, Christopher Driver, himself an Oxford graduate, noted that

> Gowns have gone, and women have come, or so nearly so that a formal governing body vote for coeducation would entail few changes in the rules ... Almost everyone – scouts [housekeeping staff], tutors, undergraduates – likes to tell you that what happens now between the sexes is what happened always, except that it is now over-exposed and over-discussed.[6]

This rejection of silliness and hypocrisy stood for a larger change of morals and manners, which was apparent partly in more egalitarian, less deferential and perhaps more abrasive forms of behaviour. This was compounded by the rise of left-wing radicalism, which invested some of

Changing manners of Oxford students in the late 1960s and early 1970s.

these things with an explicitly political significance: for the radicals, older ways of governing the college manifested the larger patterns of authority in society. In October 1969, not long after the establishment of the Joint Disciplinary Committee, the JCR complained about how it was working, citing several disciplinary decisions which revealed 'between the JCR and SCR a basic difference of opinion about the aims and methods of College discipline'. Particular concerns at that point were JCR autonomy in running the bar and the fact that the Dean, Frank Willis-Bund, had entered student rooms to remove red flags being flown on 1 May. Another incendiary issue was 'when women should be allowed to be in College'.[7] Issues of sexual morality intersected with student radicalism, and suggestions that the college was inconsistent in its attitudes.

Many of these issues crystallised in a personal attack on Willis-Bund. He had been chaplain at the college since 1945, Dean since 1952 and also served as Vice-Master: he was a prominent fixture of college life. If Howard Marks is to be believed, he was relaxed about drug use, more concerned that the Proctors (the university officers responsible for student discipline) and the police were kept out of the college, and willing, for example, to prescribe six weeks in the Drama Club as a solution to the psychological difficulties Marks experienced following his experiments with LSD. He and Marks had become friends when he supported Marks in his refusal to name drug users to the Proctors following the drug-related death of Joshua Macmillan, grandson of Harold, and he took the same line following a police raid on the shared house in which Marks was living. And while he was clear about college rules regarding the entertainment of women and staying out too late, he had explained to a bemused Ved Mehta how to get into the college late at night via a ground-floor window.[8] He was a college man with a relatively forgiving approach to many sins, remembered by Steven Lukes for bringing a wry, amused and ironic approach to both his duties and his regular encounters with human weakness. He had extended the welfare role of the Chapel to all college members and not just chapel-goers, and had discreetly administered hardship funds too.[9] However, his style was going rapidly out of fashion with the radicals.

His antipathy to left-wing student activism exacerbated these tensions. By 1968 he was very perturbed by 'left-wing revolution', and when Marks returned to Balliol as a postgraduate Willis-Bund tried to get him to put his charisma to work in discouraging his cronies from participating in radical politics. Although they dressed similarly, the revolutionaries were not the same as the hippies of 1966: Marks was a hedonist, suspicious of all political causes, and of course did not share the view that smoking marijuana was 'some sort of stupefaction imposed on the working classes by the bourgeoisie'.[10] There was undoubtedly a visible difference of sympathies between the Master and the Dean on radical politics, reported even in the *Guardian*: 'Mr Hill, the modern rebels like to think, is still fundamentally on their side.'[11]

Hill was certainly sympathetic to fresh ideas, youth culture and sexual liberation: the counter-cultural assault on bourgeois respectability. John Morrill recalled hearing Hill on the radio, in discussion with Lawrence Stone, celebrating student radicalism and youthful energy.[12] Others remembered his wry amusement at the scrawled slogans 'eggheads of the world unite' and 'gravy is bourgeois!'[13] With Bridget he attended the inaugural Womens' Liberation conference held in the Oxford Union in the spring of 1970, standing out among an audience consisting mainly of women in their twenties.[14] But he was also keen to maintain the cohesion of the college, and not always in agreement with how students expressed their radicalism. Those who knew him felt that he was ambivalent about student radicalism, having an 'instinctive sympathy for libertarian revolt … tempered by a dislike for gesture politics and self-indulgence'.[15] He was certainly more sympathetic than others though, including John Sparrow, the Warden of All Souls, another 'concerned about revolutionaries and unconcerned about marijuana smoking'.[16]

In January 1970, Martin Kettle wrote to Hill about a range of such issues, opening his letter 'Here we go again.'[17] That spring was to prove particularly testing. In March the Boat Club had won the inter-collegiate competition and celebrated in a traditional manner by setting fire to a boat and finding someone from neighbouring Trinity College who could be forced to jump over the flames. Little action had been taken though: all those involved had apparently been contrite once they sobered up. This was in sharp contrast to the harsh disciplinary measures taken against a student who had a woman in his room overnight. At the same time, Willis-Bund was accused of noting the names of students participating in the occupation of the Clarendon building, for which there could be no benign explanation. There were also accusations that he had removed post from pigeonholes, citing clutter and fire hazards but, it was assumed, actually motivated by a desire to stamp out activism, evidenced previously in relation to the red flags. The contrast between the heavy-handed disciplinary measures taken against a student who had slept with a woman and the relaxed treatment of the Boat Club's boorish behaviour proved a political flashpoint: most students felt much more strongly about the boorishness than the fornication. Much of this was reported, quite accurately, in the *Guardian*.[18]

The conflicts came to a head when Kettle proposed a JCR resolution denouncing Willis-Bund, which caused outrage in the SCR. In the end Kettle offered an apology for having criticised Willis-Bund personally rather than the office of the Dean, but the episode was very divisive: Hill noted that it discouraged senior members from participating in the Joint Disciplinary Committee,[19] and in the midst of the turmoil Tony Kenny resigned his membership.[20] Willis-Bund retired shortly afterwards and moved to All Souls. Rowse noted the 'shocking story' of Hill's behaviour, claiming that he 'adroitly slithered out of all responsibility, shuffling it off on to a committee, and another committee, leaving his Dean totally unsupported, when he was in the right'.[21] For his part, Hill wrote appreciatively in the *Annual Record* of Willis-Bund's many contributions to college life, celebrating the many 'Stories that circulate around him': 'He is known to and loved by more past and present undergraduates, I suspect, than any member of the Governing Body.'[22]

Specific conflicts like this raised the larger question of how the college should be governed. In fact, following Willis-Bund's departure, Balliol considered not appointing a replacement chaplain Fellow, 'only' deciding to continue the practice 37:11. In an apparent non sequitur, the *Observer* reported that the Master was a 'communist', both misstating his views and misrepresenting his role on the Governing Body; and John Jones recalls that Hill was strongly in favour of appointing a chaplain Fellow in the interests of pastoral care.[23]

More formal demands for student involvement in the running of the college followed. In February 1971 a JCR motion proposed that it 'affirm that Balliol is a community of both senior and junior members and calls on the College to recognise their right to share in the making of decisions which affect the lives of members'. The demand was for full executive participation on the Governing Body, consilia, Executive Committee, estates, investments and domestic sub-committees and the tutorial board.[24]

Hill had genuine sympathy for the students' demands in this area, encouraging John Prest, the senior tutor, to try to maintain civil contacts. In this he seems to have been successful. In February 1972 the JCR invited Hill and Bridget to dinner to celebrate his sixtieth birthday, and the tone of his correspondence with successive JCR presidents was generally warm.[25] Michael Roberts, who was an undergraduate at the time, remembered that 'From the vantage point of the J.C.R. [Hill] frequently looked like our best ally in assaults on the dons' bunker across the quad!'[26]

In fact, there is a lot of testimony to Hill's good relations with the students at large. He and Bridget were attentive to students of all backgrounds.[27] This was a matter of his personal style too. Ronald Hutton remembers attending a coming-up party for new research students at the History faculty in the autumn of 1976. Dress was to be 'informal', so he turned up in his then daily wear of a corduroy jacket and trousers with a collarless 'granddad shirt', grey cloth waistcoat and gypsy-style neck scarf. With him was a student from Newcastle similarly attired, but everyone else was in lounge suits. They were stared at, and everybody else backed away, including Hutton's own new supervisor. It was Hill who rescued them.[28] Howard Marks also first got to know Hill during an informal social encounter, although he was already a friend of Hill's daughter Fanny. Following a conversation in the student bar, Hill persuaded Marks to buy a bottle of whisky to bring up to the lodgings, where 'We got on remarkably well, and by the end of the evening Christopher had accepted my invitation to dinner.'[29] Hill remained very supportive of Marks following his conviction for drug dealing, and was quoted in the press as continuing to think of him as one of Balliol's 'star pupils', even if he was not willing to be interviewed about Marks's criminal career.[30]

Hill's support for student demands for a stronger voice in the governance of the college was, however, at odds with the majority view of the College Meeting, and he could be exasperated when the students failed to take advantage of the opportunities they did have.[31] Student representation may have been the issue on which he had hoped to make peace with the radicals, talking late at night over a glass of whisky with the moderates among the student body, the changes in representation emerging as if from the Putney Debates.[32] In any case, it produced his most serious breach with Governing Body, leading him to threaten resignation if it did not approve reforms. It was testament to the seriousness of the issue for him, but the response was firm – if he made such a threat again then his resignation would be accepted.[33]

Perhaps the most notorious incident of political protest during Hill's time as Master occurred in 1971. It was prompted by the visit of Edward Heath, himself a Balliol man of many parts, who continued to send Christmas cards to Hill after he became prime minister.[34] A near-contemporary of Hill's, son of a carpenter and a lady's maid, and a grammar school boy,

Heath had been prominent in student life at Balliol as a musician (he held an organ scholarship which helped fund his studies) and a politician. In the latter role he had been president both of the Oxford University Conservative Association and the Union Society, championing the opposition to the Munich agreement and hoping to foster a genuinely popular conservativism.[35] He was not just a famous old member then, but to many old members a rather admirable one whose record as a student could be a model for others.

Following a surprise election victory in 1970, Heath's government pursued policies which prefigured Thatcherism in some respects – limiting union power, making tax and spending cuts and abandoning an incomes policy. It proved hard to deliver this programme in the face of rising commodity prices, particularly after the oil crisis hit in 1973, but it nonetheless made Heath unpopular with an entire generation of student radicals. Quite shrewdly, the *Sunday Telegraph* reported that Hill had not commented on whether he had congratulated Heath on his election victory, putting this down to the 'instinctive evasiveness so often found in Marxists'. It was, the article continued, doubtful that 'the Balliol of 1970 still values such ties. For those who do not hold Left-wing views it is becoming an increasingly uncomfortable place.'[36]

However, in June 1971, when Heath came to Oxford to receive an honorary degree, his old college hosted him. The visit was marked by protests, and offensive slogans were painted on the walls of the SCR, causing hundreds of pounds worth of damage. The *Sunday Telegraph* reported that during the visit Heath had been 'ringed about by apprehensive Fellows' and that the Dean had negotiated an emergency escape route via Trinity, the neighbouring college, 'if things got too hot'. Hill, however, had given the visit a swerve, and the paper was not alone in thinking this reprehensible. It noted that the 'Marxist Master of Balliol who perhaps sensibly prefers to live in north Oxford rather than in college, was spared the embarrassment of showing civility to a Conservative prime minister. He is on sabbatical leave.'[37]

Alex Callinicos, who coordinated the protests, recalled that the spray-painting of the SCR had been spontaneous and booze-fuelled, and was not part of the original plan. When he and Simon Sedgwick-Jell were (correctly) identified as the chief culprits, Hill had given them whisky in the Master's Lodgings, along with the impression that their crime had been to get caught. Callinicos also thought Hill handled the subsequent disciplinary procedure in a way that protected them from the harshest punishments being called for. They were sent down for a year, delaying

Sedgwick-Jell's further studies, but not preventing him from graduating, and allowing Callinicos to complete his degree in due course.[38]

The JCR largely accepted that the form of the protest had been unacceptable: 'While we still strongly disapprove of the invitation of the Prime Minister as a guest of the College, in view of the pernicious policies of his government and party, we condemn the acts of vandalism committed in the College last night and apologise for the embarrassment thus caused to the College.' A formal JCR resolution followed in October, regretting the damage but also the fact that Heath had been invited in the first place, and asking that the punishments of Callinicos and Sedgwick-Jell be rescinded.[39] Claims about the violent treatment of one student protestor at the hands of Heath's security detail were at the time discounted by many Fellows as further trouble-making, but it later emerged that a student had indeed been subject to something like an assault.[40]

In 1973 and 1974 a national rent strike proposed by the NUS also proved tricky to handle. Balliol JCR took the lead among Oxford colleges. The Governing Body was sympathetic to the aims of the protest – a national campaign to increase financial support for students – but argued that a rent strike would hurt the college, not the government. As Hill wrote: 'It seems to me to hit the wrong target, and it would be a pity if friction developed between us over an issue in which we are in fact in complete agreement.' Balliol students were also at the forefront of activism in the occupation of the Indian Institute building, and another pressure point was the way the JCR was using its power to ask for 'voluntary levies'. The JCR could add such levies to its compulsory levy and had done so for charitable and campaigning purposes, but in 1974 it was asking for them to help finance the occupation of the Examination Schools. This was an obvious embarrassment to the Governing Body, although the JCR claimed a little optimistically that it in no way implied Governing Body support for the occupation. There was also pressure on a range of welfare issues that might have been seen as broadly non-political – for example, the provision of a washing machine and more flexibility about the use of vouchers for dining.[41]

A record of a general meeting of the JCR circulated by Hill in February 1974 was annotated by John Prest, the senior tutor: 'What a deplorable tone it all has'. But this may have been the nadir.[42] As student representation became accepted, relations with the JCR improved, in part for that reason. Hill signed off his annual Master's Letter in 1975 saying relations had been amicable and that a machinery for joint consultation was now working: 'The current J.C.R. Committee, whilst by no means seeing eye to eye with us on all issues, has invariably been co-operative and willing to discuss.'[43] The following year he wrote that 'Relations between the S.C.R. and the J.C.R. continued to be peaceful and harmonious.'[44]

While he had some success in mediating these conflicts, Hill was not able to achieve his most cherished reforming ambition: to oversee the admission of women. Among the men's colleges it was New College that made the first move towards co-education, voting two-thirds in favour of changing its statutes in June 1964. At that point female undergraduates constituted about 17 per cent of the Oxford population when the national figure was 37 per cent. G.E.M. De Ste Croix, a Fellow of the college, wrote in the *Oxford Magazine*: 'No one will deny that some of the women who now have to be refused admission at Oxford are abler than many of the men who are accepted.' Dining rules at New College would be relaxed immediately, and elections to the Fellowship would be opened to men and women on equal terms, since it was thought helpful to elect at least one female Fellow before going ahead. The college hoped to achieve a gender balance of 2:1 male to female undergraduates, in line with the national average, within four years of admitting the first woman.[45]

However, the collegiate structure put obstacles in the way. Women's colleges could not expand sufficiently to remedy the problem, so that some action by the men's colleges was essential. On the whole, though, the women's colleges were smaller and poorer, and feared that they would lose out if all the men's colleges went co-educational. The problem was more marked in particular subjects, because men's colleges sometimes did not offer subjects popular with female applicants at the time: Balliol, for example, had no Fellow in modern languages. If Balliol expanded it would be in subjects where female applications were already relatively scarce, posing even sharper challenges to the women's colleges. As a result, reformers in all-male colleges could not simply and unequivocally support opening up their own college to both men and women, let alone opening up all the men's colleges. Moreover, changing college statutes required Privy Council approval, and the university had to agree any approach to the Privy Council for such approval. The university was anxious about the potential for chaos if there was rapid and unmanaged change, and was likely to keep a close eye on changes to college statutes.

By 1970 the admission of women was under active discussion by a number of colleges, including Balliol. There were constructive discussions with the principal of St Anne's, but Balliol was not strong in subjects with a good supply of female applicants: Balliol's expansion would inevitably create competition in subjects with weaker demand among female applicants. At a meeting in March, however, there was no opposition to the election of female Fellows to Balliol, a necessary preliminary, most people thought, to the admission of female students.[46] The issue was the subject of a consilium in November 1970 and another in June 1971, which voted 26:2 'that the College should announce its intention to remove statutory barriers to the entry of women, with a view to admitting women at a later stage if the Governing Body after consultation with old members so decided, and provided that the interests of the existing women's Colleges were protected'.[47] Those against immediate change included not only traditionalists but also reformers who were discouraged by the practical problems, thinking that Balliol was not yet ready.

In his Master's Letter that year Hill suggested that the tide was unstoppable – co-education was already common at secondary level and in universities around the world. In fact, he wondered if Balliol could afford *not* to admit women. To him, 'Looking around the quad on a sunny afternoon, I sometimes think that it would be only a technical change to have young women permanently resident.' However, he also recognised that it would transform the college in ways 'which many of us would deplore', and that some members of Governing Body 'would prefer to die in the last ditch'. Public interest in the issue was such that the letter was reported in the *Telegraph*.[48]

The consultation with old members revealed a majority in favour of the admission of women among those who responded, but as with the Governing Body it was not a two-thirds majority. Hill had received more than fifty replies and noted some generational differences: those who had gone to Balliol after the war or during the 1950s were pretty solidly opposed, while those who arrived a decade later were pretty solidly in favour. Interestingly though, replies from those who had been at Balliol before the war were more divided, with a majority in favour of the admission of women.[49]

The university was only willing to support a small number of men's colleges in going mixed to start with: for reformers the race was to be included in this group, and to secure college agreement in time to achieve that. In Balliol it seemed that the college was in favour of making the admission of female undergraduates possible, but not of actually admitting any at this point. As the deadline approached, Oswyn Murray, then a young Fellow in Classics, raised a constitutional concern: while changing the statutes to allow the admission required a two-thirds majority, once it was done women could be admitted by a simple majority in the College Meeting. It was not an attempt at sabotage but to make sure that any changes would be made 'in a way to which no-one can object, now or later', and Murray wrote a day later commending a solution adopted at Wadham to the same problem. Time was running out for Balliol though, and Hill wrote to all Fellows on 1 November that four colleges had already amended their statutes, and that Wadham would shortly do so: if Balliol did not act pretty much immediately they would miss the boat.[50]

On 10 November the College Meeting agreed to propose a change to the statutes, but also that admission of women would only actually take place with a two-thirds majority in favour at a College Meeting. In preparation for an extraordinary meeting a week later, Murray submitted a paper noting other practical difficulties – for example the absence of any female Fellows and how ill-prepared the college was to support female undergraduates. In the event there was a majority in favour of the admission of women at that meeting, but it failed the two-thirds test by five votes: 20:17. It was agreed to prepare for the admission of women in other ways, for example by allowing for the election of female Fellows. In December the College Meeting ratified this compromise: 30:8 in favour of making it possible to elect female Fellows, 31:8 in favour of admitting female undergraduates at some future date. As a result of these hesitations, though, other men's colleges beat Balliol to it: Brasenose, Hertford, Jesus, St Catherine's and Wadham were to be the first men's colleges to go mixed, starting in 1973.[51]

Governing Body had wanted to go ahead with the amendment to its statutes, but the university planned to withhold approval unless the college agreed not to actually admit women without further consulting the university. To some Fellows this infringed the sovereignty of the College Meeting, but a constitutional crisis was averted by giving an informal commitment not to admit women for five years. Hill reported that the university wanted to review the success of the 1973 initiative before approving further moves towards co-education.[52]

The upshot was that women would not be admitted in Hill's time, but the tone of his 1972 Master's Letter was upbeat: in his view 'co-residence has come to stay'.[53] He was nonetheless disappointed by this outcome and by those he felt were responsible for Balliol missing the boat. Murray felt that there was a degree of coldness between them for several years after the crucial vote.[54] Hill predicted that further expansion of co-education would come at the end of the five-year period, but added a little ruefully that 'all that is looking forward to a period when I shall no longer be writing this annual letter'.[55] In 1973, with Hill's vigorous support, Balliol became one of the first traditional male colleges to elect a woman when it elected its first female Fellow, Carol Clark. Oswyn Murray had supported that equally enthusiastically, as a necessary preparatory step, in his view, to the admission of female undergraduates.[56]

Pressure to admit female undergraduates to the men's colleges did indeed continue to mount. In 1976, Andrew Whitehead, the enterprising chair of the co-residence committee of the Oxford Student Union, had threatened to bring a case against New College and Balliol on grounds of sex discrimination under the recent Act. Single-sex institutions could secure transitional exemption orders from the provisions of the Act, but both New College and Balliol had amended their statutes to allow for the admission of women although they were not doing so. Whitehead argued that this put them in breach of the Act, and Balliol and other colleges were forced to take legal advice.[57]

By that time, however, the university was willing to give consent to Balliol and other colleges. The first women were admitted to Balliol in 1979, a year after Hill stepped down as Master. The news coincided with the announcement of Hill's successor, Anthony Kenny, who noted 'that the desire to admit women students was one of the most cherished ambitions of Mr Hill'. Kenny regretted 'that it would not come about in Mr Hill's time but [was] honoured that it would do so after he had become Master'.[58]

At the end of his tenure, Hill took pride in improved relations with the JCR and in the modest reforms, saying that he had heartily approved of both the reduction in the power of the Master and the increased voice of junior members in the governance of the college. Increased cooperation, although regarded with misgivings by some Fellows, had 'been a great success in preserving a sense that the college is a community, not divided on we/they lines'. It prevented Fellows, who were on the Governing Body year after year, from believing that the college existed for them rather than the undergraduates. In truth, Balliol's reputation depended at least as much on its students as its Fellows: 'there are very few undergraduates indeed who do not have a real sense of responsibility for the honour and reputation of the College.' Of course, he added, common sense 'varies among the young as among the old; but I have never met an undergraduate elected to represent the J.C.R. who was not open to rational discussion'. He worried about a growing threat to the tutorial system, which was very expensive and made greater demands on Oxford tutors than teaching practices elsewhere, but in this he was a conservative: 'If

I may generalize from my own case, the stimulus and pleasure received from pupils more than compensates for any loss in time devoted to one's own interests.' He ended: '"The place exists, and I hope always will exist, for the young men", wrote Sandie Lindsay in 1949. Adding young women to young men, I should like to echo that hope in the last words I write as Master.'[59]

Hill was tight-lipped about his time as Master, and how he felt about student politics, with good reason: it is striking how often, and how accurately, Balliol's internal affairs were reported in the national press during his tenure. His correspondence as Master, as we have seen, was studiously impartial in reporting the position of Governing Body, but he could certainly be wry about the life of a college head. He wrote sardonically to Isaiah Berlin on the latter's election as the inaugural president of Wolfson College: 'Congratulations – if that is the right word. You will be second only to All Souls on the list for expropriation!' They subsequently exchanged knowing letters about fundraising and Ved Mehta's angling for a visiting position from which to enjoy a generous research grant he had been awarded.[60] In public though, Hill kept his counsel and was, as the *Guardian* had predicted, the Master of bromide.

Reviews of his Mastership by others were of course mixed, as they always are for people charged with making difficult decisions. Rowse's hostile review can be largely discounted as malicious and ill-informed.[61] Some felt, though, that Hill was a little disengaged. In moving out of the college, and acceding to reductions in the influence of the Master, he had also, by chance, put some distance between himself and some of the sharpest points of contention. He was unusual among his generation of Heads of House in taking study leave to maintain his scholarly career. John Jones recalls meeting Hill on the day that the Balliol cricket team was playing the inter-collegiate cup final and disapproving of the Master for not attending (despite Hill's own pride in once having scored the winning try for the rugby team in an inter-collegiate final): Hill was on study leave and heading back to North Oxford to write. This dilution of the day-to-day role of Master put him at some distance from the action in more controversial situations, in a way that some regarded as politically convenient. Of course a neutral might think that was reasonable, since Hill had relinquished many powers wielded by previous Masters: with less power, one might assume, comes less responsibility.

There is, however, an associated charge that this relative disengagement allowed him to dodge the really difficult controversies. All Masters, perhaps, require a certain amount of slipperiness, and Hill was probably no more guilty of that than (on his account) Lindsay had been. Murray thought Rowse's accusations on this score were clearly unfair.[62] Hill was also accused of failing to respect tradition or to maintain relations with the wider Balliol community; this was strongly implied, for example, by the *Telegraph*'s warm appreciation of David Keir following his death.[63] The paper later reported an 'acid' verdict on Hill's Mastership in the journal of the Oxford Society: Hill had profited from the success of Keir's fundraising but had not admitted 'the need to draw along with him the important establishment figures like headmasters while turning the institution inside-out'.[64]

Judgements on his handling of student discipline and behaviour are generally positive, given the acute difficulty of his position: 'avoiding confrontations wherever possible, imposing discipline when really necessary, and offering private help to some of those who got themselves into difficulties'. In fact there is quite a lot of testimony on this last point: that Hill (and Bridget) 'had always shown an exceptional willingness to defend those in personal trouble, most often where sexual behaviour and official morality clashed; a striking number of people had reason to be grateful to them for unobtrusive and tactful help in such matters'.[65] Even the acid verdict reported in the *Telegraph* concluded that Hill had been successful in dealing with 'the high noon of student revolt'.[66]

Maurice Keen, who was certainly no radical, had supported Hill's election even though Hill had warned him he might regret doing so. Keen felt that as Master Hill revealed a previously unsuspected capacity for ruthlessness, but continued to respect his integrity. Traditionalists had things to grumble about at Balliol, as everywhere in Oxford at the time, Keen thought, but no more there than anywhere else.[67] Overall, Hill seems to have been largely successful in holding the ring on a potentially very divided Governing Body, but doing that at a time when passions were running so high was impossible without 'incurring harsh criticism from one quarter or another'.[68]

As he navigated the tensions arising from student revolt, Hill was writing about the radical tradition and securing his place in it. His rate of publication had slowed in the late sixties, but the turn of the decade saw signs that his writing career was recovering. *Antichrist in Seventeenth-Century England* (1971), the published version of his Riddell memorial lectures, did not attract much attention in the broadsheets, but *God's Englishman: Oliver Cromwell and the English Revolution* (1970) certainly did. It is an odd book, meditating on the relationship between Cromwell and the revolution in a slightly elusive way. Hill had celebrated the role of Lenin and Stalin in giving shape and direction to the Russian Revolution, and he drew a contrast between Cromwell's role in the English Revolution and Napoleon's in the French. By comparison, Cromwell appears much more a man reacting to events than driving them, seen by himself and others as being in the hands of providence rather than a master of events. The central thesis is that Cromwell bound English patriotism to a sense of destiny in the state, something that underpinned Britain's role as a great power from the late seventeenth century to the mid-twentieth; but this was a product of Cromwell's actions rather than a concrete design. The book was well received, but as a biography of Cromwell it is limited, and as a Marxist meditation on the role of great men in history it is perhaps insubstantial.

Although it attracted much less attention, Hill's *Antichrist in Seventeenth-Century England* was more important for the subsequent development of his writing. The belief in the role of the antichrist was a blind alley in intellectual history, but it was profoundly important in Tudor and Stuart England. The interest of the topic lay in how the antichrist was identified, since everyone agreed about the importance of understanding his work in the world. 'Was he the Pope? Bishops? The episcopal church generally? Any state church? Any political authority maintaining a state church? Or persecuting? Monarchy? Or was it just a term of abuse to be hurled at anybody one disliked?' The significance of the identification of someone as antichrist, or some practice as antichristian, is therefore critical to understanding their thought. Hill was particularly interested in 'the contortions of a group of clerical intellectuals and lower-class sectaries', the latter providing the agenda of much of his work over the next decade and more.[69]

Overwhelmingly the most important publication of this period, however, was *The World Turned Upside Down*, which appeared in 1972. It was published in a new imprint launched by Maurice Temple Smith, who had been in line to take over at Secker and Warburg but instead launched his own imprint in 1969, gathering around him 'a group of editors and authors of exceptional strength and attractiveness'.[70] That group included Rodney Hilton, Hill's long-standing friend and comrade, who edited the series in which the book appeared. It may be that the importance of the book to the new imprint added to the urgency of the commission. John Morrill, who knew Hill well at this time, is sure that it was written from scratch in a single term of study leave.[71]

Exploring the 'revolution within the revolution', the book set out to recover the most radical voices of the mid-century crisis, and the potential they created for an alternative to the bourgeois ethic that was ultimately to triumph. The focus was on those who threw off the authority of the clergy and found their own way to religious truth. In doing so they saw scripture as an inspiration and guide, not a set of rules, and followed instead the promptings of their own conscience. They found fellowship together, and guidance from those who seemed imbued with the spirit, and their conscience might lead them to reject all kinds of human convention. The most dramatic endpoint of all this was the renunciation of sin – a concept they thought was invented and defined by men not God. This 'antinomianism' led those who felt they were pure in conscience to breach all sorts of merely human conventions about social decency, including in sexual self-expression.

Hill's heroes are vagabonds and masterless men – soldiers huddled round the campfire reading or listening to the reading of pamphlets; preachers and prophets lacking formal education but freed to speak in revolutionary conditions – all of them now liberated from the constraints of priestcraft and ecclesiastical censorship, free to foster the birth of new ideas. In fact, he consistently assumed that his writers were artisans – an elision of radical and plebeian that is often unjustified.[72] They were though, men and women largely outside the institutional power structures of church and university, responding to their own encounter with the world, generating ideas which challenged hegemonic views of sin, property, social hierarchy, gender relations and the cultural authority of their betters.

The story is told through the thought and writings of many individuals, with much less attention to the tectonic movements of Marxist political economy. The Levellers, constitutional reformers, fade into the background against the more bracing radicalism of groups with even more exciting names – Seekers, Ranters and Quakers. In the course of it all, bourgeois values concerning sex, marriage and love were swept aside by those convinced that many 'sins' were simply human conventions, rules invented to preserve respectable social arrangements, rather than expressions of God's will. In other words, the book is clearly a work of Marxist humanism – a study of people freed by their social environment to explore unconventional ideas and to create new possibilities for individual and collective fulfilment. Hill manages to bring within a single interpretive scheme an enormous range of opinion, including not just this social and religious radicalism but new ideas about how to understand the natural world. There are certainly tensions in the book – Hill had to incorporate Hobbes and Milton in appendices, their radicalism not quite fitting the overall analysis – but the effect on the reader is exhilarating. Hill really does offer a window onto the 'teeming freedom' of the revolutionary years and the excitement it induced in those who embraced it.

John Kenyon criticised the book for its obsession with 'obscure left-wing fanatics', claiming 'we are entitled to ask where all this discussion [of their thought] is getting us'. Their ideas had 'no discernible effect on the subsequent course of English development except that it perhaps made the ruling classes and the established church a mite more reactionary than they might otherwise have been'. This is somewhat beside the point – Hill said explicitly that he was not trying to characterise the mainstream of revolutionary politics, but to reveal the presence of an alternative. But Kenyon's view prefigured later criticism, arguing that to study these people was to miss the really significant action: 'This was not really a proletarian movement at all. It was an unexpected opportunity for failed shopkeepers, lazy artisans and eccentric academics to find their voice.' Meanwhile, serious people were doing serious politics elsewhere.[73]

There is no direct evidence of the influence of theoretical writings on Marxist humanism on Hill's work, but it fits with the wider cultural response and, of course, with the student radicalism he confronted in his day job. However, the book does seem more Gramscian than Marxist–Leninist in gathering together the thoughts of those challenging the cultural hegemony of the ruling class.[74] The subjective desire for freedom, for authenticity of feeling and action, for harmony of head and heart, had all been important in Hill's first move towards Marxism. More concretely, in this book, he was showing that the thought and practice of the respectable puritan reaction to Charles I's church had itself elicited an antithesis in the thought and practice of more radical groups: they sought to overthrow aspects of the Protestant ethic before it had triumphed – in the jargon, a kind of 'negation of the negation'.

At the time, the academic reception of the book was very positive, Kenyon's acerbic scepticism aside. Subsequently, most academic historians have come to regard it as flawed – asserting rather than proving the connection between ideas and particular social environments, and overstating the coherence of the worldviews and sects it discusses. The most remarkable thing about the book, however, was the chord it struck with a reading public; as Morrill recalled, 'It seemed a tract for the times.'[75] The paperback, published in 1975, sold 46,000 copies; a decade after its first publication it was selling 3,000 copies per year.[76] There were numerous translations: French in 1973, Italian (agreed in 1973 but not complete until 1981), Spanish in 1974, Portuguese and Japanese in 1982 and Bengali in 1988.[77] This was perhaps Hill's golden age, at the top of the academic world. In 1973 he was elected an honorary member of the American Academy of Sciences,[78] and delivered the Gideon Delaune Lecture on 'The medical profession and its radical critics during the interregnum.'[79]

Some clouds were gathering though. His second collection of essays, *Change and Continuity in Seventeenth-Century England* (1974), marked this eminence, but also attracted a lengthy, vituperative and controversial review by Jack Hexter. The main burden of the charge was the one made by Viner privately in 1962 – that Hill's source-mining led him to misread sources, and to connect people between whom there was, in reality, no connection. Hill was a 'lumper', interested in generalisation, rather than a 'splitter' interested in historical specificity and particularity. This led him to mislead his readers by juxtaposing statements that had little relationship with each other and did not support his assertions about what was being said. Worse, he was a determinist sort of lumper, adopting a method that enabled him to advance a thesis which, for example, required him to attribute particular beliefs to particular classes.[80]

Hill was clearly stung and wrote in the *TLS*, 'In so far as J.H. Hexter's attack on me … was personal it could be ignored.' On the more serious charge, that Hill had done a disservice to the profession, he was willing to give as good as he got.[81] Some controversy ensued, and Margot Heinemann also wrote a long letter in response, making counter-allegations about Hexter's scholarship, although it was too long to be published. Hill was nonetheless grateful for her support: 'I hope I really did get the point across that you really transformed my life over that wretched Hexter affair. I was so depressed about it all that I was just on the point of deciding not to answer at all when you rang up and put new spirit into me.'[82] There was also some wry amusement though: Richard Cobb noted some time later that 'Hexter seems to have called a truce, presumably to give his Research Team more time.'[83] Despite the sting, the Hills later entertained Hexter, and Bridget commented that 'It was difficult to hate him.'[84]

Through the rest of the 1970s Hill published on themes that were by now familiar: the history of radical religion (specifically, actually, irreligion), religious dissent, radical science and medicine, and the Levellers.[85] In part he was trying to recover a radical tradition which would embolden modern radicalism by giving it the kind of history that conservatives and orthodox thinkers received as a matter of course at school. A key article here was 'From Lollards to Levellers', published in the festschrift for Morton;[86] he also returned to the lives and thought of Milton, Marvell and Winstanley,[87] and took up his critique of the demographic approach to the family and sexuality in an article on puritanism and the family.[88]

One of Hill's more interesting historiographical experiments also comes from this time, in a collaborative article with a psychologist on the obscure visionary Arise Evans, a seventeenth-century prophet with no formal theological training and relatively humble social origins. Rather than Hill's more usual concern with the social origins of radical thought, the co-authors considered the possibility that Evans had experienced mental illness in early life, and that the social environment in which he expressed himself allowed him more licence than he might have enjoyed in previous generations. Emotionally disturbed individuals could participate actively in social life as long as their behaviour 'was not considered evidence of undue psychological impairment', and in the conditions of the 1640s and 1650s Evans was empowered. In an echo of radical psychology they concluded that he 'might well have fared worse if he had lived in less troubled times'.[89] This developed a similar thought from *The World Turned Upside Down*: 'modern psychiatry is helping us to understand that madness itself may be a form of protest against social norms, and that the "lunatic" may in some sense be saner than the society which rejects him.'[90]

However, Hill's most significant scholarly publication of the later 1970s was his book-length study of Milton, the fruit of a suggestion made to him by Faber in December 1971, and of a long-held ambition.[91] In Moscow in 1935/6, in the company of people singing revolutionary songs, he had been asked to sing an English one. Excusing himself from that, he chose instead to recite Milton's poem on 'The late massacre in Piedmont'. Through Milton he could write about the revolutionary role of intellectuals, but more importantly challenge the 'idea of continuity' in English history: the smug view that change in English history had been achieved by reasonable men acting moderately. Milton the revolutionary had defended 'divorce at pleasure' and 'complete freedom of the press', but had subsequently been embalmed, shorn of his radical credentials by later generations, just as the English past had been.[92]

Despite its long gestation, the book clearly caused Hill some pain, not least because the draft was twice the agreed length.[93] He trailed some of the key ideas in the *TLS* in 1974, causing quite a stir by arguing that

Milton should be understood as a radical, more or less a Leveller.[94] In fact the argument of the book is more subtle (or elusive) than that. Hill offers sensitive readings of Milton's prose and poetry, alert to the learned culture in which Milton (but few of us now) was immersed. Milton was a convinced opponent of popery but was also convinced that Protestant theology required reform, and his views on that were in some respects highly unorthodox. As he reflected on this across a long life, Milton lived through the personal rule of Charles I, civil war and revolution, the compromises of the 1650s and finally the Restoration, which in many ways was a defeat for him. He wrote prose tracts on social and political issues, put his polemical skills at the disposal of the Cromwellian regime and, in old age in Restoration England, composed great epic poetry: *Paradise Lost*, *Paradise Regained* and *Samson Agonistes*. The radicalism and heterodoxy he expressed resonated with the heretical third culture Hill had uncovered in *The World Turned Upside Down*, and so, despite Milton's class background and elite education, Hill sought to assimilate him to that same world of teeming freedom.

The complexities and scale of Milton's work seem ultimately to have resisted Hill's interpretative scheme, however. In the final pages he admitted that he had assumed the book would be easier to write than it proved: 'My brashness was rewarded by years of wrestling.' He had put down his pen, rather than finished, since 'every time I re-read Milton fresh aspects of his complex personality force themselves upon me'. The final chapters were headed, rather modestly, 'Towards a conclusion'. Like Hill's portrait of Cromwell, the book portrays an individual struggling in contradictory ways to make sense of the revolution. It recalls his earliest article on Marvell too, in suggesting that by understanding the dilemmas of Milton's actual social and political life, we are in a better position to understand the ambiguities and incongruities of his writing.[95]

Hill's study of Milton had far less public impact than *The World Turned Upside Down*, although it won a share of the Heinemann award in 1978.[96] It did, though, help to build his reputation among literary scholars. Although Hill tended to assert rather than demonstrate that Milton was mixing with heterodox thinkers in London's congregations and that his own ideas were shaped by these encounters, this view has largely been supported by subsequent scholarship, as has Hill's belief that Milton was the author of *De Doctrina Christiana*, which at the time was contested. That tract was very radical in its theology, and it changes how *Paradise Lost* is read, making it seem far more unorthodox than readings based on an assumption of Milton's essential theological orthodoxy.[97]

More important than these scholarly particulars, however, was Hill's determination to historicise Milton – to make him an actor in his society rather than a poet of sublime sensibility whose art escaped its immediate context. This struck a chord with literary scholars, particularly Miltonists, a group marked by resistance to the 'new criticism' of the post-war years. That tended to consider the formal properties of works, the art and genius of their composition, rather than to see them as products of a particular place and time. However, Don Wolfe, who had led work on the landmark Yale edition of Milton's prose works in the 1950s, had seen in Milton resources to resist McCarthyism – his support for freedom of the press in *Areopagitica* for example.[98] In historicising Milton, therefore, Hill was in tune with important currents in Milton studies too. He was a staunch supporter of the new journal *Literature and History*, although he was sceptical of its preoccupation with theory, being more interested in literature than the discipline of literary studies; he supplied fifty-four reviews for the journal and gave papers at two of its conferences. In 1998, a special edition on the seventeenth century was dedicated to him.[99]

Not all scholars welcomed the Milton book, though, or the approach. Blair Worden wrote a withering review for the *TLS*, arguing that the ideas that interested Hill were shared across the boundaries of the categories he imposed – radical and orthodox, plebeian and learned. Milton could not be reduced to a radical whose ideas derived from his associations with plebian religion, an association which was not in any case demonstrated in the book. Quentin Skinner, in the *New York Review of Books*, was much more positive, but he too noted that Hill's categories were distorting his analysis – leading him to ignore, for example, the effects of Milton's reading of classical literature on his poetry, and giving a reductive version of Satan in *Paradise Lost*. Here, recent scholarship has tended to confirm the criticism of Hill – that heterodox ideas might easily be the product of learned culture, and in Milton's case may well have been. Skinner did, however, welcome the attempt to place Milton in his political and social context, and was much warmer about the book overall.[100] Margot Heinemann later tried to get John Beer to present the book more sympathetically to Oxford undergraduates: the English faculty apparently recommended Blair Worden's negative review to students, and she asked for more positive ones to be added alongside it, including Skinner's.[101]

❧

It was through *The World Turned Upside Down* that Hill came closest to directly shaping the radical cultural tradition that was now at the heart of his work. Groups such as the Diggers provided a direct inspiration to counter-culture radicals. In San Francisco, for example, the name was adopted by a group who combined radical theatre with New Left, civil rights and peace movement activism. They tried to live a life free of private property, buying and selling, the memory of Winstanley and Diggers helping to bind together a counter-cultural experiment of enduring significance. In Britain the connection between such aspirations and Hill's historical writing was also quite direct. In 1973 Leon Rosselson wrote a song called 'The World Turned Upside Down', which had Winstanley's words at its heart: that the earth should be a common treasury for all. It was later re-recorded by Billy Bragg and reached number fifteen in the charts, reflecting a wider engagement by English folk singers with the radical memory of the 1640s. Bragg would later list Hill's book among the five that had most influenced him.[102] Rev Hammer wrote a folk musical about John Lilburne, while the influence of radical history is clear on the band the Levellers, as well as Attila the Stockbroker and Barnstormer 1649.

The book also resonated with radical theatre practitioners in the UK. Against the backdrop of the counter-culture, second-wave feminism, industrial strikes and confrontation between the government and unions, radical writers wanted to explore 'historic patterns of resistance, revolutionary politics, and popular rebellion', looking for ways they might speak 'to a later age of social unrest'. Caryl Churchill wrote the play *Light Shining in Buckinghamshire* under the inspiration of Norman Cohn's *The Pursuit of the Millennium*, but she also echoed the key phrase in Hill's introduction to *The World Turned Upside Down*, saying that she wanted to call attention to 'the revolution that didn't happen'.[103]

To his evident bemusement, Hill was approached in May 1973 about a dramatisation of his book by an American named, interestingly enough, William Morris. While appreciating the resonance of the name, Hill replied that he thought the book might make a documentary but not a play. Five years later he was approached by Michael Thomas, a literary agent, and this time he agreed to an adaptation. He wanted an unambiguous right to approve the script since the title was by now so much his own that 'I can't have anything using that title of which I seriously disapprove'. In return though, he would be very happy to co-operate in any way he could.[104] The result was an adaptation directed by Keith Dewhurst.

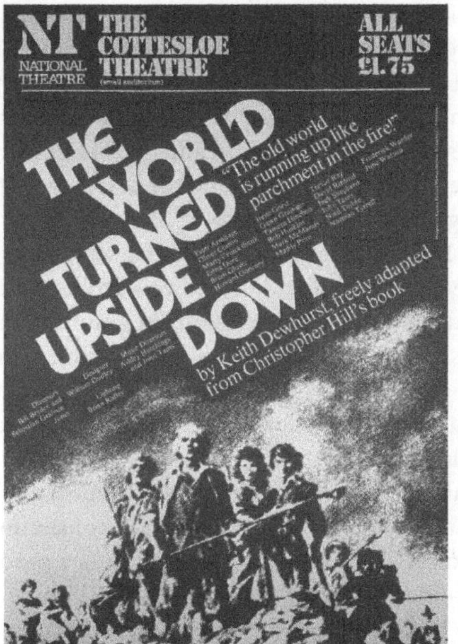

Poster for Keith Dewhurst's stage adaptation of *The World Turned Upside Down*, 1978.

Dewhurst's production also answered a need to demonstrate that the new National Theatre could speak to ordinary people in return for its lavish public subsidy. The South Bank complex had opened in 1976, dogged by adverse publicity about the cost and the director Peter Hall's salary. Initially only two of the auditoria were open, and other theatre companies complained about the share of public money going to the National Theatre, demonstrating within a month of its opening under the banner 'A National Theatre … For whom? At what cost? At whose expense?' The National Theatre's response to these objections was the Cottesloe – an intimate studio theatre where seats could not be reserved and ticket prices were low. It was intended to be both a place where other companies could perform, and a base for the informal ensemble company, the Cottesloe Company.[105]

That company acquired a reputation for what, in the light of the Digger literature, might be termed antinomian excess: the material of Hill's book was appropriate to the ethos of the company. The ambition, as Dewhurst expressed it, was to find an effective form for popular theatre that was both challenging and engaging: 'Popular theatre beats its brains out to be accessible without loss of integrity … to combine what everyone can understand with the highest possible quality of writing, acting and production.'[106] Hill attended rehearsals, helping actors understand their characters with 'absolute modesty and tact'. Along with Dewhurst he gave an interview in the *Morning Star*, and on 1 December 1978 delivered a lecture on the English Revolution, before actors from the production staged a reading of the Putney Debates.[107] The play ran for three weeks in November and December 1978 to mixed reviews, most agreeing that the balance between exposition and drama was problematic. Nonetheless, some scenes did make a clear impression; for example, that in which 'the riotous Ranters, Dionysiac religious extremists, turn a meeting into a gaudy orgy, full of mad wheeling dances, ear-splitting oaths and buttock-heaving copulation'. (Adverts for the play noted that it was 'perhaps not suitable for children'.)[108]

Coming at the end of Hill's time as Master of Balliol, as he retired from full-time academic work, the play was a consummation of ambitions he had expressed in the 1930s – celebrating a vision of society in which people could be authentically themselves, where a good society allowed people to be good, and the role of education, democracy, free thought and new ideas in bringing that about. This was matched by a public profile that reached well beyond the Cottesloe. Hill was an established figure for the reading public – a point of reference in reviews or articles on other subjects. He also featured in a twenty-six-part radio series, 'The Long March of Everyman', though the series itself was not well reviewed.[109]

Hill was by now an easily recognisable figure in the cut and thrust of the literary pages of the 1970s. He was involved in some long-running exchanges that formed part of the entertainment for that readership: with Trevor-Roper and Rowse, Laslett and Geoffrey Elton, for example. On the whole he seems to have enjoyed such jousts, writing of Rowse, for example, with some affection: 'for all his irritating idiosyncrasies, [Rowse] is another historian who sees culture as an integral part of total history, and writes the better about it because he is a total historian'.[110] Hill and Trevor-Roper maintained a courteous correspondence over decades, despite their differences and public criticism of one another's work. Having reviewed Trevor-Roper's *Religion, Reformation and Social Change* in the *Economic History Review* in 1968, Hill received a note of thanks saying: 'Like Gibbon (and you, I think, but not like – e.g. – A.L. Rowse), I like my praise "seasoned with a reasonable admixture of acid", and your admixture is very reasonable and brings out a delicious savour.'

Trevor-Roper sent another note in August 1973, warm and teasing in tone, following Hill's appearance on the radio with Lawrence Stone.[111] The same seems true of Elton. In 1967, after Hill had castigated 'what I take to be G.R. Elton's view that political and administrative history is in some sense more significant than social history or the history of culture', he received a tart riposte, but they corresponded about Tawney, and Hill evidently sent Elton copies of his work. Their public exchanges were not taken personally, it seems, and in 1978 Elton assured him that 'last year's water is under the bridge, or over the weir, or something'.[112] There was little love lost with Peter Laslett, however, who Hill claimed was a prime example of someone falling for the 'illusion of the epoch' in writing about the one class society.[113]

In these largely well-mannered combats Hill was a champion of radicals, and when Kevin Brownlow and Andrew Mollo made a film about Winstanley in 1976, he gave historical advice and reviewed it subsequently.[114] He had done more than any other scholar of his generation to bring Winstanley to the forefront of seventeenth-century studies, and he continued to write about him.[115] But Hill had a broader literary profile too: his views on the contested election to the Oxford chair of Poetry were worth quoting, for example.[116] He was by now accumulating honorary degrees too: Hull in 1966, Sheffield in 1967, UEA in 1968, Glasgow and Bristol in 1976 and York in 1978. La Sorbonne Nouvelle was to follow in 1979, Exeter in 1979 and the Open University in 1982. He was elected an honorary member of the American Academy of Sciences in 1973 and an Honored Scholar of the Milton Society of America in 1976.[117]

Some of his public commentary consisted of explicit reflection on methodology and on Marx's life, and of reviews of work by other Marxists;[118] he was also a sponsor of a new literary prize, the Isaac Deutscher Prize for contributions to the development of Marxist thought.[119] But this profile was at the service of a broader left, in a variety of progressive causes. He regularly signed open letters, against escalation of US intervention in Vietnam, for example, and in support of Abram Fischer, the South African QC put on trial for sabotage in 1966, and of Rudi Dutschke, the radical German activist trying to move to England to work on a PhD.[120] He also put his name to letters protesting against Czech suppression of intellectuals and writers after 1968 and the treatment of political prisoners, some of that work in cooperation with the Russell Foundation.[121] His instinct was to keep channels of communication open across the Iron Curtain: he wrote protesting against the British boycott of the International Congress of Historians in Moscow in 1970, which had been instituted in protest about Soviet action in Czechoslovakia.[122] He was similarly willing to express public concern about political repression in Poland, about the treatment of student protesters by the Greek authorities in 1973, and about the plight of Cypriots studying in the UK who were placed in financial difficulty by war at home.[123]

More locally, Hill took up the cudgels on behalf of British academics who in his opinion had been mistreated, particularly as a result of their political beliefs. He wrote in support of thirty-three part-time teachers at the Guildford School of Art, calling for an impartial hearing of their case against the County Council.[124] In 1970, he also weighed in when Anthony Arblaster was not appointed to a permanent position in the Politics department at Manchester, although apparently well qualified and having just completed a two-year contract in the same department. Arblaster's supporters believed it was retribution for addressing a student sit-in three months earlier, and Hill was one of those who wrote in public support.[125] Hill joined the Freedom Group, a sub-group of the National Council for Civil Liberties committed to the defence of academic freedom. A statement in the *Oxford Gazette* explained that 'in the last two years, the threat and violation of academic freedoms have included the employment of security firms at universities, the attempted employment of political informers, and sackings'. In addition to the cases of Dutschke, Arblaster and the Guildford School of Art, the statement named the non-renewal of Dick Atkinson's contract at Birmingham and employment disputes at Hornsey College of Art.[126]

At the very time Balliol was straining to deal with the tensions arising from student radicalism, therefore, Hill was himself becoming a figure in the radical tradition that his writing now focused on, and a familiar presence in the national press speaking for progressive causes. By the end of his time as Master he was the dominant figure in seventeenth-century studies and a significant public intellectual, identified with broad left progressive politics. This was to make him a target in the culture wars of the 1980s and after.

9

Retirement, Revisionism and the Experience of Defeat: 1978–2003

I knew of course that [Milton] had been defeated and that he had had a bad time after 1660, but I felt it on my pulses perhaps a bit more after the end of the student revolution and after all that died away.

Christopher Hill, interview with Penelope Corfield, 1988

As retirement from Balliol approached it was announced that Hill would take up a visiting professorship at the Open University for two years from 1978.[1] The capstone of the Wilson government's vision of education as an engine to promote welfare, full employment and social mobility, the OU was to be 'a University of the air', working by broadcast and through innovative teaching techniques. It was profoundly idealistic, committed to 'pluralism, dissent, equity and the belief that humans can and should shape the world'. It became a key point of access to higher education for those who had missed out, in close alignment with the central vision of the Robbins Report: that higher education places should be available 'for all those who are qualified by ability and attainment to pursue them and who wish to do so'.[2]

Like Lindsay before him, Hill was demonstrating a 'commitment to educational innovation'.[3] He had always been willing to use his skills beyond the walls of Balliol, through the party and the WEA, as well as at Caerleon and in numerous public talks. He had also participated in the Sussex Tapes initiative, in which prominent historians were interviewed about significant historical questions, creating, as one reviewer noted, resources 'ideal for isolated students of the Open University'.[4] He was proud of his appointment as Visiting Professor at Lancashire Polytechnic, and dedicated *A Nation of Change and Novelty*, published in 1990, to Tim Curtis, the Deputy Director there. Another collection of essays published in the 1990s listed Lancashire Polytechnic but not All Souls in the author biography.[5]

Anne Laurence remembers that many former communists were working at the OU. Unable to get university jobs in the 1950s, many party members had gone into adult education departments and from there were recruited to the OU. Certainly, Hill had long-standing connections with the OU, not least through Bridget, who had been a tutor since 1972 (one of the first in fact) and who continued there until her retirement in 1985.[6] Another connection was Arnold Kettle – former Communist Party comrade and father of Martin, student leader and activist during Hill's time as Master of Balliol – and together they collaborated in a programme on the Middleton play *Women Beware Women*.[7]

At the OU, Hill led the planning of an interdisciplinary course on seventeenth-century England covering science, art, philosophy and music alongside the topics then conventionally covered in History degree programmes. The reach of these courses was huge – 2,000 students per year. Anne Laurence, who worked closely with him in this period, remembers Hill as a consummate politician in dealing with the administration and as a constructive and egalitarian colleague, willing to join in collective discussion of course materials and happy to revise his own. The textbook for the course clearly bears Hill's stamp, but explicitly aimed to introduce students to alternative perspectives. It took them through discussions of 'structures and beliefs', the European context, economic practice and theory, the outbreak of the civil war, political thought, science and the royal society, and literature and arts.[8]

Hill wrote prolifically in retirement, continuing to probe the thought of the age and its relationship to the development of a culture helpful to capitalism. Much of this was biographical in approach, exploring contemporary writing to reveal the contradictions of the society that produced these works of imagination.[9]

His original interest in the seventeenth century had been literary, and the major achievement of this later stage of his career was in literary history. By the late 1980s, in fact, he thought 'the best history of England today is being written by literary critics and literary historians'. They are, he wrote, 'aware of the cultural crisis in England … You have only got to look at the literature to see this sense of crisis and sometimes of doom hanging over the society.' In 1979 he was invited to join the editorial board of *Prose Studies 1800–1900*, and he championed the use of literary sources by historians, noting support for that from figures such as Keith Thomas and Jack Hexter, by no means fellow Marxists.[10]

At the time he was being much criticised for failing to use manuscript materials, not least by the historian John Morrill, a leading critic of Hill's work. In response, he pointed out, not so obliquely, Morrill's weakness in the use of literary texts: 'Need I add', he said, 'I think his history lacks a dimension?' As academic history took a remorseless archival turn, the desire to bring literature and history together, he thought, was almost exclusively on the literary side.[11] This literary interest also intersected with Hill's interest in the history of dissent, notably in an exploration of the world of the Muggletonians, a sect with origins in the 1650s who held very unorthodox views. The last Muggletonian had died in 1979, leaving a large archive to the British Library.[12]

Yet in the 1980s Hill was pessimistic about the future. The threat of nuclear destruction hung over the world, and British politics in his opinion were totally controlled by the Americans. There was some hope in the 'Third World', but England, he said, 'I am very gloomy about'.[13] He told an interviewer in 1981 that although Margaret Thatcher's popularity would not last forever, he could at that point only conceive 'of some sort of ramshackle Labour government bringing the left and the right together in a fudge-over' in time for the next election (even that hope was, of course, cruelly dashed by Thatcher's sweeping victory in 1983). As for the prospect of 'real socialist change in the foreseeable future … I wish I could see it'.[14] Hill's pessimism would underpin his 1984 study, *The Experience of Defeat*, which revealed the missed opportunities of the revolution and the experiences that lay behind some of the silences of public memory after the Restoration. Like *The World Turned Upside Down*, it was a tract for the times, but it did not celebrate the present so much as commend hope for the future over regret for the past.

This was followed by a major and well-received work on John Bunyan and his social milieu, *A Turbulent, Seditious and Factious People*, which won the W.H. Smith Literary Award in 1989.[15] Many decades earlier, Hill had quoted Bunyan in a letter to Grant Duff – 'I dare not despair' – and the same feeling seemed to inform his work in the 1980s. Bunyan's message was, he said, 'that you win through not by anything except sheer dogged bloody-minded determination. It is Christ who saves you, but in order to be saved you are never to give up hope.' It is a message that had taken Bunyan into world literature and made him an inspiration, for example, to the Tai-Ping rebels in nineteenth-century China.[16]

The 1990s saw three more books: *A Nation of Change and Novelty: Radical Politics, Religion and Literature in Seventeenth-Century England* (1990), *The English Bible and the Seventeenth-Century Revolution* (1993); and *Liberty Against the Law: Some Seventeenth-Century Controversies* (1996). Despite attracting relatively little attention from academic historians, the second of these, *The English Bible*, was one of the runners-up for the NCR Book Award, beaten to the main prize by Peter Hennessy's *Never Again*.[17]

Overall, Hill's was a remarkably productive retirement, measured in pages published: more productive, in fact, than many entire careers. In addition to six books there were enough essays to fill a large part of five volumes of collected essays.[18] His earlier work continued to be reissued, sometimes updated in the light of new findings and critique: *The Century of Revolution, 1603–1714* in 1980, *Oliver Cromwell* in 1984, *Lenin and the Russian Revolution* in 1989, both *Antichrist in Seventeenth-Century England* and *Change and Continuity* in the first years of the 1990s, and *Intellectual Origins of the English Revolution Revisited* in 1997. His profile apparently guaranteed a market for republications, even if the initial sales of *Intellectual Consequences of the English Revolution* (1980) were a little disappointing.[19] He continued to meet his professional debts, writing for festschriften and offering personal appreciations, and was elected a Fellow of the Hungarian Academy in 1982; the East German Academy of Sciences followed suit in 1989.[20] He remained a prolific reviewer, primarily in *Literature and History*, but he continued to appear in the *TLS* regularly, alongside his other journalism.

Nonetheless, to historians this later work often looked like the application of familiar ideas to new (and not so new) material. As an anonymous peer reviewer of Hill's essay for a volume on radical religion wrote: 'There is a sweep and scope to the article ... Unfortunately there is a massive rehearsal of material discussed elsewhere and there is an immense amount of sleight of hand and an illusion of a case being built up where the evidence is actually incredibly thin.' Moreover, and as ever, the reviewer continued, 'populace' is heard through elite sources, 'not because it is the only way they could get a hearing, but because Hill can't or won't read unprinted sources'.[21] To literary scholars, however, Hill offered stimulation in reading Milton and Bunyan, and in paying attention to radical texts as literature: as Margot Heinemann put it, his work had freed 'students and teachers from the restrictive view of seventeenth-century literature that so many have absorbed while still at school from critical reading based on T.S. Eliot and F.R. Leavis'.[22]

At the time of Margaret Thatcher's first electoral victory in 1979, public awareness of civil war radicalism was at a high point, thanks in no small part to Hill's work in the previous decade.[23] His later work, however, came to be overshadowed by a highly successful right-wing mobilisation for radical change in British politics, accompanied by, and helping to prompt, a reaction on the left against Marxism – a polarisation and fracturing of the left coalition which allowed a free electoral run to the new conservatism championed by Thatcher. Part of that conservative message was a rejection of 1960s hedonism and liberation, alongside a hard-edged essentially neoliberal political economy. Hill was a figure in these national debates, and it became hard to separate a gathering academic scepticism about his work from this new political atmosphere.

The Thatcher governments had values, and therefore education, clearly in their sights, and their unusually ambitious hopes for cultural change implied reform of both secondary and higher education. One element in this was educational standards, a concern for which gave rise to a national curriculum and the replacement of O Levels by GCSEs. Although not unique to the Conservatives – James Callaghan had also expressed concern about the effects of comprehensive education – in the hands of Keith Joseph, the Secretary of State for Education and a leading Thatcherite, it became inseparable from a cultural assault on a left-wing establishment which, he thought, had presided over the decline. The tone was set in Joseph's speech to the Birmingham Conservative Association following the Tories' 1974 election defeat, where he launched an attack on a broad front that included among its targets universities supposedly packed with left-wing intellectuals.[24]

Following Thatcher's victory over Edward Heath in the Conservative leadership contest in 1975, the restoration of national values (as the Conservatives saw it) became the centrepiece of the Tories' reform agenda. Related to this was a suspicion of, even hostility towards, the universities. Following Thatcher's first electoral victory in 1979, there were deep funding cuts in higher education associated with a reduction of university autonomy – a process still ongoing, characterised by its critics as an odd combination of marketisation with greatly increased state control.[25]

A third election victory in 1987 gave Kenneth Baker, by then Education Secretary, the opportunity to bring in an Education Bill that established a national curriculum which would enable national monitoring of standards and school performance. While for some disciplines a national curriculum is relatively uncontroversial – there might be differences over what maths a sixteen-year-old needed to know, but they were not ideological – this was not true, of course, in history. What, from the vast store of historical knowledge, was it important for students to know? In practice the curriculum tended to become defined in terms of skills as well as content – it is easier (if not easy) to agree about the desirable skills of a good historian than what they should know – but there was a consistent pressure to make the content of the national curriculum in history support the larger programme of cultural renewal.

Hill was of course hostile to Thatcher, and his public platform as an eminent Marxist intellectual meant that he was both a point of reference for and a prominent commentator on cultural politics. For the radical left he was a talismanic figure, proof that Marxism could 'storm an important cultural citadel', and he appeared regularly on TV and radio, as well as the literary pages. He was also an active public speaker.[26] His familiarity to sixth-form students, for example, was an encouragement to them to apply to Oxford, and his inclusion in Margaret Drabble's *Oxford Companion to English Literature* was surely a mark of some distinction for a historian.[27] Setting him alongside significant literary figures and public intellectuals, he used his broadcast appearances as opportunities to comment on public issues too: to criticise the politicians who had led Britain to war in the Falklands, for instance, or to denounce the 'moral obtuseness' of global leaders in the era of Mutually Assured Destruction.[28]

In July 1981 Hill contributed to a *Guardian* 'Agenda' discussion on the role and future of the monarchy, where he extolled the republican tradition, quoting Wordsworth – 'Milton! Thou shouldst be living at this hour/ England hath need of thee' – and he was publicly associated with nuclear disarmament, the National Council for Civil Liberties, calls for the release of Nelson Mandela, and appeals on behalf of striking miners. When the *Guardian* screened the anti–nuclear war film *The Day After* in December 1983, Hill was invited to comment.[29] He signed letters and petitions in defence of student protesters and academics in Bangladesh in 1983, in support of Amnesty International's campaign against the use of torture in 1984, and against the ban on broadcasting IRA spokespeople in 1989.[30] More locally he defended the credentials of the Leveller Day held in Burford in an exchange in the *Oxford Mail* in 1976.[31]

He was also a figure of international significance, invited to Australia and New Zealand in 1981 and 1987, China in 1984 (although he was unable to travel, perhaps due to a bout of Bell's palsy), New York in 1985 and 1987, Brazil in 1988 and California in 1990.[32] The resonance of this scholarly profile was remarkably accentuated by Cold War politics. In January 1982, the *Observer* reported that a South Korean publisher, Lee Kae Bok, had been given a life sentence for attempting to 'aid the enemy'. He had reportedly been brutally tortured and forced to sign a statement prepared by the authorities; the prosecution had actually asked for the death penalty. Among his offences was the publication of Korean translations of work by Maurice Dobb, G.D.H. Cole, Herbert Marcuse and Hill. Writing a week later, Hill expressed consternation, but also noted that although the liberal press was full of support for the independent trade union movement in Poland, Solidarność, there was no similar outcry about the politics of South Korea – a clear example of Cold War double standards.[33]

Michael Foot, the Labour Party leader swept aside by Thatcher in 1983, was himself something of a devotee of the radical history practised by Hill. In a 1980s review of Fenner Brockway's *Britain's First Socialists*, he appealed to a native radical tradition in which the English Revolution figured prominently, and in direct opposition to Thatcher. 'Long before anyone had heard of Karl Marx or Methodism or Margaret Thatcher's scholarly comments on such themes, English people discussed how the nation's wealth should be commonly owned and shared, and how the ballot-box should be used to achieve these and other Leveller ambitions.'[34] Foot here ran together Leveller and Digger, and Digger and socialist, in ways that are hard to support from the historical record; but although his patronising tone about Thatcher's grasp of history was justified by the even greater simplifications of which she was guilty, it was incendiary for those on the right who saw the nation's cultural elite as a bastion of left-wing privilege and self-proclaimed superiority.

Academic history was thus rendered politically partisan, both directly and indirectly, and these were debates in which Hill figured prominently. Other academics acquired similarly charged profiles. Hugh Thomas, a major historian of twentieth-century Spain who had been a Labour Party member until 1974, became a prominent proponent of the Thatcherite vision for education, and was elevated to the House of Lords as Baron Thomas of Swynnerton, where he took the Tory whip. Geoffrey Elton was another. Eight years Hill's junior, Elton was a German Jewish refugee from the Nazis, whose family had left for Prague in 1929 and then for England in 1939, when Elton was eighteen. Arriving in the comparative calm, stability and safety of Britain, Elton developed a deep respect for the British state and law-bound political behaviour: he had made his name as champion of Thomas Cromwell, the man who bureaucratised the English state in the 'Tudor revolution', taming the caprice and tyranny of the monarchy and of Henry VIII in particular. This view of the English state and revolution, and how to write history, contrasted sharply with Hill's. Both views had much to commend them, and both were clearly responses to the traumas of the 1930s, but in the 1980s Elton's was far more congenial to the government of the day. As the *Guardian* reported in February 1988, Elton called unapologetically 'for an elitist and nationalist history ... future "servants of the state" ... should be made to examine the history of England, and the emphasis should be put on its continuity and length'.[35]

Hugh Thomas and Keith Joseph were from the early 1980s intent on promoting 'a real sense of the history of our nation' to rival what French children learned about their country. The danger, of course, was that this would be a 'state-approved view of the nation's past', that 'the state itself could become the custodian of its own myths, that schoolchildren might be brought up in the image politicians desire'. E.P. Thompson and Hill spoke out against this, calling instead for an education focused on democratic traditions and the people's struggle to claim and protect their rights.[36] Hill wrote in 1983 that 'History is too serious to be left to politicians' who would reduce it to the story of past politics, 'the "crimes, follies and misfortunes" of their predecessors'. To his credit, he also noted that it was too important to leave to professional historians, praising the work of the History Workshop that was engaging people in the writing of their own history, 'from the view point of the ruled, not the rulers, a history of the people as well as of the state'.[37] Hill had given strong support to the founders of History Workshop in 1975 and was a regular participant in its events.[38] History, he believed, should be democratic in its content and in its making.

These debates were brought to a head by the 1987 Education Bill, which proposed empowering the Secretary of State to prescribe a national curriculum and to establish working groups to define the content of specific syllabuses.[39] History was to be a core part of the curriculum, something historians tended to welcome, but there was a danger here that its content would be determined by political considerations: the journalist Ed Vulliamy quoted David Cannadine to the effect that 'no government is ever going to prescribe a version of history which challenges its power'. That influence was exerted covertly, too, since, while liberal and left-wing historians 'call themselves liberal or left-wing, the right-wing and Government rhetoric insists on being "apolitical" or "objective"'.[40]

Hill's most direct political interventions were made in the resulting debates, arguing against Thomas ('Mrs Thatcher's tame historian') for the importance of democratic, not simply patriotic, education about the British past.[41] *England's Turning Point*, a collection of much of his journalism from this period, promised 'a highly relevant contribution to current controversies surrounding the understanding and teaching of history'. Generally, though, the response from the left was hesitant and divided: better at criticising than offering a similarly coherent alternative.[42] In 1988 the historian Harvey Kaye convened a meeting to celebrate Morton's *People's History of England*, sponsored by Lawrence and Wishart. Hill was there, writing to Margot Heinemann afterwards that, 'though organized with more than usual left-wing incompetence, [it] seemed to me to be a roaring success'. Both he and Hobsbawm compared it favourably 'with the early days of the Historians Group'.[43] The journalist Richard Gott, however, was struck by the failure of those at the meeting to find an effective answer to the political mobilisation of an historical vision by the right. While the left had improved our understanding through discussions of method and the purpose of history, he wrote, it 'has not (yet) been able to forge this new vision of the past into a potent weapon of political struggle in the present'.[44]

When Thatcher was invited to celebrations of the bicentennial of the French Revolution in 1989, she took the opportunity to extol the superior virtues of the British past, prompting Hill to take her to task in the pages of the *Guardian*. She was an easy target of course, since her statements were politically programmatic and not really historical at all, but he exposed her ignorance of both English and French history, and the fragility of her historical judgements.[45] His major statement about such matters, however, was made later that year, in the Conway Memorial Lecture, subsequently published by the *Guardian*. Each generation asks new questions about the past, he said, and each generation finds new aspects of the past relevant to their experience: there was no single national past that could simply be learned. A nationally imposed curriculum risked being 'jingoistically patriotic, to stress glorious victories like the Armada, Waterloo and the Falkland Islands'. He celebrated other glories: in English literature and in triumphs over censorship. Experience like that, he said, would teach children 'the dangers of monopoly or oligopoly in opinion-forming agencies'.[46] However, this vision lacked the clarity, or at least the public resonance, of the Conservative call for a national curriculum supporting a restoration of national values.

These education debates were closely related to a late Cold War hostility to Marxism, and Hill was caught up in this too. An early symptom of this atmosphere was the report authored in 1977 by Julius Gould, a professor of sociology at the University of Nottingham, which claimed without much evidence that there was a highly organised Marxist conspiracy to subvert higher education. Although widely reported, Gould's report largely backfired, its inflated claims seeming to damage rather than advance its cause.[47] Nonetheless, *The Times* ran a series on Marxism in higher education.[48] Hill enjoyed some distinction in this controversy, as Anthony Arblaster noted: he was the sole example Gould gave of a Marxist pursuing proper scholarship. Hill kept a file on the controversy, although his own long letter in response was apparently not published.[49]

Even though Gould's report was generally seen as unpersuasive, his charges were symptomatic of what was to come. In 1979, A.L. Rowse asked out loud why so many left-wing intellectuals had fallen for Stalin's lies. Although he was sympathetic to what had drawn young, idealistic intellectuals to Marxism during the 1930s, his article was characteristic of late Cold War writing in two ways: it ran together intellectual Marxism with political treachery and spying, and it argued that former Marxists had been protected by a left-wing establishment. Thus, Hill was yoked together with Anthony Blunt, recently unmasked as a spy, while Rowse claimed he had himself been locked out of influence by the left-wing establishment because he had drawn attention to their follies. The Tories had been remiss about the cultural power of these people, he argued: 'Mrs Thatcher should look to it.'[50]

Blunt's unmasking in November 1978 marked the beginning of a period of fevered mole-hunting. In July 1979, A.J.P. Taylor gave a withering assessment of Richard Deacon's book *The British Connection: Russian Manipulation of British Individuals and Institutions*, a prominent example of the genre: 'The technique is simple: left-wing intellectuals, Socialist politicians, financiers and acknowledged agents are cooked together in a single pie, from which plums are pulled out at random.' Taylor claimed to be 'deeply hurt at having been left out': 'Surely I deserved a few words of smear', he lamented.[51] This line of attack was persistent thereafter – conflating admiration for the USSR with active disloyalty and treachery, and claiming that Marxist views had no place in British education. It was also, it seems, commonly seen as an appropriate matter for government intervention.

Marxist intellectuals were also under attack from the left. In October 1979, Conor Cruise O'Brien published a lengthy denunciation of Marxists in the *Observer*, of which he was now editor in chief. His was a complicated political position, not easy to characterise. A Catholic from the Irish Republic, born in Dublin, he had made his name in the New Left and then as an opponent of the Vietnam War, in which context he cooperated with some left-wing revolutionaries. However, he had gone on to renounce Catholicism and embrace Unionism. In his view, the two sides of the Northern Irish conflict were irreconcilable, a united Ireland unattainable, and so Republican violence was unjustifiable; as a consequence he supported hard-line measures against militant Republicans. Whatever we make of O'Brien's politics, he was clearly not in any obvious way a right-wing figure, but he was alarmed by 'militant Marxists' in the unions and Labour Party, intent on destroying the current system 'on the unproven assumption that the successor system would inevitably be vastly better'. Under challenge he distinguished them from others who thought of themselves as Marxists, including 'scholars of great intellectual power and scrupulous integrity'.[52] For him, though, Marxism was something other than Hill's scholarship on the English Revolution. If O'Brien found it hard to keep this distinction clear, spy-hunters and right-wing politicians often made little effort to do so.

Thatcher's 1983 victory led to further vituperative battles on the left. The historian and journalist David Selbourne, for example, called for a thoroughgoing reconsideration of left-wing politics in *Against the Socialist Illusion*, a book Tariq Ali characterised as 'a product of demoralisation, defeat and despair'. Selbourne had thrown in the towel, Ali wrote, and launched 'a bitter and unbalanced attack on the whole socialist project'. While Ali recognised the feeling, he thought many would recoil from where it had led Selbourne.[53]

Three years later, Selbourne was at the heart of a national debate about the dominance of the far left at British universities when he published a denunciation of Liverpool City Council's Labour leadership, alleging serious corruption. He did so, moreover, in *The Times*, then in dispute with the print unions as production of Murdoch papers was moved out of Fleet Street to Wapping to escape union regulation. At the time, Selbourne was teaching at Ruskin College – a union-supported institution associated with the left and with providing broader access to an Oxford education. There, the article was seen as a betrayal and

Selbourne faced student boycotts. He would eventually leave Ruskin, claiming unfair dismissal, and amid the ensuing litigation, Sir Albert Sloman, the first vice-chancellor of Essex University, was commissioned to report on free speech at the college. Selbourne was a Balliol graduate and had signed a letter alongside Hill criticising the government for welcoming Indira Gandhi to the UK in 1978, and Hill had a file on the dispute.[54] Although Sloman's own freedom of expression was limited by the ongoing litigation, the final report can certainly be read as expressing real doubts that Ruskin had lived up to its ideals in relation to freedom of speech.[55]

The following year, Hill was caught up more personally and publicly in these highly polarised politics when Anthony Glees, a right-wing academic specialising in the history of espionage, publicly questioned his role at the Foreign Office during the war.[56] Glees was defending the reputation of Roger Hollis, former head of MI5, in the aftermath of the revelations about the Soviet spies – Philby, Burgess, Maclean and Blunt – who had been active on Hollis's watch. His case was essentially that MI5 was under-resourced, regarded as cranky and faced an uphill struggle when people like Hill could be employed in sensitive roles without, it seemed, any questions being asked. Based on Foreign Office papers, and an interview with Hill, Glees said in the press that Hill had 'almost certainly' not been vetted, and he drew attention to Hill's friendship with Peter Smollett (who he referred to by his pre-Anglicised name, Smolka). Smollett was later revealed to be a spy, and Hill had cooperated with him in publishing his 'eulogy on Soviet Russia', *The Two Commonwealths*.[57] In the book that lay behind the press coverage, Glees gave a more nuanced account and took many of Hill's statements at face value. Nonetheless, he was clear that Hill's employment at the Foreign Office had been inappropriate. His main purpose, however, was not to denounce Hill but to defend Hollis: 'If people like Hill could be, as they were, acting perfectly legitimately, Roger Hollis's task was almost insuperable.'[58]

Hill responded to the press coverage the following week, acknowledging that the claims about him were not Glees's main point, but saying it 'must certainly be untrue' that he had not been vetted. In fact we now know from the secret service files that he had been vetted at least three times, vindicating Hill's view that 'If it was wrong to employ me, the blame attaches to MI5'. Moreover, he said, there was no secret about his political views – again something now borne out by the secret service files. As someone likely to have been approached Hill mentioned Humphrey Sumner, his tutor at Balliol, and later Warden of All Souls, who was also in the Foreign Office research department: 'He knew all about me. If he had thought me untrustworthy, I should certainly never have been employed by the FO.'[59] To the list of those who might have been asked, and who would have been well aware of Hill's politics, we could also add those working at Chatham House.

His connection with Smollett, 'to which … Glees appears to attach sinister significance', was simply that of an author and a publisher, and the book 'was published with FO approval, with the normal stipulation that a pseudonym should be used'. Again this seems to be borne out by the facts, as is the related assertion that 'treacherous actions "probably" committed by "Communist moles"' could not have involved Hill in any way: 'I had nothing to do with SOE or secret operations of any kind.'[60] In fact it seems that Hill did not know Smollett well, or remember him clearly: 'friendship' seems an exaggeration. Hill could not recall, for example, if Smollett had been in the Foreign Office. On the other hand, 'Glees thinks him a peculiarly dangerous communist, and I have no reason to think him wrong on that.'[61]

In 1993 John Saville published a comprehensive and convincing rebuttal of the accusations. He had been working on a book about Labour foreign policy after the war, and in 1990 wrote to Hill to ask about his time at the Foreign Office. Hill asked in return if he had seen Glees's book, and their subsequent correspondence reveals considerable suspicion about Glees, his motives and honesty, while Saville complained that academics were accepting this kind of work too passively, 'just like they did in the fifties'.[62] The central charge, though, was of sloppy scholarship when discussing the Foreign Office Committee on Russian Studies, which, Hill wrote, Glees apparently 'regards as a Soviet plot'.[63]

Public records at the National Archives are called 'pieces' if they consist of more than one file, and there are five pieces relating to the Committee in question; Glees, however, only referred to one of them. That in itself consisted of twenty-nine files, but Glees cited only the piece number, three times, making it very hard to follow up his claims. Had he read the files properly, he would not have claimed that the Committee was under Hill's leadership. In fact, as we have seen, the Committee on Russian Studies had three sub-committees, and Hill was secretary (not chair) of one of them, that dealing with facilities for teaching Russian studies. That sub-committee was chaired by Professor Le Gros Clark. In his role as secretary to the sub-committee, Hill was acting as principal assistant to Geoffrey Wilson, a career civil servant, who was secretary of the main committee. The chair of the main committee was Orme Sargent, then No. 2 in the Foreign Office, a fact that Glees had not mentioned. Glees had failed to say who else was on the Committee, how such committees worked, and had not explained what was in the papers Hill wrote for the Committee, nor had he been clear about the status of particular recommendations and their practical effect. The impression of Hill's dominance would have been hard to sustain if all this had been done. As Saville wrote, 'Christopher Hill took no decisions of any kind. He was in no position to take any decisions. He could insist upon no matter. He was a junior administrative officer, on a secondment that would end when the war ended.' Moreover, at the point Hill left the Foreign Office no decisions on any of these matters had been taken or implemented. In short, very little of Glees's case stood up to Saville's scrutiny, and Hill was certainly happy with the result: 'I think you have done it very convincingly and one hopes definitively. It will be very interesting to see if there is any comeback – if he reviews you, for instance. But I doubt whether his name will occur to anyone as a reviewer.'[64]

Glees had also misread the political atmosphere in which Hill had been working. Hill's recollection was that during 1944 and 1945, when the USSR was bearing the brunt of the war against Nazi Germany, 'Public opinion strongly favoured continuing friendship and co-operation after the war with both the USSR and the United States, an opinion reflected in the FO and the Government.' Indeed, he assumed he had been seconded to the Foreign Office because of his first-hand experience of the USSR, and as a 'known supporter of Anglo-Soviet friendship': the secondment certainly followed fairly quickly after the German invasion of the USSR. In fact, as Glees noted, Klugmann and other communists had been knowingly employed by the SOE.[65] Lord Gladwyn, the liberal peer, former diplomat and for a time interim Secretary-General of the United Nations, confirmed this point in response to the initial newspaper reports, noting that 'What happened after the war was another matter'. (For his part, Hill said he left the Foreign Office 'as quickly as I could' once this atmosphere changed.) Gladwyn also threw doubt on other claims made by Glees which did not involve Hill.[66]

The secret service files, released after Glees wrote his book, further undermine his case, and Hill's name did not come up in the major revelations from the Soviet archives either, for example the release of the Mitrokhin archive or the writings of Oleg Tsarev.[67] The secret service files show that it is true that Hill had not declared his party membership, but he had not been directly interviewed, so had not actively concealed it. In September 1948 Abe Lazarus had noted that Hill had been in the

Foreign Office and 'got away with it', and that Inez 'knew what was going on', but this was said in the context of an assessment of Inez's awareness of party activity (what was going on), rather than a discussion of espionage.[68] What he got away with, it seems, was being a party member in the Foreign Office, although this might suggest that worries about 'leakage' of information from Hill to party circles were not completely groundless. Hill had certainly worried that his politics might prevent him getting the job in intelligence that would get him out of an infantry command, but in fact, if the experience of Roger Simon is typical, the authorities were at least as worried about putting subversives in charge of the troops. In any case, we now know that MI5 was aware of his party membership by March 1944 at the latest, and was at that point intercepting his mail; and yet he kept his job.

These exchanges about Hill cannot be isolated from the atmosphere of Cold War recrimination in which they emerged. The mud stuck, however, and although when Hill died in 2003 none of the main obituaries mentioned the accusations, Glees himself was in the papers once more, repeating his previous claims about vetting, party membership and Smollett. He also referred to 'a number of things I thought were decidedly dodgy which carried his signature' in the Foreign Office papers. He now emphasised a proposal that at the Potsdam conference Churchill should offer to dismiss White Russian emigres teaching Russian at British universities. He also said that it had 'emerged' that Hill was a 'close associate' of Smollett, although, as we have seen, Hill had made no secret of the connection, and close associate seems an exaggeration.[69]

Hill's views about the teaching of Russian are weak evidence of communist subversion: although inflected by his political preferences, the issue was primarily academic – that depending on critics of the Soviet regime limited the pool of available talent and impaired understanding of Soviet culture.[70] In any case, as Richard Rawles pointed out in a letter to *The Times*, the plan to exclude White Russians had not been put into effect. This contrasted with the actual exclusion of communists during the 1950s: he cited the non-renewal of Andrew Rothstein's contract.[71]

One piece of new evidence was Glees's claim that when they met in 1985 Hill's first question was 'you are not going to unmask me are you?' Glees interpreted this as an admission of guilt, and claimed he promised not to do so during Hill's lifetime. In his book, however, Glees had written 'Hill firmly denies ever taking orders from any Soviet controller.' Glees also now said that during their ninety-minute conversation Hill told him he assumed he *had* been vetted but had 'escaped identification as a Communist by simply not declaring his party membership', although this conflicts with what both Glees and Hill had said publicly in the 1980s, and the evidence of the secret service files. Quoted in an *Observer* article a few days later, Glees ramped up the charges, saying that as Master of Balliol Hill may have promoted left-wing students at the expense of right-wing students, without going on record with any names (again this seems untrue). He referred to Hill's behaviour at the Foreign Office as 'sinister and disgraceful'. Hill, he said, had been demoralised at their meeting, and admitted that he was 'guilty as charged'.[72] In *The Times* he was quoted as saying Hill 'was a sad, rather pathetic figure, he appeared to have had a stroke, and I took pity on him'.[73] Hill had not had a stroke, but he was suffering from Bell's palsy, and was no doubt below his sparkling best when they met.[74] The question about whether Glees was going to 'unmask' him might not have been an admission of guilt either: many had been 'exposed' without being actually guilty, not least Hollis. Sixteen years later, Glees may have misunderstood that exchange. It is the only remaining evidence to support his case, and was strenuously denied by Corfield: 'at the 1985 meeting Hill denied Glees's charges of underhand dealings and repeated his denial in subsequent correspondence.'[75]

Hill's supporters rallied around. Hobsbawm and Saville both wrote that Hill had made no secret of his party membership before the war and that it must have been known.[76] Glees responded that it was Hill's party membership not his politics that was at stake: 'if he were to disclose to his employers that he would take orders from his CP superiors, he would have been moved at once.'[77] We now know this too is wrong. It is worth noting, however, that Glees stopped short of claiming that Hill was a spy (in fact, no one challenged the claim that Hill had no access to material of interest to the Soviets), although in the *Guardian* Glees said, without citing any evidence, 'I would not be surprised to find he had a Soviet handler.' Even in a letter to the *Observer* responding to his critics he did not allege that Hill had spied.[78]

That did not stop Andrew Roberts from claiming in the *Daily Mail* that Hill had been unmasked as a 'spy', and 'revealed as an "agent of influence" for Stalin's USSR at the very time he was in charge of the Russian desk in the Foreign Office'. He also commended Glees for his decency in not revealing this for twenty years, apparently unaware of the publicity the charges had attracted in 1987.[79] None of the press coverage mentioned Saville's rebuttal, published ten years previously, and neither did Glees.

Something bigger than Hill's conduct at the Foreign Office was at stake though. Behind much of the outrage lay the question that Roberts really wanted to pose, which had also been put by Rowse in 1979, and which was picked up in more moderate tones by Daniel Finkelstein in *The Times*: why was the British establishment more forgiving of former Stalinists than of ex-Nazis?[80] Ferdinand Mount did not hold back: referring to Hill as 'Stalin's most devoted admirer' (on the strength of Hill's 1953 article): 'surely someone who could stomach Stalin's purges, his terror, famines and his subjugation of half a continent was no more suited to guide young minds than a recently convicted paedophile.'[81]

William Rees-Mogg, the former editor of *The Times*, joined in on this point. In 1997 Mogg had included Hill among the 'race of giants' that he had been lucky enough to encounter at Balliol as an undergraduate, but he now thought the appointment of Hill as Master had brought shame on the college. He did not believe the accusation of spying, but he was shocked that while 'Balliol would not have elected an ex-Nazi as Master in the 1960s … our college elected an unrepentant ex-supporter of Stalin'. Published under the headline 'the man who disgraced Balliol', the article made no adverse claims about Hill's teaching or his conduct as Master – what was at stake was what the prominence of an ex-Stalinist revealed about British culture.[82]

Calling Hill an unrepentant Stalinist is of course grossly unfair, but in any case, and ironically enough, the fact that a communist was working in the Foreign Office while under surveillance only strengthened Glees's original argument that MI5 was up against it in hunting communists. There were a lot of them, and in 1944 and 1945 many in military and political command thought they were useful allies. That was, perhaps, a culture in which it was easy for Burgess and MacLean to function as they did and in which Hollis faced an uphill task. While it is definitely the case that Hill was fighting against fascism rather than for the British imperial state, there is no evidence that this compromised his war service, and the simplest reading of the evidence is that he did not act improperly at all. It is of course impossible to prove a negative – that he did not act subversively – but the conviction that he was an agent of influence seems to have taken flight on the currents of hot air generated in the fevered atmosphere of the late Cold War mole hunts. Its end point was to denounce former Stalinists, and the left by implication, not to sustain the accusations against Hill.

Assessments of Hill's work had become highly political as a result of these national political battles over education, values and the alleged Marxist infiltration of the establishment, and this coloured views about the growing and sustained academic criticism of key parts of his oeuvre. To undergraduates, Hill was increasingly presented as the target of revision rather than as an oracle. Geoffrey Elton noted with some satisfaction that Hill's festschrift (published in 1979) left 'two overpowering impressions: the deep affection felt for him by his pupils, and their almost total inability to endorse his own theories about the seventeenth century'.[83] Ten years later Geoff Eley and William Hunt put together an essay collection, *Reviving the English Revolution*, aimed at defending Hill from his critics, but by then the contributors were swimming against a very strong tide.[84] As Mark Kishlansky gleefully mused, in a 1996 article headlined 'Rolodex man': 'It is becoming difficult to remember how influential Christopher Hill once was.'[85]

What became known as academic revisionism had narrowly academic origins. Younger scholars in many fields were turning their back on sociological models and correlations, on grand narratives and economic explanations of political life, concentrating instead on culture, experience and subjectivity. Their key targets were determinism (a familiar charge against Marxism, but also other forms of social science interpretation) and teleology (seeing developments as inevitable and paying attention to the past only as the source of the present, rather than as a condition of life worth understanding in its own terms).

Revisionists argued that Hill had made arguments implying an inevitable path from the seventeenth century to the present, and was thus guilty of both determinism and teleology. In doing so, he had also prioritised exploring the roots of modern life in the thought and practice of people who actually lived very different lives according to very different values. Determinism and teleology had therefore led to anachronism, the use of alien values and categories to understand the lives of past societies. There was a reaction against large-scale sociological explanations which seemed to present events as inevitable, produced by tectonic social forces rather than conscious human action. Instead there was a new emphasis on detailed political narrative – on chance, contingency and personality in the course of history – and on writing about the past 'in its own terms'.[86] For John Morrill, one of the leading figures in revisionism, Lawrence Stone was the primary target, although Stone and Hill were often bracketed together (despite the oft-acknowledged differences between them).[87]

Hill's idea of a bourgeois revolution, and his related explanation for the causes of the civil war, was a major target for revisionists, but his account of radicalism was also in the firing line for exaggerating the importance, coherence and modernity of radical thinking. Revisionists downplayed the seriousness of ideological conflict in Tudor and early Stuart England because it implied that war and revolution were inevitable: an emphasis on radicalism, particularly as a cause of the breakdown of government, was in that context also seen as teleological. 'The English Revolution, 1640' has often been cited in this critique, although it was written in a hurry and published as 'a last will and testament'. As Rudrangshu Mukherjee noted in 2003: 'It was ironic that he had to live with his last will and testament for more than 60 years.'[88]

Revisionists did not retreat from structural explanation, however. Where Hill had seen a political crisis reflecting a deeper structural change in the economy, Conrad Russell (another leading revisionist) saw a functional breakdown of political institutions. He did also emphasise the beliefs and personal failings of Charles I, but the fundamental problem was a structural failure in the Stuart monarchy in trying to raise money, muster armies and manage religious policy. Part of the problem was that Charles I was king in three kingdoms, and an element of the functional failure was in managing the divergent interests of England, Scotland and Ireland. (Wales was a nation but not a separate kingdom in the seventeenth century.) Functional breakdown and the 'British problem' therefore replaced class conflict as the structural explanation for political failure. As Morrill had argued in an influential book published in 1976, the structural problem lay in the relationship between the centre and the localities, the failure of provincial society to recognise the demands of central government as legitimate. Without abandoning this line altogether, he too began to emphasise the British problem and the crisis of the Three Kingdoms in the 1980s.[89]

In his later work, Hill defended the idea that there had been a revolution, rather than his early explanation for its origins: 'I have changed my vocabulary but I do not think I have shifted far on my main "Marxist" point', that the events of the mid-century 'are aptly described as a revolution, since they led to vast changes in the history of England and of the world'.[90] He now tended to argue that it was bourgeois in effect rather than conscious inception: that the resolution of the crisis was shaped by bourgeois interests, as those interests were brought to bear in the course of the crisis. Like the French Revolution (he argued) the outcomes were shaped by what was possible in that society – they reflected the key social and economic interests of an emergent bourgeois culture. In fact his earliest lectures in Cardiff and Oxford had been framed this way; it was the attempt to assimilate Dobb into an orthodox Marxist view of the revolution that led him to try to talk about causation in a line leading from economic change to political conflict.[91] Revisionists have generally been able to claim victory about the causes of the crisis, but historians discussing the consequences of the revolution have continued to emphasise the importance of rival economic and social interests in shaping development, making some resolutions more achievable than others, even if they do not necessarily do that from a Marxist perspective.[92]

The emphasis on the British context proved powerful in a period when the future of the Union was increasingly contested, and historians who concentrated on the English dimension of this wider crisis were often accused of parochialism, regarded as themselves symptoms of the central problem of the Union, its Anglocentrism. Hill had written little about Ireland and hardly anything about Scotland – his focus was on the importance of the English Revolution. His interest in Ireland was as England's first colony, and how that imperial distraction affected the development of working-class politics at home; but he did not write directly on Ireland so much as on English attitudes towards Ireland,[93] and in fact he tended to say England where Britain or the UK would have been more accurate (although this may have been a product of his manners rather than of Little Englanderism: England as a synonym for Britain was accepted speech).[94] While Hill can hardly be accused of parochialism given the breadth of his political vision, he did seem to regard England as a coherent unit of analysis within these islands, or at least he did not escape that as an inherited category, and this made his work seem increasingly limited.

The new structural accounts were intended to offer coherent explanations for big events without resorting to determinism, teleology and anachronism. Morrill famously argued that Hill had made the wrong comparison – the crisis was not the first modern revolution but the last of the European wars of religion, a product of Reformation-era politics not a forerunner of nineteenth- and twentieth-century crises over sovereignty, citizenship and secular rights.[95] This related to the charge by other historians that seventeenth-century religious radicalism did not express secular ambitions but rather a desire to realise the will of a living God. Secular reform would liberate the godly from human constraint, the freedom they wanted was not a modern liberal individualism but a lack of interference in submitting themselves fully to God's will.[96]

Morrill's difference with Hill, in calling the crisis a war of religion, really lay in his treatment of religious conscience. Hill argued that the form taken by religious conscience reflects the society in which people have been formed as individuals. It follows that a person's political views cannot be separated from their religious and philosophical beliefs, or the other conditions of their life – family situation, the way they earn a living and so on.[97] Forms of belief are not simply theological in origin, in other words. Morrill was arguing by contrast that religion derives its force from the relationship with God, not from that wider web of relationships. There were many political issues in play in the 1640s, but when push came to shove, and particularly when it became necessary to choose which army to join, religious belief was the most decisive influence on side-taking, sometimes in fact breaking that web of relationships. Moreover, in so far as the relationship with God was moulded by human relationships, the latter cannot be reduced simply or always to class position. Although an individual arrives at their relationship with God through a life lived, that can include a much wider range of human experiences than simply that of class: as Morrill put it to me in conversation, there were indeed a lot of middling sort puritans, but that might be explained simply by the fact that there were a lot of middling sort people.

Another bone of contention was the nature of the New Model Army, which Hill had consistently presented as a potentially democratic polit- ical force, on a fairly explicit analogy with the Red Army. In contrast, Kishlansky published an influential book arguing that the Army was rad- icalised by its material and professional grievances, not by a democratic ideology, and the relationship between the Army and the Levellers in the late 1640s was subjected to sceptical re-evaluation.[98] There was a related shift from celebrating the revolution, and the Army as its radical cham- pion, to emphasising the horrors of war and the armies as the agents of those horrors. This had a Vietnam-generation edge, as Ronald Hutton said explicitly in a book which argued that gentry activists had recruited people to a fight that was not theirs, 'to the ruin of themselves and their communities'. As well as the war between roundhead and cavalier, there was in effect a second one, between the ideologues and partisans of both sides 'and the bulk of the population, which they attempted to press into service'.[99] For Hill's proto–Red Army we might substitute the army of conscripts dumped in the jungles of South East Asia.

These interpretive issues drew sustained attention to Hill's working methods: to what Viner had earlier seen as the cherry-picking of decon- textualised quotations, and Hexter as lumping. It was commonly said that Hill's method led him to radically decontextualise his evidence, reconstituting it in a framework of his own design. The criticism was put fondly but firmly by Keith Thomas: 'whatever Christopher Hill reads seems to provide him with additional support for views he already holds'.[100] Other critics, however, seemed to be accusing Hill and others of conscious falsification for ideological purposes.[101]

Many of these issues came to a head in a heated debate about the Ranters, in some ways the heroes of *The World Turned Upside Down*, who renounced sin as a human invention and responded directly to their conscience. In 1986 Colin Davis published a book which cast doubt on this whole enterprise. Examining the writings of leading Ranters he found little evidence of true antinomianism, many differences of opinion, and no sign of any connection between the individual authors. They were not a coherent sect either intellectually or in terms of organisation, he argued, and their antinomianism had been drastically overstated. He went on to suggest that this misrepresentation arose because historians had wanted to see something that wasn't there and in doing so had fallen for a seventeenth-century propaganda campaign. Reports of Ranter belief and excess did not reveal a glorious effusion of counter-culture but rather a projection of respectable fears; those fears had now become hopes and historians who accepted the truth of these claims were no less the dupes of the 'yellow press'. Davis identified Hill and Morton (in *The World of the Ranters*) as having been particularly at fault.[102] For Davis this was part of a broader reconsideration of seventeenth-century radicalism, in which he was joined by others.[103]

This assault struck at the heart of a widely shared view about the importance and interest of the radicals. The reaction was fierce.[104] Hill made his own contribution in print[105] and was withering about the book in private, writing to a colleague in Brazil that 'A man called Colin Davies [*sic*] wrote a silly book … trying to prove that the Ranters never existed. But it has given rise to a discussion which is more interesting … Don't take him seriously.'[106] Hill was, however, deeply offended by suggestions that he and Morton had more or less consciously invented the Ranter phenomenon for partisan political purposes. He had been similarly affronted by John Sparrow on these grounds in the 1960s.

The Ranter controversy became something of a centrepiece of revisionism, and Davis spoke to two of its central concerns: Hill's habit of lumping (arguing by contrast that these Ranters did not actually have a shared view or even know each other); and his anachronistic interpretation of their view of personal freedom, which Hill conflated with modern liberalism. This critique was being mounted, moreover, in relation to a group that had acquired great significance for the counter-cultural left.

In public, Hill was fairly equanimical about academic criticism from younger scholars: bumping into Blair Worden, for example, after Worden had published a review of *Change and Continuity* in the *New Statesman*, Hill 'said with that impish grin "Thank you for that very kind obituary notice."'[107] He generally adopted this tone in public when commenting on the broader phenomenon of revisionism. In an interview in 1988, for example, he acknowledged that he was facing a major counter-attack, but felt time would tell how much of his interpretation would survive. 'I think it's quite easy for a clever chap to make out a provocative case for standing something on its head. It catches the eye and people think, yes, this is a new idea and there must be something in it. Its going to take a good bit of time before things sort themselves out.'[108] In that context he welcomed the 'post-revisionist' work being undertaken by a slightly younger generation of historians who were critical of the revisionists on such issues such as the depth of political awareness and the degree of ideological consensus in early Stuart England. Nonetheless, Hill professed a willingness to learn from Russell and Morrill in particular: 'obviously I do not agree with everything they say, but they have made us all have to rethink quite a lot'.[109]

Consistent with his view of academic life in general, Hill also seems to have thought it was not really for him to reply. He wrote supportively to Ann Hughes, a colleague at the OU, about a proposed collection of essays that was to become one of the principal post-revisionist texts: *Conflict in Early Stuart England* (co-edited with Richard Cust). Hearing stories of the 'conquest of the schools' by revisionism through the medium of short, edited books, Hill encouraged Hughes to put one together in response:

> I would help in any way I could, but it is very important that this should be a post-revisionist collection – not angry old men trying to do down the young but the really young saying that the middle-aged have made a useful contribution but have overplayed their hand, and have encouraged some of the young to think it smart to overplay their hand still more.[110]

Nonetheless, when he was invited to deliver the Neale Lecture at University College, London in 1980, Hill did take the opportunity to present a lengthy response to the revisionists. 'The acceptable conclusion that the English Revolution was made by events, not by the conscious wills of men', he said, 'is no reason for refusing to try to analyse its causes'.[111] Elsewhere, he restated his position on the role of religion: his interest was in 'the effects of God on this Revolution, and its effects on God', arguing that religious belief is not a sufficient explanation for any human event, since 'any religion can serve any social purpose, because of the ambiguity of its basic texts'. The discussion should not be about 'protestantism as causing the rise of capitalism, but rather of protestantism and Puritanism being moulded by capitalist society to suit its needs'.[112] Many of his essays from these years contain a running commentary on the methodological assumptions of the revisionists and particular arguments made by them, and he tried to rebut some of the more extreme claims about his work. He was also drawn into a defence of his readings of particular issues and figures, notably Winstanley, and revisited earlier arguments or restated well-known positions.[113] This involved more direct comment on his theoretical and methodological convictions than he had offered since the 1950s, and some explicit defences of Marxism.[114]

Another element of this was a forlorn defence against the empire of the Cambridge Group. Rather in contrast to the revisionist historians, the Cambridge Group built much of its analysis of social life on a material basis (for example, the statistical preponderance of nuclear households), which Hill regarded as a partial and determinist view of social relations. In 1979 Miranda Chaytor published an article critical of the group's view, drawing on other sources to show how wider kinship networks remained important to people, even if at many points in their lives they lived in nuclear households. She received a very critical response, which Hill thought was, at least in part, bullying – a female scholar without a prestigious institutional affiliation taking on an overwhelmingly male establishment. As he admitted to Chaytor, though, his own contribution to the controversy was limited to a short notice in *Past and Present*: 'I honestly don't think I can go any further in expressing views on a matter on which my ignorance is notorious.'[115]

Hill wrote about an extraordinarily wide range of historical topics, much wider than those at stake in the revisionism debate. In his own writing, and through *Past and Present* and his support of the History Workshop, Hill helped to launch a great broadening of academic discussion and to set a number of agendas. In these other areas, however, his work was subject to a similar methodological criticism – for example, that his writing on the history of science was skewed in similar ways to his writing on civil war sects or Milton. As a result, while most academic historians would acknowledge the range and stimulus of his work, they are also likely to point to flaws in his answers to the questions he posed, which have often been overtaken by subsequent work.

By contrast, his stock remained high among literary scholars, and it was here that he was doing new work rather than defending old positions. This work in literary history was seen as fresh, although by no means uncontroversial, and his studies on Marvell, Milton, Winstanley and Bunyan remain well regarded. More broadly, his example has licensed literary scholars to explore not just the prose of Milton and Winstanley, but also the writing of innumerable less well-known authors given a voice by the opening of the presses in the revolutionary decades. Where historicism led historians away from Hill, it seems to have drawn literary scholars to him.

Hill was a big academic target. As he reached a peak of influence in Oxford in the early 1960s, the British university system was on the brink of a rapid expansion. New and expanding departments around the country were staffed from the small number of universities that dominated research – particularly Oxford, Cambridge and London. As a result they were filled with Oxford-trained historians, and the curriculum in many of them shadowed that in Oxford. In 1962, the year Hill gave his Ford Lectures, the Royal Historical Society had around 800 Fellows. Ten years later, when *The World Turned Upside Down* was published, there were nearly 1,200. In 1982, as revisionism was gathering pace, there were 1,600. This is a crude measure, since it includes independent and retired scholars, as well as people working overseas. Nonetheless, it gives some indication of the growth in the number of historians at work in British universities, primarily supplied from relatively few centres of research.[116] Hill was a point of reference not just in debates about the English Revolution, but in discussions of radicalism, history from below, the history of science and of irreligion. The dynamics of expansion therefore amplified the importance of Hill and his work, and the same was true in other parts of the English-speaking world – most US history departments taught seventeenth-century English history, if only as context for the colonial period of US history. In Australia and New Zealand too, British history often loomed large in teaching programmes, and many of the most influential historians were Oxford-trained. It is no surprise that for this rising generation Hill was an important figure against whom to react and to aspire to improve upon.

Although revisionism was driven by the normal dynamics of academic debate, it undoubtedly acquired a charge from the wider political climate. In an article for the popular magazine *History Today*, Hill responded to triumphalist claims that the fall of the Iron Curtain signalled the decisive defeat of Marxism in part by defending his analysis of the English Revolution.[117]

Academic revisionism was certainly attractive to politicians intent on achieving educational and cultural change. Kenneth Baker famously chose Davis's *Fear, Myth and History* as his book of the year in the *Observer* in November 1987, in the week following publication of his controversial Education Bill: 'A fascinating re-assessment, which argues that the Ranters didn't exist and that a myth was created in the 1650s and nurtured by Marxists this century.' By then the book was a year old, but there had been recent controversy in the *LRB*, prompted by a disdainful review by E.P. Thompson, which was perhaps in Baker's mind. His choices for the *Sunday Times* on the same day were far less annoying to the left: Peter Ackroyd's *Chatterton*, Seamus Heaney's *The Haw Lantern* and the catalogue from the Royal Academy's 'Age of Chivalry' exhibition.[118] It must have caused some chuckling to champion a book critical of a doyen of the Marxist left in the pages of the *Observer*.

When Hexter's notorious review of *Change and Continuity* was reprinted in 1979, it too was read in unmistakeably political ways. John Kenyon saw it as primarily personal, saying that Hexter's failure to take account of rebuttals to the original position 'suggests that he has missed the point altogether – or that he is inspired by some unfathomable personal animus'. Hexter's own main fault, he thought, was 'a kind of elephantine rogueishness'.[119] The animus against Hill might in fact have been to do with academic politics as much as anything else: there was some feeling at the time that it was payback for Hill's attack on Laslett, who was rumoured to have been instrumental in Hexter's appointment at Yale.[120]

Others, however, saw more obviously ideological factors at work. Raphael Samuel had believed from the start that it was part of a semi-organised assault, associated with the people behind the Gould Report. 'I think there is a real family resemblance between Gould's tract and [other recent] interventions', he wrote, 'not so much airing of a disagreement as the accusation of treason against a professional vocation'.[121] Perry Anderson, writing in the *Guardian* about the reprint, pointed out that Hexter was inconsistent in his denunciation of lumping – a vile sin in Hill was treated as a charming eccentricity in the work of Fernand Braudel. 'What explains Hexter's wild contradictions? Hill is a Marxist historian, Braudel is not. The deforming passion behind these judgements is a vengeful Cold War liberalism.'[122] Anthony Arblaster noted that the *TLS* was 'now under the anti-Marxist and anti-radical editorship of John Gross (a former assistant editor of the C.I.A.'s own *Encounter*)', which explained why it had given room to 'a comprehensive attack on Christopher Hill's whole scholarly record, complete with references to "totalitarianism", just in case anyone might miss the political point'. It also explained the space given to what Arblaster considered Blair Worden's 'inappropriately patronizing and dismissive review of *Milton and the English Revolution*'.[123]

This worked both ways, of course. Colin Davis complained that his work was being evaluated politically, not by academic standards: his motives were assumed and that avoided the necessity of actually discussing the extent to which his arguments might have merit.[124] John Adamson, a younger revisionist who was at work on a reinterpretation of the civil war as fundamentally shaped by a noble revolt, also became a regular presence in the literary pages.[125] He and Jonathan Clark, a rising star of eighteenth-century history and a significant right-wing presence in the broadsheets, were reviewed (and certainly talked about) as much for their presumed political affiliations as for their scholarship. Hill himself indulged this conflation, distinguishing between Clark, 'a Thatcherite propagandist', and Conrad Russell, who he thought was simply academically rather than politically motivated.[126]

For its foremost academic practitioners, however, revisionism expressed a commitment to academic standards rather than political partisanship, a symptom of the healthy desire of each generation to improve on the achievements of its predecessors. Russell and Morrill were clearly not Thatcherite (Russell in fact became a Liberal Democrat peer). Davis told Glenn Burgess that he felt he was working within a 'Hill paradigm' and thought Hill a 'great historian'. He had studied at Manchester where he was taught by Brian Manning, and his own politics were probably best described as old Labour.[127] But the left in general was divided, and so not particularly tied by partisan affiliation to Hill's views of the present or the past, still less to Marxism. David Selbourne had been vocal about how non- and anti-Marxists had arrived at more durable insights. Hill and other leading Marxists had, he said, quietly jettisoned their commitments: 'These Prosperos of ours have abjured their rough Marxist magic and buried their staffs in the earth, but you would not know it.'[128]

Nor was academic revisionism a coordinated campaign. There were many differences of emphasis and interpretation among the revisionists, and Kishlansky and Adamson fell out very publicly over scholarly standards in a controversy that was reported in the national press.[129] Neither were Hill's academic critics obviously supportive of the Conservative education reforms: Blair Worden, for instance, responding rather wearily to the Radio 3 series on the march of revolution, and to Hill's contribution in particular, noted that the series as a whole was history 'for the GCSE era', 'all empathy and no chronology, making difficult what it affects to make easy'.[130] Clark too could also be very dismissive of politicians' opinions about a national curriculum.[131]

Nonetheless, revisionism gained greater weight from the political atmosphere: the public attention it garnered was testimony to the charge carried by contemporary debates about the British past. Hill was a key figure for Thatcherite Conservatives keen to shift the intellectual culture. Those who saw problems in his work could be recruited to the Conservative cause, just as Selbourne's criticisms of conduct of the Labour leadership in Liverpool had been. However, the academic reaction to Hill's work should be understood as a phase in historical debate, not as a Thatcherite programme, even if there is no doubt that Thatcherites looked on with pleasure.

In retirement Hill had become the subject of academic revisionism but also a significant target in a larger programme of cultural renewal driven from the right. A highly successful Marxist who had reached the heights of the profession, he was also a public intellectual who had, for example, done more than most to bring Gerrard Winstanley – now a touchstone for the counter-cultural left – to public prominence. Eric Hobsbawm, Hill's former comrade, became a national institution after retirement; prior to that he had not had the same profile or public following. Hill's fate offers something of a contrast.

I think the only time I was in the same room as Hill was in September 1996, at an interdisciplinary conference organised by Sue Wiseman at Birkbeck College: 'Times trans-shifting: cultural politics in the English Civil War'. Hill had given the plenary lecture to a supportive audience of literary scholars and 'post-revisionist' historians. His manner fitted E.P. Thompson's much-cited description of him as the 'Dean' of English studies – fatherly, learned and reassuring. He was still active and had spoken earlier that month at an international conference on Tyndale.[132] I was too shy to approach the great man, but in any case he had caused some alarm by reading one page of his lecture twice without apparently noticing. It was an early sign of what became the serious dementia that eventually took his life six years later.

By then Bridget had died. She had told no one about her breast cancer, either at its first occurrence or at the much later recurrence. Only at the very end, when she collapsed while taking a break from caring for Christopher, was it apparent that there was anything wrong. At her eightieth birthday in April 2002, she had been 'radiant and full of plans', Corfield later recalled, and until that brief final illness 'she was at her usual seat at the Bodleian library, at her usual times in the week'. She maintained this calm despite her distress at Christopher's illness and her own 'heroic' efforts in caring for him.[133] John Jones met her by chance in Broad Street, Oxford, around that time. '[W]e had a v pleasant gossip. As we parted, she said with a smile, "You won't see me again" which I then thought enigmatic: she died soon afterwards.' That was on 31 July 2002. As Robin Briggs notes, it was perhaps a mercy that Christopher may not have known she was gone.[134] He died on 23 February 2003.

Although at his death Hill did not escape the shadow of the politics of the 1980s and post–Cold War recrimination, the response in general was much more generous, even in the right-wing press. The obituaries and recollections presented Hill as an open-minded Oxford tutor, who did not force his views on his students, and who showed concern for them without regard for their politics. He had been a friend to Howard Marks, the apolitical hippy, and Lord Selkirk, QC, one-time president of the Oxford Conservative Association and latterly a Conservative MSP, as well as to Sir John Keegan, 'a Roman Catholic and political sceptic'.[135]

10

The Past and the Present

[T]aking one's thought from other people, … seems to me the sin against the Holy Ghost.

Christopher Hill, letter to Shiela Grant Duff, February 1941

Christopher … saw the world from Balliol in the early thirties, and drew conclusions from what he saw, to which he has held without any shadow of turning, with a tenacity and loyalty, a humanity and humour, without parallel among those of us who are still alive from those days.

Richard Southern, *Balliol Annual Record*, 1978

[Christopher Hill] was the puritan that cavaliers always underestimate: loving and loved, witty, funny, perceptive, delighting in life and genuinely fond of an extraordinary variety of its human representatives.

Hugh Stretton, 'Christopher Hill: some reminiscences', 1978

I am much more interested in literature than economics. I will not say I am ashamed to say. It is just a fact, I think. I just am that way. I realised after I had slaved away at agrarian history for a long time that this was not the only Marxist approach to a civilisation.

Christopher Hill, interview with Penelope Corfield, 1988

Trevor-Roper, who knew him well, had Hill partly in mind when reflecting on the hold Marxism had over that generation of intellectuals. They grew up with economic depression and mass unemployment around them, with capitalism in apparent crisis and fascism on the rise. All that fed 'a moral reaction against the complacent philistinism of the 1920s and the private aestheticism in which their own predecessors had taken refuge'. It was a moral, not a political or intellectual reaction; in fact they were on the whole political innocents, 'but morally they felt the call to a new self-discipline', a call that appealed to bourgeois figures in particular. The Spanish Civil War gave them a sense of mission and, by 1939, of superiority – they saw themselves as an elite. 'But those whom conscience led in, conscience, if it survived, led out again.' It was partly the discovery of politics that produced this shock: communist cynicism in Spain, and the Nazi–Soviet Pact. For many, though, it was also party bureaucracy: 'the intellectual tyranny of stunted hacks'. Here Trevor-Roper definitely had Hill in mind: 'Mr Christopher Hill, for instance, seems to have had no difficulty in swallowing and defending every act of Stalin: it was the action of these local bosses which finished him.'[1] J.M. Cameron, himself a former Marxist, recalled the thirties in similar terms, and in particular the importance of the USSR as universal bogey figure among the capitalist states, and a beacon for those disaffected by them. What gave 1930s' Marxism a slightly paranoid character was in part 'a special view of the nature and role of the Soviet Union'.[2]

Hill was certainly not doctrinaire. He was a Marxist before he committed to membership of the CPGB as a political strategy, and had been hesitant about the party in the 1930s. He left it in favour of a broad left approach to progressive politics, reacting against the party's aversion to self-criticism. He came back from Moscow to write Marxist history, a more abiding legacy of the thirties than his commitment to the party, and having left the CPGB he largely avoided party commitment. Although he rejoined the Labour Party, and the Hill house displayed Labour posters in the respectable Oxfordshire village of Sibford Ferris (a rare sight), he grew less enthusiastic over time. He boycotted the 'poll tax' and kept a cutting comparing the protests to the Peasants' Revolt of 1381, but when asked at a meeting of university students in London in the late 1980s what the left should do in the face of Thatcher's electoral success 'he replied sadly: "I wish I knew."' He was, unsurprisingly, sceptical about Labour's move to the centre in search of electoral success: 'Speaking of Tony Blair, he snorted: "That young man takes too much upon himself."'[3]

Hill's allergy to doctrinaire thinking was as much Oxford as Marxist, and was in part post-Methodist. He apparently enjoyed his sparring with Trevor-Roper and Elton, and Gordon Leff remembered him in meetings of the Historians' Group as 'a guarantee against totalitarian attitudes, combining enlightened Marxism with tolerant liberalism'.[4] This academic Marxist enquiry was of a different kind than his public defences of the USSR and Stalin in the early 1950s, or his party work. A desire for authentic self-expression had led him to Marxism, shaped his interpretation of Marx, and outlasted his commitment to the political programme of the CPGB.

Certainly, as an academic, Hill fostered open debate and was happy to assess work on its own merits: his reviews show him alert to the virtues of work that he would never himself have written. As a tutor, and Master of Balliol, he was primarily a liberal academic and a democrat, a supporter of progressive causes but not particularly identifiable as Marxist. These academic values were in tension with democratic centralism as interpreted by the CPGB in the 1950s, but they were in harmony with the pursuit of self-realisation and individual flourishing that had been important to Hill in the 1930s. He had a lifelong commitment to educational work beyond Oxford, and an abiding interest in the radical thought of those outside hegemonic institutions, and it was this strand of humanism in his work that came to dominate from the 1960s onwards. Clearly he was in many ways an individualist, committed to freer personal and sexual self-expression as well as to democratic consultation and decision-making. It was these values that had led him to Marxism, in the hope of understanding how a society could better allow them; his commitment to democracy, the free exchange of ideas and accountability led him out of the Communist Party but not away from Marxism.

As Master of Balliol, Hill recognised the role of tradition and corporate unity, although he was clearly a friend of the reformers. He successfully balanced his personal preferences with the need for solidarity, although he did threaten to resign over the issue of student representation. There were perhaps casualties and a whiff of what his enemies thought of as hypocrisy, but for Maurice Keen, a self-professed traditionalist, Hill's core achievement as Master was to avoid fatal division in the college at a very difficult time.[5] His approach to teaching and life at Balliol reveals a profound and principled commitment to assisting the birth of new ideas and supporting the march of progressive thinking, but also to allowing his students to find their own voice.

In this he was famously egalitarian. 'Everyone who knew him', wrote Pennington, 'will remember the cheerful, communicative and unassuming Christopher whose vast knowledge and thought were borne so lightly'. Hill was the 'world-eminent historian who after delivering a major lecture queued for fish and chips with two former pupils and the lucid thinker who seized on whatever was valid in the blundering of others'.[6] This egalitarianism was also an element in his loyalty to the party: it was to the South Wales coalfields he went for political certainties in 1939, not the common rooms of Balliol or All Souls.

From this perspective, education served a much broader social purpose than could be achieved simply through university teaching. He shared this view with A.D. Lindsay, and the sense of being useful in the world with the Methodism of his youth as well as with Kenneth Bell and T.S. Gregory. He worked with Basque children at Caerleon and in the party's cultural programme, and was active in the WEA. He was proud of his association with the OU and Lancashire Polytechnic, and applied for jobs at Keele and Glasgow – although in fundamental ways a Balliol man, his educational ambitions were not limited to Oxford. Throughout his life he published in newspapers and magazines, and in his eighties he remained willing (for example) to talk at the Banbury public library in a programme put on for school children in their summer holidays.[7] His short book (or long chapter) on the English Revolution announced his arrival in 1940 with a new interpretation for the benefit of non-academic readers, with explicit reference to contemporary events.

Although clearly someone who lived an examined life, he was more than a little allergic to indulging that publicly. This could make him seem aloof and forbidding, for all the warmth that many people felt from him. He was relaxed, friendly and egalitarian in manner, but also reserved and proper, more than a little shy. Political caution added another layer of reserve to this temperamental disposition. In general, 'he believed in the duty to "bear witness" publicly',[8] and even the secret services thought that neither he nor Inez had made any secret of their politics in the early Cold War years.[9] But during the 1930s and more especially the 1950s he had witnessed what he saw as political victimisation in academia, and during the fifties (he told Mehta) only tenure at Balliol had protected him.[10]

After leaving the CPGB, therefore, he refused to give ammunition to critics of British communism or Marxism. A late, and clear, statement of his rejection of Stalinism came, perhaps significantly, in an interview in New Zealand, where he was probably less conscious of a British audience: 'I was a sucker for Stalinism until I found out a lot more about it. I thought the Communist Party held out an alternative. I was wrong.'[11] So, while it is patently wrong to claim that he was 'unrepentant' about his Stalinism, his repentance was quiet; he did not want it to give encouragement to the enemies of the left or of those with whom he had suffered. Nor did he easily reveal his connections or relationships with other radicals. As he said of the Ranters and other radicals: 'Illegal and persecuted movements have a habit, unfortunate for the simple-minded historian, of not leaving around too much written evidence of their organization … and contacts.'[12] Being Master of Balliol gave him a third reason for personal reserve. During his time as Master the internal life of Balliol was frequently and accurately reported in the national press: he had good reason to be tight-lipped about college life.

For many people Hill was defined by his Marxism, although, ironically enough, his Marxism was itself quite ill-defined – he was tight-lipped about this too. As early as 1965 he wrote to Isaiah Berlin: 'Let's skip talking Marxism for a bit: I don't know where I am about that.'[13] In general, but particularly in the context of the culture wars of the 1980s, he was more enigmatic: 'to the question "Are you still a Marxist?", one of his answers was "I don't quite know: does it matter?"'[14]

One reason for this frustrating refusal to set out his view systematically was stylistic: he said on several occasions that after a conversation with a party activist in the early 1950s he had avoided Marxist jargon, and (also stung by a jibe from Tawney) had concentrated instead on effective communication. It was clearly more than that, however. He had plenty of opportunities to explain his position, declining several invitations from admirers to set out his views, but he obviously had a general aversion to theorisation.[15]

This reticence also derived from a deep antipathy to hyper-intellectualism, a source both of his long-standing suspicion of philosophy and of his dislike of All Souls. Of himself he wrote, 'I am not a political philosopher, just a historian interested in 17th century England: I am chary of philosophical generalisations.'[16] This may also have reflected a feeling that it was not his strength. When Berlin sought reconciliation between them in the mid-1960s, Hill confessed that 'the real truth is that I am frightened of you and your sort of cleverness, and can't compete, and feel clumsy and resentful, and curl up. The political thing is secondary, not exactly an excuse but an alibi.'[17]

This dislike of purely conceptual discussion, however, was clearly not a symptom of a lack of interest in ideas; indeed he later described his 1950s self as 'a 17th-century historian for whom ideas were an essential part of history'.[18] But this suspicion was consistent with his methodological assumption that ideas were to be understood in the context of the society that made them work, not as timeless truths. That is what he thought about puritanism and about Marxism: he was interested in the 'meaning of Marxism not as dogma but [a] guide to action'.[19]

Hill's Marxism was a product of what he saw as a crisis of bourgeois culture in the 1930s, offering a framework to understand not just the crisis of global capitalism and bourgeois states but also the personal alienation felt by intellectuals and others. It made sense of such diverse phenomena as sexual repression, the dumping of coffee into the Atlantic and the attitude of Imperial Britain to the rise of Nazi Germany. It was not a straightforward replacement for the Methodism of his youth. In fact, having lost his own faith, he was resistant to all forms of dogmatism including that of secularists like Archibald Robertson, who 'tended to have a very religious approach to irreligion, substituting one form of dogmatism for another'.[20]

Rather than a reaction to his loss of faith, his Marxism was a reaction against what he saw as the smug liberalism which seemed so inadequate in the face of the 1930s crisis. He wanted to find meaning and direction in human affairs where H.A.L. Fisher had seen none, and to puncture the complacent liberal myth of continuity and gradualism in English development. Writing in 1965, he thought the case had been made that the English and French Revolutions were comparable, and that there was merit in the comparison, but bemoaned the fact that the English Revolution was still assumed to have had no intellectual origins. He was attracted by the idea of radical change, and the role of ideas in that, and so disliked the view that the English Revolution 'just happened, in the typically British empirical way in which we always like to imagine ourselves muddling through: in a fit of absence of mind'.[21] This had implications for the present: ideas and reason could improve the world; it was not necessary to despair, as liberals did, or to submit ourselves to God's mercy, as traditionalists had when confronted by the failures of human reason.

During the 1930s his conclusion that bourgeois civilisation was in its terminal crisis led him to an interest in its seventeenth-century origins – the intellectual revolution that had produced bourgeois culture and the social conditions in which that revolution had been possible. A characteristic lecture on this theme sets out eleven revolutions in the seventeenth century, of which only one is an 'economic revolution'. The others are intellectual, political and constitutional, religious, moral, legal, historical (in the sense of changing ideas about how to write history), political-theoretical, literary and philosophical. Another is 'women'. It was the interaction of these many transformations that interested him, not the determining force of the economic revolution (eighth on the list as it happens).[22]

Ideas were at the centre of his analysis, therefore, but they had to be understood in their total social, economic and cultural context. This was dialectical materialism – an interest in the interaction of ideas with their material environment. It is a position defined in opposition to economic determinism, which derives the content of ideas from their material context. It is a subtle distinction, one Hill's work did not always honour, but also one that has evaded many of his critics.

Criticism of Hill's position as determinist makes light of his constantly stated view on this dialectic between ideas and their social, cultural and material environment. It also seems to reflect a hostility to his Marxism rather than to materialism more generally, since other at least equally obviously determinist arguments often pass with less objection. For example, Laslett explained the mental world he recovered – patriarchal, deferential, localised – from the material environment (the economic and demographic centrality of the nuclear household), but has not (it seems to me) been criticised for determinism. Similarly, revisionist historians argued for the importance of the county in shaping the consciousness of the gentry community. Bound together by marriage within the county and by participation in its political institutions – the one class of Laslett's 'one class society' – the political imagination of the county gentry was, characteristically, similarly geographically circumscribed. This is questionable, and has been very extensively questioned, but this 'county community school' was not accused of determinism in the way that Hill has been. Criticism of determinism is more often a shorthand for hostility to Marxism than a real aversion to determinism.

For Hill, the two partially distinct strands of the crisis of bourgeois culture in the 1930s gave rise to partially distinct strands in his writing: one concerned with political economy, revolution and the state, the other with authenticity of expression, the struggle of individual thinkers to reconcile the contradictions in their society and to imagine new worlds. It is the first strand – the history of the state and its relation to economic change – that has attracted most criticism for its determinism. His work on that issue, at least in 'The English Revolution, 1640', took the established political narrative and tried to marry it to Dobb's analysis of the changing mode of production, and the result does seem deterministic.

However, the question of authenticity and personal flourishing, the alienation that many feel from the roles that society demands of them, was closer to Hill's heart. This was also a core Marxist concern. Berlin wrote to Hill in the mid-1960s that he had become more interested in the phenomenon of alienation in understanding Marxism, asking 'Have you views on that subject? Alienation I mean?'[23] It was a shrewd question since it goes to the heart not only of Hill's own biography, but his biographical writings on others.

His work on the struggles of individuals to make sense of the contradictions of a society in transition more successfully avoids determinism, or the appearance of it. A less familiar example might make this case: a lecture on the poet Richard Crashawe (or Crashaw) (1613–49) contrasted what Hill saw as the escapism of Crashawe's devotional poetry with Gerrard Winstanley's active political engagement. Winstanley saw love as the product of human strength and a powerful source of social and political change, and on that basis led the establishment of a commune giving life to a 'new law of righteousness'. Crashawe, by contrast, had seen love as the antidote to human weakness, and looked to heaven for consolation and love in the afterlife rather than seeking to transform this world. It was the exact reverse of Winstanley's insistence on 'Glory here'. In that sense, Hill argued, 'Crashawe represents the dead end of religious devotional poetry in England, for its social basis had been blown away by Cromwell's cannon. The contradiction between escapist aspirations and economic facts lost its agonizingly eloquent literary expression once the poets had lost their private incomes.' Understanding the tensions in these works, Hill thought, would come from an understanding of the society which gave rise to them: 'the contradictions between old-established customs and modes of thought and morality and the new economic realities that were upsetting them, to the conflict between two worlds feudal and capitalist, which fought the issue out in civil war'.[24]

Criticism of this strand of Hill's work is not usually that his reading of the texts is crude, but that in the end his reading of the tensions in the thought of particular writers was predetermined – Crashawe stands for a particular class and its experience, for example. Similarly, in his readings of Milton he is continually tempted to attribute the latter's radicalism to his encounter with artisan culture and plebeian irreligion, rather than to the learned culture in which Milton was immersed throughout his life. The readings of each text are sensitive and revealing, but in the end Hill's interpretation always falls one way. In some ways, the journey becomes more interesting than the destination, but this is not the crude determinism of which Hill was often accused. Rather, for him, of all the aspects of a biography that might produce alienation and a divided heart, class is the one that always matters in the end.

Hill consistently said that the appeal of Marxism lay in the connections it made, that it was a total history which avoided the idealism of

Gardiner's Puritan revolution without falling for economic determinism, like that in play in the gentry controversy in the 1950s. Marx, he said, had recognised the existence of a material world, and that our ideas derive from it, but also that our ideas are not simply *given* by the material world. Hill disliked materialism because it encouraged the fatalism he despised in 1930s liberals, and preferred to believe that we shape the material world as much as we are shaped by it. He gave the example of atomic energy, which 'is not in itself either bad or good: its effect on humanity depends on the uses to which it is put, and those depend on the organisation of society. The organisation of society depends on you, me, and millions of others.' People create the world in which they live: as Marx put it, 'What distinguishes the worst architect from the best of bees is this, that the architect raises his structure in imagination before he creates it in reality.'[25]

The critical point for the historian, however, was that imagination is a product of society and not just individual genius: what the architect can imagine in any epoch is a product of their engagement with the material world and the whole web of social relations built upon it. This helped resolve the apparent paradox of Marx's calling on people to struggle to achieve what his own analysis of history had concluded was inevitable: the collapse of capitalism.[26] Hill wanted us to be active in the world, which made him reject determinism. That led him to advocate what he called 'cultural' history, meaning by that the analysis of the whole of society rather than abstracted elements of it.[27]

It is not at all clear, however, that Hill was himself able to live up to these precepts. Most glaringly, in talking about Marx's influence on historical writing Hill argued that it had pushed historians beyond literary texts (chronicles, memoirs, letters, diaries and newspapers) towards documentary records (public records, parish registers, charters, inscriptions) and even archaeological sources, although this was a move Hill is himself notorious for not having made.[28] Moreover, the materialism in Hill's dialectic was limited. A new generation of economic and social historians from the 1960s produced work that is technically superior, relying less on what Elton called the journalism of the age and more on detailed study of administrative records, quantitative data and manuscript sources. Hill was in the hands of contemporary commentators and moralists, since he did not ground his research on the records of actual social situations or economic enterprises. He was clearly on the losing side of that battle.

Later in his career he committed himself less firmly to Marxism – perhaps in response to the highly political constructions placed on the term in that polarising culture. A manuscript note attached to the draft of his lecture on 'Marx's virtues' distinguished his Marxism from the construction placed on it by some politicians:

Am I a Marxist? 20 years in the British C.P., left 1957 because too Soviet (not wanting it to be Chinese, but British). Am I a Marxist today? K[arl] M[arx] thanked God he wasn't. Certainly qua historian find KM a most useful guide, not because gives answers but because gives questions. If I have doubts about politics, it is only because some self-styled Marxist politicians seem to me to distort M. by ignoring Lenin's dictum, 'Not a dogma but a guide to action'. The one thing one cannot get from M. is a series of ready-made truths about history (or anything else) which can be learnt by heart then applied. Favourite motto = 'de omnibus dubitandum', our scepticism should be universal. KM not a Marxist.

Writing on the centenary of 1867 and the fiftieth anniversary of 1917 he thought Marxism had become a state religion, and he wanted to emulate the Protestants by going back to the original texts to counter 'the corruptions of established churches'.[29] Thompson, talking about the future of radical history in New York in 1985, with Hill also on the platform, had said he was bored of Marxism, while Selbourne writing six years later saw it as a sign of the failure of Marxism that Hill used quotation marks around the term.[30] The obituary for Hill in *The Times* captures his development: gradually his Marxism 'mellowed into the considered and lively humanism, albeit with a Marxist tinge, that shaped his major work'.[31] He found Marx and other Marxists helpful, but was more ambivalent about the broader phenomenon of Marxism, and its reception.

Hill was a Marxist humanist but also perhaps a Marxisant liberal. He valued a humane style of historical writing, demonstrating a sympathy with the dilemmas of real people in the past. He admired Thompson for this:

Himself a poet, Thompson saw the importance of literature as a source for economic and social history. He opposed all kinds of determinism – economic, demographic or vulgar Marxism – in order to stress the importance of individual people. A pioneer of history from below, he treated people not as items in a statistical table or as blind masses driven merely by hunger and economic necessity. He studied them as living suffering and struggling human beings.[32]

Hill had also admired Morton for his humanity, and he remembered his own tutors for their open-mindedness and respect for the opinions of others. He wrote warm academic references for Maurice Keen, commending his 'sympathetic insight into the human problems of men and women in the past, and a sensitivity and delicacy in his analysis of those problems'.[33] Keen, it need hardly be said, was no Marxist.

Through Christopher Hill we can track the reactions of the British left to changing domestic and international politics, and how that inflected views of the past, from the potentially transformative power of institutional change in the 1930s and 1950s, through the high hopes for science and technology in the 1960s, an interest in the counter-culture and radical ideas in the later 1960s and 1970s, to the experience of defeat in the 1980s. In following this trajectory, Hill had by the 1970s himself become a figure in the radical tradition he was now championing. This was the difference that he had hoped to make.

He did not write to order (aside from some 'hack party stuff' in the 1950s),[34] but he did write in the hope of being relevant. Consciousness of the past lent meaning to the present and the possibility of imagining new directions in the future. Although Hill had seemed to catch 'the mood of the Sixties with preoccupations that echoed the antinomianism of the 1640s', by 1991 Jonathan Clark felt that 'his vision … seems strangely dated'.[35] One reason for that was that the English Revolution lost its public prominence, as academic revisionism renounced campaigning zeal: the ambition for political relevance had (the revisionists thought) exercised a distorting effect on the historian's work. To write about the past 'on its own terms' reflected an ambition to free it from the prison of our own preoccupations, to show proper respect to the experience of those who actually lived it, and to learn by encountering alternative worldviews rather than searching for the roots of our own. The Thatcher years also saw a reaction on the left against Marxism, so that a core loyalty to Hill and his vision was not the focus of a response to Thatcherism.

More than that, though, progressive academic writing was turning away from political economy and the state. Hill's work had followed the trajectory of left-wing interest in the past from the 1930s to the 1980s, but since then issues other than those he wrote about have preoccupied the left, particularly structural inequalities based on race, sexuality and gender. Hill, by contrast, was revising an account of constitutional development and exploring the divided hearts of (almost exclusively male) writers seeking to make sense of the origins of bourgeois culture. Moreover, he did so through writing almost entirely about England. Recent interest in connected, entangled, global history has made that preoccupation with the formation of the British state seem a matter of local interest. Hill wrote comparative rather than global history (with the comparison often implicit): the main actor in his macro-historical writing was the British state, driven by its class character. In this way, too, his writing has seemed less relevant to a globally minded audience.

He was alert to some of these developments, of course. The move with which he most wanted to be associated in his later career was the growing interest in 'history from below'. There, although he had anticipated developments, his writing did not really lead the way. Revisionists tended to offer a counter-assumption, that the people were apolitical, and that the arguments among the gentry were inflicted upon them. This seems to have been an assumption of the localist school championed by Morrill, while Conrad Russell, in a very extreme moment, suggested that soldiers on their way north to fight the Scots in 1639 might have burned altar rails because they were cold rather than because they thought altars should not be railed off in a popish manner. Subsequent work on the revolution and the Reformation has demonstrated awareness of national and international events in local society, and how that shaped responses to local problems. This is much beyond anything Hill achieved, not least because he did not use the sources that are most revealing of the realities of plebeian life.[36] Moreover, a younger generation of scholars working on archival sources was to prove more influential in the study of popular politics away from the national story: they were in many ways the academic descendants of the Cambridge Group that Hill so disliked.[37]

Several women played an important part in Hill's life: Bridget, of course, but also his mother, his sister, Margaret James, Shiela Grant Duff, Dona Torr, Inez Waugh, Sheila Rowbotham, Margot Heinemann. These were powerful intellects, to whom he owed a lot and with whom he exchanged academic and political opinions; but he did not write women's history. He went with Bridget to the inaugural Women's Liberation conference at the Oxford Union in 1970, and his lack of engagement with the rapid growth of women's history is therefore quite striking. As he wrote in 1985: 'Women's history, I suppose, is the best advertisement for the beneficial result of asking of the past questions which arise from the present.' He was ashamed, he said, of accepting that it should be taken for granted that in seventeenth-century England political demands were made only in the name of men. He now saw that 'to understand that society we have to ask *why* it was taken for granted ... Once we ask the question, other questions are opened up', and that would prompt 'a bigger rethink of the past than even Feminist historians have yet realized'.[38]

In fact, he could have been prompted to write women's history very early on: as early as 1958 one of his star pupils, Keith Thomas, had written an important article on the double standard – roughly, the habit of attributing sexual misbehaviour to the moral weakness of women rather than of men. Certainly, writing *The World Turned Upside Down* could have provided an opportunity to consider gender relations: he wrote it, after all, while pressing for Balliol to admit women. However, he got a hostile reception at a very well-attended History Workshop Conference on 'Women in History', in May 1973, about which Samuel had subsequently written apologetically.[39] At the 1985 meeting in New York, it was Joan Scott who showed the way: 'What was absent ... was an understanding of gender', she said, 'not just as a physical or social fact, but as a way of organizing power and talking about the social relations of power'.[40]

Hill's impatience with hypocritical bourgeois respectability underpinned his sympathy with the sexual manners of the new generation, and that might have led to a contribution to the history of sexuality. He thought Laslett, working on the records of the church courts, had developed a very exaggerated sense of the constraints on seventeenth-century sexuality and that, for example, 'some Ranters at least expressed tolerably permissive opinions'. The roots of sexual repression were deep, but that was because the counter-pressure also had a history: would a man or woman who held such views have expressed them in the church courts?[41] These historical and political commitments made him a friend of the emergent field of the history of sexuality, and in particular of the pioneering work of Alan Bray on the history of male homosexuality.[42] But he did not himself make a lasting contribution to this literature.

Similarly, he had been alert to the possibilities of histories of race, saying in 1985: 'Now that so many British citizens are the descendants of slaves, British historians have a duty to assess such matters, just as German historians are trying to come to terms with the equally horrific phenomenon of Nazism and its acceptance in the 1930s' – this was the key issue to be addressed in the field.[43] However, despite his interest in the slave trade as a source of capital formation, and his association with figures central to the New Left, he did not write about these issues.

By the time of his death, many of these topics loomed larger in contemporary politics than the ones he had written about. His writing had moved with the left from the 1930s to the 1980s, but by the 1990s he could not capture the left's concerns as he had done in his heyday. As he lost his position at the forefront of progressive writing he was at the same time under political attack and the subject of sustained academic critique. His work no longer captured a political mood as it had done in the 1970s.

For Hill, writing history was a political act, and the resonance of his work on the British left was what he had set out to achieve. As the Cold War reached its crescendo in the late 1980s, his very success attracted hostility as the polarising politics of left and right, and sometimes equally rancorous divisions on the left, put Marxist intellectuals in the spotlight. He could not really have complained that his work was politicised in this way, although he had always championed academic over political evaluation of historians' work. In his lifetime, though, the politics came to overwhelm the reception of his writing. He was very productive in retirement, but that body of work is less often read, particularly by historians. His image has been frozen, almost, in the posture of the 1980s: an attachment on the left associated with solidarity; dismissal in the centre and on the right based on anti-Marxism; and a position at an angle to subsequent progressive history.

There is still much to admire in his achievement, however. The *Telegraph* obituary concluded that 'perhaps his greatest achievement was … in the liberating diversity of his scholarship and his contribution to the history of ideas'.[44] Hill was a liberal Marxist intellectual with a strong moral purpose, not the crude determinist so many have set up as a straw man for the benefit of their undergraduates. He retained that strong moral purpose throughout his career, alongside a conceptual commitment to a total account of the force of new ideas, not a determinist one, even if he did not always live up to it. His work is flawed, but few historians since have attempted to match its totalising ambition and moral seriousness as a contribution to the improvement of the world around us, nor its ambition to contextualise the strengths and weaknesses of the modern British state in a coherent understanding of its past.

Acknowledgements

This project was supported primarily by the University of Sheffield, which granted the research leave during which I wrote the preliminary draft. It was completed during my tenure of a British Academy/Wolfson Research Professorship, and I am very grateful to the Academy and the Wolfson Foundation for that support. After this book was submitted to Verso I was elected to a Fellowship at All Souls College, for which I am enormously grateful. Somewhat in breach of convention, therefore, I would like to say that all views about the college expressed in the text are Hill's and not my own.

Archivists and librarians have been unfailingly helpful: at the Balliol College archives, the Bodleian Library, the British Library, Exeter University Library Special Collections, the Hull History Centre, the Institute of Education Special Collections, Keele University Library Special Collections, LSE Special Collections, the Modern Records Centre at the University of Warwick, Nottingham University Special Collections, the Parliamentary Archives, and the People's History Museum, Manchester. Anna Bayman was very generous in fielding questions and giving me access to the archives of *Past and Present*. For advice on the Eric Hobsbawm and Doris Lessing archives I am grateful to Richard Evans and Patrick French respectively. I quote from the Berlin papers in the Bodleian Library with the permission of the Trustees of the Isaiah Berlin Literary Trust, the Literary Estate of Lord Dacre of Glanton and the Estate of Goronwy Rees. I am grateful to Henry Hardy for his help with these permissions. Material from the Sparrow papers in All Souls College Library is reproduced by permission of the Warden and Fellows of All Souls College, Oxford.

John Merrick, at Verso, has been a very supportive, knowledgeable and insightful editor. I am also particularly grateful to Bill Braddick, Jill Pritchard, Lyndal Roper, Paul Slack and Miles Taylor, who read drafts of the book: it is much improved as a result.

In the course of my research I benefited enormously from conversations with those who knew Hill. It is fortunate for me that his niece, Penelope Corfield, herself a major historian, has written about him with great insight. She has been extremely generous with her time and knowledge, and I am particularly grateful for her help. Even though I am an academic with experience of senior administrative roles, I find some aspects of life at Oxford University hard to grasp. I am particularly grateful to John Jones for guiding me through the Balliol archive with such remarkable expertise and generosity, and to Paul Slack and Keith Thomas, both of whom knew Hill well, and the Oxford in which he moved. For advice on other topics I am very grateful to Christopher Andrew, Miranda Carter, the late Justin Champion, Judith Curthoys, Susanne Dell, Miriam Dobson, Simon Eliot, Richard Hollies, Henry Irving, Ian Kershaw, Jon Lawrence, Peter Mandler, Kevin Morgan, Bob Moore, Marcus Nevitt, Jenny Rees, Steve Smith, Anna Towlson and Benjamin Ziemann. Many others who knew Hill and his academic and political milieux have been generous with their help, advice and insight, in particular Robin Briggs, Glenn Burgess, Tom Corns, Richard Davenport-Hines, Andrew Foster, Ann Hughes, Ronald Hutton, Alan Knights, John Lanchester, Anne Laurence, Nicholas McDowell, John Morrill, Oswyn Murray, David Norbrook, Wilf Prest, John Rees, the late Patrick Renshaw, Quentin Skinner, Nigel Smith, Nicholas Tyacke, John Walter and Blair Worden. I have also spoken to a number of people who knew Hill as students or personally, outside these professional contexts: Felicity Armstrong, Alex Callinicos, Lynn Farleigh, Martin Kettle, Jeannie Moyo, Tim Stretton and John Woodvine. For help with texts in Italian and German I am grateful to Umberto Albarella, Dave Laffan and Henk de Berg.

Above all, though, I am deeply grateful to Sarah, Cora and Mel for their love and support.

A Note on Citations and Abbreviations

KV/2 files are made available by the National Archives in digital form – the page number given here directs the reader to the image number in the pdf file, not the original pagination. The files are paginated in reverse order – the most recent documents are at the top of the file, and I have generally put references in chronological rather than numerical page order. The Grant Duff papers are cited as they are dated in the Bodleian collection, even though some letters bear the same date and some are (in my view) misdated; citing them as they are catalogued is of most assistance in finding them, however. Citing Hill's published essays is a deceptively complicated task. Many of his articles were republished with amendments, including changes to the title. Where I have directly quoted from an essay I have tried to refer to the version as it stood at the point in time I am writing about, although on some occasions I have quoted the new material. For most purposes, however, the republications are actually most useful to the reader – easier to find and frequently incorporating corrections and the results of later reflection. In general, therefore, I have noted the date of the original publication but cited the republished version. Hill's books were also often republished with silent but significant amendments; again, I have tried to quote from the text as it stood at the point in time I am writing about. A list of abbreviations used in the citations follows:

Balliol	Balliol Archives
Beer	Samuel Beer, 'Christopher Hill: some reminiscences', in Donald Pennington and Keith Thomas (eds), *Puritans and Revolutionaries: Essays in Seventeenth-Century History presented to Christopher Hill* (1978), 1–4
Berlin papers	Bodleian MS Berlin
Briggs	Robin Briggs, 'Hill, (John Edward) Christopher (1912–2003)', *ODNB*
Corfield, 'As I knew him'	Penelope J. Corfield, 'Christopher Hill: the Marxist historian as I knew him', © Penelope J. Corfield (2003; 2018) (at penelopejcorfield.com)
Corfield, 'Bridget Hill'	Penelope J. Corfield, 'Bridget Hill: historian and feminist', © P.J. Corfield (2002; 2019) (at penelopejcorfield.com)
Corfield, 'All one'	Penelope J. Corfield, '"We are all one in the eyes of the Lord": Christopher Hill and the historical meanings of radical religion', *HWJ*, 58 (2004), 110–27 (at penelopejcorfield.com)
Corfield, 'Intellectual trajectory'	Penelope J. Corfield, 'Christopher Hill's intellectual trajectory: from Biblical Protestantism to humanist Marxism', © Penelope J. Corfield (2003, 2005) (at penelopejcorfield.com)
Corfield interview	'Interviews with Historians: Christopher Hill with Penelope Corfield, 1988' (at penelopejcorfield.com) [citations from transcript in Heinemann papers, 2/3/1]
Corfield, 'Balliol College'	'Christopher Hill: Marxist history and Balliol College', *Balliol Annual Record*, 2009, 39–41 (at penelopejcorfield.com)

Corfield, 'Methodism and Marxism'	Corfield, 'Christopher Hill: Methodism and Marxism', *The Historian*, 87 (2005), 21–2 (at penelopejcorfield.com)
CPGB	Communist Party of Great Britain
Dell papers	Bodleian MS. Eng c 7768 'Edmund's Papers', 1938–48
DNB	*Dictionary of National Biography*
EcHR	*Economic History Review*
EHR	*English Historical Review*
Grant Duff papers	Bodleian MS Grant Duff
Heinemann papers	Special Collections and Archives, Goldsmiths University of London, Margot Heinemann papers, HEIN
HJ	*Historical Journal*
Hill, *Collected Essays*, i	*The Collected Essays of Christopher Hill,* 1: *Writing and Revolution in 17th Century England* (1985)
Hill, *Collected Essays*, ii	*The Collected Essays of Christopher Hill,* 2: *Religion and Politics in 17th Century England* (1986)
Hill, *Collected Essays*, iii	*The Collected Essays of Christopher Hill,* 3: *People and Ideas in 16th and 17th Century England* (1986)
Hill, *Change and Continuity*	*Change and Continuity in 17th-Century England* (1974)
Hill, *Nation of Change*	*A Nation of Change and Novelty: Radical Politics, Religion and Literature in Seventeenth-Century England* (1990)
Hill papers	Balliol Archives, Hill papers
Hill, *Puritanism*	*Puritanism and Revolution: Studies in Interpretation of the English Revolution of the 17th Century* (1986), first published 1958

Hill, *Turning Point*	*England's Turning Point: Essays on 17th Century English History* (1998)
Hilton	Rodney Hilton, 'Christopher Hill: some reminiscences', in Pennington and Thomas (eds.), *Puritans and Revolutionaries*, 6–10
HWJ	*History Workshop Journal*
JBS	*Journal of British Studies*
Jones, *Balliol*	John Jones, *Balliol College: A History*, 2nd edition, revised (2005)
Keen	Maurice Keen, 'Christopher Hill: some reminiscences', in Pennington and Thomas (eds.), *Puritans and Revolutionaries*, 17–21
Kettle interview	Interview with Martin Kettle, *Guardian*, 28 October 1988, p. 31
LRB	*London Review of Books*
MQ	*Modern Quarterly*
MRC	Modern Records Centre, University of Warwick
NYRB	*New York Review of Books*
ODNB	*Oxford Dictionary of National Biography*
P&P	*Past and Present*
P&P papers	Bodleian Library, MS *Past and Present*
Pennington	Donald Pennington, 'John Edward Christopher Hill, 1912–2003', *Proceedings of the British Academy*, 130 (2005), 23–49
PHM	People's History Museum
Rowse, 'Hill'	Exeter University Library, Special Collections, 113/1/2/4/4086, memoir of Christopher Hill
Saville papers	Hull History Centre, DJS

SocCR	Society for Cultural Relations between the People of the British Commonwealth and the USSR
Stretton	Hugh Stretton, 'Christopher Hill: some reminiscences', in Pennington and Thomas (eds), *Puritans and Revolutionaries*, 10–17
THES	*Times Higher Education Supplement*
TLS	*Times Literary Supplement*
TNA	The National Archives
WEA	Workers' Educational Association
Whale	Gwendolyn B. Whale, 'Christopher Hill: some reminiscences', in Pennington and Thomas (eds), *Puritans and Revolutionaries*, 4–6

Notes

Preface

1   TNA, KV/2/3941, pp. 121, 167.
2   Corfield, 'Intellectual trajectory', p. 1.

1. Methodism, Modernism, Marxism and the
Crisis of Bourgeois Culture: 1912–36

1   Hill papers, 1.
2   Ibid.
3   Beer, p. 4; Pennington, p. 24.
4   Corfield, 'Intellectual trajectory', p. 3; Beer, p. 4.
5   Corfield, 'All one', p. 113; 'Intellectual trajectory', pp. 3–4.
6   Rowse, 'Hill', unpaginated.
7   Corfield, 'As I knew him', p. 2; Corfield interview, p. 1.
8   TNA, KV/2/3941, pp. 183, 142.
9   For rugby, Hill papers, 2 (includes reply card for selection for York RUFC); Beer, p. 1;
    Corfield, 'As I knew him', pp. 2–3.
10 Grant Duff papers, 38/1, from Balliol [3 April 1940]; see also Corfield interview, pp.
    1–2.
11 Beer, p. 4.
12 Corfield interview, p. 29. See also Ved Mehta, *Up at Oxford* (1993), p. 156.
13 Beer, p. 1.
14 Hill papers, 25.
15 Beer, p. 2.
16 Patrick Renshaw, personal communication; Pennington, p. 24; *THES*, 16 December
    1994, p. 14.
17 Beer, p. 1.
18 Sir Richard Southern, *Balliol Annual Record, 1978*, pp. 11–12; TNA, KV/2/3941, p. 142.
    He appears to have visited Freiburg-im-Breisgau in 1936 too: Hill papers, 4.
19 For example, Hill papers, 45–7. For notes on Marx, Engels and Hegel taken in German
    see ibid., 45 and 46. In 1962 he requested a copy of F. Chabod, *La politica di Paulo Sarpi*,

P&P papers, Box 343, unpaginated: note following editorial board meeting, 6 October 1962. For the poem, see below p. 261 n 60.

20 R.W. Southern, 'Galbraith, Vivian Hunter (1889–1976)', *ODNB*.

21 Corfield, 'All one', p. 125 n. 14; Pennington, p. 25.

22 *THES*, 16 December 1994, p. 14; Corfield interview, p. 4. Hill's *Daily Telegraph* obituary (27 February 2003, p. 29) claims that Galbraith and Bell had driven to York because he had got '100%' in his entrance exam. It may be that parts of the oral tradition have been conflated here.

23 Grant Duff papers, 38/4, from Cheltenham [19 February 1941].

24 Oswyn Murray, *Holywell Manor: An Anecdotal History* (2007), pp. 27–8.

25 Jones, *Balliol*, p. 268; Murray, *Holywell Manor*, p. 29.

26 Balliol, deceased members files, K.N. Bell, clipping from *Oxford Magazine*, 15 November 1951, pp. 80–1, at p. 81.

27 Pennington, p. 25.

28 Murray, *Holywell Manor*, p. 25; see also Hill papers, 21, 'Balliol in the 1930s'.

29 See below, pp. 161–5, 200.

30 Stretton, p. 13.

31 J.E.C. Hill, 'Lindsay, Alexander Dunlop, first Baron Lindsay of Birker (1879–1952)', *DNB*. A fuller draft survives in Keele University Special Collections and Archives, GB172 Lindsay papers, L145. For the foreword see A.S.P. Woodhouse, *Puritanism and Liberty* (1938), and for its use at Balliol, Alastair MacLachlan, *The Rise and Fall of Revolutionary England: An Essay on the Fabrication of Seventeenth-Century History* (1986), pp. 36–7, 335 n. 19.

32 Hill, 'Lindsay'; Hill, *Listener*, 18 November 1971, pp. 696–7

33 Hill, 'Lindsay'.

34 *Listener*, 18 November 1971, pp. 696–7.

35 Ibid.

36 Hill, 'Lindsay'. For the comparison, Stretton, pp. 15–16; quoted by A.J.P. Taylor, *Observer*, 21 November 1971, p. 33.

37 Corfield, 'Methodism and Marxism', p. 2.

38 Corfield, 'Intellectual trajectory', p. 4.

39 Beer, p. 4.

40 Corfield, 'Intellectual trajectory', p. 20 n. 16; Corfield, *Guardian*, 6 March 2003, p. 29.

41 Grant Duff papers, 38/1, from York [30 December 1939], from Balliol [later 1939].

42 Grant Duff papers, 38/1, from York [10 April 1940].

43 TNA, KV/2/3943, pp. 53–4, 7 June 1953.

44 Balliol, deceased members files, Raphael Samuel, from Samuel, 7 July 1978, from Hill, 13 July 1978.

45 Corfield, 'Intellectual trajectory', p. 5.

46 Corfield interview, pp. 30–1; Corfield, 'Intellectual trajectory', pp. 5–6; Corfield, 'Methodism and Marxism', pp. 3–4.

47 Corfield, 'All one', p. 115.

48 Christopher Hill, *Intellectual Origins of the English Revolution* (1965), p. ix; Hill papers, 247, from Gregory, 12 June 1963, 18 June 1963.

49 Corfield, 'Methodism and Marxism', p. 4.

50 Corfield, 'All one', p. 114.

51 Corfield interview, p. 3; Mehta, *Up at Oxford*, p. 157.

52 *Observer*, 11 June 1989, p. 13; Pennington, p. 26. For these political circles see Brian Harrison (ed.), *The History of the University of Oxford*, vol. viii: *The Twentieth Century* (1994), pp. 395–400.

53 Corfield interview, p. 6. Beer says that Hill was not a member of the October Club (Beer, pp. 1–2), but this is contradicted by Hill's statement in Corfield interview, p. 6.

54 For the meeting with Laski see Beer, p. 3; Rowse, 'Hill', unpaginated; A.L. Rowse, *Historians I Have Known* (1995), pp. 105–6.

55 Hilton, p. 7.

56 Healey, quoted in Pennington, p. 26.

57 Beer, p. 3.

58 Eric Hobsbawm, *Interesting Times: A Twentieth Century Life* (2002), p. 97, emphasis in original.

59 John Morrill, personal communication; Heinemann papers, 2/3/1, to Heinemann, 30 March 1984. See also Margot Heinemann, 'How the words got on the page: Christopher Hill and seventeenth-century literary studies', in Geoff Eley and William Hunt (eds), *Reviving the English Revolution: Reflections and Elaborations on the Work of Christopher Hill* (1988), 73–97, at p. 77.

60 I am grateful to Tom Corns, John Lanchester and David Norbrook for discussing this with me.

61 Heinemann papers, 2/3/1, to Heinemann, 30 March 1984.

62 Corfield, 'Intellectual trajectory', p. 7.

63 *Listener*, 10 August 1967, p. 172.

64 Hill papers, 2, 22, 23, 27.

65 Hill papers, 35, loose paper.

66 Ibid., loose paper.

67 Ibid., p. 1.

68 Ibid. For notes on music see also Hill papers, 28, 37 at p. 15 (Dvořák: 'Just misses being a great rev[olutionary] symphony, no doubt for the usual political reasons', referring in part to its racial politics).

69 Hill papers, 28, unpaginated. These notes are in the back of a school geography notebook, in what seems a later hand. The quoted comments are on a separate page folded in.

70 T.S. Eliot, 'The metaphysical poets', reprinted in Anthony Cuda and Ronald Schuchard (eds), *The Complete Prose of T.S. Eliot: The Critical Edition* (2014), 375–85, at pp. 376, 380. The essay was first published in *TLS*, 20 October 1921.

71 *Listener*, 10 August 1967, p. 172.

72 Eliot, 'The metaphysical poets', p. 381.

73 Heinemann papers, 2/3/1, to Heinemann, 30 March 1984. See also Heinemann, 'How the words got on the page', in Eley and Hunt (eds), *Reviving the English Revolution*, pp. 76–7.

74 Hill papers, 109, 142. He has notes on Freud's *New Introductory Lectures on Psychoanalysis*, first published 1933: item 142.

75 TNA, KV/2/3941, p. 14, 20 February 1952.

76 Beer, p. 2; Hill papers, 35, pp. 16, 21.

77 Hill papers, 35, p. 5.

78 Hill papers, 34, p. 4.

79 Corfield, 'Intellectual trajectory, pp. 4, 6. Beer says with certainty that Hill was a Marxist by the spring of 1935, p. 3. Some loose notes on D.H. Lawrence are on the back of financial statement of 23 March 1933, although his fuller notes on *Lady Chatterley's Lover* have a note folded in which is written on University College Wales notepaper, suggesting a date after 1936: Hill papers, 28, 34.

80 Beer, pp. 1–2.

81 Hill papers, 35, pp. 2, 9, 13, 14.

82 For example, Hill papers, 37, 45, 46, 56, 130.

83 Hill papers, 37, at p. 37.

84 *Listener*, 10 August 1967, p. 172.

85 For his notes on Lenin and historical materialism see Hill papers, 45.

86 *Listener*, 10 August 1967, p. 172.

87 Corfield interview, p. 4; *Listener*, 10 August 1967, p. 172.

88 Hill papers, 21, '1930s'.

89 *Listener*, 10 August 1967, p. 173.

90 Hill papers, 21, '1930s'.

91 *Daily Telegraph*, 13 May 1965, p. 19; Harrison (ed.), *History of the University of Oxford*, pp. 24–5, 167–8, 400; *The Isis*, 15 February 1933, pp. 1, 7; Martin Ceadel, 'The "King and Country" debate, 1933: student politics, pacifism and the dictators', *The Historical Journal*, 22:3 (1979), 397–422.

92 Hill papers, 21, '1930s'; Corfield interview, p. 9. Briggs and Pennington both say that Hill was unsuccessful in trying to enlist for the International Brigade: Briggs; Pennington, p. 26.

93 Hill papers, 21, '1930s'.

94 *Guardian*, 3 October 1988, p. 20.

95 Hill papers, 21, '1930s'.

96 Southern, *Balliol College Record, 1978*, p. 11. He is quoting Benjamin Jowett talking about the crisis of a hundred years earlier that led some into the Oxford Movement.

97 Barbara Epstein, 'The rise, decline and possible revival of socialist humanism', in David Alderson and Robert Spencer (eds), *For Humanism: Explorations in Theory and Politics* (2017), 17–67, at p. 17.

98 Pennington, p. 25; *The Times*, 28 April 1933, p. 16.

99 LSE Special Collections, Fabian Society/J/38/2; Chorley/2/1, New Fabian Research Bureau Political Section, minutes of meeting 14 November 1933.

100 LSE Special Collections, Fabian Society/J/38/4; Chorley/2/4. It is not clear when he became involved, but he is not mentioned in the minutes or records of Fabian conferences held during 1933.

101 LSE Special Collections, Fabian Society/J/38/2.

102 Corfield interview, pp. 2–3, 35.

103 Berlin papers, 104, fos. 206–7, 26 November 1935; 105, fos. 12–13, Hill to Berlin, 1 February 1936.

104 Mehta, *Up at Oxford*, p. 156; Hill, *Turning Point*.

105 Briggs; Pennington; see also Rowse, *Historians*, pp. 105–6. For Sumner see R.J.W. Evans, 'Sumner, (Benedict) Humphrey (1893–1951)', *ODNB*.

106 TNA, KV/2/3941, p. 185. The note was not added to the file until December 1954, apparently at the time of his visit to Moscow, see below, pp. 116–19. For his hair, see Grant Duff papers, 38/4, from Cheltenham [19 February 1941].

107 Kettle interview.

108 Hill gave this date of his joining in a note to the party leadership: TNA, KV/2/3944, p. 10a. There is a page missing between pp. 10 and 11 of the scanned image: I am grateful to the staff of TNA for access to the original and to Mabel Winter photographing the missing page. The same joining date is given in the delegate list of the 21st National Party Conference in November 1949: TNA, KV/2/3941, p. 46. The files contain a report from a redacted informant that Hill was prominent in the communist student movement during the 1930s but this seems misleading, at least if that implies that he was a party member while an undergraduate: TNA, KV/2/3941, p. 27. Corfield says that he joined in 1934, the date repeated in Pennington and Briggs: Corfield, 'All one', p. 115; Pennington, p. 26; Briggs.

109 For the 'Golden Age' and his later disavowal of those illusions, see Hill papers, 21, '1930s'. See also Kettle interview.

110 Mehta, *Up at Oxford*, p. 157; Kettle interview.

111   TNA, KV/2/3941, pp. 181–2.
112   Hill papers, 3 (unpaginated); Irene Corfield, Obituary, *Guardian*, 14 May 2013 (by Penelope Corfield), accessed online.
113   Hill papers, 3.
114   For the affair, Grant Duff papers, 38/1, single page from a longer letter [undated]; from Cheltenham [3 April 1941] (Taya); Briggs.
115   Hill papers, 3.
116   See John F. N. Bradley, *The Czechoslovak Legion in Russia, 1914–1920* (1991), chs. 4–5. I am grateful to Steve Smith for discussing this with me.
117   Hill papers, 3.
118   Ibid.
119   Ibid.; Saville papers, 2/1/14, Hill to Saville, 24 June 1984.
120   Hill papers, 3.
121   Kevin Morgan, *Against Fascism and War: Ruptures and Continuities in British Communist Politics, 1935–41* (1989), ch. 1; James Eaden and David Renton, *The Communist Party of Great Britain since 1920* (2002), chs. 1–2.
122   Hill papers, 3.
123   Ibid.
124   Berlin papers, 104, fos. 222–3, from Moscow, 14 December 1935; 105, fos. 12–13, from Moscow, 1 February 1936.
125   Hill papers, 3.
126   Ibid.
127   Berlin papers, 105, fos. 12–13, from Moscow, 1 February 1936.
128   Hill papers, 3.
129   TNA, KV/2/3944, pp. 31, 50.
130   Morgan, *Against War and Fascism*, ch. 1; Eaden and Renton, *Communist Party*, ch. 2; Jim Fyrth (ed.), *Britain, Fascism and the Popular Front* (1985), esp. chapters by Fyrth, Myant and Heinemann.
131   TNA, KV2/3944, p. 10.
132   *Manchester Guardian*, 7 June 1935, p. 9; Hill, 'Lindsay'; Gary McCulloch, 'Alexander Dunlop, first Baron Lindsay of Birker (1879-1952)', *ODNB*. Lindsay was Oxford correspondent for the *Manchester Guardian* for five years during the 1930s: Hill, 'Lindsay'.
133   Hill papers, 3.

2. Academic Life, Communism and the Authentic Self: 1936–40

1   Whale, p. 5; Pennington, p. 26; Hill, 'Lindsay'; Southern, 'Galbraith'.
2   Whale, p. 5.
3   TNA, KV/2/3941, p. 142.
4   Grant Duff papers, 38/2, from Balliol, 'Tuesday' [before summer 1940]; from Balliol [before summer 1940].
5   Whale, p. 5.
6   Berlin papers, 105, fos. 92–3, Hill to Berlin, 16 October 1936.
7   Whale, p. 5; Berlin papers, 105, fo. 284, Hill to Berlin, 4 December [1937].
8   Whale, p. 5.
9   Berlin papers, 105, fos. 92–3, Hill to Berlin, 16 October 1936.
10   Hill papers, 128, fos. 2, 98.
11   R.G. Usher, *A Critical Study of the Historical Method of Samuel Rawson Gardiner* (1915); cited by Hill in 'Historians on the rise of British capitalism', *Science and Society*, 14:4 (1950), 307–21, and 'Recent interpretations of the Civil War' (1956), in Hill, *Puritanism*.

For a more sympathetic view of Gardiner's method see Mark Nixon, *Samuel Rawson Gardiner and the Idea of History* (2010).

12   A.L. Rowse, *Spectator*, 19 August 1938, p. 303. For Hill's review see *Spectator*, 12 August 1938, pp. 275–6, and the author's reply, *Spectator*, 19 August 1938, pp. 305–6.

13   See C.H. George, 'Christopher Hill: a profile', in Eley and Hunt (eds), *Reviving the English Revolution*, pp. 15–29, at p. 16. Hill kept his notes on Namier's Ford lectures, although I have not located them: Bodleian MS 12215/4, fo. 530, Sutherland to Hill, 29 May 1962; Hill papers, 123, Sutherland to Hill, 4 January 1963. He commended Namier in 'Recent interpretations'. I am grateful to Steve Pincus for pointing this out to me. For Namier see Miles Taylor, 'The beginnings of modern British social history?', *HWJ*, 43 (1997), 155–76, esp. 157–9; D.W. Hayton, *Conservative Revolutionary: The Lives of Lewis Namier* (2019).

14   For the chronological error see draft manuscript on the New Model Army, Hill papers, 140, p. b.

15   Whale, p. 6; for Paynter, David Smith, *Balliol Annual Record, 1978*, p. 18; TNA, KV/2/3944, p. 10; Corfield interview, p. 9; for the Left Book Club see Morgan, *Against Fascism and War*, pp. 254–76.

16   Berlin papers, 105, fo. 284, Hill to Berlin, 4 December [1937]; Grant Duff papers, 38/2, from Balliol, 'Thursday' [before summer 1940]; Hill papers, 5; see 'Telling our stories – voices from the Basque refugee oral histories: (6f) life in the colonies. Josefina Savery talks about her time in Caerleon' (cdn.southampton.ac.uk); for the Christmas card lists see Hill papers, 21.

17   Berlin papers, 105, fo. 284, Hill to Berlin, 4 December [1937].

18   Whale, p. 6.

19   Berlin papers, 274, fo. 12, Rees to Berlin [1929–33] [1933]; Kenneth O. Morgan, 'Rees, (Morgan) Goronwy (1909–1979)', *ODNB*. For the relationship see Jenny Rees, *Looking for Mr Nobody: The Secret Lives of Goronwy Rees* (1994), esp. chs. 4–5.

20   Berlin papers, 254, fo. 90, Grant Duff to Berlin [summer 1933]. Rees's memoirs are largely anonymised and there is no obvious reference to Hill; Goronwy Rees, *A Chapter of Accidents* (1972).

21   Shiela Grant Duff, *The Parting of Ways: A Personal Account of the Thirties* (1982); Klemens von Klemperer, *A Noble Combat: The Letters of Shiela Grant Duff and Adam von Trott zu Solz 1932–1939* (1988).

22   Jones, *Balliol*, pp. 279–80, 331.

23   Grant Duff papers, 38/1, postcard [early 1939]; [8 December 1939]; [later 1939].

24   Ibid., 38/2, Hill to Mrs Grant Duff [5 January 1940]; for discretion see 38/2, from Balliol spring [1940].

25   Ibid., 38/2, from Balliol [8 April 1940].

26   Ibid., 38/2, from York [4 April 1940].

27   Ibid., 38/2, from York [10 April 1940].

28   Ibid., 38/1 [December 1939], annotated by SGD, 'after my motor accident?'

29   Ibid., 38/1, from York [30 December 1939].

30   Ibid., 38/1, from Balliol [later 1939]. Pritt had worked with the Fabian Research Bureau and was a prominent pro-Soviet commentator on the international situation, later expelled from the Labour Party for defending the Soviet pact with Hitler and the Soviet invasion of Finland: Kevin Morgan, 'Denis Nowell Pritt (1887–1972)', *ODNB*.

31   Grant Duff papers, 38/1, from York [25 December 1939]; [late 1939?]; from York [23 December 39].

32   Ibid., 38/1, from York [30 December 1939].

33   Klemperer is a little coy on the subject, having acknowledged the sensitivity of

publishing their letters: *Noble Combat*, esp. pp. 5–6. For Grant Duff's view of the relationship see *Parting of Ways*, esp. 55–64 (describing her visit to his family in 1934), pp. 198–213 (the increasing tensions between them as a result of impending war). She later thanked Hill for prompting her to write the book: Grant Duff papers, 38/5, Grant Duff to Hill [11 November 1987].

34   Rees, *Looking for Mr Nobody*, p. 75.
35   Grant Duff papers, 38/1, from York [30 December 1939].
36   Ibid., 38/1, single page from a longer letter [undated].
37   Ibid., 38/1, from Balliol [later 1939]. This is presumably a reference to an early version of his essay on 'Andrew Marvell and his society', eventually published in 1946. He had high hopes for it: 'The Marvell article seemed to me to be about something enormously important when I wrote it, but it doesn't communicate itself very well does it?'
38   Ibid., 38/2, card from Balliol [February 1940]
39   Ibid., 38/1 [4 December 1939].
40   Ibid., 38/3, from Aldershot [2 September 1940].
41   Ibid., 38/3, from Aldershot [6 September 1940].
42   Ibid., 38/1, single page from a longer letter [undated].
43   Ibid., 38/3, from Aldershot on Balliol paper [Autumn 1940].
44   Ibid., 38/2, from Ramillies on Balliol paper [4 August 1940].
45   Ibid., 38/4, from 2 Malvern Place, Cheltenham [early 1941], April 1941?
46   Ibid., 38/3, from Aldershot [15 October 1940].
47   Ibid., 38/3, from Ashburton [December 1940]; 38/1, from Balliol [later 1939].
48   Ibid., 38/3, from Aldershot [8 September 1940]; from Cheltenham [5 February 1941].
49   Ibid., 38/3, from Ashburton [December 1940].
50   Ibid., 38/4, from Cheltenham [3 April 1941].
51   Ibid., 38/4, from Cheltenham [22 April 1941]; 38/4, from Cheltenham Station [late 1942].
52   Ibid., 38/4, from Cheltenham [May 1941].
53   Ibid.
54   Ibid., 38/4, from Cambridge [24 August 1943?].
55   Ibid., 38/5, from Northmoor Road [August 1946]. I found no mention of Hill in her correspondence with Berlin during the 1950s, although some of Berlin's correspondence is closed.
56   Grant Duff papers, 38/4, from Cheltenham [16 February 1941].
57   Mehta, *Up at Oxford*, p. 142, see also p. 154.
58   Grant Duff papers, 38/1 [December 1939].
59   Ibid., 38/3, from Aldershot [15 September 1940].
60   'Du bist mir wie ein Frülingstraum/ Zur Weihnachtszeit geträumt;/ Ein Apfel auf zu hoch 'nen Baum;/ Ein Spielzung aufgeraümt./ So ist es schön; denn wer nicht hat,/ Der kann nicht wissen wie/ Das Haben is der Liebe Tot:/ Sei mir vollkommen nie': ibid., 38/2 [29 August 1940]. For Freud see 38/2, card from Balliol [Feb 1940]; card from Balliol [1940]. For Rilke see ibid., 38/3, from Ashburton [December 1640].
61   Ibid., 38/2, from Balliol [3 April 1940]; 38/3, from Ashburton [25 December 1940].
62   Ibid., 38/2, from York [5 April 1940].
63   Ibid., 38/1, from Balliol [later 1939].
64   Ibid., 38/4, from Cheltenham [19 February 1941].
65   Ibid., 38/1, from Balliol [December 1939].
66   Hilton, p. 6.
67   C.E. Gore, '250th anniversary of the "Glorious" revolution', *Communist International* (November 1938), 22–9, at pp. 23, 28–9, 29.
68   *Spectator*, 14 October 1938, pp. 614–16.

69   Hilton, p. 6.

70   'Soviet interpretations of the English Interregnum', *EcHR*, 8 (1938), 159–67 and 'The agrarian legislation of the Interregnum' (1940), in Hill, *Puritanism*. Reviews: *EcHR*, 8 (1938), 203–4; *EcHR*, 10 (1940), 162–4.

71   Reviews: *Spectator*, 21 October 1938, p. 668; *Spectator*, 12 August 1938, p. 275; *Science and Society*, 3 (1939), 261–3; *Modern Quarterly*, 1:1 (1938), 91–4.

72   Christopher Hill, 'A Whig Historian' (H.A.L. Fisher), *Modern Quarterly*, 1:3 (1938), 275–84, at p. 284; review of D.L. Keir, *The Constitutional History of Modern Britain, 1485–1937* and M.A. Thompson, *A Constitutional History of England*, iv: *1642–1801*, *Modern Quarterly*, 2:2 (1939), 198–205.

73   Corfield interview, pp. 10–11.

74   V.G. Kiernan, 'Torr, Dona Ruth Anne (1883–1957), historian', *ODNB*.

75   Kiernan, 'Torr'; *Times*, 18 January 1957, p. 11; David Renton, 'Opening the books: the personal papers of Dona Torr', *HWJ*, 52 (2001), 236–49. For the intellectual climate in the party see Margot Heinemann, 'The People's Front and the intellectuals', in Fyrth (ed.), *Britain, Fascism and the Popular Front*, 157–86, esp. pp. 174–5, 177–80; for Chris see Balliol, MCOP 24ii, Hill to Brickhill, 17 January 1974. He signed as Chris in some party contexts, for example, KV/2/3945, p. 112, Hill to Payne, 25 October 1955, and published as Chris in *Challenge*, 21 January 1956, ibid., p. 100.

76   Hill addressed his letter to Saville about the festschrift formally: 'Dear John Saville' and signed 'Christopher Hill': Saville papers, 2/1/14, Hill to Saville, 28 March [?].

77   Saville papers, 2/1/22, Torr to Hill, 25 September [1947]; Saville papers, 2/1/14, Hill to Dorothy Thompson, 10 October 1994.

78   Claire Harman, 'Rickword, (John) Edgell (1898–1982)', *ODNB*.

79   *London School of Economics and Political Science Register, 1895–1932* (London, 1934), p. 94; Margaret James student file, LSE Institutional Archives; *Nottingham Evening Post*, 18 October 1943, p. 1; 19 October 1943, p. 1. She had had a serious fall the previous year at the Head Sorting Office, *Nottingham Evening Post*, 13 May 1942, p. 1 (column 5). I am grateful to Anna Towlson for these references. Hill commended James's book in his draft MS on the New Model Army, Hill papers, 140, p. b and passim. For their correspondence about the war see below, pp. 57–62.

80   Christopher Hill et al., *Twelve several papers delivered at the Humanities Research Centre of the Australian National University* (1981), at pp. 180–1 (I am grateful to Wilf Prest for sharing a copy with me); Hill, *Change and Continuity*, p. xi. John Buckatzsch had studied at Balliol before taking up a Fellowship in the Department of Applied Economics in Cambridge in 1947. At the time of his early death in 1954, he was Senior Officer at the Institute of Economics in Oxford. (*Times*, 24 April 1947, p. 7; *Times*, 10 October 1947, p. 7; *Times*, 19 June 1953, p. 8; *Times*, 9 August 1954, p. 1; *Listener*, 26 May 1955, p. 955). His pioneering work on occupational structure and the distribution of national wealth anticipated work from the 1960s onwards now associated with the Cambridge Group. See Hill, 'Sex, marriage and parish registers' (1978), in Hill, *Collected Essays*, iii. I am grateful to Richard Smith for discussing Buckatzsch's work with me.

81   'The English Revolution', in Christopher Hill (ed.), *The English Revolution 1640: Three Essays* (1940), 9–82, at pp. 80–1. He made a critical change to this formulation in later editions: '[T]he period 1640–60 saw the destruction of *one kind of state* and the introduction of a *new* political structure within which capitalism could freely develop', *The English Revolution 1640: An Essay* (third edition, 1955, repr. 1979), at p. 61.

82   'The English Revolution', p. 14.

83   Ibid., pp. 17, 46.

84   Ibid., p. 81.

85 Grant Duff papers, 38/3, from Aldershot [2 September 1940].
86 *New Statesman and Nation*, 24 August 1940, p. 193. For the debate among Marxists see below, pp. 93–5. Orwell commended James's essay as the pick of the bunch.
87 *TLS*, 7 September 1940, p. 436.
88 A.L. Merson, 'Problems of the English bourgeois revolution', *Marxism Today* (October 1963), 310–15, at p. 312.
89 Kettle interview; Corfield interview, pp. 16–17.

3. Fighting the Wrong War: 1939–45

1 Hill papers, 29; 131, fo. 18; 149 (Dobb). For Angell and the King and Country debate, see Ceadel, 'The "King and Country" debate, 1933'.
2 Hill papers, 131, fo. 18, cutting from *New Statesman*, 6 April 1935.
3 PHM, CP/IND/POLL/2/7 (card collection 'Ercoli and War'). The CPGB published a manifesto in the *Daily Worker*, 7 October 1939, p. 2: ibid.
4 Grant Duff papers, 38/1, from York [25 December 1939]. Gustave Bouvet was an anarchist who had attempted to assassinate the French president Alexandre Millerand in 1922.
5 Hill papers, 21, '1930s'. For the peace ballot see Helen McCarthy, 'Democratizing British foreign policy: rethinking the peace ballot, 1934–35', *JBS*, 49:2 (2010), 358–87.
6 Helen McCarthy, *The British People and the League of Nations: Democracy, Citizenship and Internationalism, c. 1918–45* (2011).
7 Kiernan, 'Torr', *ODNB*; asked by a sixth-form student in the Master's lodgings in Balliol, in 1967 or 1968, what he thought of the Nazi–Soviet Pact he 'just said "it was the worst day in my life" – without expanding further': Paul Slack, personal communication.
8 Kevin Morgan, *Harry Pollitt* (1993), ch. 4; Morgan, 'Pollitt, Harry (1890–1960)', *ODNB*.
9 Hill papers, 21, '1930s'.
10 Grant Duff papers, 38/1, from York [25 December 1939].
11 Grant Duff papers, 38/2, Hill to Margaret James [1939–40], fo. 1r–1v.
12 Ibid., fo. 3r–3v.
13 Ibid., fo. 4r.
14 Ibid., fo. 4r–4v.
15 Ibid., 38/1, from York [25 December 1939].
16 Ibid., 38/2, Hill to Margaret James [1939–40], fo. 5r–5v.
17 Ibid., 38/1, from York [25 December 1939].
18 Hill papers, 21, '1930s'.
19 Grant Duff papers, 38/1, from York [25 December 1939].
20 Ibid., 38/2, Hill to Margaret James [1939–40], fo. 8r.
21 Ibid., 38/1, from York [25 December 1939].
22 Ibid., 38/2, Hill to Margaret James [1939–40], fo. 6r.
23 Ibid., fo. 6v; 38/1, from York [25 December 1939].
24 Morgan, *Against Fascism and War*, pp. 106–10.
25 Grant Duff papers, 38/1, from York [25 December 1939].
26 Ibid., 38/2, Hill to Margaret James [1939–40], fo. 7r.
27 Ibid., 38/1, from York [25 December 1939].
28 Ibid., 38/2, Hill to Margaret James [1939–40], fo. 8r–8v.
29 Ibid., 38/1 [19 December 1939].
30 Ibid.
31 Morgan, *Against Fascism and War*, chs. 6–7; Eaden and Renton, *The Communist Party*, chs. 2–3.

32   Grant Duff papers, 38/1, from York [23 December 1939].

33   *Spectator*, 19 December 40, p. 78. See also 5 January 1940, p. 6; 12 January 1940, p. 46; 26 January 1940, p. 110, 2 February 1940, p. 148. Not all correspondence was enraged – some correspondents expressed wry amusement at the radicalism of youth.

34   Ibid., 12 January 1940, p. 46.

35   *New Statesman and Nation*, 18 May 1940, p. 644.

36   Hill papers, 21, '1930s'.

37   John Saville, *The Politics of Continuity: British Foreign Policy and the Labour Government, 1945–46* (1993), p. 214.

38   TNA, KV/2/3941, p. 143, for the vettings see pp. 121, 168, 179, 180, 184.

39   Grant Duff papers, 38/3, from Aldershot [Autumn 1940].

40   Ibid., 38/3, from Aldershot [26 December 1940].

41   Ibid., 38/2, from Ramillies [29 July 1940].

42   Ibid., 38/2, from Ramillies [24 July 1940].

43   Ibid., 38/3, from Aldershot [26 September 1940]; 38/4, from Asburton [18 January 1941].

44   Ibid.

45   Ibid., 38/2, from Ramillies [22 August 1940].

46   Ibid., 38/3, from Aldershot [11 September 1940].

47   Ibid., 38/2, from Ramillies [23 August 1940]. Naming the parts of the Bren gun was essential so that they could be disassembled and reassembled effectively. It was widely regarded as a rite of passage, and is memorialised in Henry Reed's poem 'Naming of parts'. I am grateful to Bill Braddick for this reference.

48   Grant Duff papers, 38/2, from Ramillies [25 July 1940].

49   Ibid., 38/2, from Ramillies [25 August 1940]; 38/3, from Aldershot [18 September 1940].

50   Ibid., 38/3, from Ashburton [12 December 1940].

51   Ibid., 38/3, from Aldershot [24 September 1940].

52   Ibid., 38/2, from Ramillies [29 July 1940]; Julian Baldick, 'Zaehner, Robert Charles (1913–1974)', *ODNB*.

53   Grant Duff papers, 38/3, from Aldershot [8 September 1940]. Austin in fact went on to have a distinguished war, including a key role in the preparations for the Normandy landings: P.M.S. Hacker, 'Austin, John Langshaw (1911–1960)', *ODNB*.

54   Grant Duff papers, 38/2, from Ramillies [24 July 1940].

55   Ibid., 38/2, from Ramillies [9 August 1940]; from Ramillies [13 August 1940].

56   Ibid., 38/3, from Aldershot [18 September 1940].

57   Ibid., 38/3, from Aldershot [2 September 1940].

58   Ibid., 38/3, from Aldershot [24 September 1940].

59   Ibid., 38/3, from Ashburton [12 December 1940].

60   Ibid., 38/3, from Aldershot [24 September 1940].

61   Ibid., 38/3, from Aldershot [8 September 1940].

62   Ibid., 38/3, from Aldershot [26 September 1940].

63   Ibid., 38/2, from Ramillies [18 August 1940].

64   Ibid., 38/3, from Aldershot [8 September 1940].

65   Ibid., 38/3, from Aldershot [Autumn 1940].

66   Ibid., 38/3, from Aldershot station [9 September 1940].

67   Ibid., 38/3, from Aldershot [12 September 1940].

68   Ibid., 38/2, from Ramillies [14 August 1940]; 38/2 from Ramillies [18 August 1940].

69   Ibid., 38/3, from Aldershot [26 September 1940]; 38/3 from Aldershot [28 September 1940].

70   Ibid., 38/4, from Ashburton [7 January 1941]; 38/4 from Cambridge [24 August 1943?].

71   Ibid., 38/3, from Aldershot [8 September 1940].

72   Ibid., 38/2, from Aldershot [20 September 1940].

73 Ibid., 38/3, from Aldershot [Autumn 1940].

74 Ibid., 38/2, from Ramillies [25 July 1940].

75 Ibid., 38/2, from Aldershot [8 August 1940].

76 Ibid., 38/3, from Aldershot [12 September 1940].

77 Ibid., 38/2, from Ramillies [24 July 1940].

78 Ibid., 38/2, from York [10 April 1940]; see also 'filthy war', 38/4, from Cheltenham [7 April 1941].

79 Ibid., 38/3, from Aldershot [16 September 1940]; *Scrutiny*, 9 (1940), 277–84.

80 Grant Duff papers, 38/3, from Ashburton [12 December 1940].

81 Ibid., 38/3, from Aldershot [15 September 1940]; 38/3 from Aldershot [1 October 1940].

82 Ibid., 38/3, from Aldershot [3 October 1940].

83 Ibid., 38/3, from Aldershot [15 October 1940].

84 TNA, KV/2/3941, p. 143.

85 Grant Duff papers, 38/4, from Ashburton [7 January 1941].

86 Ibid., 38/4, from Ashburton [20 January 1941].

87 Zaehner was subsequently employed in intelligence in Persia: Baldick, 'Zaehner'. For his importance to Hill for advice about intelligence work, see Grant Duff papers, 38/4, from Ashburton [18 January 1941]; from Ashburton [20 January 1941].

88 Ibid., 38/4, from Cheltenham Station [late 1942], misdated?

89 Ibid., 38/4, from Ashburton [18 January 1941].

90 Eaden and Renton, *Communist Party*, ch. 3; Morgan, *Against Fascism and War*, postscript and conclusion; Monty Johnstone, 'The CPGB, the Comintern and the war, 1939–1941: filling in the blank spots', *Science and Society*, 61:1 (1997), 27–45.

91 TNA, KV/2/3941, p. 143.

92 Ibid., pp. 173–7.

93 Ibid., pp. 169–72.

94 Ibid., pp. 143, for the vetting, p. 168.

95 Grant Duff papers, 38/4, from Cambridge [24 August 1943?].

96 TNA, KV/2/3941, pp. 121, 141, 144.

97 Bill and Ann Braddick, personal communication. For the Ministry of Information campaign see Egilboy [Marc Wiggam], 'Awkward allies: the ministry's domestic policy for the Soviet Union' (moidigital.ac.uk). I am grateful to Simon Eliot and Henry Irving for discussing this campaign with me.

98 TNA, KV/2/3941, p. 122.

99 Corfield, 'As I knew him', p. 9. A report written by Hill for the Foreign Office in April 1945 on the Soviet Union and the trade union movement was put on his file, although it seems to read like a report that any informed official might have written. It discounted the view that the World Trade Union Congress could take up the role in international communism left vacant following the end of the Comintern: TNA, KV/2/3941, pp. 107–9.

100 Saville, *Politics of Continuity*, pp. 212–14.

101 Saville papers, 2/1/14, Hill to Saville, 21 January 1988.

102 Balliol, MISC131, Hill to Jones, 4 February 1992.

103 Berlin papers, 112, fo. 112, Berlin to Hill, 29 May 1945; 112, fo. 140, Hill to Berlin, 16 June 1945. See Gerald Stone, 'Slavonic Studies at Oxford: a brief history' (mod-langs.ox.ac.uk).

104 Berlin papers, 112, fo. 140, Hill to Berlin, 16 June 1945. For the earlier exchanges: Berlin papers, 105, fos. 92–3, Hill to Berlin, 16 October 1936; Grant Duff papers, 38/4, from Cheltenham [5 February 1941].

105 Ibid., 112, fo. 112, Berlin to Hill, 29 May 1945.

106 Ibid., 112, fo. 140, Hill to Berlin, 16 June 1945.

107   Saville, *Politics of Continuity*, pp. 213–14.

108   Hill, *Independent*, 15 January 1994, p. 29.

109   K.E. Holme, *The Two Commonwealths: The Soviets and Ourselves* (1945), at p. 5. Hill identified himself as the author in 'Hobbes and English political thought', in Roy Wood Sellars, V.J. McGill and Marvin Farber (eds), *Philosophy for the Future: The Quest of Modern Materialism* (1949), pp. 13–32 (republished in Hill, *Puritanism*).

110   Holme, *Two Commonwealths*, at p. 42.

111   Grant Duff papers, 38/2, from Balliol [before summer 1940].

112   TNA, KV/2/3941, pp. 121, 134, 135–6, 145, 146–7, 155–6, 159–62, 164–5, 167.

113   Ibid., pp. 121–4, at p. 124.

114   Ibid., pp. 121, 124. For his marriage to Inez see below, pp. 111–12.

115   Ibid., p. 123–4.

116   Ibid., p. 120.

117   Corfield, 'As I knew him', p. 9.

118   Grant Duff papers, 38/4, from Cheltenham [7 April 1941].

119   Roger Simon, TNA, KV 2/3925, pts 1 and 2. For Johnston see pt. 1, p. 141; for Simon's own summary of his career see pt. 1, p. 101.

120   TNA, KV/2/3941, pp. 79–84.

121   Nottingham University Special Collections, DG 3/6, 'Notes on the state' by C. Hill; Douglas Garman to Hill, 3 September 1945.

122   Eaden and Renton, *Communist Party*, chs. 3–4; Morgan, *Against Fascism and War*, postscript and conclusion.

4. Cold War, Marxism and the British Past: 1945–53

1   *Balliol Annual Record, 1978*, p. 21.

2   Corfield interview, p. 13.

3   In Hill's case see for example TNA, KV/2/3941, pp. 59, 50.

4   Hill, *Independent*, 15 January 1994, p. 29; TNA, KV/2/3941, pp. 137–8, 133.

5   *New Statesman and Nation*, 27 March 1948, p. 254. A cutting was retained by the security services: TNA, KV/2/3941, p. 85.

6   Ibid., pp. 79–84, at p. 82.

7   'England's democratic army', *Communist Review* (June 1947), 171–8, at p. 171.

8   Hilton, p. 6.

9   TNA, KV/2/3941, p. 49.

10   *New Statesman and Nation*, 20 May 1950, p. 576; TNA, KV/2/3941, p. 41; *New Statesman and Nation*, 27 May 1950, p. 607; *Manchester Guardian*, 4 August 1950, p. 4.

11   Hobsbawm, *Interesting Times*, p. 185.

12   Mehta, *Up at Oxford*, p. 158. For the general context see Matthew Gerth, *Anti-Communism in Britain during the Early Cold War: A Very British Witch-Hunt* (2023).

13   *TLS*, 12 December 1952, p. 816.

14   *TLS*, 19 December 1952, p. 837. For Lindsay's reply see ibid., p. 853; *Modern Quarterly*, new series, 8:3 (1953), 186–9.

15   TNA, KV/2/3943, pp. 69–70.

16   Stretton, p. 13.

17   TNA, KV/2/3942, pp. 45–6, at p. 46.

18   Berlin papers, 274, fo. 114, Trevor-Roper to Berlin, 24 August 1955.

19   Ibid., 274, fo. 116, Trevor-Roper to Berlin, 1 May 1956. For extended discussion of the accusations about Rees see Rees, *Looking for Mr Nobody*.

20   All Souls Library, Ms Sparrow 9, from Hill, 2 March 1952. I am grateful to Richard Davenport-Hines for this reference.

21 Ibid., from Hill, 10 March 1952. I am grateful to Richard Davenport-Hines for this reference.

22 Rees, *Looking for Mr Nobody*, pp. 181–90; Morgan, 'Rees, (Morgan) Goronwy', *ODNB*. For example, Berlin papers, 274, fo. 70, Rees to Berlin, Monday [19 March 1956; postmark 20 March 1956]; fo. 71, Rees to Berlin, 24 April 1956; fo. 72, Berlin to Rees, 27 April 1956. Rees had previously claimed to share Berlin's exasperation with communists: 274, fos. 49–50, Rees to Berlin, 10 October [1949];

23 Saville papers, 2/1/14, Hill to Saville, 24 June 1984. There is a copy of Meyer's testimony enclosed.

24 TNA, KV/2/3941, pp. 12, 31–2, 48.

25 TNA, KV/2/3942, pp. 3–5, 20–6, 29–30, 47–8 (Underdown and Peter Marshall); pp. 35–6, 40–2 (Berentzen); KV/2/3943, pp. 48–9, 46, 39–40 (Lingard), pp. 30, 28 (Pearl), pp. 9, 6; KV/2/3944, p. 68 (Dorothy Marshall).

26 TNA, KV/2/3942, pp. 9, 11.

27 Ibid., p. 10. Checks were resumed in April 1953: KV/2/3943, pp. 3, 71.

28 TNA, KV/2/3944, pp. 57–9 for the bibliography.

29 TNA, KV/2/3942, p. 49 (High Wycombe), p. 38 (Banbury).

30 Ibid., pp. 12–14, 18–19 (Klugmann), p. 16 (Anglo-French conference); KV/2/3943, p. 77 (St John). See also KV/2/4291.

31 TNA, KV/2/3371, p. 8.

32 Heinemann papers, 7/12: R.P. Dutt, 'Intellectuals and communism', *Communist Review* 4:9 (September 1932), 421–30. For context see John McIlroy, 'The establishment of intellectual orthodoxy and the Stalinization of British Communism 1928–1933', *P&P*, 192 (2006), 187–226, esp. pp. 217–23.

33 Alastair MacLachlan, *The Rise and Fall of Revolutionary England: an Essay on the Fabrication of Seventeenth-Century History* (1986), p. 62. See also David Parker (ed.), *Ideology, Absolutism and the English Revolution: Debates of the British Communist Historians 1940–1956* (2008), p. 55.

34 Heinemann papers, 7/18 Harry Pollitt, at pp. 3, 6, 7, 11. For Pollitt see Morgan, *Harry Pollitt*.

35 Eaden and Renton, *The Communist Party*, ch. 4.

36 PHM, CP/CENT/CULT/1/1, Minutes of the Cultural Committee, 15 May 1947.

37 TNA, KV/2/3941, p. 154.

38 Ibid., p. 152. Hill also cooperated with Bernal in facilitating communist discussion and sociability in London, e.g. ibid., p. 30; PHM, CP/IND/MONT/5/3, Minutes of MQ editorial board, 4 February 1945, 18 July 1946.

39 PHM, CP/CENT/CULT/1/1, Minutes of the Cultural Committee, passim. The secret services noted his membership of the editorial board in 1950: TNA, KV/2/3941, p. 45; KV/2/3944, p. 61, where he is listed as a member from 1947 until his resignation in January 1954.

40 PHM, CP/IND/MONT/5/3, Minutes of MQ editorial board, 18 May 1951.

41 PHM, CP/CENT/CULT/1/3.

42 PHM, CP/CENT/COMM/9/4.

43 PHM, CP/CENT/CULT/1/1, Minutes of the Cultural Committee, 19 April 1947.

44 'Anglická revoluce [The English Revolution]', *Sborník pro Hospodářské a Sociálni Dějiny*, 2:1–2 (1947), 1–17; 'L'oeuvre des historiens marxistes anglais sur l'histoire britannique du 16e et du 17e siècles [The work of Marxist historians on 16th and 17th century British history]', *La Pensée*, ns, 28 (1950), 51–62; review of T.S. Willan, *The Muscovy Merchants of 1555*, *Anglo-Soviet Journal*, 14 (1953), 40; comment on review of M. Dobb, *Studies in the Development of Capitalism*, *Revue Historique*, 205 (1951), 174–7; 'The English Revolution and the brotherhood of man' (1953, English translation 1954), in Hill, *Puritanism*.

45   TNA, KV/2/3941, pp. 56, 57.

46   *TLS*, 19 December 52, p. 837. Not all the audience members were impressed: *TLS*, 26 December 1952, p. 853 (Kosminsky); TNA, KV/2/3944, p. 63 (Chesneux), p. 8 (Genoux).

47   TNA, KV/2/3941, pp. 20, 25–6.

48   *Times*, 20 March 2003, p. 34.

49   TNA, KV/2/3944, p. 11.

50   TNA, KV/2/3941, pp. 128. See also pp. 117–18.

51   Ibid., pp. 112–15.

52   'Society and Andrew Marvell', *Modern Quarterly*, new series, 1:4 (1946), 6–31, at pp. 6, 9, 10 (republished in Hill, *Puritanism*).

53   'Hobbes and English political thought' (1949), in Hill, *Puritanism*.

54   'The English Revolution and the state', *Modern Quarterly*, new series, 4:2 (1949), 110–28, at p. 115.

55   'Time and Mr Toynbee', *Modern Quarterly*, new series, 2:4 (1947), 290–307, at p. 303.

56   'The myth of western civilisation', *Modern Quarterly*, new series, 5:2 (1950), 172–4.

57   Adam Sisman, *Hugh Trevor-Roper: The Biography* (2010), p. 274.

58   'Marxism and history', *Modern Quarterly*, new series, 3:2 (1948), 52–64.

59   'The materialist conception of history', *University*, 1 (1951), 110–14, at p. 112.

60   'Lenin: theoretician of revolution', *Communist Review* (February 1947), 59–64; 'The Restoration spirit', *New Theatre*, 4 (1947), 16–17; 'The fight for an independent foreign policy', *Communist Review* (February 1948), 46–52; 'Historians and the rise of British capitalism', *Science and Society*, 14:4 (1950), 307–21; 'The transition from feudalism to capitalism, II', *Science and Society*, 17:4 (1953), 348–51.

61   Between 1942 and 1953 he wrote reviews for *Our Time, Communist Review, Modern Quarterly, The Anglo-Soviet Journal, Science and Society*.

62   'The English civil war interpreted by Marx and Engels', *Science and Society*, 12:1 (1948), 130–56. (Italian translation in *Societa*, 4 (1948), 33–63).

63   'The English Revolution and the state'; 'Land in the English Revolution', *Science and Society*, 13:1 (1949), 22–49. In 1946 he had summarised the findings of Lavrovsky on the land market: 'Professor Lavrovsky's study of a seventeenth-century manor', *EcHR*, 16:2 (1946), 125–9.

64   PHM, CP/CENT/CULT/5/11, Minute Books of the Historians' Group, October 1946–January 1951.

65   Quoted in Pennington, p. 31.

66   Kiernan, 'Torr', *ODNB*. See also Corfield interview, pp. 13–14.

67   Hilton, p. 9. For a general account see Parker (ed.), *Ideology*, introduction. MacLachlan, *Rise and Fall*, ch. 3, discusses the internal party dynamics shaping the discussions of the group from a largely hostile perspective, and although useful on some points, as Parker shows, misreads the discussions.

68   Hill papers, 234, 'A.L. Morton', p. 2.

69   PHM, CP/CENT/CULT/5/11, Minute Books of the Historians' Group, October 1946–January 1951; Minute Books of the Historians' Group, minutes of 1946 conferences. See also Parker (ed.), *Ideology*, p. 10; Corfield interview, pp. 13–14.

70   Parker (ed.), *Ideology*, pp. 10, 31–53; MacLachlan, *Rise and Fall*, pp. 44–6. See also Tim Rogan, *The Moral Economists: R.H. Tawney, Karl Polanyi, E.P. Thompson, and the Critique of Capitalism* (2017), pp. 138–40.

71   Hill attended lectures by Dobb in January 1945, TNA, KV/2/3941, p. 153; for their personal relationship see Saville papers, 2/1/14, Hill to Saville, 16 April 1988.

72   TNA, KV/2/3941, pp. 105–6. He was positive about the revised edition: *Daily Worker*, 24 February 1949. See also Rogan, *Moral Economists*, p. 139.

73 Hill papers, 234, 'A.L. Morton', at p. 2.
74 Saville papers, 2/1/14, Hill to Saville, 4 May 1979.
75 Parker (ed.), *Ideology*, pp. 32–3; MacLachlan, *Rise and Fall*, 59–63.
76 Matthew Stibbe, *Debates on the German Revolution of 1918–19* (2023), pp. 58–62.
77 Ibid., p. 61. For Dutt's file on the controversy see PHM, CP/IND/DUTT/8/8.
78 Dell papers, fos. 156–8, from the Secretariat of the CPGB, 26 November 1940, 6 December 1940, at fo. 157.
79 Parker (ed.), *Ideology*, pp. 32–3, 37–8; Corfield interview, p. 14.
80 Hilton, p. 9.
81 TNA, KV/2/3941, pp. 76–8.
82 Kettle interview.
83 Parker (ed.), *Ideology*, introduction.
84 *Lenin and the Russian Revolution* (1947). For Trotsky see pp. 148–50, 157–8 and 220–1.
85 *The Independent*, 15 January 1994, p. 29.
86 Rowse, 'Hill', unpaginated. He was only slightly less withering in print: *Historians I Have Known* (1995), p. 106; Berlin papers, 169, fo. 9, Hill to Berlin, 4 July 1962. Unusually, the letter was typed, a measure perhaps of coolness between them although the tone is of attempted reconciliation.
87 *Listener*, 21 October 1965, pp. 613–14, at p. 614.
88 *TLS*, 10 April 1948, p. 205; J. Middleton Murray responded robustly: *TLS*, 24 April 1948, p. 233.
89 *TLS*, 21 July 1950, p. 453; 'The myth of western civilisation'.
90 TNA, KV/2/3941, pp. 90–101, 14. The latter article was criticised for drawing a distinction between 'Elizabethans' in different eras, but not historicising the bourgeoisie and capitalism in the same way: *Guardian*, 23 December 1952, p. 4.
91 TNA, KV/2/3941, p. 75; see also pp. 60, 58; KV/2/3943, pp. 56–60; KV/2/3944, pp. 13, 17.
92 TNA, KV/2/3941, pp. 43–4.
93 Corfield, 'Intellectual trajectory', 20 n. 27. Hill wrote to Berlin at the time of the operation: Berlin papers, 104, fos. 222–3, 14 December 1935; 105, fos. 12–13, 1 February 1936.
94 J.D. Bernal, 'Stalin as Scientist', *Modern Quarterly*, 8:3 (summer 1953), 133–42. There was much discussion of Lysenko on the editorial board of *Modern Quarterly* in the early 1950s: PHM, CP/IND/MONT/5/3, Minutes of MQ editorial board.
95 'Stalin and the science of history', *Modern Quarterly*, 8:4 (autumn 1953), 198–212, at pp. 209, 212.
96 PHM, CP/CENT/CULT/5/12, Minute Books of the Historians' Group, March 1951– March 1954, where discussion of the article pre-dates the attachment of Hill's name to the suggestion.
97 Grant Duff papers, 38/4, from York [May 1941].
98 Trevor-Roper, *New Statesman and Nation*, 9 September 1944, pp. 171–2. Hill retaliated in a letter commenting on Trevor-Roper's work, *New Statesman and Nation*, 5 June 1948, p. 460.
99 Introduction to Leonard Hamilton (ed.), *Gerrard Winstanley: Selections from His Works* (1944), pp. 4–5.
100 'Hobbes and English political thought', at p. 26.
101 Parker (ed.), *Ideology*, pp. 21–2.
102 Christopher Hill and Edmund Dell (eds), *The Good Old Cause: The English Revolution of 1640–60. Its Causes, Course and Consequences* (1949).
103 Dell papers, fos. 169, 483.
104 Ibid., fos. 260–5, 407–9, 607–10, 628–36.

105   Ibid., fo. 279, Hill to Dell, 19 February 1947.

106   Ibid., fo. 283, 24 May 1947.

107   Ibid., fo. 259, note from 23 July 1947.

108   Ibid., fo. 290, 2 December 1948. See also Dell's correspondence with the Provost: fos. 624, 625.

109   Ibid., fo. 290, 2 December 1948.

110   Ibid., fo. 287, 22 May 1948.

111   Ibid., fo. 284, n.d. For related correspondence see fos. 259, 288, 598–611. He remained in contact with Dell, at least in connection with reprints, and Dell wrote having read Hill's recent book *God's Englishman*: 'You will agree that I use my new found leisure well': Hill papers, 257, from Dell, 22 August 1970.

112   *Good Old Cause*, pp. 19, 21, 477.

113   TNA, KV/2/1843, p. 32. Thompson's main purpose was to restore Christopher Caudwell's reputation for historical analysis, partly on the grounds that he had anticipated Hill's arguments no later than 1936 in *Illusion and Reality*.

114   TNA, KV/2/3941, p. 12.

115   C. Hill, R.H. Hilton and E.J. Hobsbawm, 'Past and Present: origins and early years', *P&P*, 100 (1983), 3–14, at p. 9. (Hill and Hilton clearly saw this as primarily Hobsbawm's work: Hobsbawm papers, 937/6/2/4).

116   Hill, Hilton and Hobsbawm, 'Past and Present', p. 9.

117   Hobsbawm, *Interesting Times*, pp. 230–1. See also Hill, Hilton and Hobsbawm, 'Past and Present'. For the Historians' Group discussion see PHM, CP/CENT/CULT/5/12, Minute Books of the Historians' Group, March 1951–March 1954, meetings of 18 May and 8 June 1951; CP/CENT/CULT/8/1, first notebook, p. 3. See also Bill Speck, *TLS*, 15 November 1996, pp. 33–4.

118   Hobsbawm, *Interesting Times*, pp. 282–7, at p. 285.

119   Enquiry from Livia Ciavarella, a student at the Catholic University of Milan: P&P papers, box 342, unfoliated, Aston's reply is 11 July 1979.

120   The Editorial Board, *P&P*, 1:2 (1952), p. iii.

121   Ibid., p. iv.

122   *EHR*, 67:262 (1952).

123   *The Cambridge Historical Journal*, 10:3 (1952).

124   TNA, KV/2/3943, p. 66. For other intercepted *P&P* correspondence see ibid., pp. 62.

125   *P&P*, 4 (1953), p. 1. A report on the 10th International Congress of Historians in 1955 restated many of the ambitions of the founding editorial statement and celebrated the renewed dialogue between East and West, something to which both Hill and Hobsbawm had themselves contributed: *P&P*, 8 (1955), pp. 83–90.

126   PHM, CP/CENT/CULT/6/01, Minute Books of Historians' Group, May 1954–December 1956, meetings of 8 July 1956, 21 October 1956 and 28 October 1956.

127   Hill, Hilton and Hobsbawm, 'Past and Present', pp. 11–1; Minutes of the Editorial Board, 19 July 1958. I am grateful to Anna Bayman for allowing me access to the minutes.

128   Hill, Hilton and Hobsbawm, 'Past and Present', pp. 12; Minutes of the Editorial Board, 19 July 1958; Editorial note, *P&P*, 14 (1958), p. 93.

129   Corfield interview, pp. 20–1.

130   'Puritans and the poor' (1952), in Hill, *Puritanism*; Communication on 'Puritans and the poor and William Perkins', *P&P*, 3 (1953), 53–4.

131   'Benlowes and his times', *Essays in Criticism*, 3:2 (1953), 143–51 (see also Hill, *Collected Essays*, i).

132   *TLS*, 29 May 1953, p. 353.

133   TNA, KV/2/3943, pp. 55, 63, 68.

134 'The Barebones Parliament: a revaluation', *Listener*, 23 July 1953, pp. 142–3; TNA, KV/2/3943, pp. 42–5. The programme was broadcast on 6 July 1953 and 9 July 1953: *Manchester Guardian*, 6 July 1953, p. 11, 9 July 1953, p. 9.

135 *Listener*, 23 July 1953, at p. 143.

136 TNA, KV/2/3943, p. 41.

137 'Clarendon and the civil war' (1953), in Hill, *Puritanism*.

138 TNA, KV/2/3943, pp. 53–4; see above, pp. 9–10.

139 TNA, KV/2/3941, p. 46.

140 It has been more conventional to see these as stages in the development of his writing: my reading is closer to that of Parker (ed.), *Ideology*, introduction.

5. Personal and Political Crises: 1953–7

1 TNA, KV/2/3941, p. 72.

2 Grant Duff papers, 38/3, from Aldershot [15 September 1940]. For Roger see also 38/1 [December 1939]; 38/2, from Ramillies [25 July 1940]; 38/2, card from Balliol [1940]; 38/3, from Aldershot [8 September 1940]; 38/3, from Ashburton [12 December 1940]. I have not been able to identify who this is. One possibility is Roger Schönbaum: 38/2, from York [3 April 1940]; another Roger Mynors, who could at the time have given her lunch in Balliol, as promised in 38/2, from Balliol [before summer 1940].

3 Ibid., 38/4 [4 March 1941]; from Cheltenham [7 April 1941].

4 Mike Daunt, *The Bounder: The Riotous True-Life Adventures of a Bon Viveur* (2016), pp. 115–6.

5 Corfield, 'As I knew him', p. 4.

6 *Times*, 20 March 2003, p. 34.

7 Corfield interview, p. 25.

8 See above, p. 75.

9 Saville papers, 2/1/14, Hill to Saville, 7 May 1984.

10 TNA, KV/2/3941, pp. 133, 137–8.

11 Ibid., pp. 146–7.

12 Corfield, 'As I knew him', p. 3.

13 TNA, KV/2/3941, pp. 72–4.

14 Ibid., pp. 65–8.

15 Ibid., p. 38.

16 Possibly Daunt's aunt: Daunt, *Bounder*, p. 120.

17 TNA, KV/3/3943, pp. 51–2.

18 Ibid., p. 28.

19 Ibid., p. 23.

20 Ibid., pp. 8, 10, 11, 13, 14, 19; KV/2/3944, pp. 67, 42.

21 TNA, KV/2/3943, p. 23.

22 Corfield, 'As I knew him', pp. 3–4.

23 Grant Duff papers, 38/5, from Balliol, 5 December [1950s].

24 TNA, KV/2/3943, p. 23.

25 Ibid., pp. 36–8.

26 Corfield interview, p. 19.

27 'Cavaliers, Roundheads – or neither?', *Amateur Historian*, 1:1 (1952), 13–17.

28 PHM, CP/CENT/CULT/5/12, Minute Books of the Historians' Group, March 1951–March 1954, meetings of 8 January 1953, 22 March 1953, 19 April 1953, 21 June 1953; CP/CENT/CULT/06/01, Historians' Group, May 1954–December 1956, rough minutes of Working Committee and full Committee of the Historians' Group, meeting 20

March 1955. See also the discussion of weak support for the publication 'Our history', 9 October 1955.

29 Dell papers, fo 129, n.d.; fo. 151, n.d.

30 PHM, CP/CENT/CULT/5/11, Minute Books of the Historians' Group, October 1946–January 1951, 10 December 1949, 14 January 1950. By 1953 Dell was a member of the Labour Party.

31 *Balliol Annual Record, 1978*, p. 21.

32 PHM, CP/CENT/CULT/5/11, Minute Books of the Historians' Group, October 1946–January 1951, 10 April 1948.

33 PHM, CP/CENT/CULT/06/01, Historians' Group, May 1954–December 1956, rough minutes of Working Committee and full Committee of the Historians' Group.

34 TNA, KV/2/3944, p. 48.

35 Hobsbawm papers, 937/4/4/3 (unpublished obituaries), Hill, 7/3/2003, p. 1. Hobsbawm's Moscow diary consists mostly of personal reflections on life in Russia: Hobsbawm papers, 1215/26, Moscow Diary 1954–5. For Tanya and Kostya see above, pp. 24–30.

36 Hobsbawm, *Interesting Times*, pp. 196–201, at pp. 197, 198, 200.

37 TNA, KV/2/3944, pp. 30, 34–7, 38, 53, 62; ibid., p. 38; ibid., p. 10.

38 Ibid., pp. 28, 45–6.

39 Ibid., p. 26, *World News*, 23 July 1955.

40 Institute of Education, Special Collections, SIM/6/1/5; *Universities Quarterly*, pp. 332–41.

41 TNA, KV/2/3944, pp. 24–5. The copy sent to Saville is in Saville papers, 1/13, Hill to Saville, 22 July 1955.

42 TNA, KV/2/3945, p. 112.

43 F.D. Klingender, 'Students in a changing world', *Bulletin of Economic Research*, 6:1 (1954), 1–33, notes in Hill papers, 81.

44 I am grateful to Felicity Armstrong, Jeannie Moyo and David Cursons for discussing Fanny's time at St Christopher School with me.

45 TNA, KV/2/3944, p. 19; KV/2/3945, 102, 107–9.

46 *Guardian*, 13 August 2002, p. 16.

47 Ibid.; *Times*, 2 September 2002, p. 7[S]. For Christopher and Stephen see Parker (ed.), *Ideology*, pp. 10, 11, 22; *Balliol Annual Record, 1978*, p. 21.

48 Corfield, 'Bridget Hill', pp. 2, 4; *Guardian*, 13 August 2002, p. 16.

49 Corfield, 'Bridget Hill', p. 2.

50 Ibid., pp. 3–4; Corfield, 'As I knew him', pp. 7–8.

51 Grant Duff papers, 38/2, from York, 5 April 1940.

52 TNA, KV/2/3945, pp. 86, 98.

53 Ibid., p. 101.

54 Ibid., p. 88, letter to the *Daily Worker*, 27 March 1956.

55 Ibid., pp. 86–7, 76.

56 Ibid., pp. 48–56, 61; for the cutting from *World News* see KV/2/3946, pp. 91–3.

57 Ibid., p. 60.

58 Ibid., pp. 47, 69.

59 Hilton, pp. 9–10. He noted that the party was able to do that later, in relation to Czechoslovakia.

60 *Listener*, 16 December 1976, pp. 787–8, at p. 788.

61 Ibid. See also Heinemann papers, 7/8.

62 See Richard J. Evans, *Eric Hobsbawm: A Life in History* (2019), esp. pp. 337–53.

63 Michael Kenny, *The First New Left: British Intellectuals after Stalin* (1995), pp. 16–18; MacEwen, *Listener*, 16 December 1976, pp. 787–8, at p. 788. See also PHM, CP/CENT/

CONG/11/05, 'Communist Party Executive Committee statement on "The Reasoner"', 13 September 1956. For Saville's recollections see *Socialist Register* (1994), pp. 20–31.

64 Saville papers, 1/65, Samuel to Saville, June 1956 (Saville's date, although this seems mistaken – Polish anti-Stalinists had been repressed in June, but the Hungarian rising only started in October).

65 TNA, KV/2/3945, p. 37.

66 Saville papers, 1/43, Kiernan to Hill, 12 November 1956.

67 Ibid., 1/65, Hobsbawm to Saville [1956].

68 Ibid., 2/1/14, Dorothy Thompson to Hill, 21 October 1994.

69 PHM, CP/CENT/CONG/11/05, 'Communist Party Executive Committee statement on "The Reasoner"', 13 September 1956, pp. 4–5.

70 Eaden and Renton, *The Communist Party*, p. 123.

71 Saville papers, 2/1/14, Dorothy Thompson to Hill, 21 October 1994.

72 Ibid., 2/1/14, Hill to Dorothy Thompson, 30 October 1994.

73 TNA, KV/2/3945, p. 72, 31 July 1956. I have not been able to locate a copy of the letter.

74 Saville papers, 1/65, Hill to Saville, 11 November 1956.

75 *New Reasoner*, 4 (1957), 107–13; *New Reasoner*, 5 (1957), 115–18.

76 Saville papers, 1/67, Hill to Saville, 24 May 1957.

77 Kenny, *First New Left*, ch. 1; Duncan Thompson, *Pessimism of the Intellect: A History of New Left Review* (2007), ch. 1.

78 Saville papers, 2/1/14, Hill to Dorothy Thompson, 30 October 1994.

79 TNA, KV/2/3945, p. 34.

80 The letter to the *Daily Worker* was circulated for signature with a covering letter signed by Hill and Hilton. It asked for approval for the plan to send it to the *New Statesman* and *Tribune* if the *Daily Worker* would not print it within a short period. A second letter followed saying that the *Daily Worker* had refused and disputing the grounds on which it had done so, along with a third letter, from Hilton, refuting the Political Committee's statement about the *Daily Worker* letter: Saville papers, 1/43, from Hill and Hilton, 15 November 1956; from Kiernan 19 November 1956; from Hill, 3 December 1956; and from Hilton, 8 December 1956.

81 TNA, KV/2/3945, pp. 27, 36, 37, 41–4, at pp. 27, 37.

82 Ibid., p. 40.

83 Ibid., pp. 25, 26.

84 Ibid., p. 11.

85 Ibid., p. 24.

86 Ibid., p. 23; *New Statesman and Nation*, 1 December 1956, p. 701.

87 Ibid. For Abramsky's attempted intervention: TNA, KV/2/3945, p. 39. The letter was signed by Abramsky, Hobsbawm, Hyman Levy, Robert Browning, Paul Hogarth, Jack Lindsay, Henry Collins, George Houston, Hugh MacDiarmid, Hill, Kiernan, Ronald Meek, Hilton, Doris Lessing and Thompson. Saville and Thompson had already left the party; Thompson's signature was noted by the party leadership to be in itself inappropriate, and was presumably one reason why Abramsky's amendment was not accepted.

88 TNA, KV/2/3212, pt. 1, pp. 94 (5 December 1956), 76–7 (3 December 1956), 31–5 (meeting of 25 January 1957).

89 TNA, KV/2/3945, pp. 18, 19, 20.

90 Ibid., pp. 14–17, transcript of letter to *World News*, 4 December 1957.

91 TNA, KV/2/4280, pp. 57–8; *World News*, 15 December 1956.

92 Ibid.

93 Saville papers, 1/65, Hobsbawm to Saville [1956] and [late 1956?].

94 TNA, KV/2/3945, pp. 7–8.

95 Saville papers, 2/1/14, Hill to Dorothy Thompson, 30 October 1994.

96 TNA, KV/2/3946, pp. 89–90, *Observer*, 27 January 1957, pp. 1, 9. For an earlier draft of the report with the comments of the minority appended, see correspondence between Hill and Klugmann, PHM, CP/IND/KLUG/01/06 and TNA, KV/2/3945, pp. 27–33.

97 *Times*, 23 April 1957, p. 4.

98 TNA, KV/2/3946, p. 88. Hill was also involved in correspondence with *World News* about misrepresentation of the minority view about the possibility of ordinary members shaping party policy: ibid., pp. 85–7.

99 Ibid., p. 77.

100 For the records of the conference, including materials circulated to delegates and full transcripts of all the speeches, see PHM, CP/CENT/CONG/10/05–11, CP/CENT/CONG/11/01–12.

101 TNA, KV/2/3946, pp. 79, 82, 83.

102 *Times*, 15 April 1957, p. 7; *Manchester Guardian*, 23 April 1957, p. 2.

103 *Manchester Guardian*, 23 April 1957, p. 2; *Daily Telegraph*, 23 April 1957, p. 13.

104 *Times*, 15 April 1957, p. 7.

105 PHM, CP/CENT/CONG/11/03. See also ibid., 11/02, 04 (for the undelivered speech).

106 TNA, KV/2/3212, pt. 1, pp. 28–47, meeting 25 February 1957; KV/2/3213, pt. 2, p. 42, 1 May 1957.

107 TNA, KV/2/3212, pt. 1, pp. 39, 33, meeting 25 January 1957.

108 PHM, CP/CENT/CONG/10/10 for the memo; CP/CENT/CONG/10/06 for the transcript of his speech.

109 *Tribune*, 26 April 1957, p. 5. For the exchange with Gollan, see TNA, KV/2/3212, pt. 1, p. 46, 13 February 1957. For the transcript of the speech see PHM, CP/CENT/CONG/10/08.

110 *Tribune*, 26 April 1957, p. 5.

111 PHM, CP/CENT/CONG/10/09. Reported in *Daily Telegraph*, 23 April 1957, p. 13; *Manchester Guardian*, 23 April 1957, p. 2.

112 *Daily Telegraph*, 23 April 1957, p. 13; *Manchester Guardian*, 23 April 1957, p. 2.

113 *Daily Telegraph*, 23 April 1957, p. 13.

114 For drafts of the speech see TNA, KV/2/3946, pp. 68–74, which include annotations in his own hand. A version (quoted here) was printed in *World News*, ibid., pp. 58–9, 56, 55. For a cutting see PHM, CP/CENT/CONG/11/02. For the transcript see PHM, CP/CENT/CONG/10/09. It is not a fair copy, perhaps because that had been sent to the *World News*.

115 PHM, CP/CENT/CONG/11/11, Max Engelinck's notes on Hill's speech. Gollan also took accurate and neutral notes: CP/CENT/CONG/10/10.

116 *Times*, 23 April 1957, p. 4. For the transcript of Hunter's speech see PHM, CP/CENT/CONG/10/09.

117 *Herald Tribune*, 23 April 1957, pp. 1, 8; *Times*, 23 April 1957, p. 4.

118 PHM, CP/CENT/CONG/10/09; CP/CENT/CONG/11/12.

119 *Times*, 15 April 1957, p. 7. This is the verdict, implied or explicit, of the rest of the liberal press too: *Times*, 23 April 1957, p. 4; *Daily Telegraph*, 23 April 1957, p. 13; *Herald Tribune*, 23 April 1957, pp. 1, 8; *Manchester Guardian*, 23 April 1957, p. 2.

120 TNA, KV/2/3946, p. 65.

121 Rowse, 'Hill', unpaginated.

122 Corfield, 'Intellectual trajectory', pp. 9–10.

123 Rowse, 'Hill', unpaginated. Rowse claimed to have cheered him up by reporting on a recent meeting with Hill's mother, at which he 'brightened in a moment, relieved at no reference to what was on his mind'.

124   For Thompson's letter, Corfield, 'As I knew him', pp. 4–5.
125   Saville papers, 2/1/14, Hill to Dorothy Thompson, 30 October 1994.
126   Ibid., 1/67, Hill to Saville, 24 May 1957.
127   Ibid., 1/71 Heinemann to Saville, n.d.
128   TNA, KV/2/3946, pp. 63–4, 75, 76.
129   Heinemann papers, 1/1, items 2, 21; Heinemann/7/6.
130   See, in general, Hobsbawm, *Interesting Times* and Evans, *Hobsbawm*.
131   *Observer*, 29 September 1985, p. 9.
132   TNA, KV/2/3946, p. 54.
133   Heinemann papers, 7/20 Heinemann to Andy Croft, 18 September 1979. Her novel, *The Adventurers* (1962), feels like a post-facto justification of the decision to remain in the party. I am grateful to John Merrick for this suggestion.
134   TNA, KV/2/3946, pp. 54, 66, 62, 65.
135   *Daily Telegraph*, 9 August 1957, p. 13; Corfield, 'Bridget Hill', p. 2.
136   TNA, KV/2/3946, pp. 40–6.
137   Ibid., p. 49.
138   Ibid., pp. 36, 38.
139   Ibid., pp. 10, 13–15, 28.
140   *Times*, 23 October 1957, p. 11.
141   TNA, KV/2/3946, pp. 30, 53.
142   MRC, Papers of Lawrence Daly, MSS.302/3/13 (Thompson to Daly, 17/09). Saville defended the tactic in 'A note on West Fife', *New Reasoner*, 10 (1959), 9–13.
143   TNA, KV/2/3946, p. 18.
144   Ibid., p. 27.
145   Ibid., p. 9.
146   TNA, KV/2/3941, p. 103.
147   Grant Duff papers, 38/4, from Cheltenham [6 February 1942].
148   Hill, 'Notes and comments', *P&P*, 20 (1961), 4–5, at p. 4.
149   TNA, KV/2/3946, pp. 34, 44. It was Bridget who had 'immediately decided to have another child': *Guardian*, 13 August 2003, p. 16.
150   Pennington, p. 44; John Watts, personal communication; Sarah Randall, personal communication.
151   Briggs.

6. Science, Radicalism, Revolution and Progress: 1957–65

1   *Sunday Telegraph*, 10 January 1965, p. 5. Balliol lies approximately halfway along a line running east to west from Wadham to Worcester.
2   Jones, *Balliol*, p. 289; Hill, 'Lindsay', *ODNB*.
3   Robin Briggs, personal communication.
4   John Carey, *The Unexpected Professor: An Oxford Life in Books* (2014), pp. 156–7.
5   Keen, p. 19; Pennington, p. 37.
6   Jones, *Balliol*, p. 286.
7   Briggs.
8   Keen, p. 18; for other memories of his tutorial style see *Balliol Annual Record, 1978*, pp. 16–20.
9   Stretton, p. 11; Pennington, p. 29; Corfield, 'Balliol College', p. 4.
10   Pennington, p. 29.
11   Bill Braddick, personal communication.
12   TNA, KV/2/3944, p. 42.

13 Briggs.

14 Keen, p. 17.

15 Grant Duff papers, 38/2, from Balliol, 'Thursday' [before summer 1940]; 38/2, from Balliol [before summer 1940] 'Saturday'.

16 Dell papers, fo. 277, 13 November [1946].

17 Balliol, deceased members files, Raphael Samuel, letter 13 July 1964. Hill's academic references are also in the file, noting both Samuel's brilliance and his waywardness.

18 *Times*, 7 March 2003, p. 42; for the illness, see Balliol, deceased members' files, John Keegan.

19 *Times*, 11 March 2003, p. 21.

20 Keen, p. 19; Stretton, p. 11.

21 Keen, p. 19.

22 'A.B. Rodger', *Balliol College Record*, 1962, 35–7; Hill, 'Lindsay'.

23 Keen, p. 18; Corfield, 'Balliol College', p. 3.

24 Mehta, *Up at Oxford*, pp. 142, 156; Alex Callinicos, personal communication.

25 TNA, KV/2/3943, p. 23.

26 Based on M.F. Roberts, 'Christopher Hill: A Select Bibliography, 1938–1977', in Donald Pennington and Keith Thomas (eds), *Puritans and Revolutionaries: Essays in Seventeenth-Century History Presented to Christopher Hill* (1978), pp. 382–402, and standard library searches.

27 *Daily Worker* reviews: 25 February 1954 (of Brunton and Pennington); 25 November 1954; 29 December 1955; 'The transition from feudalism to capitalism, II'.

28 *Telegraph*, 23 March 1955, p. 4; *Listener*, 31 March 1955, p. 588; *Daily Mail*, 18 May 1956, p. 14.

29 *Guardian*, 25 May 1960, p. 8; 'Republicanism after the Restoration', *New Left Review*, 1:3 (1960), 46–51.

30 'Recent interpretations of the Civil War' (1956), in Hill, *Puritanism*. See also 'A propos d'un article recent sur Cromwell' [by Trevor-Roper], *Annales*, 9 (1956), 490–2. He also commented on this debate in *Encounter*, 11 (1958), 76.

31 Christopher Hill, *Economic Problems of the Church: From Archbishop Whitgift to the Long Parliament* (1956), at pp. ix, x.

32 Ibid., p. v.

33 Ibid., p. 348.

34 Ibid., at pp. xii, 348, 351. He more or less repeated this formulation in C. Hill and G.J.M. Pearce, 'History and denominational history', *Baptist Quarterly*, 22:2 (1967), 65–71, at p. 66 (republished in Hill, *Collected Essays*, ii).

35 'The Norman Yoke' (1954), in Hill, *Puritanism*.

36 See also Rogan, *Moral Economists*, ch. 4.

37 'Clarissa Harlowe and her times' (1955), in Hill, *Puritanism*.

38 'The mad hatter' (1957); 'John Mason and the end of the world', *History Today*, 7:11 (1957), 776–80, at p. 780 (both in Hill, *Puritanism*).

39 Hilton, p. 9.

40 Corfield interview, pp. 20–1.

41 *Guardian*, 13 August 2002, p. 16; *Times*, 2 September 2002, p. 25; Corfield, 'Bridget Hill'.

42 Hill, *Puritanism*.

43 Corfield interview, pp. 16–17.

44 Mehta, *Up at Oxford*, p. 158; John Rees and Lee Humber, 'The good old cause; an interview with Christopher Hill', *International Socialism*, 56:2 (1992), pp. 125–34.

45 Parker (ed.), *Ideology*, p. 14; see also Hill, 'Marxism and history'.

46 *Economic Problems*, at pp. 351–2.

47 *Oliver Cromwell 1658–1958*, Historical Association Pamphlet G 38 (1958); *Listener*, 4

September 1958, p. 8. See also 'Colonel John Hutchinson, 1615–1664: a tercentenary tribute', *Transactions of the Thoroton Society of Nottinghamshire*, 69 (1966 for 1965), 79–87.

48 Christopher Hill, *The Century of Revolution, 1603–1714* (1961) (here quoting second edition, 1980, pp. 4, 266).

49 'La Révolution Anglaise du XVIIe siècle: essai d'interprétation [The seventeenth-century English Revolution: interpretative essay]', *Revue historique*, 221 (1959), 5–32. He later contributed the introduction to Trevor Aston (ed.), *Crisis in Europe: Essays from Past and Present* (1965).

50 *Balliol Annual Record, 1978*, p. 19.

51 Hill, *Century of Revolution*, p. 266.

52 'The many-headed monster in late Tudor and early Stuart political thinking' (1966), in Hill, *Change and Continuity*.

53 H.N. Brailsford, *The Levellers and the English Revolution* (1961), edited and prepared for publication by J.E.C. Hill, at p. v.

54 The secret services kept a cutting of the *Times* announcement: KV/2/3946, p. 24, May 1961.

55 TNA, KV/2/3943, pp. 36–7.

56 Hill reviewed Mason's *A History of the Sciences* very positively in *Oxford Left* (Michaelmas 1954), 49–51.

57 Tudor Jones, *Remaking the Labour Party: From Gaitskell to Blair* (1996), ch. 4; Robert Sheldon, 'Dell, Edmund Emmanuel (1921–1999)', *ODNB*.

58 Paul Betts and Stephen A. Smith (eds), *Science, Religion and Communism in Cold War Europe* (2016), esp. intro, chs. 5, 11, 12.

59 *Listener*, 24 March 1960, pp. 549–50.

60 'Hobbes and English political thought' (1949), in Hill, *Puritanism*.

61 'William Harvey and the idea of monarchy', *P&P*, 27 (1964), 54–72; 'Puritanism, capitalism and the scientific revolution (debate)', *P&P*, 29 (1964), 88–97; 'William Harvey (no parliamentarian, no heretic) and the idea of monarchy', *P&P* 31 (1965), 97–103; 'Science, religion and society in sixteenth and seventeenth centuries', *P&P*, 31 (1965), 110–12.

62 Hill, *Intellectual Origins*, at pp. 1, 3, 299.

63 Serialised in the *Listener*, 31 May to 5 July 1962. For the broadcasts see, *Listener*, 24 May 1962, p. 909. See also *Listener*, 13 July 1962, p. 6.

64 'The politics of John Milton', *Listener*, 12 September 1963, pp. 383–5.

65 *Observer*, 20 January 1963, p. 35.

66 Christopher Hill, *Society and Puritanism in Pre-Revolutionary England* (1964).

67 'Puritans and "the dark corners of the land"' (1963), in Hill, *Change and Continuity*; 'Propagating the gospel', in H.E. Bell and R.L. Ollard (eds), *Historical Essays, 1600–1750, Presented to David Ogg* (1963), pp. 35–59.

68 Hill papers, 255, letter from Gregory, 31 May 1964 (Hill suggested E.P. Thompson, Ivan Roots, Keith Thomas and E.W. Ives). The script is in Hill papers, 249; *Observer*, 29 August 1965, p. 18.

69 *Observer*, 29 August 1965, p. 18.

70 Roberts, 'Christopher Hill: A Select Bibliography', pp. 382–402, and standard library searches.

71 Pennington, p. 33.

72 Briggs; Stretton, p. 12; Paul Slack, Keith Thomas, personal communication.

73 'Protestantism and the rise of capitalism', in F.J. Fisher (ed.), *Essays in the Economic and Social History of Tudor and Stuart England in Honour of R.H. Tawney* (1961), 15–39 (reprinted in Hill, *Change and Continuity*).

74   Steven Lukes, personal communication. Hill corresponded with Tawney's literary executors following Tawney's death, causing them to worry that he was angling to edit the papers: LSE Special Collections, Tawney/27/14, folder 2, 5; Tawney/27/19, folder 1. In fact, he was trying to find out if Tawney's Ford Lectures had survived, and he later put copies of the notes on the lectures taken by one of his pupils at their disposal (Hill himself had not been able to attend them since he was in the USSR that year).

75   'Protestantism and the rise of capitalism', at pp. 18, 27, 36, 37.

76   Hill papers, 167, Viner to Hill, 31 July 1961, at pp. 3–4.

77   Hill, *Intellectual Origins*, pp. 14, 16.

78   'Stalin and the science of history', p. 199. For his reviews of the relevant works by Fisher and Toynbee see above, pp. 49–50, 88–9.

79   Hill, 'A one-class society', *History and Theory*, 6:1 (1967), 117–27, at p. 122 (republished in Hill, *Change and Continuity*).

80   Corfield interview, p. 23.

81   Briggs.

82   See above, pp. 121–2, 127.

7. Master of Balliol and Modernisation in British Universities: 1965–69

1   *Sunday Telegraph*, 10 January 1965, p. 5.

2   *Sunday Times*, 24 January 1965, p. 13. See also *Financial Times*, 22 January 1965, p. 14.

3   Stretton, pp. 13–15. Corfield notes that Keir had expressed public disapproval of the divorce, but Keir's opinion was not of any account in the election of his successor, and I have not found any evidence that Hill's divorce was an issue for the electors: Corfield, 'Balliol College'.

4   *Sunday Times*, 24 January 1965, p. 13.

5   *Sunday Times*, 15 December 1963, p. 27. For Meiggs see Murray, *Holywell Manor*, esp. ch. 5.

6   *Daily Telegraph*, 23 May 1964, p. 8; *Financial Times*, 6 November 1964, p. 14; *Sunday Telegraph*, 10 January 1965, p. 5.

7   *Sunday Times*, 24 January 1965, p. 13.

8   Ibid.

9   *Sunday Times*, 31 January 1965, p. 18; Balliol, MISC 108 (b) correspondence with Cobb about Hill election.

10   Briggs.

11   *Daily Mail*, 22 January 1965, p. 3.

12   *Daily Telegraph*, 22 January 1965, pp. 1, 14. Hill had actually said 'snug', not 'smug': see above p. 135. The *Mirror*, unlike most other papers, noted quite accurately the reason for his resignation from the CPGB: *Daily Mirror*, 22 January 1965, p. 12. The *Financial Times* also made the connection with Lindsay, 22 January 1965, p. 14.

13   *Guardian*, 22 January 1965, p. 1; *Financial Times*, 22 January 1965, pp. 1, 14. *The Times* gave accurate biographical detail and did not editorialise: *Times*, 22 January 1965, p. 12.

14   *Sunday Times*, 24 January 1965, p. 13.

15   Briggs. For the Cold War hardliners, Corfield, 'Balliol College', p. 1.

16   Jones, *Balliol*, p. 290.

17   Ibid., pp. 290–2; Mehta, *Up at Oxford*, pp. 59–63, 135–7.

18   Jones, *Balliol*, p. 292.

19   Ibid., p. 294 n. 48. Rowse claimed that Keir 'hated the job': Rowse, 'Hill', unpaginated.

20   Corfield, 'Balliol College', p. 2.

21 Keir also publicly stated the importance of Hill's Balliol affiliation, including his decisive try for the rugby team: *Sunday Times*, 24 January 1965, p. 15; *Financial Times*, 22 January 1965, p. 14; *Sunday Times*, 24 January 1965, p. 13.

22 Jones, *Balliol*, p. 307.

23 *Daily Telegraph*, 13 May 1965, p. 19; *Observer*, 16 May 1965, p. 12.

24 *Daily Telegraph*, 13 May 1965, p. 19; see also *Times*, 13 May 1965, p. 8.

25 *Daily Telegraph*, 14 May 1965, p. 18; see also ibid., 15 May 1965, p. 9.

26 Ibid., 13 May 1965, p. 19.

27 *Daily Mail*, 16 June 1965, p. 6; *Times*, 15 May 1965, p. 12; *Daily Telegraph*, 17 May 1965, pp. 1, 32; *Observer*, 20 June 1965, p. 11; Harrison (ed.), *History of the University of Oxford*, p. 408 and plate 14.3.

28 *Times*, 16 May 1965, p. 10; 17 May 1965, p. 8.

29 *Times*, 23 December 1965, p. 5.

30 *Times*, 19 April 1965, p. 10; *Guardian*, 14 May 1965, p. 14.

31 Correspondence and Copy of Memorial Presented to Prime Minister Harold Wilson Urging the Acceptance of the Wolfenden Committee Recommendations, LSE Library, 7/31. For the report: Parliamentary Archives, HL/PO/JO/10/11/588.

32 *Balliol Annual Record*, 1974, p. 6; *Balliol Annual Record*, 1977, p. 9.

33 *Balliol Annual Record*, 1978, p. 11.

34 *Sunday Times*, 15 December 1963, p. 27; *Guardian*, 25 April 1970, p. 9.

35 For context see Peter Mandler, *The Crisis of Meritocracy: Britain's Transition to Mass Education since the Second World War* (2020), ch. 5; Harrison (ed.), *History of the University of Oxford*, ch. 26.

36 *Balliol Annual Record*, 1965, at p. 6.

37 Ibid., at pp. 6, 8.

38 *Balliol Annual Record*, 1966, pp. 4–7, at p. 7. The letter was reported in the *Daily Telegraph*, 3 December 1966, p. 8.

39 Mandler, *Crisis of Meritocracy*, pp. 63–4 (Crowther), ch. 5 (Robbins); *Times*, 10 July 1967, p. 9.

40 *Balliol Annual Record*, 1966, p. 7.

41 *Guardian*, 25 April 1970, p. 9; *Balliol Annual Record*, 1978, p. 9.

42 *Times*, 4 August 1967, p. 7.

43 Ibid., p. 7; *Daily Telegraph*, 3 December 1966, p. 8.

44 Jones, *Balliol*, pp. 314–15. For the 'sumptuous' refit enabled by the appeal, see *Guardian*, 25 April 1970, p. 9.

45 *Guardian*, 30 July 1969, p. 9; *Balliol Annual Record*, 1968, pp. 6–7; Pennington, p. 37; this was possibly the prompt for his lecture on the 1930s: Hill papers, 21, '1930s'. These initiatives were noted by the *Guardian*, 25 April 1970, p. 9. It may have been the meeting at which Paul Slack remembers Hill referring to news of the Nazi–Soviet Pact as the worst day of his life: see above, pp. 58–9.

46 *Balliol Annual Record*, 1968, p. 7; *Balliol Annual Record*, 1970, p. 6.

47 David Leigh, *High Time: The Life and Times of Howard Marks* (1984), p. 27; Howard Marks, *Mr Nice* (2017 edn), p. 72.

48 Jones, *Balliol*, pp. 301–2. Oswyn Murray, personal communication.

49 *Balliol Annual Record*, 1967, p. 6.

50 Ibid., p. 6; *Balliol Annual Record*, 1969, p. 6.

51 P&P papers, Box 343, Minutes of and extraordinary meeting of the board on 6–7 July 1968.

52 *P&P*, 41:1 (1968), at p. 211.

53 Roberts, 'Christopher Hill: A Select Bibliography', pp. 382–402; Hill, 'Lindsay'; 'John Morris', *P&P*, 75 (1977), 3–4.

54 Hobsbawm papers, 937/7/5/2/9, Hill to Hobsbawm, 19 October 1964; *Listener*, 10 August 1967, pp. 172–3.

55 For the importance of economic history in shaping approaches to modern British social history, see Miles Taylor, 'The beginnings of modern British social history', *HWJ*, 43:1 (1997), 155–76, esp. 162–4.

56 Review of Peter Laslett, *The World We Have Lost*, *History and Theory*, 6:1 (1967), 117–27, at p. 121 (republished as 'A one-class society?', in Hill, *Change and Continuity*).

57 The suggestion is Glenn Burgess's, cited in John Morrill, *Revolt in the Provinces: The People of England and the Tragedies of War 1630–1648*, second edition (1999), p. 3.

58 Hill papers, 196, for other examples see items 199, 205.

59 LSE Special Collections, 7SHR/A/1, letter from Hill, 23 April 1970.

60 Hill review in *History*, new series, 37 (1952), 166; Hill papers, 251, Laslett to Hill, 1 August 1956; Laslett, *Guardian*, 10 November 1962, p. 7; Laslett hostile review of *World Turned Upside Down*: *Times*, 22 June 1972, p. 12; and of *Change and Continuity*: *Guardian*, 23 January 1975, p. 14. Hill returned to the attack in 'Sex, marriage and parish registers' (1978), in Hill, *Collected Essays*, iii.

61 Corfield interview, p. 8.

62 'Catherine Macaulay and the seventeenth century', *Welsh History Review*, 3:4 (1967), 381–402.

63 Hill and Pearce, 'History and denominational history', in Hill, *Collected Essays*, ii.

64 'Sir Isaac Newton and his society' (1967), in Hill, *Change and Continuity*; 'The intellectual origins of the Royal Society: London or Oxford?', *Notes & Records of the Royal Society*, 23:2 (1968), 144–56; '"Reason" and "reasonableness" in 17th century England' (1969), in Hill, *Change and Continuity*.

65 'Pottage for freeborn Englishmen: attitudes to wage labour in the sixteenth and seventeenth centuries' (1967), in *Change and Continuity*.

8. Youth Culture and Student Rebellion: 1969–78

1 Balliol, MCOP24 ii, correspondence about the occupation of the Indian Institute and subsequent recriminations February 1974; letter from Balliol JCR to St Anne's JCR, 30 May 1974. See also JCR 10. For national press interest see *Guardian*, 25 April 1970, p. 9. Alan Knight, personal communication.

2 [Hugh Trevor-Roper], *The Letters of Mercurius* (1970).

3 Jones, *Balliol*, pp. 302–3, 306; Stretton, pp. 11, 16.

4 Murray, *Holywell Manor*, pp. 24, 28–9; A.B. Rodger's obituary did not dwell on the circumstances of his departure from the college: ibid., pp. 24–7; see also Jones, *Balliol*, p. 283.

5 Balliol, MCOP 24ii, Hill to Kettle, 21 November 1969; Hill to all members of the Executive Committee, 23 March 1970; JCR 10, Pradeep K. Mitra (JCR president) to Hill, 13 May 1970.

6 *Guardian*, 25 April 1970, p. 9.

7 Balliol, MCOP 24ii, Statement of the Balliol JCR Committee, 10 October 1969.

8 Marks, *Mr Nice*, pp. 44–58; Mehta, *Up at Oxford*, pp. 72–3. See also Leigh, *High Time*, pp. 9–11, 23.

9 Steven Lukes, personal communication; Jones, *Balliol*, p. 308.

10 Marks, *Mr Nice*, pp. 67–8.

11 *Guardian*, 25 April 1970, p. 9.

12 John Morrill, 'Which World Turned Upside Down?', *Prose Studies*, 36:3 (2014), 231–42,

at p. 231. A version of the discussion was published in the *Listener*, 4 October 1973, pp. 448–51.

13 Corfield, 'Balliol College', p. 2; *Times*, 26 February 2003, p. 30.

14 *Guardian*, 13 August 2003, p. 16.

15 Briggs.

16 Marks, *Mr Nice*, p. 68; Rowse reports a falling out between Hill and Sparrow over some left-wing, anti-All Souls (but also homophobic) graffiti: Rowse, 'Hill', unpaginated.

17 Balliol, MCOP 24ii, Kettle to Hill, 19 January 1970.

18 *Guardian*, 25 April 1970, p. 9.

19 Balliol, MCOP 24ii, Hill to president and members of JCR committee, 23 March 1970; handwritten statement by Martin Kettle, 17 March 1970.

20 Balliol, MCOP 24ii, letter from Pradeep K. Mitra (JCR president) to Hill, 13 May 1970; statement by Pete Hutchinson explaining the background to the motion, March 1970.

21 Rowse, 'Hill', unpaginated.

22 *Balliol Annual Record*, 1972, pp. 7–8.

23 *Observer*, 9 April 1972, p. 38; Balliol, MCOP 24ii, consilium about the Deanship, March 1971; John Jones, personal communication.

24 Balliol, MCOP 24ii, Motion for Extraordinary General Meeting of JCR, 12 February 1971; Simon Sedgwick-Jell to Hill, 4 March [1971]; The College as a Community, n.d. [1973?]. See also MCOP 47, where the issue of student representation looms large.

25 Balliol, JCR 10, Phillip McDonagh to Hill, 1 January 1972; Christopher Brickhill to Hill, 22 May 1974.

26 *Balliol Annual Record*, 1978, p. 20.

27 Corfield, 'Balliol College', p. 2; Keen, p. 20; Balliol, deceased members files, Maurice Keen, appreciation of Bridget Hill; Jones, *Balliol*, p. 294; *Balliol Annual Record*, 1978, p. 18.

28 Ronald Hutton, personal communication.

29 Marks, *Mr Nice*, p. 69; Leigh, *High Time*, pp. 27–8.

30 *Times*, 30 July 1988, p. 5. For the campaign in support of parole and serving his sentence in Britain, see Balliol, MISC 297.3; MISC 131, Hill to Jones, 4 February 1992; Jones to Hill, 5 February 1992.

31 Balliol, JCR 10, Hill to JCR president, 25 November 1968.

32 Corfield, 'Balliol college', pp. 2–3.

33 Jones, *Balliol*, p. 294; Balliol, MISC 108 (c). The letters confuse the cause of the threatened resignation with the admission of women, but it was certainly occasioned by the votes on student representation: I am grateful to John Jones and Oswyn Murray for their advice on this point.

34 Hill papers, 8.

35 Douglas Hurd, 'Heath, Sir Edward Richard George [Ted]', *ODNB*; Harrison (ed.), *History of the University of Oxford*, pp. 392–3.

36 *Sunday Telegraph*, 28 June 1970, p. 2.

37 *Sunday Telegraph*, 27 June 1971, p. 2.

38 Alex Callinicos, personal communication. Oswyn Murray agreed that Hill had protected them from the wrath of the Governing Body; personal communication. For Sedgwick-Jell see 'Other lives', *Guardian*, 1 January 2015.

39 Balliol, MCOP24ii, from Ken Jones (JCR president) to the Vice-Master, 22 June 1971; Jones to Hill, 20 October 1971.

40 Oswyn Murray and Steven Lukes, personal communication.

41 Balliol, MCOP 24ii.

42 Ibid., record of general meeting of JCR, 3 February 1974.

43 *Balliol Annual Record, 1975*, p. 8.
44 *Balliol Annual Record, 1976*, p. 10.
45 Balliol, MCOP 17, cutting from *Oxford Magazine*, 15 October 1964.
46 Ibid., memo from Principal of St Anne's to Master of Balliol, 2 January 1970; note of meeting 5 March 1970.
47 Ibid.; see also Jones, *Balliol*, pp. 308–9.
48 *Balliol Annual Record, 1971*, pp. 8–9; *Daily Telegraph*, 11 October 1971, p. 14.
49 *Balliol Annual Record, 1972*, p. 7; for the letters see Balliol, MCOP 18.
50 Balliol, MCOP 17, Murray to Hill, 9 October 1971 and 10 October 1971.
51 Jones, *Balliol*, pp. 308–11; Balliol, MCOP 17.
52 Balliol, MCOP 17; *Balliol Annual Record, 1972*, p. 7.
53 *Balliol Annual Record, 1972*, p. 7.
54 Oswyn Murray, personal communication. Steven Lukes remembers Murray's intervention, too.
55 *Balliol Annual Record, 1972*, p. 7.
56 John Jones and Oswyn Murray, personal communication.
57 *Times*, 2 March 1976, p. 3; *Guardian*, 2 March 1976, p. 5; Balliol, MCOP 17.
58 *Daily Telegraph*, 18 June 1977, pp. 15, 19.
59 *Balliol Annual Record, 1978*, p. 10.
60 Berlin papers, 173, fo. 258, Hill to Berlin, 27 June 1966; 177, fo. 148b, Hill to Berlin, 10 February 1967; ibid., fo. 157b, Berlin to Hill, 13 February 1967; 190, fo. 381, Berlin to Hill, 8 December 1970; ibid., fo. 390, Hill to Berlin, 14 December 1970.
61 For balance, see Trevor-Roper's satirical portrait of the embittered Rowse in late career: Richard Davenport-Hines and Adam Sisman (eds), *One Hundred Letters from Hugh Trevor-Roper* (2014), pp. 153–7; Peter Raina, *John Sparrow, Warden of All Souls College, Oxford* (2017), pp. 493–6. I am grateful to Robin Briggs for these references.
62 Hill, 'Lindsay'; Oswyn Murray, personal communication. Stretton made the comparison with Lindsay directly: Stretton, pp. 15–16.
63 *Daily Telegraph*, 5 October 1973, p. 18.
64 *Daily Telegraph*, 10 October 1979, p. 14.
65 Briggs; see also Stretton, p. 16; Corfield, 'Balliol College', p. 2.
66 *Daily Telegraph*, 10 January 1979, p. 1.
67 Keen, pp. 19, 20; Corfield, 'Balliol College', p. 1.
68 Keen, p. 20.
69 *Antichrist in Seventeenth-Century England* (1971), pp. 3, 177.
70 *Sunday Times*, 16 March 1969, p. 55
71 Morrill, 'Which World?', p. 231.
72 For the limitations of Hill's class analysis and judgement of the educational background of the writers he discusses, see Nicholas McDowell, 'Decorum personae: *The World Turned Upside Down* and the Praise of Folly', *Prose Studies*, 36:3 (2014), 219–30.
73 Kenyon, *Spectator*, 8 July 1972, pp. 54–5, at p. 55.
74 Although he had read Lenin's *State and Revolution* closely in the 1930s; that was itself in part a reflection on Engels's *Family, Private Property and the State*, on which he also kept notes: Hill papers, 45.
75 Morrill, 'Which World?', p. 232.
76 Barry Reay, 'The World Turned Upside Down: a retrospect', in Eley and Hunt (eds), *Reviving the English Revolution*, pp. 53–71, at p. 56.
77 Hill papers, 264.
78 *Times*, 26 February 2003, p. 30.
79 Hill papers, 210, 11 May 1973.
80 Hexter, *TLS*, 24 October 1975, pp. 1250–2.

81 *TLS*, 7 November 1975, p. 1333.

82 Cobb and Heinemann comments, *TLS*, 14 November 1975, p. 1360; Hexter and Hammersley comments, *TLS*, 28 November 1975, pp. 1419–20; Hobsbawm and Zagorin comments, *TLS*, 12 December 1975, p. 1489; Heinemann papers, 2/3/1, Hill to Heinemann, 3 November 1975.

83 Balliol, deceased members files, Richard Cobb, Cobb to Hill, 25 November 1975.

84 Pennington, p. 41.

85 'Plebeian irreligion in seventeenth-century England' (1969), in Hill, *Turning Point*; 'The radical critics of Oxford and Cambridge in the 1650s' (1972), in Hill, *Change and Continuity*; 'The Levellers', in David Rubinstein (ed.), *People for the People: Radical Ideas and Personalities in British History* (1973), pp. 30–6 (with a foreword by Michael Foot); 'Irreligion in the "Puritan" revolution', The Barnett Shine Foundation Lecture, QMC, London, Dept of Economics, 1974; 'Occasional conformity' (1977), in Hill, *Collected Essays*, ii; Foreword to A.L. Morton (ed.), *Freedom in Arms: A Selection of Leveller Writings* (1975), pp. 12–13.

86 'From Lollards to Levellers' (1978), in Hill, *Collected Essays*, ii.

87 'John Pym', *Encyclopaedia Britannica: Macropaedia*, 15 (1974), 312–13; 'Milton and Marvell' (1978), in Hill, *Collected Essays*, i; 'The religion of Gerrard Winstanley' (1978), in Hill, *Collected Essays*, ii.

88 'Inglaterra: Puritanos en familia', *Historia*, 16:2 (1977), 105–15.

89 Christopher Hill and Michael Shepherd, 'The case of Arise Evans: a historico-psychiatric study', *Psychological Medicine*, 6 (1976), 351–58, at p. 157. See also Hill's essay on Evans in *Change and Continuity*.

90 *The World Turned Upside Down: Radical Ideas during the English Revolution* (1972), p. 16.

91 Hill papers, 253.

92 Corfield interview, pp. 32–4.

93 Heinemann papers, 2/3/1, Hill to Heinemann, 27 June 1975, 19 and 24 September 1975.

94 'Milton the radical', *TLS*, 29 November 1974, pp. 1330–2; subsequent correspondence: *TLS*, 13 December 1974, p. 1416; 31 January 1975, p. 112; 14 February 1975, p. 168; 7 March 1975, p. 252.

95 *Milton and the English Revolution* (1977), p. 471.

96 *Daily Telegraph*, 21 June 1978, p. 18; *Times*, 21 June 1978, p. 19.

97 Thomas Corns, 'Milton and Winstanley', in Peter Lake and Jason Peacey (eds), *Insolent Proceedings: Rethinking Public Politics in the English Revolution* (2022), pp. 184–97; David Lowenstein, 'Milton among the religious radicals and sects: polemical engagements and silences', *Milton Studies*, 40 (2001), 222–47; Gordon Campbell and Thomas N. Corns, *Milton and the Manuscript of de Doctrina Christiana* (2007).

98 Sharon Achinstein, 'Cold War Milton', *University of Toronto Quarterly*, 77:3 (2008), 801–36.

99 Pennington, p. 43; R.C. Richardson, 'Complementarities: Christopher and Bridget Hill and literary history', *Literature and History*, third series, 13:1 (2004), 1–8; Richardson edited the special edition, *Literature and History*, 7:2 (1998); Heinemann, 'How the words got on the page', in Eley and Hunt (eds), *Reviving the English Revolution*, pp. 73–97.

100 Worden, *TLS*, 2 December 1977, pp. 1394–5; Skinner, *NYRB*, 23 March 1979; Nicholas McDowell, *Poet of Revolution: The Making of John Milton* (2020).

101 Heinemann papers, 2/3/1.

102 *Guardian*, 20 January 1997, p. 3.

103 Marcus Nevitt, 'The theatre of the World Turned Upside Down', *Prose Studies*, 36:3 (2014), 185–98, at pp. 185, 186.

104   Hill papers, 264, William Morris to Hill, 22 May 1973; Hill to Morris, 31 May 1973; Hill to Michael Thomas, 17 July 1978. Perhaps ironically, given his insistence here, shortly before his own book was published Hill found to his embarrassment that Ian Donaldson had published a book called *The World Upside Down*: Hill to Ian Donaldson, 5 October 1972. He wrote to Heinemann: 'I wasn't even aware I had cribbed his title. So I had to write to him very apologetically and have been careful ever since': Heinemann papers, 2/3/1, Hill to Heinemann, 30 March 1984.

105   Nevitt, 'The theatre', pp. 190–1.

106   Quoted in ibid., p. 191; see also *Observer*, 29 October 1978, p. 31; for the ethos of the company: John Woodvine and Lynn Farleigh, personal communication.

107   Nevitt, 'The theatre', p. 191; *Guardian*, 1 December 1978, p. 18.

108   Michael Billington, *Guardian*, 3 November 1978, p. 11. See also *Observer*, 5 November 1978, p. 28; *Times*, 3 November 1978, p. 9; *Financial Times*, 3 November 1978, p. 19; *Daily Telegraph*, 3 November 1978, p. 15; *Daily Mail*, 7 November 1978, p. 31; *TLS*, 24 November 1978, p. 1367. For the advert: *Guardian*, 27 October 1978, p. 26.

109   *Listener*, 18 November 1971, p. 683–4; *Sunday Telegraph*, 6 February 1972.

110   *TLS*, 24 November 1972, pp. 1431–2, at p. 1432.

111   Hill papers, 181, Trevor-Roper to Hill, 15 June 1968; 225, Trevor-Roper to Hill, 17 August 1973. See, in general, Sisman, *Hugh Trevor-Roper*, pp. 208, 262–3, 265–6, 274, 287, 344, 362. See also Hill papers, 242, 249. For their political differences see above, p. 81 (Trevor-Roper to Berlin). Trevor-Roper was very critical of *Intellectual Origins: History and Theory*, 5:1 (1966), 61–82.

112   *TLS*, 24 November 1972, pp. 1431–2, at p. 1431. Elton sent a personal note of rebuke: Hill papers, 180, Elton to Hill, 25 December 1972. Following public exchanges in the *TLS*, Elton reassured Hill that he bore no personal grudge: *TLS*, 18 February 1977, p. 184; 4 March 1977, p. 244; 18 March 1977, p. 308; Hill papers, 271, Elton to Hill, 3 February 1978. For other evidence of their relationship, see Hill papers, 14, 224, 332. Hill was generous in response to criticism of *Intellectual Origins* by Quentin Skinner, ibid., 249, Hill to Skinner, 9 June 1965 and Skinner to Hill, 14 June 1965.

113   'Partial historians and total history', *TLS*, 24 November 1972, pp. 1431–2, at p. 1431 (republished in Hill, *Collected Essays*, iii and Hill, *Turning Point*).

114   Hill papers, 243; *P&P*, 69 (1975), 132.

115   *Winstanley: The Law of Freedom and Other Writings* (1973); Hill, 'Religion of Gerrard Winstanley'.

116   *Sunday Times*, 16 July 1978, p. 33.

117   Hill papers, 212, article on Hill published by Lancashire Polytechnic; Hill papers, 229. See also *Times*, 17 February 1966, p. 15; *Guardian*, 31 May 1966, p. 5; *Daily Telegraph*, 9 October 1976, p. 16.

118   *Listener*, 10 August 1967, pp. 172–3; *TLS*, 24 November 1972, pp. 1431–2; 'La revolucion Inglesa', *Historia*, 16:1 (1976), 100–9; 'Forerunners of socialism in the seventeenth-century English Revolution', *Marxism Today*, 21 (1977), 270–6; 'Answers and questions' (1977), in Hill, *Collected Essays*, iii.

119   *Times*, 23 October 1968, p. 12; *TLS*, 24 October 1968, p. 1205.

120   *Times*, 25 April 1966, p. 7; *Times*, 30 June 1966, p. 10; *Times*, 24 January 1967, p. 9; *Times*, 30 March 1966, p. 11. The *Sunday Telegraph*, 2 August 1970, p. 2, reported Dutschke's application to Kings, Cambridge, noting that if unsuccessful he would no doubt be welcome at Hill's Balliol. See also *Times*, 12 January 1971, p. 13.

121   *Times*, 2 October 1971, p. 13; *Times*, 10 March 1972, p. 7; *Times*, 17 July 1972, p. 6; *Guardian*, 18 July 1972, p. 5A; *Times*, 23 October 1972, p. 13; *TLS*, 22 October 1974, p. 1317.

122   *Times*, 28 November 1968, p. 9, with R.B. Wernham.

123   *Times*, 9 June 1977, p. 15; *Times*, 27 March 1973, p. 8; *Times*, 29 November 1974, p. 19.
124   *Times*, 2 September 1970, p. 9.
125   *Guardian*, 19 October 1970, p. 1.
126   *Guardian*, 5 March 1971, p. 6.

9. Retirement, Revisionism and the Experience of Defeat: 1978–2003

1   *Times*, 14 January 1976, p. 16.
2   Daniel Weinbren, *The Open University: A History* (2014), chs. 1–2, at p. 7; Mandler, *Crisis of Meritocracy*, ch. 5, at p. 73; for the OU and access to higher education, see pp. 113, 132–3, 135.
3   Corfield, 'Balliol College', p. 5.
4   *Sunday Times*, 24 October 1971, p. 38. With Donald Pennington, 'Science and society' and 'Cromwell', Sussex Tapes, record H 3 (1971); with Donald Pennington, 'Seventeenth-century England: change and revolution', Audio Learning Ltd, cassette: English history no. 4 (1975).
5   Hill, *Nation of Change*, p. x; Hill, *Turning Point*.
6   Anne Laurence, personal communication; *Guardian*, 13 August 2002, p. 16.
7   *Observer*, 15 February 1981, p. 48.
8   Pennington, p. 45. W.R. Owens (ed.), *Seventeenth-Century England: A Changing Culture*, vol. ii: *Modern Studies* (1980). For examples of the course materials, see A203 block 5, *Political Ideas* (1981) and A203 Block 6, *The Sixteen-Fifties* (1981). See also Heinemann, 'How the words got on the page', in Eley and Hunt (eds), *Reviving the English Revolution*, pp. 94–5.
9   'Covenant theology and the concept of "a public person"' (1979), in Hill, *Collected Essays*, iii; essays on Francis Quarles (1980), John Wilmot, Earl of Rochester (1980), Thomas Traherne (1980), 'George Wither and John Milton' (1980), Samuel Pepys (1983), all in Hill, *Collected Essays*, i, along with his earlier piece on Benlowes [above, p. 107], now combined with Quarles; 'Dr. Tobias Crisp, 1600–1643' (1982), in Hill, *Collected Essays*, ii; 'Archbishop Laud and the English Revolution' (1990), in Hill, *Nation of Change*; 'Catharine Macaulay's *History* and her Catalogue of Tracts', *Seventeenth Century*, 8:2 (1993), 269–85.
10   Corfield interview, p. 27; Hill papers, 172; Hill, 'Literature and the English Revolution', *Seventeenth Century*, 1:1 (1986), 15–30 (republished in Hill, *Nation of Change*).
11   Ibid., p. 15.
12   Christopher Hill, Barry Reay and William Lamont, *The World of the Muggletonians* (1983); 'John Reeve and the origins of Muggletonianism', in Ann Williams (ed.), *Prophecy and Millenarianism: Essays in Honour of Marjorie Reeves* (1980), pp. 305–33; 'The Muggletonians', *P&P*, 104 (1984), 153–63 and discussion (for Reeve see Hill, *Collected Essays*, ii); 'Robinson Crusoe' (1980), in Hill, *Collected Essays*, ii; 'Quakers and the English Revolution' (1992), in Hill, *Turning Point*.
13   Corfield interview, pp. 35–6.
14   *New Zealand Listener*, 11 April 1981, pp. 49–50, at p. 50. I am grateful to Glenn Burgess for sharing his copy of this interview with me.
15   *Daily Telegraph*, 17 March 1989, p. 15. He had trailed the subject in 'John Bunyan and the English Revolution', *Marxist Perspectives*, 2 (1979), 8–26; See also 'John Bunyan and his public', *History Today*, 38:10 (1988), 13–19.
16   Corfield interview, p. 37.
17   *Daily Telegraph*, 21 May 1993, p. 18.
18   Hill, *Collected Essays*, i–iii; Hill, *Turning Point*; Hill, *Nation of Change*.

19   Hill papers, 274, from Juliet Gardiner, 20 April 1988.

20   'Gerald Aylmer at Balliol', in John Morrill, Paul Slack and Donald Woolf (eds), *Public Duty and Private Conscience in Seventeenth-Century England: Essays Presented to G.E. Aylmer* (1993), pp. 1–7; Hill papers, 212, article on Hill published by Lancashire Polytechnic; Hill papers, uncatalogued for the East German Award.

21   Hill papers, 295. The book was J.F. McGregor and Barry Reay (eds) *Radical Religion in the English Revolution* (1984); correspondence in November 1982.

22   Heinemann, 'How the words got on the page', in Eley and Hunt (eds), *Reviving the English Revolution*, p. 76.

23   See, for example, the interview with Leon Rosselson, *Guardian*, 21 August 1981, p. 10.

24   *Sunday Times*, 20 October 1974, p. 1. For the broader context, see Dennis Kavanagh and Anthony Seldon (eds), *The Thatcher Effect* (1989), esp. chapters by J.R.G. Tomlinson, 'The schools'; Peter Scott, 'Higher education'; and Ivor Crewe, 'Values: the crusade that failed'.

25   *Washington Post*, 3 February 1982, p. A14.

26   Corfield, 'Intellectual trajectory', pp. 14–15.

27   *Guardian*, 11 October 1983, p. 13; Margaret Drabble, *Oxford Companion to English Literature*, fifth edition (1985), p. 461.

28   *Guardian*, 18 November 1982, p. 14; 1 March 1984, p. 12.

29   *Guardian*, 27 July 1981, p. 7, quoting William Wordsworth, 'London, 1802'; 2 May 1977, p. 5; 10 December 1984, p. 4; 10 December 1983, p. 5; 27 February 1985, p. 5; 12 December 1983, p. 17.

30   *Times*, 29 March 1983, p. 13; 4 April 1984, p. 21; *Daily Telegraph*, 15 August 1989, p. 2.

31   Hill papers, 202.

32   Hill papers, 13, 14, 17. For New York, *TLS*, 29 November 1985, p. 1354; Grant Duff papers, 38/5, from 110 Bleecker St [19 October 1987?]; *TLS*, 29 November 1985, p. 1354; Australian National University summer school, February 1981: Hill et al., *Twelve several papers*; *New Zealand Listener*, 11 April 1981, pp. 49–50; I am grateful to Wilf Prest and Glenn Burgess for sharing copies of these publications with me; Hill, letters, *Observer*, 22 March 1987, p. 22.

33   *Observer*, 24 January 1982, p. 6; 31 January 1982, p. 14.

34   *Observer*, 18 May 1980, p. 30.

35   *Guardian*, 6 February 1984, p. 13.

36   *Guardian*, 20 June 1983, p. 13.

37   *Guardian*, 30 July 1983, p. 15. For Hill on the History Workshop movement: Pennington, pp. 43–4.

38   Balliol, deceased members files, Raphael Samuel, letter from Hill, 13 May 1975.

39   For the broader context see David Cannadine, Jenny Keating and Nicola Sheldon, *The Right Kind of History: Teaching the Past in Twentieth-Century England* (2011), ch. 5.

40   *Guardian*, 17 November 1987, p. 15.

41   *Guardian*, 6 February 1984, p. 13.

42   Although alternatives were presented, such as a history based around the story of citizens' rights: *Guardian*, 3 August 1987, p. 7.

43   Heinemann papers, 2/3/1, Hill to Heinemann, 10 July 1988.

44   *Guardian*, 11 July 1988, p. 19.

45   *Guardian*, 15 July 1989, p. 23.

46   *Guardian*, 29 May 1989 (reprinted in Hill, *Turning Point*).

47   *Economist*, 24 September 1977, pp. 24–5; *Times*, 30 September 1977, p. 17.

48   *Times*, 14 November 1977, p. 1.

49   Arblaster, *Balliol Annual Record, 1978*, pp. 15–16; Hill papers, 230.

50   *Daily Mail*, 22 November 1979, p. 6.

51 *Observer*, 22 July 1979, p. 37.

52 *Observer*, 28 October 1979, p. 9.

53 *Guardian*, 7 February 1985, p. 10.

54 *Guardian*, 11 November 1978, p. 6; Hill papers, 20.

55 House of Commons Library, DEP 3300, Report by Sir Albert Sloman on academic freedom at Ruskin College, Oxford, 1987.

56 Anthony Glees, *Secrets of the Service: British Intelligence and Communist Subversion 1939–51* (1987), pp. 279–88.

57 *Observer*, 15 March 1987, p. 13.

58 Glees, *Secrets*, pp. 279–88, at p. 288; *Observer*, 15 March 1987, p. 13. In the book, Glees states that Hill had been taken into intelligence without being vetted: *Secrets*, p. 280.

59 *Observer*, 22 March 1987, p. 22; Evans, 'Sumner, (Benedict) Humphrey', *ODNB*.

60 *Observer*, 22 March 1987, p. 22.

61 Saville papers, 2/1/14, Hill to Saville, 10 May 1992 and Hill to Saville, 16 December 1993. Smollett had been put in touch with Hill via the CPGB, however, in relation to the cultural work of the party: KV/2/3941, p. 170.

62 Saville papers, DJS/2/1/14, Correspondence file with Christopher Hill, quotation from Saville to Hill, 7 December 1993. Saville offered Christopher and Bridget a veto over the final text, in which case instead of including it in the book he would deposit it in the library with a thirty-year embargo: ibid., Saville to Bridget and Christopher Hill, 26 August 1990. See also DJS/3/13, Foreign policy and the Labour government.

63 Saville papers, DJS/2/1/14, Hill to Saville, 3 September 1990.

64 Saville, *The Politics of Continuity*, pp. 212–17, at p. 217; Saville papers, 2/1/14, Hill to Saville, 5 December 1993.

65 See above, p. 71; Hill, *Observer*, 22 March 1987, p. 22. He later wrote to Saville: 'I presume the text to which this is an appendix will have reminded readers of the story of pro-Russian feeling in England at all levels in 1944 and early 45? Glees relies on us all thinking in cold-war terms, and many of his readers will be liable to fall into that trap.' Saville papers, 2/1/14, Hill to Saville, 10 May 1992.

66 *Observer*, 22 March 1987, p. 22.

67 For Christopher Andrew's initial thoughts about Hill's file on its release in 2014, see National Archives, Security Service file release October 2014 (nationalarchives.gov.uk).

68 TNA, KV/2/3941, p. 72.

69 *Guardian*, 6 March 2003, p. 9. Saville had not known of this proposal in considering Glees's original charges, which did not include this one. Glees, *Secrets*, pp. 284–5 is ambiguous, suggesting that the proposal at Potsdam was to discuss academic exchange, not the dismissal of White Russians. Saville did not find any proposal to dismiss White Russians actually in post, simply not to employ more: *Politics of Continuity*, p. 217.

70 See above, pp. 72–3.

71 *Times*, 11 March 2003, p. 21.

72 *Times*, 5 March 2003, p. 3; *Observer*, 9 March 2003, p. 31; Glees, *Secrets*, p. 280.

73 *Times*, 5 March 2003, p. 3.

74 Corfield, personal communication; Corfield, 'As I knew him', p. 5. See also Grant Duff papers, 38/5, from 110 Bleecker St, New York [19 October 1987?].

75 Corfield, 'Intellectual trajectory', p. 23 n. 62.

76 *Guardian*, 6 March 2003, p. 9; 10 March 2003, p. 21.

77 *Observer*, 16 March 2003, p. 30; *Times*, 5 March 2003, p. 3.

78 *Guardian*, 6 March 2003, p. 9; *Observer*, 16 March 2003, p. 30.

79 *Daily Mail*, 8 March 2003, p. 12.

80 *Times*, 3 March 2003, p. 43; *Daily Mail*, 8 March 2003, p. 12.

81   *Sunday Times*, 9 March 2003, p. 18.

82   *Times*, 10 March 2003, p. 18; 10 November 1997, p. 22.

83   G.R. Elton, 'Catching up-British History: 1: Tudors and Stuarts', *TLS*, 23 November 1979, p. 27.

84   Eley and Hunt (eds), *Reviving the English Revolution*.

85   *LRB*, 31 October 1996.

86   For a good conceptual discussion (from a revisionist-friendly perspective) see Glenn Burgess, 'On revisionism: an analysis of early Stuart historiography in the 1970s and 1980s', *The Historical Journal*, 33:3 (1990), 609–70.

87   Morrill, *Revolt in the Provinces*, pp. 1–10.

88   *Times*, 8 April 2003, p. 30.

89   Some of the key works are: Conrad Russell, *The Causes of the English Civil War* (1990); Russell, *Unrevolutionary England, 1603–1642* (1990); Russell, *The Fall of the British Monarchies 1637–1642* (1991); Morrill, *Revolt of the Provinces* [first edition, 1976]; Morrill, *The Nature of the English Revolution* (1993).

90   'Premature obsequies', *History Today*, 41: 4 (1991), 44–7 at p. 45 (republished in Hill, *Turning Point*).

91   'A bourgeois revolution?' (1980), in Hill, *Collected Essays*, iii.

92   Michael J. Braddick, *State Formation in Early Modern England* (2000); Steve Pincus, *1688: The First Modern Revolution* (2009).

93   'Seventeenth-century English radicals and Ireland' (1985), in Hill, *Nation of Change*. Early lectures on Ireland and Scotland do not seem to have made their way into print: Hill papers, 171, 173, although he did write on the bicentenary of the '45 for *Modern Quarterly*: see above, p. 86.

94   Mehta, *Up at Oxford*, p. 109.

95   Morrill, *Nature of the English Revolution*, part one and ch. 14.

96   Morrill, *Revolt of the Provinces*, pp. 1–10; J.C. Davis, 'Puritanism and revolution: themes, categories, methods and conclusions', *The Historical Journal*, 34:2 (1991), 479–90; Davis, 'Radicalism in a traditional society: the evaluation of radical thought in the English commonwealth 1649–1660', *History of Political Thought*, 3:2 (1982), 193–213; Davis, 'Religion and the struggle for freedom in the English Revolution', *The Historical Journal*, 35:3 (1992), 507–30.

97   See, for example, *TLS*, 10 August 1967, pp. 172–3; Hill, *Economic Problems of the Church*, p. 348.

98   Mark A. Kishlansky, *The Rise of the New Model Army* (1979); Michael Mendle (ed.), *The Putney Debates of 1647: The Army, the Levellers and the English State* (2001).

99   Ronald Hutton, *The Royalist War Effort 1642–1646*, second edition (1999), pp. xvi, 201, 203.

100 *Guardian*, 9 March 1993, p. A8.

101 This may not have been the intention, but it was the effect of the use of language like 'fabrication' and 'invention': MacLachlan, *The Rise and Fall of Revolutionary England*; J.C. Davis, *Fear, Myth and History: the Ranters and the Historians* (1986).

102 Davis, *Fear, Myth and History*.

103 Conal Condren, 'Afterword: radicalism revisited', in Glenn Burgess and Matthew Festenstein (eds), *English Radicalism 1550–1850* (2007), pp. 311–37.

104 Gerald Aylmer, 'Did the Ranters exist?', *P&P*, 117 (1987), 208–19; J.C. Davis, 'Fear, myth and furore: reappraising the "Ranters"', *P&P*, 129 (1990), 79–103; and the essays in *P&P*, 140 (1993), 155–210.

105 'The lost Ranters? A critique of J.C. Davis' (1987), in Hill, *Nation of Change*.

106 Hill papers, 14, to Selma Colonna, Pontifícia Universidade de São Paulo, 25 October 1991. He retained a positive view of Davis personally, who had previously contacted

him for advice on arranging a viewing of Kevin Brownlow's Winstanley film in New Zealand: Hill papers, 243, Davis to Hill, 22 February 1976. Davis was, Burgess thought, one of the organisers of the New Zealand leg of Hill's visit to Australia and New Zealand in 1981: Glenn Burgess, personal communication.

107 Blair Worden, personal communication. For the review see *New Statesman*, 24 January 1975, pp. 113–14.

108 Kettle interview.

109 Corfield interview, pp. 24–5.

110 Hill to Ann Hughes, 1 July 1984 (I am grateful to Ann Hughes for lending me her letters from Hill). The result was Richard Cust and Ann Hughes (eds), *Conflict in Early Stuart England: Studies in Religion and Politics, 1603–1642* (1989). Hill commended it (along with other work of that generation) for restoring the centrality of principled difference to the historiography of early Stuart England: Christopher Hill, The *English Bible and the Seventeenth-Century Revolution* (1993), pp. 48–9.

111 'Parliament and people in early 17th century England', 4 December 1980: *TLS*, 24 October 1980, p. 1212. For the fuller academic version: 'Parliament and people in seventeenth-century England', *P&P*, 92 (1981), 100–24 at p. 124; and subsequent debate: *P&P*, 98 (1983), 151–8 (republished in Hill, *Collected Essays*, iii).

112 'God and the English Revolution' (1984), in Hill, *Collected Essays*, ii.

113 See the essays on 'Political discourse in early seventeenth-century England' (1986), 'The word "Revolution" in seventeenth-century England' (1986) and 'Winstanley and freedom' (1986), in Hill, *Nation of Change*; and 'The religion of Gerrard Winstanley: a rejoinder', *P&P*, 89 (1980), 147–51. 'From Marprelate to the Levellers' (1982) and 'Censorship and English literature', in *Collected Essays*, i; 'Science and magic in seventeenth-century England' (1983), in *Collected Essays*, iii; 'Irreligion in the "puritan" revolution', in McGregor and Reay (eds.), *Radical Religion*, pp. 191–211; 'Freethinking and libertinism: the legacy of the English Revolution' (1995), in Hill, *Turning Point*.

114 'Braudel and the state', *New Society*, 26 June 1980; 'Braudel and the state', *New Statesman*, 20 July 1984; 'Karl Marx and Britain' (1983) (all in Hill, *Collected Essays*, iii); 'Premature obsequies'. For Braudel see also *History and Theory*, 8 (1969).

115 Hill papers, 231, to Chaytor, 6 December 1980; 'Household and kinship', *P&P*, 88 (1980), 142.

116 *Transactions of the Royal Historical Society*, fifth series, 12 (1962), 173–92; 22 (1972), 196–225; 32 (1982), 23–74.

117 'Premature obsequies'.

118 *Observer*, 29 November 1987, 'Bazaar', p. 1. There was extensive press coverage of the proposed education reforms that month. Thompson's review is in *LRB*, 9 July 1987. Davis and Jonathan Scott replied in *LRB*, 17 September 1987, and there was further correspondence in the editions of 1 October (Thompson) and 15 October (Nigel Smith). I am grateful to John Morrill for discussion of this point.

119 *Observer*, 23 September 1979, p. 37.

120 A suggestion made to me independently by both Christopher Thompson and John Morrill.

121 Balliol, deceased members files, Raphael Samuel, from Samuel, 23 September 1977, 27 September 1977. *HWJ* published an editorial: 'The attack', *HWJ*, 4:1 (1977), pp. 1–4.

122 *Guardian*, 13 September 1979, p. 11.

123 *Balliol Annual Record*, 1978, p. 16.

124 *TLS*, 6 March 1987, p. 241.

125 J.S.A. Adamson, 'The baronial context of the English civil war', *Transactions of the*

Royal Historical Society, fifth series, 40 (1990), 93–120; Adamson, 'Politics and the nobility in civil war England', *The Historical Journal*, 34 (1991), 231–55.

126   Kettle interview.

127   Glenn Burgess, personal communication.

128   *TLS*, 10 May 1991, pp. 7–8, at p. 7.

129   *Sunday Telegraph*, 2 June 1991, p. 17.

130   *Daily Telegraph*, 5 March 1991, p. 14. Brian Young reviewed the programme very warmly in the *Financial Times*, 9 March 1991, p. xvii: 'I cannot speak too well of the whole series.'

131   *Sunday Telegraph*, 20 August 1989, p. 23. See also his endorsement of Raphael Samuel as offering more solid intellectual foundations for Labour than other successors of great left-wing scholars such as Hill and Thompson: *Times*, 23 February 1995, p. 36.

132   *TLS*, 23 August 1996, p. 24.

133   Corfield, 'Bridget Hill'; *Guardian*, 13 August 2002, p. 16.

134   Balliol, deceased member's files, Maurice Keen, copy of an email covering Keen's appreciation of Bridget. I am grateful to John Jones for permission to cite this email; Briggs.

135   Sir John Keegan, *Times*, 7 March 2003, p. 42; Lord Selkirk, *Times*, 11 March 2003, p. 21; Balliol deceased members files, John Keegan, for the record of his illness and the warm correspondence he had with Hill in later life. Hill wrote positive academic references for him too.

10. The Past and the Present

1   *Sunday Times*, 1 November 1959, magazine, p. 15.

2   *Listener*, 21 October 1965, pp. 613–4, at p. 614.

3   John Woodvine, personal communication; Hill papers, 12; Corfield, 'Intellectual trajectory', p. 14; Corfield, 'All one', p. 126 n. 39; Corfield, 'As I knew him', p. 5.

4   Pennington, p. 33.

5   Keen, pp. 20–1.

6   Pennington, p. 49.

7   Hill papers, 304.

8   Corfield, 'Intellectual trajectory', p. 23.

9   TNA, KV/2/3941, p. 38; see also KV/2/3944, p. 42.

10   Mehta, *Up at Oxford*, p. 158.

11   Interview in *New Zealand Listener*, 11 April 1981, pp. 49–50, at p. 49. I am grateful to Glenn Burgess for sharing a copy of this interview with me.

12   'The lost Ranters? A critique of J.C. Davis', *HWJ*, 24 (1987), 134–40, at p. 138.

13   Berlin papers, 172, fos. 98–9, Hill to Berlin, 30 January 1965. For the attempts at reconciliation see also 169, fo. 9, Hill to Berlin, 4 July 1962 and fo. 21, Berlin to Hill, 9 July 1962. In the latter Berlin writes: 'I am glad that now the ice is broken, the water underneath it is not altogether cold.'

14   *Times*, 26 February 2003, p. 30.

15   For example, suggestions from John Saville that he might write a book on Marxism and history in 1965, or a review of civil war historiography for the *Socialist Register* in 1973: Saville papers, 1/104, Hill to Saville, 13 May 1965; Saville to Hill, 4 July 1973 and Hill to Saville, 7 July 1973.

16   'Premature obsequies', republished in Hill, *Turning Point*, at p. 292. This passage was not in the original: *History Today*, 41:4 (1991).

17   Berlin papers, 172, fos. 98–9, Hill to Berlin, 30 January 1965.

18 Hill papers, 236.

19 Dell papers, fo. 290, Hill to Dell, 2 December 1948.

20 Balliol, deceased members files, Raphael Samuel, from Samuel, 7 July 1978, from Hill, 13 July 1978.

21 Hill, *Intellectual Origins*, p. 1.

22 Hill papers, 197.

23 Berlin papers, 169, fo. 21, Berlin to Hill, 9 July 1962.

24 Hill papers, 183, p. 27 (actually the first page of the notebook, but the concluding paragraph of the lecture).

25 *Listener*, 10 August 1967, pp. 172–3, at pp. 172, 173.

26 Ibid.

27 *TLS*, 24 November 1972, pp. 1431–2.

28 *Listener*, 10 August 1967, pp. 172–3, at p. 173.

29 Hill papers, 306, handwritten p. 1. The published version excludes this passage: *Listener*, 10 August 1967, pp. 172–3.

30 *TLS*, 29 November 1985, p. 1354; *TLS*, 10 May 1991, pp. 7–8, at p. 7.

31 *Times*, 26 February 2003, p. 30.

32 Hill papers, 194.

33 Balliol, deceased members files, Maurice Keen, 28 May 1957.

34 Pennington, p. 29.

35 *Times*, 18 May 1991, section, p. 21.

36 See John Walter, 'Popular iconoclasm and the politics of the parish in Eastern England, 1640–1642', *The Historical Journal*, 47:2 (2004), 261–90 (for Russell pp. 261–2); Walter, *Understanding Popular Violence in the English Revolution: The Colchester Plunderers* (1999); Walter, *Covenanting Citizens: The Protestation Oath and Popular Culture in the English Revolution* (2017). See also Lake and Peacey (eds), *Insolent Proceedings*.

37 Key works include Keith Wrightson and David Levine, *Poverty and Piety in an English Village: Terling, 1525–1700* (1979); Wrightson, *English Society, 1580–1680* (1982); and John Walter, *Crowds and Popular Politics in Early Modern England* (2006).

38 Hill, *Nation of Change*, pp. 245–6.

39 Hill papers, 188.

40 Abby Wetton Kleinbaum, *New Directions for Women*, 15:2 (1986), p. 10. The meeting was reported in the *TLS*, 29 November 1985, p. 1354.

41 Review of Peter Laslett, *The World We Have Lost*, History and Theory, 6:1 (1967), 117–27, at p. 121 (republished as 'A one-class society?', in Hill, *Change and Continuity*).

42 Review of Alan Bray, *Homosexuality in Renaissance England* (1984), in Hill, *Collected Essays*, iii. See also review of B.R. Burg, *Sodomy and the Perception of Evil: English Sea Rovers in the Seventeenth-Century Caribbean*, NYRB, 12 May 1983.

43 *TLS*, 23 June 1989, p. 700.

44 *Daily Telegraph*, 27 February 2003, p. 29.

Index